THE IRON MEN
OF BASEBALL

THE IRON MEN OF BASEBALL

Major League Leaders in Consecutive Games Played, 1876–2005

Marty Friedrich

McFarland & Company, Inc., Publishers
Jefferson, North Carolina, and London

All photographs unless otherwise noted are from
National Baseball Hall of Fame Library, Cooperstown, N.Y.

LIBRARY OF CONGRESS CATALOGUING-IN-PUBLICATION DATA

Friedrich, Marty.
The iron men of baseball : major league leaders in
consecutive games played, 1876–2005 / Marty Friedrich.
p.   cm.
Includes bibliographic references and index.

ISBN-13: 978-0-7864-2431-3
(softcover : 50# alkaline paper) ∞

1. Baseball players—United States—Biography—Dictionaries.
2. Baseball—United States—History—Dictionaries.
I. Title.
GV865.A1F75 2006   796.357'640922—dc22 [B]   2006020685

British Library cataloguing data are available

©2006 Marty Friedrich. All rights reserved

*No part of this book may be reproduced or transmitted in any form
or by any means, electronic or mechanical, including photocopying
or recording, or by any information storage and retrieval system,
without permission in writing from the publisher.*

On the cover: Cal Ripken Jr. of the Baltimore Orioles

Manufactured in the United States of America

*McFarland & Company, Inc., Publishers
Box 611, Jefferson, North Carolina 28640
www.mcfarlandpub.com*

To my loving wife, Joanne,

For all of your love, support and
understanding while I followed
my dream

Acknowledgments

We all have dreams. One of my dreams has been to put a book together that draws on my love of baseball and history. Now that dream has come true. This book has been in the making for many years, and as a result, I have many people to thank.

To begin with, I must thank my great-great-aunt, Kate Sehrer. This woman was the first person to introduce me to the great game of baseball. I remember when I was a little boy, she showed me the sports section of the newspaper and taught me how to read the box scores. Aunt Kate (my great-grandmother's youngest sister) played softball many years before I was born, and I remember her mentioning to me the pure joy she felt in playing ball. She was a big baseball fan right up to her death in 1983 at the age of 98.

Next is my mom, Nancy, who supported me in all my baseball exploits when I was in Little League. She also greatly contributed to my being a lifelong Yankees fan. In August 2004, my mom passed away after a brief illness. She was aware that I was under contract to write a book about baseball and was looking forward to seeing the publication. I will miss her a great deal.

I shall not fail to mention my dad, Martin Sr., who on so many occasions gave me a ride to the library to do my research.

I also thank my two closest friends, Gary Wodarczak and Timothy Osberg. With the friendship of these two guys, my love for baseball, and sports in general, only grew larger.

A special thanks to my fellow mail carrier at work, Joe Marochi. Whenever I needed to check or verify information, Joe would lend me his *Total Baseball* encyclopedia or even personally research the info for me. I never believed someone could be a bigger fan of the game than I am; I was wrong. Joe would take vacation days during the playoffs and World Series so he and his late wife could stay up and watch (and score) the games. They don't come any better then Joe!

When I joined the Society for American Baseball Research (SABR) in 1988, I didn't realize how important a role this organization would play in helping me to accomplish my dream. The following SABR members (most of whom I have never met in person) were very helpful as I put this book together, immediately responding to my never ending inquiries for information: Rich Topp, Bob Tiemann, Pete Palmer, Eric Enders, Tom Ruane, Dave Smith, Dave Vincent, the folks at the Baseball Hall of Fame Research Library, the SABR's lending library coordinators, and the late Bob Davids.

A big thank you goes to my father-in-law, Joe, and brothers-in-law, Tom and Sam, for the trips to Toronto to see our team (the Yankees) and the enjoyment and company spent while watching the games on television.

And finally, I thank my loving wife, Joanne, and my two boys, Joe and Ryan, for their love and extreme patience. I know the noise of my personal microfilm reader's reel-to-reel drove you guys nuts some nights. I apologize, but I know you knew it was worth the irritation.

Table of Contents

Acknowledgments vi
Preface 1

1. Paul Hines — 3
2. Davy Force — 5
3. John Glenn — 6
4. John Peters — 8
5. Jim O'Rourke — 9
6. John Clapp — 11
7. Cal McVey — 13
8. Paul Hines — 15
9. John Morrill — 17
10. Jack Burdock — 19
11. Bill Phillips — 21
12. Jim O'Rourke — 22
13. Joe Hornung — 23
14. Bill Gleason — 26
15. Jimmy Wolf — 27
16. Steve Brady — 29
17. Charley Jones — 30
18. Curt Welch — 32
19. Jim O'Rourke — 34
20. Bill McClellan — 36
21. Henry Larkin — 38
22. George Pinkney — 40
23. Sid Farrar — 42
24. Dave Foutz — 44
25. Hub Collins — 46
26. Germany Smith — 47
27. Bid McPhee — 49
28. Tommy McCarthy — 51
29. Jake Beckley — 53
30. Hugh Duffy — 55
31. Steve Brodie — 56
32. George Van Haltren — 59
33. Kid Gleason — 61
34. Gene DeMontreville — 63
35. Duff Cooley — 64
36. Hugh Duffy — 66
37. George Van Haltren — 67
38. Jimmy Slagle — 69
39. Jesse Burkett — 70
40. Jimmy Collins — 72
41. Jimmy Barrett — 75
42. Topsy Hartsel — 77
43. Freddy Parent — 78
44. Candy LaChance — 80
45. Buck Freeman — 82
46. Bill Bradley — 84
47. Lee Tannehill — 85
48. Freddy Parent — 87

Table of Contents

49. Sherry Magee	89	
50. George Stone	91	
51. Jiggs Donahue	92	
52. Tom Jones	94	
53. Ed Konetchy	96	
54. John Hummel	97	
55. George McBride	98	
56. Eddie Grant	100	
57. Eddie Collins	102	
58. Zack Wheat	104	
59. George McBride	105	
60. Ed Konetchy	107	
61. Clyde Milan	108	
62. Owen "Chief" Wilson	110	
63. Sam Crawford	111	
64. George Cutshaw	114	
65. Ray Chapman	116	
66. Del Pratt	118	
67. Eddie Collins	119	
68. Fred Luderus	121	
69. Everett Scott	123	
70. Joe Sewell	126	
71. Lou Gehrig	129	
72. Pete Fox	132	
73. Frankie Crosetti	134	
74. Stan Hack	136	
75. Frank McCormick	137	
76. Rudy York	139	
77. Danny Litwhiler	141	
78. Mickey Vernon	143	
79. Billy Herman	144	
80. Bill Nicholson	146	
81. Bobby Doerr	148	
82. Stan Musial	150	
83. Phil Cavarretta	152	
84. Tommy Holmes	154	
85. Eddie Lake	156	
86. Mickey Vernon	157	
87. Frankie Gustine	159
88. Vern Stephens	160
89. Gil Hodges	162
90. Granny Hamner	164
91. Eddie Yost	165
92. Roy McMillan	167
93. Stan Musial	169
94. Nellie Fox	171
95. Ernie Banks	174
96. Vada Pinson	176
97. Rocky Colavito	177
98. Brooks Robinson	179
99. Ron Santo	181
100. Bill White	182
101. Ken Boyer	184
102. Johnny Callison	185
103. Curt Flood	187
104. Leo Cardenas	188
105. Billy Williams	189
106. Sandy Alomar	192
107. Roy White	194
108. Eddie Brinkman	195
109. Mike Schmidt	197
110. Dave Cash	199
111. Pete Rose	201
112. Steve Garvey	203
113. Pete Rose	206
114. Alfredo Griffin	208
115. Dale Murphy	209
116. Cal Ripken Jr.	211
117. Albert Belle	216
118. Vinny Castilla	218
119. B. J. Surhoff	220
120. Johnny Damon	221
121. Sammy Sosa	223
122. Shawn Green	225
123. Luis Gonzalez	226
124. Miguel Tejada	228

Appendices

A: Chronological Listing of Baseball Iron Men   231

B: Season by Season Review of Baseball Iron Men   235

C: Longest Consecutive Playing Streaks (500 or More Games)   243

D: Start Dates for Streaks of 500 or More Consecutive Games Played   245

E: Miscellaneous Consecutive Games Played Records   249

F: Season by Season Review of Major Leaguers Who Played All Their Team's Games   253

Bibliography   273

Index   275

Preface

For as long as I can remember, I have been a New York Yankees fan. The Yankee who I admired most was Lou Gehrig because of the way he conducted himself both on and off the baseball diamond. He was a hard worker who came from a loving family, loved baseball and was a devoted husband. He is definitely one of the true greats of the game.

Gehrig's most famous achievement in baseball was playing 2,130 consecutive games between June 1925 and April 1939. Most baseball fans and members of the media thought this record would stand forever.

In the mid–1980s, I noticed that another player with similar traits to those Gehrig possessed had put together a consecutive games played streak that had gone over 500 games and counting. As the seasons passed, the streak continued, and eventually the media came to report regularly on the continued health and determination of "The Iron Man," a nickname that recalled Gehrig, still known to baseball fans as "The Iron Horse." In September 1995, Cal Ripken, Jr., broke Gehrig's record when he played in his 2,131st consecutive game. Eventually, Ripken's streak would be extended to 2,632 games before he ended it voluntarily in Baltimore by sitting out of the game against the Yankees on September 20, 1998.

As this was occurring, I wondered if there was a cumulative list of players who had held Gehrig's title of "Major League Baseball Iron Man"—a title I created, as there is of course no official recognition of these men—from the beginning of major league baseball play in 1876. Although I came across an all-time list with 500 or more consecutive games played, there was no cumulative list in existence, let alone one from 1876 to the present. I decided to compile such a list. I went through every season and noted every player who played every game (taking into consideration games that were forfeited before becoming official and also traded players who played every game that particular season for the two teams they played for). I borrowed *The Sporting Life*, *The Sporting News* and *New York Clipper* microfilms from the SABR Lending Library and checked the players for the beginning and ending dates of their playing streaks by going through each box score.

While I used the opening of the 1876 season as the starting point for the major league Iron Men listing, I must give due respect to at least four players who achieved Iron Man status in the National Association. My main reason for omitting these players is that the instability of the National Association's schedule during the league's existence from 1871 through 1875 makes it extremely difficult to compile a complete and accurate listing. The four players were Dave Eggler, who had a 205-game streak from May 18, 1871, to May 4, 1875; Harry Schafer, who compiled a 213-game streak from May 5, 1871, to April 26, 1875; Al Spalding, who set the National Association's record for most consecutive games with a 266-game streak from May 5, 1871, to August 19, 1875; and Dickey Pearce, who was that league's last Iron Man with his 203-game streak

Preface

from August 22, 1872, to the closure of the league's final season on October 29, 1875. Pearce would have been the first Iron Man listed in this book if he hadn't missed the 1876 St. Louis season opener.

The main portion of this book is the historical and statistical review of each major league player who for any length of time held the distinction of having played in the longest uninterrupted string of games, whether within or across seasons. There have been 124 major league baseball Iron Men (some of them achieving the title more than once) from Paul Hines in 1876 to Miguel Tejada, whose streak began in 2000 and continues as this book goes to press. The Iron Men are numbered and listed chronologically with information addressing each streak's beginning and ending dates (always the date of the game that followed the streak's final game), number of consecutive games played and other basic statistical and biographical information.

The streak data included are games played, at-bats, runs scored, hits, doubles, triples, home runs, runs batted in, bases on balls, strikeouts, batting average, slugging average and stolen bases. In some stats columns, complete data are not available for certain years because that information was not collected during those particular seasons. Other years, statistical data were compiled, but the game-by-game data used to form the yearly information were either misplaced or destroyed. This is especially true with streaks involving partial seasons in the National League from 1876 through 1890. I went through the Tattersall Collection of National League box scores from 1876 through 1890 to compile the statistics included in this book, poring over the game-by-game National League box scores from 1876 through 1890 that involved the players who had long streaks. Nevertheless, some stats columns are filled but others are not. In addition, some stats from the National League (from 1904 through 1919) and the American League (from 1906 through 1919) are missing from the daily official averages. All stats from the 1920 season to the present are accounted for and listed in each streak's batting statistics. I am hoping that eventually, with the research being done by Dave Smith and Retrosheet.org, all box scores will be accurately scored and the stats counted. For all other years, the daily batting logs contained in the Information Concepts Corporation sheets and the official American and National leagues' game-by-game sheets maintained at the Baseball Hall of Fame Research Library were used.

The appendices provide additional information about the annual list of men who played all their team's games, the Iron Men streak information and other consecutive games played streaks.

Although not all media representatives place much importance on long consecutive playing streaks, it must be noted that, as of this writing, 20 players who were baseball's active leaders in consecutive games played have gone on to baseball immortality by being elected to the Baseball Hall of Fame (and this doesn't include Cal Ripken, Jr., a decision that will be a no-brainer when he is eligible for election; Pete Rose, if his lifetime ban is ever lifted; Gil Hodges, Steve Garvey, and Dale Murphy — all of whom may eventually be elected to the Hall of Fame). Of the Hall of Famers, seven were selected by the Baseball Writers Association of America and 13 were picked by the Hall of Fame's Veterans' Committee.

A player who doesn't miss a game during an entire season is a rare breed. As the seasonal review of perfect attendance (Appendix F) shows, in most years only six or seven players (sometimes fewer) play the entire schedule of games. These long playing streaks and perfect attendance occurrences should be given some kind of recognition.

The Iron Men

1. Paul Hines

Born: March 1, 1852, Washington, D.C. *Died*: July 10, 1935; Hyattsville, Maryland *Bats*: Right *Throws*: Right *Height*: 5 feet, 9½ inches *Weight*: 173 *Major league debut*: April 20, 1872 (Baltimore at Washington [NA]) *Last major league game*: July 3, 1891 (Cincinnati at Washington [AA])

Major league Iron Man from: April 25, 1876, to September 13, 1876 *Consecutive games played*: 226 *Games as major league Iron Man*: 59 (consecutive games 168 through 226) *Teams played for during streak*: Washington Nationals (NA) (1873), Chicago White Stockings (NA) (1874–1875) and Chicago White Stockings (NL) (1876) *Primary position played*: Outfield *Game missed before streak*: Played all his team's games during 1872 season but his team folded on July 22, 1872 *First game played of streak*: April 14, 1873 (Washington vs. Maryland at Baltimore) *Last game played of streak*: September 12, 1876 (Chicago at Hartford) *Game missed to end streak*: September 13, 1876 (Chicago at Hartford)

Consecutive Game Streak's Statistical Totals

Year	G	AB	R	H	2B	3B	HR	RBI	BB	SO	AVG	SLG	SB
1873	39	181	33	60	6	3	1	29	1	2	.331	.414	0
1874	59	271	47	80	10	2	0	34	4	4	.295	.347	4
1875	69	308	45	101	14	4	0	36	1	0	.328	.399	6
1876	59	284	57	92	20	3	2	—	1	2	.324	.437	—
Total	226	1044	182	333	50	12	3	99	7	8	.319	.398	10

Paul Hines had one of the longest playing careers in the early history of major league baseball, performing from 1872 to well into the 1891 season. He was a regular player for just about his entire time as a member of eight big league teams. Although he did play in the infield and other outfield positions on various occasions, a great majority of his time was spent patrolling centerfield. He became known for his spectacular running catches of flies to the outfield. Additionally, he was one of that era's most durable players as he missed just two games in his first eight years. His ballplaying career started out in his hometown of Washington, D.C., as a member of the independent Washington Nationals. When the Nationals secured a spot with the National Association in 1872, his big league career commenced with the team's season opener in Washington on April 20 against the Baltimore Canaries. The Nationals lasted just 11 games that year before folding in the middle of July. Hines played in all those contests and batted .224, but he became unemployed with the team's demise.

When another franchise was granted to Washington in 1873, Hines was back on the playing rolls manning left field for the new team in D.C., also called the Nationals. His playing streak that earned him the distinction as major league baseball's first recognized Iron Man started with the 1873 opener on April 14. Although he actually had not missed a game in 1872, he played only a small portion of that year because the team had folded and did not appear on the playing field for any other big league team over the last four and a half months of that season. In 1873, the Nationals' manager, Nick Young, used Hines in left field. Among the regular players, he led the club in hitting (.331) as the Nationals won only eight games out of 39 contests and finished in seventh place. He made the move to the Chicago White Stockings, one of the new teams in the league, in 1874. While the team played near the .500 level and came in fifth place, his batting dropped to a .295 average as he switched over to primarily handling the centerfield duties (although he was used in the infield several times). His hitting bounced back in 1875 as he attained a .328 average, a figure good enough to easily pace the sixth-place White Stockings' hitters. When the final year of the National Association came to an end in late October 1875, Hines found himself trailing only shortstop Dickey Pearce of the St. Louis Brown Stockings for the longest games played streak. Pearce's mark stood at 203 games while Hines trailed with 167 contests.

When the dust had settled during the off-season, the National League was formed to succeed the defunct National Association as the premier professional baseball league. Both St. Louis and Chicago kept their teams and became members of the new league. Chicago had improved dramatically as they signed on four new key players: Cal McVey, Ross Barnes, Deacon White and the best pitcher in the game, Al Spalding. The White Stockings had raided the ultrapowerful and talented Boston Red Stockings, who had lost only eight games the previous year in the 1875 campaign, to get these players. The Brown Stockings had settled on Denny Mack as the club's shortstop and this caused Pearce to miss St. Louis' season and home opener against the Cincinnati Reds on April 25, 1876, in addition to stopping his playing run at 203 games. Hines immediately took possession of the longest playing streak which continued to lengthen as the National League's first season progressed. It was not till there were less then 10 games left on the White Stockings' schedule that Hines sat out the team's game in Hartford against the Dark Blues on September 13, 1876. This caused his Iron Man streak of games to stop after 226 straight contests. He returned to the lineup after missing just that one contest for three more games before resting against the Boston Red Caps on September 23. He started his second playing streak (that eventually earned him a second Iron Man title) on September 26, 1876. Since Hines was a two-time Iron Man and also an active player for many more years at the

Paul Hines: Major league baseball's first Iron Man. He put together streaks of 226 and 242 games to claim Iron Man honors on two occasions.

2. Davy Force

Born: July 27, 1849; New York, New York *Died*: June 21, 1918; Englewood, New Jersey *Bats*: Right *Throws*: Right *Height*: 5 feet, 4 inches *Weight*: 130 *Major league debut*: May 5, 1871 (Boston at Washington [NA]) *Last major league game*: August 20, 1886 (Boston at Washington [NL])

Major league Iron Man from: September 13, 1876 to May 19, 1877 *Consecutive games played*: 225 *Games as major league Iron Man*: 8 (consecutive games 218 through 225) *Teams played for during streak*: Baltimore Canaries (NA) (1873), Chicago White Stockings (NA) (1874), Philadelphia Athletics (NA) (1875), Philadelphia Athletics (NL) (1876), New York Mutuals (NL) (1876) and St. Louis Brown Stockings (NL) (1877) *Primary positions played*: Shortstop and third base *Game missed before streak*: July 11, 1873 (Baltimore vs. Baltimore Marylands at Newlington Park, Maryland) *First game played of streak*: July 21, 1873 (Baltimore at Philadelphia Athletics) *Last game played of streak*: May 17, 1877 (St. Louis at Chicago) *Game missed to end streak*: May 19, 1877 (St. Louis at Chicago)

Consecutive Game Streak's Statistical Totals

Year	G	AB	R	H	2B	3B	HR	RBI	BB	SO	AVG	SLG	SB
1873	24	111	39	48	7	1	0	20	5	1	.432	.514	0
1874	59	294	61	92	9	0	0	26	3	1	.313	.344	4
1875	77	386	78	120	22	5	0	49	7	5	.311	.394	6
1876	61	287	48	66	6	0	0	17	5	3	.230	.251	—
1877	4	17	0	5	1	0	0	—	0	0	.294	.353	—
Total	225	1095	226	331	45	6	0	*112*	20	10	.302	.354	*10*

Davy Force was a top-notch infielder who played at the major league level for 15 seasons. During this time, he was a member of nine teams but close to half of his time was spent in the uniform of the Buffalo Bisons. He started playing ball at 18 with an amateur team out of Washington, D.C., called the Olympics. When the National Association (baseball's first true professional league) was formed in 1871, the Olympics secured one of nine franchises granted to take part in the league's first season. Force played shortstop and batted lead off. He hit for a .278 average and led the league's shortstops in putouts, assists and fielding.

Force moved over to the Troy Haymakers for the 1872 campaign. The franchise was financially shaky although the team was playing at a .600 winning percentage. As July was coming to an end, the club threw in the towel and folded. Force was picked up by the Baltimore Canaries and finished the year as their third baseman. Despite being shuttled between teams, he had one of his best years offensively as he hit for a .418 average (second in the league behind Boston's Ross Barnes' .430 average), along with being third in hits and on base percentage. He stayed with Baltimore as their third baseman for a second year. On July 21, 1873, in an away game against the Philadelphia Athletics, he started his consecutive playing streak with 24 games left in Baltimore's 1873 schedule. He hit .365 as the Athletics closed out the year with a 34–22 record and a third-place finish behind the Boston Red Stockings and the Philadelphia White Stockings. Force moved to Chicago for the 1874 season as a member of the new team called the White Stockings. He played either shortstop or third base during the entire schedule of 59 games as the team finished in fifth place. His .313 average was good for second place on the club behind fellow infielder Levi Meyerle's .394 hitting clip. Next, it was on to the Philadelphia Athletics where he batted .311 and led the league's shortstops with 116 putouts, 22 double plays and an .887 fielding accuracy. The National Association folded after the 1875 season and the National League was soon born. The Athletics were one of the teams making the move over to the new league. Force retained his role as the club's excellent fielding shortstop. At the tail end of the 1876 campaign, Paul Hines of the White Stockings sat out his team's September 13 game against the Hartford Dark Blues. This occurrence resulted in Force becoming the owner of the longest playing streak actively running with 218 contests to his credit. Although he played in all the seventh-place Athletics' games that year, he also was used by the New York Mutuals in one game at the tail end of the season. The Athletics went from being in third place with a 53–20 record during the National Association's final year to a disappointing seventh place with a 14–45 mark in the inaugural season of the National League. Force's performance at the plate showed a drastic drop of over 80 percentage points as he finished with his lowest batting average (.230) to date. His fielding was not affected though as he again led all shortstops with 110 putouts. He moved to the St. Louis Brown Stockings for the 1877 campaign where he replaced the departed shortstop Denny Mack. It was just four games into the 1877 season that Force's playing streak ended on May 19 after 225 games while the Brown Stockings were visiting the White Stockings. He mildly recovered from his 1876 off year offensively by elevating his hitting to a .262 average for the 1877 campaign. He also won his third fielding title at shortstop with a .914 percentage.

Force departed the majors after the season and played in 1878 for the Buffalo Bisons of the International Association. The following year (1879), the Bisons' ownership decided to take a chance at the major league level and secured a franchise in the National League. Force stayed with the Bisons during the team's entire seven-year run in the majors. He was the Bisons' starting shortstop except for the 1880, 1881 and 1885 seasons when he played more games at second base. The main highlight of his time with Buffalo was the exemplary fielding he achieved in winning three more fielding championships at shortstop in 1879, 1882 and 1884. If it was not for his great fielding skills, he probably would not have been kept in the majors because his .241 batting average in 1882 was the best he achieved in his seven seasons in Buffalo. Twice he finished with marks well below the .200 level and four other seasons his batting average ranged between .206 and .225. He was released from the Bisons when the team dissolved in November 1885. Soon after, the Washington Senators signed him to a contract. In his final major league season, he hit only .182 as he played in just over half of the Senators' games. After leaving the big leagues, he played and managed in the minors for a couple of years before retiring as an active participant. He also umpired for another season before giving up the game permanently. A short time later, he was working for the Otis Elevator Company where he stayed gainfully employed for many years.

3. JOHN GLENN

Born: 1849; Rochester, New York *Died*: November 10, 1888; Sandy Hill, New York *Bats*: Right *Throws*: Right *Height*: 5 feet, 8½ inches *Weight*: 169 *Major league debut*: May 13, 1871 (Washington at Cleveland [NA]) *Last major league game*: September 28, 1877 (Chicago at Cincinnati [NL])

Major league Iron Man from: May 19, 1877, to September 4, 1877 *Consecutive games played*: 209 *Games as major league Iron Man*: 38 (consecutive games 172 through 209) *Teams played for during streak*: Chicago White Stockings (NA) (1874–1875) and Chicago White Stockings (NL) (1876–1877) *Primary positions played*: Outfield and first base *Game missed before streak*: July 15, 1874 (Philadelphia White Stockings at Chicago) *First game played of streak*: July 18, 1874 (Philadelphia White Stockings at Chicago)

Last game played of streak: August 25, 1877 (Chicago at St. Louis) *Game missed to end streak*: September 4, 1877 (Chicago vs. Hartford at Brooklyn)

Consecutive Game Streak's Statistical Totals

Year	G	AB	R	H	2B	3B	HR	RBI	BB	SO	AVG	SLG	SB
1874	31	135	19	34	5	0	0	13	2	1	.252	.288	0
1875	69	308	46	75	8	0	0	27	3	6	.244	.269	10
1876	66	276	55	84	9	2	0	32	12	6	.304	.351	—
1877	43	178	29	42	4	1	0	—	3	—	.236	.270	—
Total	209	897	149	235	26	3	0	72	20	13	.262	.298	*10*

John Glenn's playing career spanned only seven seasons as he played at the major league level in the National Association and the National League from 1871 to 1877. He originally started out playing just in the outfield, but by his third season he switched to playing first base for a couple of seasons. He eventually was used at both positions although most of his playing time was in the outfield. The National Association started in early May 1871. Within a few days, Glenn was making his big league debut in the Washington Olympics' lineup as the team's right fielder on May 13, 1871. By the end of that first season, he had played in 26 contests and finished among the team leaders in hitting with a .308 batting average as Washington finished in fifth place with a 15–15 record.

Glenn was still on the Olympics' roster, this time as their left fielder, when the 1872 season started. The team played a partial schedule of nine games when the club disbanded in late May. He played in all these contests but had no club to play for as June rolled around as a result of the Olympics' demise. Soon after, he signed on with the Washington Nationals. He got into only one of their games before that team also folded in July. He had only 43 total at-bats in the 11 games and finished the year batting with just a .186 average. The next year (1873) found him still in Washington with the city's new team in the National Association. This was the season he made the change to first base. He didn't miss a single contest in 1873 as he played all 39 of the Washington Nationals' games at the first sack. He hit .263 for the year as the club won only eight games and finished in seventh place in the final standings. The Nationals did not come back for a return engagement in 1874. Glenn finally left Washington and became a member of the new team in Chicago called the White Stockings. During 1874, he rotated quite frequently between first base and right field. His Iron Man consecutive playing streak commenced in Chicago on July 18 against Philadelphia. He had one of his better years with the bat as he hit .283 and drove in a career-best 32 runners (he also achieved this total in 1876). The White Stockings, in the meantime, completed their first year with a fifth-place finish. After two seasons of playing mostly first base, Glenn reverted to primarily manning left field in 1875 for the White Stockings although he still put in around 40 percent of his on-field time at the initial base. There was not much to show for in that season as he batted .244 and the White Stockings finished a dismal seventh. The National Association expired after five years of operation with the end of the 1875 season. The White Stockings transferred over to the newly formed National League for the 1876 campaign. Chicago also signed four key players (Al Spalding, Deacon White, Ross Barnes and Cal McVey) that year from the dominating 1875 Boston Red Stockings. With these new additions, Chicago captured the first National League title as the team finished six games ahead of the second-place St. Louis Brown Stockings. The presence of these high-profile players also rubbed off on Glenn as he had his best offensive year since his rookie campaign by hitting .304 and having career highs in the runs, hits, doubles, triples and RBI categories. Additionally, his free pass total of 12 walks tied him with teammate Cap Anson for the fourth-best total in the league. Glenn became the major league Iron Man less than two weeks into the 1877 season when Brown Stockings' Davy Force sat out his team's May 19 game in Chicago against the White Stockings. Glenn would hold on to the Iron Man title through most of the season until the first week of September when an injury caused him to miss the September 4 contest against the Hartford Dark Blues.

Glenn played just seven more games before his career ended with the closure of the 1877 season. With the exception of his abbreviated playing time in 1872, his .228 batting average in his last year turned out to be a career low along with it being the lowest mark among all the fifth-place White Stockings' starters.

4. JOHN PETERS

Born: April 8, 1850, New Orleans, Louisiana, *Died*: January 4, 1924, St. Louis, Missouri *Bats*: Right *Throws*: Right *Height*: 5 feet, 7 inches *Weight*: 180 *Major league debut*: May 23, 1874 (New York at Chicago [NA]) *Last major league game*: June 11, 1884 (St. Louis at Pittsburgh [AA])

Major league Iron Man from: September 4, 1877, to September 6, 1878 *Consecutive games played*: 274 *Games as major league Iron Man*: 72 (consecutive games 203 through 274) *Teams played for during streak*: Chicago White Stockings (NA) (1874–1875), Chicago White Stockings (NL) (1876–1877) and Milwaukee Cream Citys (NL) (1878) *Primary positions played*: Second base and shortstop *Game missed before streak*: August 5, 1874 (New York at Chicago) *First game played of streak*: August 8, 1874 (New York at Chicago) *Last game played of streak*: August 31, 1878 (Indianapolis at Milwaukee) *Game missed to end streak*: September 6, 1878 (Milwaukee at Indianapolis)

Consecutive Game Streak's Statistical Totals

Year	G	AB	R	H	2B	3B	HR	RBI	BB	SO	AVG	SLG	SB
1874	24	102	14	25	3	0	0	7	0	0	.245	.275	0
1875	69	297	40	85	16	2	0	34	0	3	.286	.354	12
1876	66	316	70	111	14	2	1	47	3	2	.351	.418	—
1877	60	265	45	84	10	3	0	41	1	7	.317	.377	—
1878	55	246	33	76	6	1	0	22	5	8	.309	.341	—
Total	274	1226	202	381	49	8	1	151	9	20	.311	.366	12

Baseball historians have determined that John Peters was one of baseball's best fielding shortstops during the formative years of the National League. He was a regular player for nine of his 11 major league years as a member of five teams. After playing for a couple of amateur and independent teams in St. Louis, Peters joined the Chicago White Stockings of the National Association for the 1874 season. He made his debut in a White Stockings' home game against the New York Mutuals on May 23, 1874. It was in another Chicago home game against those same Mutuals nearly three months later (August 8) that Peters initiated his consecutive playing streak. He took in 55 games his rookie season and hit for a .289 average while rotating between shortstop and second base. In what was Chicago's first year of play in the major leagues (excluding the Chicago team that played during the 1871 season), the White Stockings finished in fifth place with a 28–31 record.

Starting with the 1875 season (with the lone exception being the 1878 campaign), Peters would man only the shortstop position for the remainder of his playing career. Although he hit a solid .286 average and provided a steady presence at shortstop in 1875, it did not help Chicago much; the team won just 30 of the 67 decided games and were 35 games behind the powerful Boston Red Stockings while being in sixth place when the season ended. Soon after, the National Association folded and Chicago moved over to the newly formed National League. Peters had his best season careerwise both offensively and defensively during the 1876 season. He achieved career highs in batting average (.351), runs (70), hits (111) and runs driven home (47). His hit total was also second overall in the league behind teammate Ross Barnes' 138 base knocks. At shortstop, he led the position with a career best .932 fielding percentage and 16 double plays. The team also performed quite well and won the first National League championship by six games over the second-place St. Louis Brown Stockings. Of course, it did not hurt that Chicago had signed four key members of the 1875 Red Stockings team to play for them in 1876. Peters had another solid year at the bat and in the field in 1877 as he hit .317 (good for third place on the team behind Cal McVey and Cap Anson), led the team with 41 RBI (only Boston's Deacon White had more with 49 runs driven in) and led all shortstops in games played, putouts, assists and double plays. Additionally, when fellow White Stocking John Glenn sat out Chicago's game against the Hartford Dark Blues on September 4, 1877, Peters took over the active lead in consecutive games with a streak of 203 contests played. After capturing the league title the previous season, the White Stockings finished in next to last place in 1877 as the club performed at a .441 percentage level and were nearly 16 games off the winning pace set by the Boston Red Caps. Peters made a change in scenery after four years with the White Stockings when in 1878 he moved over to the new National League franchise stationed in Milwaukee, the Cream Citys. The season turned out to be a disaster for the team as Milwaukee was cemented deep in the basement with a 15–45 record. Peters was second on the club with a .309 average and played more games at second base than at shortstop in 1878. His playing streak ended late that season on September 6 in Indianapolis after 274 games played.

Once his playing streak was concluded, Peters' batting and production numbers started a steady decline. Except for hitting .288 during the 1882 season, his average never climbed higher than .245. He returned to the White Stockings for one year (1879), then played for the Providence Grays in 1880 where he again led the shortstops in games played, putouts and fielding. He took one final turn in the National League with the Buffalo Bisons in 1881 before going over to the new American Association where he played his last full major league season (1882) with the Pittsburgh Alleghenys. Although he made some cameo appearances with the Alleghenys in 1883 and 1884, he spent the great majority of those years in the minors.

5. JIM O'ROURKE

Born: September 1, 1850, Bridgeport, Connecticut *Died*: January 8, 1919, Bridgeport, Connecticut *Bats*: Right *Throws*: Right *Height*: 5 feet, 8 inches *Weight*: 185 *Major league debut*: April 26, 1872 (Middletown at Troy [NA]) *Last major league game*: September 22, 1904 (First Game) (Cincinnati at New York [NL])

Major league Iron Man from: September 6, 1878, to May 13, 1879 *Consecutive games played*: 225 *Games as major league Iron Man*: 14 (consecutive games 212 through 225) *Teams played for during streak*: Boston Red Stockings (NA) (1875), Boston Red Caps (NL) (1876–1878) and Providence Grays (NL) (1879) *Primary position played*: Outfield *Game missed before streak*: July 31, 1875 (New Haven at Boston) *First game played of streak*: August 4, 1875 (Philadelphia White Stockings at Boston) *Last game played of streak*: May 10, 1879 (Providence at Buffalo) *Game missed to end streak*: May 13, 1879 (Providence at Chicago)

Jim O'Rourke

Consecutive Game Streak's Statistical Totals

Year	G	AB	R	H	2B	3B	HR	RBI	BB	SO	AVG	SLG	SB
1875	28	128	42	42	5	4	3	27	3	2	.328	.500	6
1876	70	312	61	102	17	3	2	43	15	17	.327	.420	—
1877	61	265	68	96	14	4	0	23	20	9	.362	.445	—
1878	60	255	44	71	17	7	1	29	5	21	.278	.412	—
1879	6	30	10	10	2	1	0	—	1	1	.333	.467	—
Total	225	990	225	321	55	19	6	*122*	44	50	.324	.436	6

Jim O'Rourke had one of the longest playing careers in major league history. In a Hall of Fame career that spanned 23 seasons, he played just about every position as a member of seven big league teams. He was very popular among the fans for his dedication in playing the game and the honesty he showed, both on and off the field. He earned the nickname "Orator Jim" because of his unique (and sometimes very long-winded) responses to even the simplest of questions. While he was still an active player, he continued his college education and eventually earned a law degree from Yale University. He is also the only player in the history of major league ball to put together three separate consecutive games-played streaks that eventually were long enough for him to become baseball's Iron Man on each occasion. With a career that lasted so long, it is ironic that he made his debut (in the National Association) with a team that existed less than one year. When the Middletown Mansfields opened its only season of play in 1872, O'Rourke played his first of nearly 2,000 regular season major league career games on April 26 of that year in Troy, New York, against the Haymakers. By the middle of August, the Mansfields disbanded after playing just 24 contests. O'Rourke got into 23 of those games (most notably at shortstop) and hit for a .273 average. By the next season, he earned a spot on the powerful Boston Red Stockings' roster as their first baseman and alternate outfielder. He would spend seven of the next eight seasons playing for the Boston franchise in both the National Association and the National League.

O'Rourke played on his first championship team in 1873 when the Red Stockings edged out Philadelphia by four games as Boston claimed the first prize for the second straight year. The Red Stockings were so offense laden that O'Rourke's .350 batting average was good for only fifth place on the club. His 21 doubles were the

J. H. O'ROURKE, CATCHER AND CENTRE FIELD.

Jim O'Rourke: This Hall of Famer is the only player in major league history to hold the Iron Man title three times. He held the all-time record of consecutive games until it was broken by Boston's Joe Hornung.

second-highest total in the league behind teammate Ross Barnes' 31 two-baggers. In 1874, he played all but one contest the entire year as he was used strictly at first base. Although his batting average dropped to a .314 mark, he still had plenty of offense in his bat as he was the top home run hitter in the league with five round-trippers along with having the second-highest totals in runs (82), total bases (150) and RBI (61). He finished behind Boston teammate Cal McVey in each of these categories. The Red Stockings were still the dominant team in the league as the club again cruised to a third consecutive league title. The next season (1875), manager Harry Wright switched O'Rourke from playing first base to rotating between third base and centerfield. His first Iron Man streak started with the Red Stockings' home game on August 4, 1875, against the Philadelphia White Stockings. He played the final 28 games on the team's schedule. O'Rourke's hitting fell under the .300 level, with a .296 average, for the first time since his rookie year. He repeated as the home run hitting champion with six clouts along with being among the league leaders again in runs scored and runs knocked in. The Red Stockings completely dominated the other teams in the league by finishing with a near-perfect 71–8 record and handily winning a fourth title in as many years. O'Rourke handled the centerfield position in the team's first season with the National League. He led the club in several categories, most notably his .327 batting average. Unfortunately, with the Red Stockings losing four key players (first baseman Cal McVey, second baseman Ross Barnes, catcher Deacon White and pitcher Al Spalding) to the Chicago White Stockings, Boston slipped to a fourth-place finish in the standings and were 15 games behind the pennant-winning White Stockings. Although he was still the team's center fielder in 1877, O'Rourke alternated more frequently that year between left and center fields. Even though he did not have a single homer that year, the 1877 season was probably was one of his better years in the big leagues. He finished with a career-best .362 average (which was good for fourth place among all league batters) and led the league with 68 runs, 20 walks and a .407 on base percentage. With Deacon White returning to the Boston lineup after a one-year hiatus in Chicago, the newly named Red Caps found themselves in a familiar position by the end of the season as the club climbed back on top of the league standings with a seven-game edge over the controversial second-place-finishing Louisville Grays. He took over the role as the sport's most durable player late in the 1878 season when the Milwaukee Cream Citys' infielder John Peters' streak concluded on September 6 in Indianapolis. After having such an excellent year with the bat the previous year, O'Rourke finished 1878 with just 71 hits as his batting plummeted over 80 percentage points to a .278 average. The team was still able to capture its sixth title in seven years by finishing four games ahead of the Cincinnati Reds. O'Rourke decided to leave Boston after the 1878 season due to a financial conflict he had with the team's management and signed on to play for the Providence Grays in 1879. He was assigned the right field spot in the lineup, replacing the departed Dick Higham. O'Rourke's playing streak ended after 225 games, just six games into the new year, when he sat out the May 13, 1879, contest in Chicago against the White Stockings.

O'Rourke's next playing streak started in the latter stages of the 1879 season. Further information about his second and third playing streaks plus the remainder of his playing career are contained in later profiles of this great player.

6. JOHN CLAPP

Born: July 17, 1851, Ithaca, New York *Died*: December 18, 1904, Ithaca, New York *Bats*: Right *Throws*: Right *Height*: 5 feet, 7 inches *Weight*: 194 *Major league debut*: April 26, 1872 (Middletown at Troy [NA]) *Last major league game*: September 28, 1883 (Detroit at New York [NL])

John Clapp   12

Major league Iron Man from: May 13, 1879, to June 25, 1879 *Consecutive games played*: 212 *Games as major league Iron Man*: 19 (consecutive games 194 through 212) *Teams played for during streak*: St. Louis Brown Stockings (NL) (1876–1877), Indianapolis Blues (NL) (1878) and Buffalo Bisons (NL) (1879) *Primary positions played*: Catcher and outfield *Game missed before streak*: October 28, 1875 (St. Louis at Philadelphia Athletics [NA]) *First game played of streak*: April 25, 1876 (St. Louis at Cincinnati) *Last game played of streak*: June 24, 1879 (Cleveland at Buffalo) *Game missed to end streak*: June 25, 1879 (Cleveland at Buffalo)

Consecutive Game Streak's Statistical Totals

Year	G	AB	R	H	2B	3B	HR	RBI	BB	SO	AVG	SLG	SB
1876	64	298	60	91	4	2	0	29	8	2	.305	.332	—
1877	60	255	47	81	6	6	0	34	8	6	.318	.388	—
1878	63	263	42	80	10	2	0	29	13	8	.304	.357	—
1879	25	104	20	32	5	1	0	—	2	4	.308	.375	—
Total	212	920	169	284	25	11	0	92	31	20	.309	.360	—

John Clapp was a stocky player who caught and played in the outfield with National Association and National League teams between 1872 and 1883. During his years in the big leagues, he wasn't one to stay around long in one place as was evidenced by his playing with eight teams in 11 years. He also displayed leadership traits that were used when he managed six of those eight teams. He first played in the amateur ranks before becoming a professional in the National Association in 1872 with the Middletown Mansfields. In addition to being the club's catcher, he also served as the team's manager. Clapp hit for a .278 average in 19 contests as the team had a 5–19 record when it disbanded in mid–August of that first year.

Clapp immediately moved over to the Philadelphia Athletics the following year where he stayed for three seasons. His assignment with the Athletics turned out to be his longest tenure with one team during his playing career. He took over the catching duties from Fergy Malone and Mike McGeary, who had shared that chore in 1872. Clapp had another good season with the bat by hitting .304 while the Athletics finished with a winning .549 winning percentage and a fifth-place finish. Clapp returned to the Athletics for a second season and although he was still the primary catcher, he shared that responsibility occasionally with shortstop McGeary. His average fell to a .291 batting mark, but he hit three homers which was good enough to lead the club. If it were not for three Boston Red Stockings (O'Rourke, McVey and White), his home run total would have been good enough to top all league hitters. The Athletics were still about a dozen games behind the top-finishing Red Stockings in 1874 as the squad came in third place with a .600 winning percentage. Clapp fully concentrated on catching in 1875 but he slumped often and, as a result, his batting average fell to .264. The Athletics finished third for the second straight year with a 53–20 record but were still 15 games off the winning pace set by the Red Stockings, who topped off the standings with an amazing 71–8 record. Although the Athletics were one of the franchises retained for the new National League, Clapp found himself on the move when he switched over to the St. Louis Brown Stockings. Since he had sat out the Athletics' 1875 season finale on October 28, his Iron Man consecutive playing streak started with the new league's startup on April 25, 1876, when the Brown Stockings opened up the year in Cincinnati against the Reds. Clapp hit .305 while holding down the team's catching duties. His batting average was good for second place on the team behind center fielder Lip Pike's .323 mark. That year, Clapp also led all league catchers in putouts (333) and passed balls (52). The Brown Stockings had a good season as well as the squad came in with a 45–19 record which was good for second place behind the first-place Chicago White Stockings. The next year (1877), Clapp found himself the team's key run producer with 34 RBI along with pacing St. Louis with a .318 average. The Brown Stockings regressed in the standings to fourth place in the six-team league with a 28–32 record. After two years in St. Louis, Clapp jumped at the chance to be a manager a second time when he was offered the role with the new league franchise in Indianapolis, called the Hoosiers. He decided to take advantage of his position as manager to primarily play left field instead of the more physically grueling position of catcher. He hit above the .300 level for the third straight year with a .304 average and extended his playing streak to 187 games (good enough for the second-longest mark behind Jim O'Rourke). His tenure with the Hoosiers was not much of a success though as he guided them to a fifth-place outcome, some 17 games behind the first-place Boston Red Caps. When Indianapolis dropped out of the league after the 1878 season, Clapp again changed teams. He signed as a player-manager with the Buffalo Bisons, another new National League team. Two weeks into the 1879 season, Clapp took over the longest active run of consecutive games when the Providence Grays' O'Rourke missed a game on May 13. Clapp's time as the top Iron Man lasted just under 20 games when his 212 game playing streak ended on June 25 due to an injured finger. He was the last player to play every National League contest since the league's formation in 1876. The year turned out to be his best season as a manager as he guided the Bisons to a 46–32 record and a solid third-place finish behind the Grays and Red Caps.

After one season, Clapp left Buffalo and over the next two years played and managed the Cincinnati Reds and Cleveland Blues, but the final results both times were finishes at or near the bottom of the standings. He spent the 1882 season out of the major leagues with the independent New York Metros' team before returning to the big leagues in 1883 to manage and play with the new team in New York, the Gothams. In what turned out to be his final major league season, he played just 20 games and hit for a minuscule .178 average while guiding New York to a sixth-place outcome in the final standings. He gave up baseball after the 1883 season and several years later returned to his native Ithaca, New York, and became a member of the city's police force.

7. CAL MCVEY

Born: August 30, 1850, Montrose, Iowa *Died*: August 20, 1926, San Francisco, California *Bats*: Right *Throws*: Right *Height*: 5 feet, 9 inches *Weight*: 170 *Major league debut*: May 5, 1871 (Boston at Washington [NA]) *Last major league game*: September 30, 1879 (Cincinnati at Cleveland [NL])

Major league Iron Man from: June 25, 1879, to May 1, 1880 *Consecutive games played*: 262 *Games as major league Iron Man*: 56 (consecutive games 207 through 262) *Teams played for during streak*: Chicago White Stockings (NL) (1876–1877) and Cincinnati Reds (NL) (1878–1879) *Primary positions played*: First base, third base and catcher *Game missed before streak*: May 8, 1876 (Chicago at St. Louis) *First game played of streak*: May 10, 1876 (Cincinnati at Chicago) *Last game played of streak*: September 30, 1879 (Cincinnati at Cleveland) *Game missed to end streak*: (major league career ended after 1879 season)

Consecutive Game Streak's Statistical Totals

Year	G	AB	R	H	2B	3B	HR	RBI	BB	SO	AVG	SLG	SB
1876	60	294	60	105	14	0	1	—	2	4	.357	.415	—
1877	60	266	58	98	9	7	0	36	8	11	.368	.455	—
1878	61	271	43	83	10	4	2	28	5	10	.306	.395	—
1879	81	354	64	105	18	6	0	55	8	13	.297	.381	—
Total	262	1185	225	391	51	17	3	*119*	23	38	.330	.409	—

Cal McVey

Although Cal McVey played at the major league level for just nine seasons, he was a member of four championship teams during those years. He was an excellent hitter who had the versatility to play just about any position. He had played for Harry Wright in Cincinnati before the National Association became baseball's first official professional league. When McVey was recruited to play for the Boston Red Stockings. Harry Wright was there already as the team's manager. McVey's first year proved very successful as he was the league leader with 66 hits along with finishing in second place in batting (.431), runs knocked in (43) and times on base (67). On defense, he served as pitcher Al Spalding's catcher and led the position in games played.

McVey's second year in the league saw his batting severely plummet to a .321 average. His RBI total was still up there as he drove in 44 runners and contributed to the club's winning the league pennant in 1872. He moved over to the Baltimore Canaries the next year where he was chosen to take the managerial reins. Although he played most games as catcher, he served as a utility player and used himself at a variety of positions. By the second week of July, he was replaced as manager by the team's second baseman, Tom Carey. McVey recovered from his sophomore slump as he rediscovered his batting stroke and upped his average to .380 along with pacing Baltimore with a .490 slugging percentage. After one season in Baltimore, he returned to the Red Stockings in 1874. With Deacon White now handling the catching duties for the Red Stockings' primary pitcher, Al Spalding, McVey took over the right field position, replacing Bob Addy who departed for the Hartford Dark Blues. McVey wound up having another solid season by finishing the year with a .359 batting average (good for runner-up to batting champion Levi Meyerle's .394 mark) and achieving league-leading marks in runs (91), hits (123), runs batted in (71), times on base (124), total bases (165) and extra-base hits (30). His efforts that year were also one of the main reasons the Red Stockings captured another National Association title. His superior play followed through to the next season (1875) as he played in all of Boston's games (he shifted over to primarily play first base) and again

Cal McVey: This Cincinnati player appeared in the final 262 games of his big league career. He left the majors after the 1879 season and moved to California.

was the league's leader in RBI, extra-base hits and total bases along with adding on the most doubles and best slugging percentage to his resume. He concluded the National Association's final year by being on his third championship team in five seasons as the Red Stockings left all their competitors in the dust with an astounding 71–8 record. When the National League started up play in April 1876, McVey jumped over to the new league with three other Red Stockings teammates and signed on to play for the Chicago White Stockings, who were being managed by his former battery mate, Al Spalding. Two weeks into the new season he started his consecutive playing streak (returning to the lineup after missing three games) on May 10, 1876, in Chicago where the White Stockings were playing the Cincinnati Reds. He finished the year with a .347 average as he appeared in the final 60 games on the schedule. For the fourth time in six years McVey was on a first-place club as Chicago won the very first National League title by six games over the St. Louis Brown Stockings. In 1877 he was one of the very few bright spots for the White Stockings as the team completely collapsed by finishing with a 26–33 record and barely missed coming in last as the club claimed fifth place. His team high .368 average was good for third place in the league behind former Boston teammate Deacon White's .387 and Hartford's John Cassidy's .378 batting performances.

This was his final season in Chicago as he moved to the Cincinnati Reds in 1878 as their new manager and third baseman. Although he hit for only a .306 average, his leadership as manager turned around a Reds club that the two previous seasons had finished dead last in the standings. The squad just missed a last-to-first scenario by trailing the first-place Boston Red Caps by a mere four games in the final standings. Amazingly, when the 1879 season rolled around, his former Red Stockings' teammate Deacon White was the Reds' new skipper. White's reign lasted just 18 games and by June 10, McVey was again the team's manager. He switched to primarily playing first base in 1879 although he took a crack at several other positions during the course of the year. Two weeks after being renamed the Reds' manager, he assumed major league baseball's Iron Man title on June 25 from Buffalo's playing manager and catcher John Clapp. McVey finished the year with a career-low .297 batting average as he led the Reds to an overall fifth-place result. He also extended his playing streak to 262 games when the curtain came down on the 1879 season. Before the beginning of the 1880 season, McVey voluntarily ended his streak as he gave up his major league playing career so he could move to California. He went on to play with and manage baseball teams for several years in the Pacific Coast leagues.

8. Paul Hines

Born: March 1, 1852, Washington, D.C. *Died*: July 10, 1935, Hyattsville, Maryland *Bats*: Right *Throws*: Right *Height*: 5 feet, 9½ inches *Weight*: 173 *Major league debut*: April 20, 1872 (Baltimore at Washington [NA]) *Last major league game*: July 3, 1891 (Cincinnati at Washington [AA])

Major league Iron Man from: May 1, 1880, to June 29, 1880 *Consecutive games played*: 242 *Games as major league Iron Man*: 33 (consecutive games 210 through 242) *Teams played for during streak*: Chicago White Stockings (NL) (1876–1877) and Providence Grays (NL) (1878–1880) *Primary positions played*: Outfield and second base *Game missed before streak*: September 23, 1876 (Boston at Chicago) *First game played of streak*: September 26, 1876 (Hartford at Chicago) *Last game played of streak*: June 28, 1880 (Providence at Buffalo) *Game missed to end streak*: June 29, 1880 (Providence at Buffalo)

Paul Hines

Consecutive Game Streak's Statistical Totals

Year	G	AB	R	H	2B	3B	HR	RBI	BB	SO	AVG	SLG	SB
1876	2	10	2	5	1	0	0	—	0	1	.500	.600	—
1877	60	261	44	73	11	7	0	23	1	8	.280	.375	—
1878	62	257	42	92	13	4	4	50	2	10	.358	.486	—
1879	85	409	81	146	25	10	2	52	8	16	.357	.482	—
1880	33	146	34	57	12	0	0	—	5	3	.390	.473	—
Total	242	1083	203	373	62	21	6	*125*	16	38	.344	.457	—

Hines' second consecutive playing streak that qualified him to be the major league's Iron Man started just a couple of weeks after his initial playing streak ended on September 13, 1876. It was the September 26 contest that started his new playing streak as the Chicago White Stockings hosted the Hartford Dark Blues. He finished with a .331 average and had league highs with 21 doubles and a .923 fielding percentage for outfielders. He also was tied with teammates Cap Anson and Ross Barnes for second place in the league with 59 runners driven in. Another Chicago teammate, Deacon White, topped the league by bringing home 60 runners. The White Stockings were so powerful offensively that the club scored over 150 more runs than their closest competitor, the Red Caps, in the runs scored category. The White Stockings also won the 1876 National League championship by six games over the St. Louis Brown Stockings.

The 1877 season was a below-average year for both Hines and the White Stockings. His hitting fell off 51 percentage points (down to a .280 average) while Chicago completely fell apart at the seams. The club won only 26 games (half of what the squad won the previous year) and came in fifth place, just a few games ahead of the cellar-dwelling Cincinnati Red Stockings. That year turned out to be Hines' final season with Chicago. When the 1878 season arrived, he was the center fielder on the new National League team in Providence called the Grays. Hines had a spectacular year as he won baseball's first Triple Crown by leading the league with a career best .358 batting average, four homers and 50 runs driven home. His .486 slugging percentage and 125 total bases also led all league hitters. Providence also made quite an impression their first year in the league by finishing in third place, only eight games behind the first-place Boston Red Caps. In 1879, Hines had another great year as he repeated as the league's batting champion with a .357 average along with leading in at-bats, hits, total bases, times on base and most games played by an outfielder. He was also among the league leaders in on-base percentage, runs scored and doubles. Additionally, he played his sixth season (in the last seven years) without missing a game and extended his streak to 209 games. Providence also surprised many fans by outpacing the Red Caps by five games to capture the National League title. With the opening of the 1880 season on May 1, Hines became the Iron Man of the majors for the second time in his career. He replaced Cal McVey, who left the Cincinnati Reds and the major leagues at the conclusion of the 1879 campaign and moved to California. Hines' second tour as Iron Man lasted two months and ended after 242 games when an injured arm caused him to sit out the Grays' June 29, 1880, contest in Buffalo. He finished the year by pacing the Grays' hitters with a .307 average. He also was the club's top man in several other statistical categories, including at-bats where his total was second in the league behind the White Stockings' Abner Dalrymple. Defensively, he was the top-fielding outfielder in the league with a .927 average and had the most double plays with seven twin killings. Although the White Stockings ran away with the title in 1880 by 15 games, Providence still had a good year by finishing in second place with a 52–32 record.

Hines kept playing for many more seasons but never compiled another playing streak to qualify as the Iron Man. He patrolled center field for the Grays through to the team's final year in 1885. During this time, he played the full slate of games in 1882 and 1884 and led the National League in doubles in 1881 (27) and 1884 (36). With the demise of the Grays after the 1885 season, Hines was obtained by the Washington Senators in March 1886. He put in two productive years for the Senators, hitting above .300 each season before being traded to the Indianapolis Hoosiers after the 1887 campaign. He stayed with the Hoosiers for a couple of seasons before serving brief stints with the Pittsburgh Alleghanys, Boston Beaneaters and finally the Washington Senators (of the American Association). He was the oldest active major league ballplayer his last two years (1890 and 1891) in the big leagues. With a playing career that had started back in 1872, he played his last major league contest in the American Association on July 3, 1891, in Washington against the Cincinnati Porkers. He played in the minors for three more years after that before permanently retiring from the game in 1896. He returned to his hometown and soon after got a job (via presidential appointment) with the United States government.

9. John Morrill

Born: February 19, 1855, Boston, Massachusetts *Died*: April 2, 1932, Brookline, Massachusetts *Bats*: Right *Throws*: Right *Height*: 5 feet, 10½ inches *Weight*: 155 *Major league debut*: April 24, 1876 (Boston at Philadelphia [NL]) *Last major league game*: July 8, 1890 (Cleveland at Boston [PL])

Major league Iron Man from: June 29, 1880, to May 20, 1881 *Consecutive games played*: 302 *Games as major league Iron Man*: 64 (consecutive games 239 through 302) *Team played for during streak*: Boston Red Caps (NL) *Primary positions played*: First base and third base *Game missed before streak*: October 21, 1876 (Hartford at Boston) *First game played of streak*: April 30, 1877 (Boston vs. Hartford at Brooklyn) *Last game played of streak*: May 18, 1881 (Boston at Cleveland) *Game missed to end streak*: May 20, 1881 (Boston at Chicago)

Consecutive Game Streak's Statistical Totals

Year	G	AB	R	H	2B	3B	HR	RBI	BB	SO	AVG	SLG	SB
1877	61	242	47	73	5	1	0	28	6	15	.302	.331	—
1878	60	233	26	56	5	1	0	23	5	16	.240	.270	—
1879	84	348	56	98	18	5	0	49	14	32	.282	.362	—
1880	86	342	51	81	16	8	2	44	11	37	.237	.348	—
1881	11	40	2	5	1	0	0	—	0	2	.125	.150	—
Total	302	1205	182	313	45	15	2	*144*	36	102	.260	.327	—

John Morrill held down the first-base job of the Boston Red Caps and Beaneaters for most of a 13-year span from 1876 to 1888. He also proved his versatility by playing every position on the baseball diamond many times over a 15-year major league career. Having played amateur ball for just one year, the Red Caps signed him to a contract starting with the inaugural season of the National League in 1876. He made his debut in the Red Caps' second game on April 24, 1876, in Philadelphia. Unfortunately, Boston would rather have forgotten the game as the team was massacred by the hometown Athletics by a 20–3 score. Red Caps' manager Harry Wright rotated Morrill that first season by using him at second base or performing the catching duties. Morrill proved his capability to hit major league pitching as he finished with a very respectable .263 average although he had one of the lowest RBI totals on the team with just 26 runs driven home. He only sat out just four contests his rookie year, one of which was the season finale in Boston against the Hartford Dark Blues on October 21, 1876.

John Morrill 18

With the startup of the 1877 season, Morrill began his consecutive string of playing games on April 30, 1877, when the Red Caps played the Hartford Dark Blues in the season opener in Brooklyn. He put in most of his time that year at first or third base although he did take the occasional turn in right field. Even though he still was not bringing many runs home, Morrill provided the steady presence in the field and had his second-best career season as a hitter with a .302 average. Boston in the meantime easily coasted to its first National League title by seven games over the Louisville Grays. Although his 1878 performance resulted in a .240 average (a drop of over 60 points from his 1877 efforts), the Red Caps won a second straight title as the league champions, outlasting the Cincinnati Reds by four games. Morrill played first base and led the position with 36 double plays. The next year (1879), the Red Caps preferred rookie Ed Cogswell at first base and shuttled Morrill between third base and as a backup for Cogswell at first. He rebounded from his poor performance in 1878 by hitting .282 and more than doubling his RBI total with 49 runners brought home (even though the schedule contained 24 more games). Trying for a third consecutive title, the Red Caps came up five games short and finished in second place as the Providence Grays won the 1879 National League title. Morrill took over the Iron Man title a few months into the 1880 season when Providence's Paul Hines sat out the June 29 contest due to an injured arm. Morrill established a new all-time record for most consecutive games played on August 17, 1880, when his streak reached 263 games and he bypassed the record previously held by Cal McVey. Morrill finished the season by playing his fourth straight year without missing a contest and further extending the record to 291 games. His performance that year might have justified a day or two off from the schedule as his hitting fell off again, this time to a .237 average although he was just one RBI short of having a team high in that particular statistic. He also led all first basemen with 26 assists. The Red Caps suffered their first losing season with a .476 winning percentage and a sixth-place finish. Morrill finally sat out a game when the Red Caps played in Chicago against the White Stockings on May 20, 1881, thereby ending a streak that just two games prior had achieved 300 games (the first playing streak to achieve this mark). He had only five hits (and a .125 batting average) in the first 11 games that season and his sitting out the contest was understandable. He held onto the all-time record until it was broken by Jim O'Rourke during the 1883 season.

JOHN F. MORRILL,
Boston Club, First Base.

John Morrill: He was the first player to cross over the 300-straight-game barrier in May 1881. His streak ended days later at 302 games.

After his streak ended, Morrill stayed with Boston for another seven years. His best year overall was the 1883 season when he hit a career-best .319 and finished second to Buffalo's Dan Brouthers in slugging percentage, total bases and triples. Additionally, he led first basemen with a .974 fielding average, the only time in his career that he led in fielding. Besides playing first base and serving as the team captain, he also took the managerial reins in 1882, succeeding Harry Wright. He guided the club to a third-place tie that season but gave way the next year (1883) to Jack Burdock. By the end of July 1883, he was back at the helm replacing Burdock and guiding the newly named Beaneaters to the National League pennant. He stayed on as manager through the end of the 1888 season but did not come close to another pennant as Boston was a perennial middle-of-the-pack finisher. After a prominent 13-year career with the Boston franchise, he was sold to the Washington Senators at the start of the 1889 campaign. He took in only 44 games for the Senators and was hitting an anemic .185 when he was given his release in midseason. He appeared in a couple of games the next year with the Boston Reds of the renegade Players League before calling it a career in 1890. He stayed in baseball for several more years, doing some umpiring and sportswriting before going into private business selling sporting goods.

10. Jack Burdock

Born: April 1852, Brooklyn, New York *Died*: November 27, 1931, Brooklyn, New York *Bats*: Right *Throws*: Right *Height*: 5 feet, 9½ inches *Weight*: 158 *Major league debut*: May 2, 1872 (Brooklyn at Middletown [NA]) *Last major league game*: July 23, 1891 (Brooklyn at Boston [NL])

Major league Iron Man from: May 20, 1881, to June 7, 1881 *Consecutive games played*: 276 *Games as major league Iron Man*: 10 (consecutive games 267 through 276) *Teams played for during streak*: Hartford Dark Blues (NL) (1877) and Boston Red Caps (NL) (1878–1881) *Primary position played*: Second base *Game missed before streak*: July 25, 1877 (Hartford at Cincinnati) *First game played of streak*: July 26, 1877 (Hartford at Chicago) *Last game played of streak*: June 4, 1881 (Buffalo at Boston) *Game missed to end streak*: June 7, 1881 (Buffalo at Boston)

Consecutive Game Streak's Statistical Totals

Year	G	AB	R	H	2B	3B	HR	RBI	BB	SO	AVG	SLG	SB
1877	25	115	14	32	2	0	0	—	1	7	.278	.296	—
1878	60	246	37	64	12	6	0	25	3	17	.260	.358	—
1879	84	359	64	86	10	3	0	36	9	28	.240	.284	—
1880	86	356	58	90	17	4	2	35	8	26	.253	.340	—
1881	21	77	7	16	3	0	0	—	2	5	.208	.247	—
Total	276	1153	180	288	44	13	2	96	23	83	.250	.316	—

During the early portion of major league baseball history, Jack Burdock was one of the sport's best second basemen. He had a long playing career that lasted 18 seasons as he toiled for five teams. The majority of his peak years were spent in a Boston Red Caps or Beaneaters uniform. His career started with the Brooklyn Atlantics of the National Association where he hit for a .270 average and played in every contest as he held down the shortstop job during his rookie season in 1872.

He returned to Brooklyn the following season but he switched over to play second base due to the Atlantics' acquisition of shortstop Dickey Pearce, who had come from the New York Mutuals. Burdock had a decent year with a .253 average and his putouts, errors and games played at second base led the league in 1873. The 1874 season found him on the New

York Mutuals' roster, where he took over third base from John Hatfield, who was moved to the outfield. After playing for just a season with the Mutuals, where he hit for a .279 average and led the league's third basemen in fielding percentage and putouts, Burdock moved on to the Hartford Dark Blues in 1875. It was there that he made the permanent career switch to playing second base. The Dark Blues were looking for a new second baseman since Bob Addy had left to play for the Philadelphia franchise. Burdock had the second-highest batting average (.294) on the team next to left fielder Tom York. In 1875, Burdock also won his first of six fielding titles at second base. Although the National Association went out of business after the 1875 campaign, Hartford was one of the franchises that moved over to the National League in 1876. That first year in the National League, Burdock played the full slate of Dark Blue games and led the second basemen in games played and putouts. It was at the halfway point of the 1877 season when he started up his consecutive playing streak during a Hartford game in Chicago against the White Stockings. In what was to be his final year with Hartford, he had a solid .260 average and came in third place in the league's at-bats department. Additionally, his 185 putouts and .903 fielding percentage were league highs for second basemen. Hartford came in third place, 10 games off the pennant-winning pace of the Red Caps. By the time the next season rolled around, Burdock was a member of those same Red Caps. He took over the club's second base spot from George Wright, who moved over to shortstop. As the Red Caps repeated as league champions, Burdock won the Triple Crown for fielders at his position as his putout, assist and fielding numbers (along with double plays) easily outpaced all other second basemen. The following year (1879), his batting average had fallen to .240 as Boston came up short by five games of capturing another title as the Providence Grays came in first. Burdock brought his batting up to a .253 average in 1880 and again led the National League's second basemen in games played, putouts and fielding. He closed out the year by extending his consecutive playing string to 255 games. The Red Caps had a disappointing season as the Boston franchise experienced its first under .500 percentage season with a 40–44 record and a sixth-place finish. The following year when teammate John Morrill missed the May 20, 1881 game, Burdock inherited the Iron Man title. His time as major league baseball's most active durable player came to an end just 10 games later when his playing streak was snapped at 276 games on June 7 in a Red Caps' home game against the Buffalo Bisons. He had gotten off to a rather poor start that year as was indicated by his .208 batting average and his benching was justified.

    Although his playing streak finally came to an end, Burdock spent many more years with Boston. He managed Boston during the first few months of the 1883 season (succeeding Morrill) before returning the managerial reins to Morrill. Burdock's career year at the plate (1883) was also the year he was the club's offensive driving force. It also happened to be the same season the team changed their name to the Beaneaters. His team-leading .330 batting average and 88 runners driven home contributed directly to helping the Beaneaters win the 1883 National League championship. His RBI total in 1883 was the second best in the league behind Buffalo's first baseman Dan Brouthers, who drove in 97 runners. He stayed with the Beaneaters for close to five more years until the opening months of the 1888 season when he moved over to the Brooklyn Bridegrooms of the American Association to supplant Bill McClellan at second base. His performance with the Bridegrooms turned out to be a major disappointment as he batted only .122 and scored just 15 runs in 70 games. He returned to the minor leagues in 1889 for three more seasons except for a final three major league games with Brooklyn in 1891. He retired after the conclusion of the 1891 season. Although his playing career spanned over three decades, his baseball skills in the latter stages of his playing career were negatively affected by his excessive use of alcohol.

11. Bill Phillips

Born: 1857, St. Johns, New Brunswick, Canada *Died*: October 7, 1900, Chicago, Illinois *Bats*: Right *Throws*: Right *Height*: 6 feet *Weight*: 202 *Major league debut*: May 1, 1879 (Providence at Cleveland [NL]) *Last major league game*: October 14, 1888 (second game) (Kansas City at Louisiana [AA])

Major league Iron Man from: June 7, 1881, to August 23, 1882 *Consecutive games played*: 275 *Games as major league Iron Man*: 126 (consecutive games 150 through 275) *Team played for during streak*: Cleveland Blues (NL) *Primary position played*: First base *Game missed before streak*: July 21, 1879 (Boston at Cleveland) *First game played of streak*: July 23, 1879 (Boston at Cleveland) *Last game played of streak*: August 19, 1882 (Cleveland at Worcester) *Game missed to end streak*: August 23, 1882 (Cleveland at Troy)

Consecutive Game Streak's Statistical Totals

Year	G	AB	R	H	2B	3B	HR	RBI	BB	SO	AVG	SLG	SB
1879	42	186	24	43	4	2	0	—	2	3	.231	.274	—
1880	85	334	41	85	14	10	1	36	6	29	.254	.365	—
1881	85	357	51	97	18	10	1	44	5	19	.272	.387	—
1882	63	273	34	72	14	6	4	—	4	8	.264	.403	—
Total	275	1150	150	297	50	28	6	80	17	59	.258	.366	—

Bill Phillips was one of the best-fielding first basemen around during the 1880s. He participated in the major leagues for 10 seasons. He was born in Canada but moved to the United States as a child. He started out playing for independent teams but eventually made it to the majors when Cleveland was granted a National League franchise in 1879. When he made his debut in Cleveland on May 1, 1879, against the Providence Grays, Phillips became the first Canadian to play in the major leagues. His consecutive playing streak started around the midway point of his rookie season while the Boston Red Caps were visiting the Blues on July 23, 1879. Phillips justified his presence on the club by posting the team's third-highest batting average (.271) behind catcher Doc Kennedy's .290 mark. Phillips drove in 29 runners and had team highs in at-bats, runs and hits for the sixth-place Blues. He also led league first basemen with 75 games played. His rookie season turned out to be the only year where he was used at different playing positions as he was used as catcher in 11 games and played in the outfield on a couple of occasions. The rest of his career was spent at first base except for one brief appearance as a catcher during the 1882 season.

Phillips suffered a moderate sophomore slump in 1880 as his batting average fell to .254 but he did increase his run productive total by driving home 36 runners. At first base, he did not miss a single inning and led the position in double plays along with appearing in the most contests. While his hitting numbers had shown a slight decline, Cleveland improved dramatically from their inaugural season as the club won 20 more games and finished in third place, behind the Chicago White Stockings and the Providence Grays. Phillips' playing streak had grown to only 150 games when he replaced Red Caps' second baseman Jack Burdock as major league baseball's new Iron Man on June 7, 1881. He was the top run producer on the team with 44 runs knocked in. His batting average rebounded to a .272 mark and his 10 triples were good for second best in the league behind Buffalo Bisons' catcher Jack Rowe, who had 11 three-baggers. Phillips again led in games played at first base for the third successive season and repeated as the leader in double plays. On the other hand, the Blues went in reverse as the club finished in seventh place, just three games ahead of the last-place Worcester Ruby Legs. Phillips' playing streak came to an end after 275 contests on August 23, 1882, when he missed the game against the Troy Trojans. Ironically, he was the only Blues' infielder to miss a game that season. His 47 runs driven home was good enough to repeat as the team's RBI king while he also clubbed a career-best four homers. In what turned out to be a closely contested pennant race, the Blues finished in fifth place but were only a dozen games behind the league-leading White Stockings.

Phillips capably handled the first base duties for the Blues for two more seasons until the club passed away after the 1884 season. During that season, the Brooklyn Trolley Dodgers of the American Association used three players at their first base position. With the Dodgers in desperate need of a first baseman, Phillips was available and made the switch to the American Association. He held down that position for three years, highlighted by his career-best .302 average during his first season (1885) in a Dodgers uniform and the 101 runs he drove home in 1887 while still in Brooklyn. He also put together Gold Glove–caliber seasons at first base in 1885 and 1887. The Dodgers sold him to the Kansas City Cowboys in mid–January 1888. His one year in Kansas City turned out to be his final major league season. He missed only three games, fielded first base with a .980 percentage and led the position with 1,476 putouts for the last-place Cowboys. He had his problems at the plate as he produced a career-low .236 average. Soon after the season closed, the Cowboys released him. He returned to Canada to play for a season with Hamilton of the International Association before retiring permanently after the 1889 season.

12. Jim O'Rourke

Born: September 1, 1850, Bridgeport, Connecticut *Died*: January 8, 1919, Bridgeport, Connecticut *Bats*: Right *Throws*: Right *Height*: 5 feet, 8 inches *Weight*: 185 *Major league debut*: April 26, 1872 (Middletown at Troy) *Last major league game*: September 22, 1904 (first game) (Cincinnati at New York)

Major league Iron Man from: August 23, 1882, to July 3, 1883 *Consecutive games played*: 319 *Games as major league Iron Man*: 61 (consecutive games 259 through 319) *Teams played for during streak*: Providence Grays (NL) (1879), Boston Red Caps (NL) (1880) and Buffalo Bisons (NL) (1881–1883) *Primary positions played*: Catcher, first base, third base and outfield *Game missed before streak*: August 15, 1879 (Providence at Troy) *First game played of streak*: August 19, 1879 (Syracuse at Providence) *Last game played of streak*: July 2, 1883 (Buffalo at Chicago) *Game missed to end streak*: July 3, 1883 (Buffalo at Chicago)

Consecutive Game Streak's Statistical Totals

Year	G	AB	R	H	2B	3B	HR	RBI	BB	SO	AVG	SLG	SB
1879	27	116	21	45	5	3	1	—	2	0	.388	.509	—
1880	86	363	71	100	20	11	6	45	21	8	.275	.441	—
1881	83	348	71	105	21	7	0	30	27	18	.302	.402	—
1882	84	370	62	104	15	6	2	37	13	13	.281	.370	—
1883	39	173	37	57	15	0	0	—	4	5	.329	.416	—
Total	319	1370	262	411	76	27	9	*112*	67	44	.300	.415	—

O'Rourke's second Iron Man streak started in the latter stages of the 1879 season during a Providence Grays' home game on August 19 against the Syracuse Stars. He played the final 27 games on the Grays' 1879 schedule and checked out with a great year during his only season with the Grays as he improved his batting average 70 percentage points to a .348 mark. This was good enough to tie with Cincinnati's King Kelly for second place as O'Rourke's teammate Paul Hines led the league with a .357 average. O'Rourke's .371 on-base percentage however was tops among all National Leaguers. With Providence having the league's top two hitters in their starting lineup along with excellent pitching, the Grays won the National League title by five games over the Red Caps.

O'Rourke resolved the financial problems he had in 1878 with Boston's management during the off-season and returned to the Red Caps for the 1880 season. His older brother, John, was happy that O'Rourke was returning to Boston so that they could become teammates. John actually replaced his younger brother in center field when Jim left the team for the Grays. The 1880 season turned out to be Jim O'Rourke's seventh and final year playing for the Boston franchise. Although he played every contest that year, Boston's manager, Harry Wright, used him more in a utility role as O'Rourke took turns filling in at catcher, first base, third base and the outfield. He led the Red Caps in every offensive statistic except doubles and batting average. His home run total of six round-trippers was tops in the league, tied with Harry Stovey of the Worcester Ruby Legs. His average however plummeted back to .275 (a drop of 73 percentage points) even though it was the third-best average in the club. Boston did not challenge for the title as the squad finished in sixth place, 27 games off the lead and ahead of just two teams, the Buffalo Bisons and the Cincinnati Reds. One of those teams (Buffalo) offered O'Rourke the chance to both manage and play for the club. He took the Bisons up on the offer and became their player-manager in 1881, replacing Sam Crane at the helm. While O'Rourke was hitting .302 and leading the Bisons in hits, runs and walks, the team responded well to their rookie manager's leadership. The squad finished in third place and nearly doubled their win total from the 1880 campaign. O'Rourke became the Iron Man for a second time with an active streak of 259 games when Bill Phillips of the Cleveland Blues missed a contest on August 23, 1882, ending his 275-game streak. O'Rourke turned in another solid performance as he hit .281 and led Buffalo to a 45–39 record and another third-place finish. Additionally, for the first time in four seasons, he concentrated on playing one position as he manned center field in the lineup for 77 of the 84 games played during the 1882 season. When his streak reached 303 consecutive games the following season on June 8, 1883, he replaced John Morrill as the all-time leader in consecutive games. Less than a month later, his record 319-game playing streak came to an end while the Bisons were visiting the Chicago White Stockings on July 3, 1883. He would hold the all-time record for just one more week. Boston's Mike Hornung's streak reached 320 straight contests on July 10, establishing a new record. O'Rourke closed the year hitting a solid .328 and achieving totals in at-bats and runs scored that paced the Bisons. Although the Bisons came in fifth place in 1883, the pennant race was very competitive as only about 10 games separated the first-place Boston Beaneaters and the fifth-place Bisons.

A few years later O'Rourke would become the majors' Iron Man for a third time. He is the only player in major league history to be baseball's Iron Man on three occasions. Information about his third streak and the rest of his baseball playing career are discussed in a later narrative.

13. JOE HORNUNG

Born: June 12, 1857, Carthage, New York *Died*: October 30, 1931, Howard Beach, New York *Bats*: Right *Throws*: Right *Height*: 5 feet, 8½ inches *Weight*: 164 *Major league debut*: May 1, 1879 (Boston at Buffalo [NL]) *Last major league game*: October 3, 1890 (New York at Chicago [NL])

Major league Iron Man from: July 3, 1883, to September 13, 1884 *Consecutive games played*: 464

Joe Hornung

Games as major league Iron Man: 150 (consecutive games 315 through 464) *Teams played for during streak*: Buffalo Bisons (NL) (1879–1880), Boston Red Caps (NL) (1881–1882) and Boston Beaneaters (NL) (1883–1884) *Primary positions played*: Outfield and first base *Game missed before streak*: August 30, 1879 (Chicago at Buffalo) *First game played of streak*: September 1, 1879 (Chicago at Buffalo) *Last game played of streak*: September 11, 1884 (Buffalo at Boston) *Game missed to end streak*: September 13, 1884 (Cleveland at Boston)

Consecutive Game Streak's Statistical Totals

Year	G	AB	R	H	2B	3B	HR	RBI	BB	SO	AVG	SLG	SB
1879	19	80	15	23	4	3	0	—	0	5	.288	.413	—
1880	85	342	47	91	8	11	1	42	8	29	.266	.363	—
1881	83	324	39	78	12	8	2	25	5	25	.241	.346	—
1882	85	388	67	117	14	11	1	50	2	25	.302	.402	—
1883	98	446	107	124	25	13	8	66	8	54	.278	.446	—
1884	94	424	94	113	24	9	4	—	12	55	.267	.394	—
Total	464	2004	369	546	87	55	16	*183*	35	193	.272	.395	—

Joe "Ubbo Ubbo" Hornung played left field for 12 seasons in the major leagues for four teams. He possessed a strong throwing arm and was one of the best defensive fielders in the game. By his outspokenness about the players from his era, it is safe to say he came from the old school. He took great pride in playing the game gloveless. He also earned his nickname by yelling it out whenever he collected a hit or made a great fielding play. When he came to the plate to hit, he usually had a cocky smirk on his face that sometimes rattled the opposing pitchers. He was an average hitter (at best) who struck out often (although he never led the league in that category) and showed little patience when hitting. This was evidence by the rather paltry sum of 120 career walks in over 4,900 plate appearances. His career started in Canada in 1877, where he played for the London Tucumsehs of the International Association. Midway through the following year, when the London team closed up shop, he stayed in the league by joining the Buffalo Bisons. He was still with them when Buffalo become a member of the National League, starting with the 1879 season. He made his debut in the majors when the Bisons were defeated 5–0 by the Boston Red Caps on May 1, 1879. With the exception of just one game, he played in every Bisons contest during his rookie year. The only game he sat out was the Bisons' home game against the Chicago White Stockings on August 30. During the following game on September 1, 1879, against those same White Stockings, Hornung started his consecutive playing streak which would eventually become the first to cross over the 400-game barrier. He hit for a .266 average and drove in 38 runners while helping the Bisons finish a respectable third place in the final standings.

Hornung repeated his .266 average in 1880 and posted team highs in RBI and triples but the Bisons rapidly sunk to seventh place in the standings, just ahead of the last-place Cincinnati Reds. After a two-year internship with the Bisons, he moved to the Boston Red Caps, starting in 1881. During his first year in Boston, his batting average dropped down to .241 although he still was able to lead the Red Caps with eight triples along with hitting two of the team's five homers. He led the outfielders with 198 putouts and won his first of five fielding titles with a .948 percentage. The roster changes the Red Caps had made during the off-season did not help much as the club repeated their sixth-place finish from the previous year. Hornung accomplished a career-best .302 batting average in 1882 while leading the team in hits and triples and finishing second to Chicago's Abner Dalrymple in the at-bats column. Additionally, he played the most games and was the best fielder of all outfielders during the 1882 campaign. The Red Caps, in the meantime, jumped a few spots in the standings and finished tied with the Bisons for third place overall. During the off-season, Boston changed the club's name to the Beaneaters. In midseason of the following year, Hornung took over the Iron Man role from Buffalo's Jim O'Rourke on July 3, 1883. A week later, he established a new major league record of consecutive games played when he played his 320th straight contest on July 10. He closed out the season by further extending the record (another 50 games) to 370 contests. Boston's new name seems to bring the club some luck as they won their first pennant since 1878. Hornung was a big factor in that team's fortunes as he was the league leader in at-bats and runs scored and topped the club with eight homers while batting .278. His record run of consecutive games finally came to an end late in the 1884 campaign when he sat out the Beaneaters' home game on September 13 against the Cleveland Blues. His 464-game streak remained the all-time major league mark until it was surpassed by Brooklyn Bridegrooms' third baseman George Pinkney on May 27, 1889. The game he missed to stop the streak was the only contest in which his name did not appear in a box score all season. He batted .268 and topped Boston with 10 triples and seven homers. The 518 at-bats and 119 runs scored (which also were team highs) he achieved during the 1884 season were the second-highest total among the league leaders in those categories. Although the Beaneaters did not repeat as league champions, they did finish in second place, comfortably ahead of all the other teams except the pennant-winning Providence Grays.

Joe Hornung: The Boston Beaneater became the first to achieve 400 straight contests. His streak ended in September 1884 at 464 games. The mark was the all-time record until it was broken by Brooklyn Bridegrooms' third baseman George Pinkney in May 1889.

Hornung's tenure with the Beaneaters lasted another four years. His most noteworthy achievement during this time was that he had the highest fielding percentage among all National League outfielders during the 1886 and 1887 seasons. He left Boston after the 1888 campaign and signed on to play left field for the Baltimore Orioles of the American Association. He spent just one year with Baltimore before returning to the National League to play for the New York Giants in what turned out to be his final big league season. Starting in 1891, he played five more years in the minors, starting with the Buffalo team of the Eastern League before retiring in 1895. After hanging up his cleats, he umpired for a few seasons in the minor leagues.

14. BILL GLEASON

Born: November 12, 1858, St. Louis, Missouri *Died*: July 21, 1932, St. Louis, Missouri *Bats*: Right *Throws*: Right *Height*: 5 feet, 8 inches *Weight*: 170 *Major league debut*: May 2, 1882 (Louisville at St. Louis [AA]) *Last major league game*: June 18, 1889 (Louisville at Baltimore [AA])

Major league Iron Man from: September 13, 1884, to May 30, 1885; May 30, 1885, to June 6, 1885 (tied with Jimmy Wolf); June 6, 1885, to April 25, 1886 *Consecutive games played*: 406 *Games as major league Iron Man*: 139 (consecutive games 268 through 313, consecutive games 314 through 319 (tied with Jimmy Wolf), consecutive games 320 through 406) *Team played for during streak*: St. Louis Browns (AA) *Primary position played*: Shortstop *Game missed before streak*: (Never played in major leagues before start of streak) *First game played of streak*: May 2, 1882 (Louisville at St. Louis) *Last game played of streak*: April 24, 1886 (Louisville at St. Louis) *Game missed to end streak*: April 25, 1886 (Louisville at St. Louis)

Consecutive Game Streak's Statistical Totals

Year	G	AB	R	H	2B	3B	HR	RBI	BB	SO	AVG	SLG	SB
1882	79	347	63	100	11	6	1	—	6	—	.288	.363	—
1883	98	425	81	122	21	9	2	42	15	—	.287	.393	—
1884	110	472	97	127	21	7	1	—	27	—	.269	.350	—
1885	112	472	79	119	9	5	3	53	29	—	.252	.311	—
1886	7	31	5	9	2	0	0	5	4	—	.290	.355	1
Total	406	1747	325	477	64	27	7	*100*	81	—	.273	.353	*1*

Bill Gleason was a shortstop who played eight years in the American Association with the St. Louis Brown Stockings or Browns (1882–1887), Philadelphia Athletics (1888) and Louisville Colonels (1889). He gained a reputation as an excellent contact hitter and an aggressive base runner. After playing in the semipro and minor leagues for a half dozen years, he and his older brother, Jack, joined the big leagues with the formation of the American Association. The brothers shared the left side of the Brown Stockings' infield with Jack playing third base and Bill manning the shortstop position. Bill's major league debut in the Brown Stockings' home game against the Colonels on May 2, 1882, was also the start of his playing streak. He didn't sit out a single inning in the club's officially played 79 games and led the team in several batting categories including his .288 average. Additionally, he turned out to be the busiest shortstop in the league by recording the highest totals of games played (79), putouts (131), assists (294), errors (85) and double plays (23). While he was posting some league highs, the Browns were at the other end of the spectrum as they finished fifth out of six teams in the final standings.

In his sophomore year in the majors, Gleason achieved similar stats in 1883 and went a second straight year without missing an inning at shortstop. He took over the Browns' lead off hitter role in the lineup early in the year, replacing Jack who was sent over to the Colonels. The team's hitting improved, and as a result his .287 batting average was good for only fourth place on the squad. Even so, he still was able to top the team in at-bats, hits, doubles and triples along with again leading all shortstops in games played. The 24-point jump in the team's batting directly resulted in their competing for the league's title. In a very close pennant race, Philadelphia edged the Browns by a single game for the league's title. As the following year was winding down, Gleason had a 268-game streak actively running when he took over the Iron Man role from Mike Hornung, whose record run of 464 games came to an end on September 13, 1884. Gleason concluded the year playing every game at shortstop for the third straight season. While his batting average dropped to .269, the Browns finished

27 games above .500 but the club's .626 winning percentage was good for only a fourth-place showing and was eight games behind the first-place New York Metros. About two months into the 1885 season, Jimmy Wolf of the Colonels caught up to Gleason in consecutive games played. Wolf started his streak three games later then Gleason, but on May 30, 1885, the Colonels had played three more games at that point of the season. The tie remained for a span of six games until Gleason broke the deadlock and retook the lead on June 6 and stayed ahead of Wolf's pace for the rest of the year. For the third time in four seasons, Gleason did not miss a single inning at shortstop. He topped the league shortstops in games played for a fourth consecutive year. He led the team with 119 hits but his .252 average was the lowest he had ever hit up to that time. The Browns' dynasty of the late 1880s had just started as they won their first of four consecutive American Association titles in 1885, running away with the championship by 16 games over the second-place Cincinnati Red Stockings. St. Louis faced the National League champion Chicago White Stockings in the World's Series. The series ended up a stalemate as each team won three games and tied one. Gleason banged out six hits in seven games in the series for a .231 average. His consecutive playing streak came to an end after 406 contests, and just seven games into the 1886 season, when he missed the first game of his career on April 25 as he sat out the Browns' 16–10 victory over the Colonels. The Browns again cruised to another title by a dozen games over the Pittsburgh Alleghenys. St. Louis had a repeat engagement with the White Stockings in the 1886 World's Series. The Browns won the world championship this time in six games. Although he only hit .208 against Chicago, Gleason contributed to the Browns' cause by driving in five runs.

Gleason played one more season with the Browns in 1887 as the club claimed a third straight title. The more powerful Browns were stunned in the World's Series by the Detroit Wolverines of the National League as the Wolverines claimed 10 of the 15 games played. Gleason played in all but two contests but was not much of an offensive factor as he contributed just eight hits and finished with a .163 batting average. He also was having an awful series defensively with his sloppy play at shortstop but his outstanding grab of a line drive hit by Detroit's Sam Thompson in the third inning of the 10th game turned the Wolverines' chance for a big inning into a triple play. The Browns went on to win the game by an 11–4 score. Gleason was traded a few weeks after the series to Athletics. He put in one year with Philadelphia and part of another with the Colonels before calling it quits. He spent a couple of years in the minor leagues before permanently retiring and returning to his hometown of St. Louis.

15. Jimmy Wolf

Born: May 12, 1862, Louisville, Kentucky *Died*: May 16, 1903, Louisville, Kentucky *Bats*: Right *Throws*: Right *Height*: 5 feet, 9 inches *Weight*: 190 *Major league debut*: May 2, 1882 (Louisville at St. Louis [AA]) *Last major league game*: August 21, 1892 (Baltimore at St. Louis [NL])

Major league Iron Man from: May 30, 1885, to June 6, 1885 (tied with Bill Gleason) *Consecutive games played*: 397 *Games as major league Iron Man*: 6 (consecutive games 314 through 319) (tied with Bill Gleason) *Team played for during streak*: Louisville Colonels (AA) *Primary position played*: Outfield *Game missed before streak*: May 4, 1882 (Louisville at St. Louis) *First game played of streak*: May 5, 1882 (St. Louis at Louisville) *Last game played of streak*: April 17, 1886 (Louisville at Cincinnati) *Game missed to end streak*: April 18, 1886 (Cincinnati at Louisville)

Consecutive Game Streak's Statistical Totals

Year	G	AB	R	H	2B	3B	HR	RBI	BB	SO	AVG	SLG	SB
1882	76	309	44	93	11	8	0	—	9	—	.301	.388	—
1883	98	389	59	102	17	9	1	—	5	—	.262	.360	—
1884	110	486	79	146	24	11	3	73	4	—	.300	.414	—
1885	112	483	79	141	23	17	1	52	11	—	.292	.416	—
1886	1	4	1	1	0	0	0	1	0	—	.250	.250	0
Total	397	1671	262	483	75	45	5	*126*	29	—	.289	.397	0

Jimmy "Chicken" Wolf was one of the most reliable players of his era. He played for 10 of his 11 seasons in the majors with the Louisville Colonels of the American Association. Although he was the right fielder in about 90 percent of the games in which he appeared, he showed his dexterity by filling in at whatever position his manager needed him for. He barely had a year in the professional ranks when he joined the Colonels. Louisville was one of six clubs granted a franchise in the newly established American Association for the 1882 season. He took up his position in right field. He made his debut on May 2, 1882, while the Colonels were visiting the St. Louis Brown Stockings. Two days later, he sat out the May 4 game (the Colonels' third game of the year). He started his consecutive playing streak the next day on May 5 in a Colonels' home game against St. Louis. Not missing another game that first season, he helped lead the Colonels to a respectable third place as they finished 13 games behind the first-place Cincinnati Red Stockings. Wolf fully justified his presence in Louisville's lineup as he hit for a .299 average and led all outfielders with 21 assists.

His second season was not nearly as successful as his rookie year. His batting average dropped to a .262 mark as the Colonels claimed fifth place in the eight-team league. He also topped all outfielders in double plays that year by doubling off six runners with his accurate throwing arm. He rebounded in 1884 as his batting average was back at .300. He also drove in 73 runners and had a team-high 11 triples. Although he led the league with 486 at-bats, his on base percentage suffered because of his impatience at the plate. In nearly 500 at-bats, he walked a mere four times. This averaged out to a walk every 121.5 times at the plate. His performance still helped keep the Colonels in the race for the league's title. The final outcome was a third-place finish again, but seven and a half games out of the top position. The start of the 1885 season found him in close pursuit of St. Louis' Bill Gleason, who was the possessor of the longest active streak of consecutive games in the majors. Wolf caught up to Gleason in consecutive games on May 30, 1885. The pair stayed tied for the Iron Man title for the next six games until June 6 when Gleason retook the lead. Gleason maintained the lead and stayed ahead of Wolf's pace for the rest of the year. While maintaining his batting average close to the .300 mark with a .292 average, Wolf repeated as the team's leader in at-bats and triples. Playing for their fourth manager in as many years and even with the presence of Wolf and the power-hitting Pete Browning in the team's lineup, the Colonels regressed to fifth place and were 26 games off the pennant-winning pace set by the St. Louis Browns. Wolf missed the second game of the 1886 season when he was out of the lineup (for the first time in 397 contests) during a Louisville home game against Cincinnati on April 18. Wolf never caught up to Gleason again in consecutive games. Ironically, Wolf would have become the Iron Man a week later (April 25) if his streak had been active because Gleason's streak came to an end that day.

Wolf stayed in a Colonels uniform for six more solid-performing years. He was one of the team's most respected players. The Colonels had a horrid year in 1889; they went through four managers and finished 27–111 in last place. Wolf took over the managerial reins on April 30 from Dude Esterbrook and guided them to a 14–51 record before being replaced in late

July by Dan Shannon. Wolf had his best year in 1890 (and just a couple of years before retirement). He led the American Association in batting with a .363 average along with top marks in hits (197) and total bases (260). He finished as the runner-up in RBI with 98 runners driven in and tied with several players with 29 doubles. Wolf's efforts that year helped Louisville make the worst-to-first climb up the ladder. The Colonels ran away with the title by beating out the Columbus Buckeyes by 10 games. Louisville faced the Brooklyn Bridegrooms in the 1890 World's Series. Although the series wound up deadlocked after seven games with each team winning three games along with a tie, Wolf was one of the most valuable players as he collected nine hits, batted .360 to lead the Colonels and topped all players with eight runners driven home. He played his 10th straight year in the American Association before the league closed up shop after the 1891 season. Wolf played just a few games in 1892 in the National League for the St. Louis Browns. Most of the year though was spent playing for Syracuse in the Eastern League. He returned to the Eastern League the following year and ended his playing days with Buffalo where he hit for a solid .343 batting average. He hung up his baseball gear and returned to Louisville and took a job with the city's fire department. He died four days after turning 40 due to the residual effects of a head injury he suffered while on the job for the fire department.

16. STEVE BRADY

Born: July 14, 1851, Worcester, Massachusetts *Died*: November 1, 1917, Hartford, Connecticut *Bats*: Unknown *Throws*: Unknown *Height*: 5 feet, 9½ inches *Weight*: 165 *Major league debut*: July 23, 1874 (Hartford at New York [NA]) *Last major league game*: October 5, 1886 (New York at Cincinnati [AA])

Major league Iron Man from: April 25, 1886, to May 3, 1886 *Consecutive games played*: 328 *Games as major league Iron Man*: 4 (consecutive games 325 through 328) *Team played for during streak*: New York Metropolitans (AA) *Primary positions played*: First base and outfield *Game missed before streak*: (Out of major leagues since 1875 season before start of streak) *First game played of streak*: May 1, 1883 (New York at Baltimore) *Last game played of streak*: May 1, 1886 (New York at Philadelphia) *Game missed to end streak*: May 3, 1886 (Baltimore at New York)

Consecutive Game Streak's Statistical Totals:

Year	G	AB	R	H	2B	3B	HR	RBI	BB	SO	AVG	SLG	SB
1883	97	432	69	117	12	6	0	—	11	—	.271	.326	—
1884	112	485	102	122	11	3	1	—	21	—	.252	.293	—
1885	108	434	60	128	14	5	3	58	25	—	.295	.371	—
1886	11	42	5	8	0	1	0	4	3	—	.190	.238	4
Total	328	1393	236	375	37	15	4	62	60	—	.269	.326	4

Steve Brady had a relatively brief major league playing career. He was an all-purpose player who had the skills to play most any position but would eventually settle in the outfield. He started out in the National Association and played in that league's last two years of existence. Once the National League was formed, Brady was out of a job because no teams from the new league needed his services. It would be years later before he would return to the big leagues with the New York Metros of the American Association. He made his debut with the Hartford Dark Blues on July 23, 1874, in Hartford's 13–5 loss to the New York Mutuals. He played third base in most of the 27 contests in which his name appeared in the lineup. His performance that rookie season resulted in a .314 batting average and 14 runners driven home. Hartford, on the other hand, won only 16 games in 53 decisions while finishing in next-to-last place.

The next season, Brady switched to the new club in Washington. The club's life span turned out to be quite short as by the middle of July the team disbanded. Brady took in 21 games with Washington but collected only 13 hits and closed the year out with a paltry .137 average. He stayed out of the major leagues until the beginning of the 1883 season when he secured a place on the roster with one of the new teams in the American Association, the New York Metros. When the Metros opened the season in Baltimore on May 1, 1883, Brady started his consecutive playing streak. He mostly was used at first base although the team's skipper, Jim Mutrie, platooned him in right field for 16 games. He hit .271 and led the club with 432 at-bats while the team finished in fourth place, 11 games off the pace set by the front-running Philadelphia Athletics. Mutrie did some shuffling of playing positions on his team at the beginning of the 1884 season. Brady went from first base and took over the right field spot from Chief Roseman, who moved to center field, replacing the departed John O'Rourke. Brady played every game for the Metros for a second straight season. He hit .252 and had the second-highest number of at-bats (485) in the league as Louisville's Jimmy Wolf edged him with just one more time at the plate. The Metros experienced unexpected success and surprised many by capturing the American Association pennant in just the franchise's second year of play. They finished six and a half games ahead of the Columbus Buckeyes. The first recorded World's Series was held in late October that year and saw the Metros face off against the much stronger Providence Grays of the National League. The series was not much of a contest as the Grays demolished the Metros and swept them in three games. The Grays' performance was so dominating that the Metros scored just three runs compared to the Grays' 20 runs. Brady took part in all three games with very little to show for it. He went hitless in 10 at-bats with a run scored. He went another season in 1885 without missing a contest (his third consecutive year) but had not taken the lead in consecutive games thanks to Bill Gleason of the St. Louis Browns, who had just completed his fourth year without sitting down. Brady finished second on the club with a .295 average, hit three of his four career homers and posted a career number in RBI with 58 runners brought home. After winning the league title the previous year, the Metros plummeted to seventh place under the guidance of new manager Jim Gifford. Early in the 1886 campaign, Brady finally took over the Iron Man role when Gleason missed a contest on April 25. Brady did not hold onto the title for very long because just four games later he missed the May 3 contest, which was a Metros' home game against the Baltimore Orioles. This closed out his playing streak at 328 games.

After his streak was finally halted, Brady finished out the 1886 season with the Metros by playing an additional 113 games. He finished with a .240 batting average along with 112 hits and 39 runs driven in. New York was nowhere to be found in the pennant race as they were 38 games behind the league leader in the final standings as well as repeating a seventh-place finish for the second consecutive year. His major league experience ended with the closure of the 1886 season. His entire career consisted of just 490 games where he had 2,030 official at-bats and finished with an overall .261 batting average during his six years of play.

17. CHARLEY JONES

Born: April 30, 1850, Alamance County, North Carolina *Died*: Date and place of death is unknown *Bats*: Right *Throws*: Right *Height*: 5 feet, 11½ inches *Weight*: 202 *Major league debut*: May 4, 1875 (Chicago at Keokuk [NA]) *Last major league game*: April 26, 1888 (Louisville at Kansas City [AA])
Major league Iron Man from: May 3, 1886, to July 29, 1886 *Consecutive games played*: 333 *Games*

as major league Iron Man: 70 (consecutive games 264 through 333) *Team played for during streak*: Cincinnati Reds (AA) *Primary position played*: Outfield *Game missed before streak*: August 20, 1883 (Cincinnati at New York) *First game played of streak*: August 21, 1883 (Cincinnati at Philadelphia) *Last game played of streak*: July 28, 1886 (Cincinnati at New York) *Game missed to end streak*: July 29, 1886 (Cincinnati at Brooklyn)

Consecutive Game Streak's Statistical Totals:

Year	G	AB	R	H	2B	3B	HR	RBI	BB	SO	AVG	SLG	SB
1883	25	112	25	42	7	5	5	26	4	—	.375	.661	—
1884	112	472	117	148	19	17	7	71	37	—	.314	.470	—
1885	112	487	108	157	19	17	5	35	21	—	.322	.462	—
1886	84	343	53	83	13	8	6	34	40	—	.242	.379	3
Total	333	1414	303	430	58	47	23	166	102	—	.304	.460	3

Charley Jones was one of the early stars of major league baseball, but on a few occasions controversy seemed to follow him. He played in the National Association, National League and American Association during his 12-year career. He started out in the National Association with the Keokuk Westerns where he made his debut on May 4, 1875. The team folded after just thirteen games. He played one more game that year with the Hartford Dark Blues. He had a .255 batting average in the limited time he played. The National Association passed away soon after and by the next spring the National League was established and operating.

Jones made the 1876 Cincinnati Reds' squad as the team's starting center fielder. The Reds were a pathetic team as their record indicated. They won only nine games in 65 contests and if it were not for Jones, the club would not have hit a single homer all year. Jones led the team's offense in just about every category. He drove in 38 of the team's 132 RBI that were scored, 17 of the 51 doubles, four of the 12 triples and all four homers. Jones returned to Cincinnati the next season and shifted over to left field. The club was on the verge of folding less than 20 games into 1877 when Jones decided to sign a contract to play with the Chicago White Stockings. After appearing in just two contests with Chicago, Cincinnati quickly reorganized and Jones was returned to the club. He finished the year hitting .313 and for the second straight season accounted for most of his team's offense. Jones got some help in 1878 after two years of virtually carrying the offensive fortunes of the team on his back. As he again paced the team with three homers and 39 runs batted in, the Reds (under their new manager, third baseman Cal McVey) showed tremendous improvement as they went from last place to placing a close second behind the Boston Red Caps in the league's final standings. He switched teams in 1879 as he landed on the Red Caps' roster as their new left fielder, replacing longtime Boston player Andy Leonard. Although most of his offensive numbers would not be his personal bests, Jones had his career year as he led the league in home runs, RBI (tied with teammate John O'Rourke), walks and extra-base hits. His nine home runs also set the all-time single-season mark for most homers. He held on to this record until Harry Stovey of the Philadelphia Athletics smacked 14 homers in 1883. Jones' slugging and total bases were also the second highest figures in the final stats. He also won his only fielding title when he led all outfielders with a .933 percentage. He was having another fine year in 1880 with a team-leading .300 average when he got into a salary disagreement with the club's owner as the season was coming to an end. The owner decided to suspend Jones from the team (and later expelled him from the league) due to his insubordination. Jones' banishment from playing baseball cost him two years of his playing career. Although Jones never played again in the National League, he finally returned to the major leagues when he was given the right to play during the 1883 season. He quickly signed with the American Association's Cincinnati Reds team and was assigned as the club's center fielder. He initiated his consecutive playing streak later that year when Cincinnati visited Philadelphia on August 21, 1883. He had not lost his power swinging touch during his layoff as he hit a career-high 10 homers (good enough for second place behind Philadelphia's Stovey) along with a .294 batting average. Jones helped keep the Reds in the pennant race but the team came in third place, five games behind the first-place Athletics. The following year (1884), Jones upped his batting average 20 points to a .314 mark and topped the league in times on base, on base percentage and putouts by an outfielder. Cincinnati, in the meantime, fell back a couple of spots to fifth place in a race that saw the league's top seven at times separated by only 14 games. Jones followed that up by hitting .322 in 1885 as well as leading the league with 487 at-bats and finishing second to Louisville's Pete Browning in total hits. While he had no problems getting on base (he led the team with 108 runs scored), his RBI totals fell way off as he drove home only 35 runners in 112 games. More clutch hitting might have helped the second-place Reds make the race for the title closer to the runaway Browns, who easily claimed the first-place prize. With the 1886 season less than three weeks old, Jones replaced the New York Metros' Steve Brady on May 3 as baseball's most durable player. He retained the Iron Man title for 70 games until his own streak ended after 333 games when he sat out a 6–4 loss in Brooklyn against the Trolley Dodgers on July 29, 1886. His final .270 average that year was his lowest batting mark since his rookie season, although he did improve his run production by driving home 68 runners. The Reds finished in fifth place as the St. Louis Browns again ran away with the league's title.

In the middle of the 1887 season, Cincinnati sold Jones to the Metros. He finished the year in New York and was given his release at the season's end. He signed on with the Kansas City Cowboys, played just six games in left field and was released before the end of April. He tried to negotiate a deal to play in the minors but nothing ever was finalized. His alcohol use played a major role in the rapid decline of his playing skills. With his playing days over, he worked as a sheriff and then as an election inspector. His final whereabouts are unknown. Many years of research by baseball historians have not been able to uncover the particulars of his demise. The last known date of his existence was in August 1909 when a banquet was to be held for him in New York to help raise funds for his well-being. At that time, he was already a semi-invalid. His disappearance is quite puzzling, being that Jones was one of baseball's top players in his time along with being extremely popular with the fans.

18. CURT WELCH

Born: February 10, 1862, Williamsport, Ohio *Died*: August 29, 1896, East Liverpool, Ohio *Bats*: Right *Throws*: Right *Height*: 5 feet, 10 inches *Weight*: 175 *Major league debut*: May 1, 1884 (Toledo at Louisville [AA]) *Last major league game*: May 23, 1893 (Cincinnati at Louisville [NL])

Major league Iron Man from: July 29, 1886, to September 9, 1886 *Consecutive games played*: 334 *Games as major league Iron Man*: 32 (consecutive games 303 through 334) *Teams played for during streak*: Toledo Blue Stockings (AA) (1884) and St. Louis Browns (AA) (1885–1886) *Primary position played*: Outfield *Game missed before streak*: (never played in major leagues before start of streak) *First game played of streak*: May 1, 1884 (Toledo at Louisville) *Last game played of streak*: September 8, 1886 (second game) (St. Louis at Pittsburgh) *Game missed to end streak*: September 9, 1886 (St. Louis at Pittsburgh)

Consecutive Game Streak's Statistical Totals:

Year	G	AB	R	H	2B	3B	HR	RBI	BB	SO	AVG	SLG	SB
1884	109	425	61	95	24	5	0	—	10	—	.224	.304	—
1885	112	432	84	117	18	8	3	69	23	—	.271	.370	—
1886	113	470	97	134	27	9	1	63	26	—	.285	.387	48
Total	334	1327	242	346	69	22	4	*132*	59	—	.261	.355	*48*

Curt Welch is at or near the top of the list of most baseball historians' choices as the premier defensive outfielders of the 19th century. The reasoning for this was that he had a great skill at judging fly balls and easily tracking down deep drives, even though he played a somewhat shallow outfield. His entire professional career lasted just 13 years, 10 of which were spent in the major leagues. He was much traveled during this time as his records indicated he was employed by seven big league ball clubs. After playing just one year in the minors, he made the majors in 1884 as the starting center fielder for the new American Association team, the Toledo Blue Stockings. When he made his big league debut during Toledo's season opener in Louisville against the Colonels on May 1, 1884, it also marked the beginning of his consecutive playing streak. He hit only .224 his rookie year but did produce 24 doubles, good enough for second place on the Blue Stockings' squad. His 207 putouts in the outfield was the league's highest mark for that position. The Blue Stockings turned in an eighth-place performance with a 46–58 record in the club's only year in the American Association. The association dropped Toledo along with four other clubs as it trimmed down to just eight teams for the 1885 season.

Welch then signed on to play with the soon-to-be-powerhouse St. Louis Browns. The Browns' manager, Charlie Comiskey, immediately made Welch the club's new center fielder, replacing Fred Lewis. Welch responded well to playing on a winning team as he improved his batting average to .271 in addition to leading all outfielders with a .946 fielding percentage, 236 putouts and 112 games played. For all intents and purposes, there really was no pennant race in 1885 as the Browns easily coasted to the league championship by 16 games. The Browns faced Cap Anson and his Chicago White Stockings in the 1885 World's Series. The series turned out to be a draw after seven games with each team winning three with one tie. Welch was not much of a factor offensively as he only had four hits in 27 at-bats in the seven games for a .148 average. Midway through the following season, he became baseball's Iron Man when he took over the active lead in consecutive games played from Charley Jones of the Cincinnati Reds, who missed his team's July 29, 1886, game in Brooklyn. Welch's time as Iron Man lasted six weeks; with about a month left on the 1886 schedule, he missed his first major league game when he sat out the Browns' September 9 game in Pittsburgh against the Alleghenys. His playing streak was snapped that day after playing 334 straight contests. It also turned out to be the only game that Welch's name did not appear in the Browns' lineup that season. He finished the year batting .281 and again repeated as the outfielders' leader in fielding and putouts. The Browns easily glided to another title, finishing a dozen games ahead of the second-place Alleghenys. The Browns were up against the White Stockings again and this time beat them by a 4–2 count in a best-of-seven series to win the world title. Welch's bat was performing quite well as he went 7 for 20 for a .350 mark, which was the second-best average in the series behind teammate Tip O'Neill's .400 mark.

Although he had another good solid year in 1887 with a .278 average, Welch's mark was the second lowest among the regular players on the offensive-laden Browns, saved only by catcher Jack Boyle's anemic .189 performance. Defensively, Welch again led all outfielders for the fourth successive year in putouts. The Browns had another easy time winning the

American Association title (for the third straight year) as they finished 14 ahead of their closest competitor, the Cincinnati Reds. They faced the National League champion Detroit Wolverines in the 1887 World's Series. The Wolverines surprised most everyone by winning 10 of the 15 games to claim the world championship. Welch had 12 hits in 58 at-bats for a .207 average and topped all the Browns' players with six runners driven home. After three years with the mighty Browns, Welch was traded to the Philadelphia Athletics in November 1887. He spent four more years in the American Association with the Athletics and the Baltimore Orioles. Those years were highlighted by his leading the league in doubles in 1889 and being hit by the most pitches in 1888, 1890 and 1891. With the folding of the American Association after the 1891 season, he moved over to the National League with the Orioles. His stay with the Orioles was short-lived as he left in midseason 1892 and finished out the year with the Cincinnati Reds. His major league career closed in 1893 when he played 14 contests in left field for the Louisville Colonels. By the end of May 1893, his services were no longer needed and the Colonels released him. He wound up in the minors and played around 200 games at that level over the next couple of years before leaving the game. His rapid decline in playing skills was directly related to his problem handling alcohol. In today's world, he would have been an alcoholic and might have gotten the help to beat the addiction and restart his playing career. At the end, his life was in shambles and the severe abuse of alcohol (consumption) claimed his life on August 29, 1896, at the young age of 34 years.

19. JIM O'ROURKE

Born: September 1, 1850, Bridgeport, Connecticut *Died*: January 8, 1919, Bridgeport, Connecticut *Bats*: Right *Throws*: Right *Height*: 5 feet, 8 inches *Weight*: 185 *Major league debut*: April 26, 1872 (Middletown at Troy) *Last major league game*: September 22, 1904 (first game) (Cincinnati at New York)

Major league Iron Man from: September 9, 1886, to September 17, 1886 *Consecutive games played*: 288 *Games as major league Iron Man*: 5 (consecutive games 284 through 288) *Teams played for during streak*: Buffalo Bisons (NL) (1884) and New York Gothams (NL) (1885–1886) *Primary positions played*: Catcher, first base and outfield *Game missed before streak*: June 27, 1884 (Philadelphia at Buffalo) *First game played of streak*: June 28, 1884 (Philadelphia at Buffalo) *Last game played of streak*: September 16, 1886 (Washington at New York) *Game missed to end streak*: September 17, 1886 (Washington at New York)

Consecutive Game Streak's Statistical Totals:

Year	G	AB	R	H	2B	3B	HR	RBI	BB	SO	AVG	SLG	SB
1884	71	310	75	107	20	5	3	—	20	13	.345	.471	—
1885	112	477	119	143	21	16	5	42	40	21	.300	.442	—
1886	105	440	106	136	26	6	1	34	39	21	.309	.402	14
Total	288	1227	300	386	67	27	9	76	99	55	.315	.435	14

O'Rourke's third Iron Man playing streak started in Buffalo on June 28, 1884, in a game against the Philadelphia Quakers. He maintained a steady presence in left field that season but took several turns at pitching, catching, first base and third base. He finished second to the Chicago White Stockings King Kelly in hitting with a .347 average and in reaching base on 197 occasions. He also had 162 hits, a league-high mark he shared with Ezra Sutton of the Boston Beaneaters, and easily topped the Bisons in runs scored with 119 completed trips home (another mark in which he came in second place behind Kelly). In his fourth and final season as the Bisons' skipper, he led the Herd to another respectable third-place finish. During the off-season, he left the Buffalo scene when he was lured over to the New York Giants with a contract that made him the highest-paid player in the league. He played every contest that first year in New York and hit a league-leading 16 triples, finished runner-up to the league leaders in the runs scored and at-bats, batted an even .300 and provided excellent coverage of center field. His goal of helping the Giants to the league pennant came up just two games short as the New Yorkers played second fiddle in the standings to the White Stockings. Giants' manager Jim Mutrie decided to rotate O'Rourke between center field and catcher in 1886 so regular backstop Buck Ewing could get the occasional rest from his regular catching duties. In the last month of the season, O'Rourke became the only player in major league history to achieve the Iron Man title for a third time when St. Louis Brown center fielder Curt Welch sat out a contest on September 9, 1886. O'Rourke's Iron Man reign this time was very short because just a week later he suffered a season-ending hand injury during the September 16 game against the Washington Statesmen. This injury left him unable to field and properly grip the bat to hit. As a result, his playing streak was over after 288 straight contests. He finished tied for second place on the club with a .309 batting average and still was able to top the team with 106 runs scored, even though he missed the final 19 games on the 1886 schedule.

O'Rourke still had several more productive years left in the major league scene. In 1887, he hit .285 while serving as the typical utility player as he played a relatively even number of games at catcher, third base and in the outfield. It was during this time that he finished his college education, graduating from Yale University's law school. The following year (1888), he split the catching duties again with Ewing and helped the Giants win the National League pennant by nine games over the White Stockings. The Giants faced the perennial American Association champion St. Louis Browns in the World's Series and defeated them 6–4 in a closely contested affair. O'Rourke had a mediocre series as he went 8-for-36 for a .222 average with just one run batted in. He played left field during the 1889 season and improved his batting average nearly 50 points with a .321 mark. He also drove home 81 runners and led the team in at-bats and doubles. Every player's contribution counted that year as the Giants repeated as National League champs as New York edged the Boston Beaneaters by one game. In the World's Series, the Giants beat the Brooklyn Bridegrooms 6–3 to claim their second consecutive world championship. O'Rourke was definitely one of the Giants' more valuable players as he smacked 14 hits, batted .389, clobbered homers in games three and seven and drove in seven runs. When the major league players rebelled during the upcoming off-season, O'Rourke left the National League and signed on to play right field for the New York Giants of the Players League. He feasted on that league's pitching by hitting .360 in addition to parking nine homers and driving home 115 runs (both totals of which were career highs). After one season, tempers cooled on the labor front and a peace was agreed upon by the players and the major leagues involved. He returned to the National League Giants and amazingly played in every team game that season at 41 years old. This was the eighth (and final time) he went an entire year without sitting out a contest. That year (1891), he also became the oldest active player in major league baseball, a title he would hold for the next three seasons until his retirement after the 1893 season. He proved he was still productive with the bat in 1891 as he led the Giants with 95 runs batted in. His RBI total was good enough to tie with the Beaneaters' Billy Nash and Harry Stovey for second place behind league leader Cap Anson of the Chicago Colts. O'Rourke put in one more year with the Giants before going over to the Washington Senators to serve as player-manager. The Senators were definitely the cellar dwellers as the club won only 40 games while under O'Rourke's guidance. With the closure of the 1893 season, he retired as a player and was chosen to do umpiring duties the next season. In 1895, he resumed being a player when he went back to the minors and joined the new Connecticut League. He played in that league for another 15 years for his hometown team in Bridgeport while eventually serving simultaneously as a player, manager, team owner and league president. When he finally did depart the baseball scene as he was nearing 60 years old, O'Rourke used the college degree he earned from Yale University Law School to practice law in Bridgeport along with keeping active in community affairs. He was selected a member of baseball's Hall of Fame by the old timers' committee in 1945.

20. BILL MCCLELLAN

Born: March 22, 1856, Chicago, Illinois *Died*: July 3, 1929, Chicago, Illinois *Bats*: Left *Throws*: Left *Height*: 5 feet 5½ inches *Weight*: 156 *Major league debut*: May 20, 1878 (Indianapolis at Chicago [NL]) *Last major league game*: October 17, 1888 (Cleveland at Philadelphia [AA])

Major league Iron Man from: September 17, 1886, to June 7, 1887 *Consecutive games played*: 333 *Games as major league Iron Man*: 54 (consecutive games 280 through 333) *Teams played for during streak*: Philadelphia Quakers (NL) (1884) and Brooklyn Trolley Dodgers (AA) (1885–1887) *Primary positions played*: Second base, third base and shortstop *Game missed before streak*: July 28, 1884 (Providence at Philadelphia) *First game played of streak*: July 30, 1884 (Boston at Philadelphia) *Last game played of streak*: June 5, 1887 (Cleveland vs. Brooklyn at Ridgewood, NY) *Game missed to end streak*: June 7, 1887 (Cleveland at Brooklyn)

Consecutive Game Streak's Statistical Totals:

Year	G	AB	R	H	2B	3B	HR	RBI	BB	SO	AVG	SLG	SB
1884	46	188	25	42	6	1	1	—	12	12	.223	.282	—
1885	112	464	85	124	22	7	0	46	28	—	.267	.345	—
1886	141	595	131	152	33	9	1	68	56	—	.255	.346	43
1887	34	140	45	50	13	2	0	14	29	—	.358	.479	31
Total	333	1387	286	368	74	19	2	*128*	125	12	.265	.350	74

Bill McClellan played for just eight seasons at the major league level. He was one of the smallest players in the league. He was also a rarity in that he threw left-handed and played his entire career in the infield, with the exception of 54 appearances he made in the outfield. In the early years of 19th century baseball, it was not uncommon to see left-handed infielders and catchers play their positions on a regular basis. Playing records indicate that 13 lefties (including McClellan) served as regular positioned infielders between 1871 and 1896. In McClellan's case, it was probably due to the fact that he was a southpaw that his playing time in the majors was so short. His first season in the majors was in 1878 when the Chicago White Stockings were in need of a second baseman to replace Ross Barnes. The team's playing manager, Bob Ferguson, decided on McClellan to fill the spot. He made his debut on May 20 in a White Stockings home affair against the Indianapolis Hoosiers. He stayed the whole year and hit a rather unimpressive .224 (the lowest average on the team among the regular players) but provided adequate fielding at second base for the fourth-place White Stockings. His services were retained for just the one year as by the next season his second base spot was filled on the roster by Joe Quest, who came over from the Hoosiers.

McClellan played in the minor leagues for the next two years before returning to fill the shortstop position for the Providence Grays. Providence was also in need of a shortstop to replace John Peters, who went over to the Buffalo Bisons. As was with his experience with the White Stockings, McClellan stayed just the one year with the Grays. By hitting an anemic .166, he had the league's lowest batting average among all the regular players. For the next year, minor league ball was his calling, despite the fact he sufficiently manned the Grays' shortstop position. With Philadelphia finally returning to the National League in 1883 (with the transfer of the Worcester franchise), McClellan had returned to the majors for the third time. He filled the shortstop role, hit .230 and finished second on the team with 33 RBI for the cellar-dwelling Quakers. He returned in 1884 for a second season with the Quakers and by the midseason mark started his playing streak in a Quakers home game on July 30 against the Boston Beaneaters. Many of his final 1884 numbers finished at the top of the team's leaderboard (including hits and at-bats) as he improved his batting average to .258 (second in the club behind Jack Manning's .271 average). He also posted league-leading figures at the shortstop position with 111 games played, 165 putouts, 313 assists and 83 errors. The Quakers showed much improvement by winning 22 more games than in 1883 and jumped two spots from the cellar to sixth place, even though the club still was 45 games behind the Grays, who easily won the pennant. McClellan left the Quakers and the National League after the 1884 season and joined the Brooklyn Trolley Dodgers of the American Association. He took over third base on the 1885 Dodgers' roster, replacing Fred Warner. By midseason, he and second base teammate George Pinkney exchanged playing positions in the lineup. This move might have been because McClellan was a southpaw and Pinkney was a more natural choice at the hot corner. This decision did not affect either players' time in the lineup. In fact, both men eventually put together playing streaks that saw them achieve the Iron Man title. McClellan posted a career-high .267 batting average as he played the full slate of games and contributed to the Dodgers finishing in fifth place, an improvement of four spots in the standings. The following season he didn't miss a single inning as he hit .255, scored a team-high 131 runs and led all second basemen with 141 games played. Additionally, he had the second-highest league total in doubles (behind his successor as Iron Man, Henry Larkin) and at-bats (behind teammate Pinkney). He became the major league Iron Man (and the first left-handed player to achieve this honor) in the latter stages of the season when on September 17, 1886, the New York Giants' Jim O'Rourke suffered a season-ending hand injury. McClellan went on to finish the season with a 299-game streak intact. Although there was not much of a pennant race because the St. Louis Browns cruised to another title in the American Association, the Dodgers continued to show improvement as they were 16 games behind the Browns, which was good enough for a third-place finish. A couple of months into the following campaign, Dodgers skipper Charlie Byrne gave McClellan a one-game rest on June 7, 1887, during a home game against the Cleveland Blues. The decision resulted in McClellan's streak ending after 333 games. He finished out the year missing just one other contest. He drove in 53 Dodger runners, scored 109 runs and batted .263. He also led second basemen in games played (136) for the second successive season. Although he had another decent year, his contributions did not prevent the Dodgers from dropping down to sixth place after two seasons of progress.

During the off-season, Brooklyn changed its name to the Bridegrooms. McClellan was still the team's regular second baseman when the 1888 season opened; however, new manager Bill McGunnigle was about to make a change that affected McClellan's career. In midseason, the Bridegrooms acquired oldtimer Jack Burdock from the Beaneaters of the National League and inserted him into the regular second base position, replacing McClellan. This decision was made specifically because McClellan was a southpaw. He became Burdock's backup but the decision was so final that McClellan was soon gone from the team. The choice to replace

1888 Brooklyn Bridegrooms team photograph. This team had five men on the roster that were Iron Men at some point during their playing careers: Jack Burdock (second baseman) top row, second from left; Dave Foutz (right fielder and first baseman) top row, fourth from left; George Pinkney (third baseman) bottom row, first from left; Germany Smith (shortstop) bottom row, third from left; Bill McClellan (second baseman) bottom row, first from right (Transcendental Graphics/ruckerarchive.com).

McClellan at second base turned out to be a mistake for the Bridegrooms as Burdock hit a measly .122 and scored only 15 runs in 70 games played. He had replaced a man in the line-up who scored 109 runs the previous season. McClellan finished out the year (and his major league career) with the Cleveland Blues. Too short to play first base and too old to play the outfield, his big league career came to an abrupt end because he was a left-handed infielder.

21. Henry Larkin

Born: January 12, 1860, Reading, Pennsylvania *Died*: January 31, 1942, Reading, Pennsylvania *Bats*: Right *Throws*: Right *Height*: 5 feet, 10 inches *Weight*: 175 *Major league debut*: May 1, 1884 (Philadelphia at Pittsburgh [AA]) *Last major league game*: August 4, 1893 (Washington at Philadelphia [NL])

Major league Iron Man from: June 7, 1887, to August 15, 1887 *Consecutive games played*: 318 *Games as major league Iron Man*: 55 (consecutive games 264 through 318) *Team played for during streak*: Philadelphia Athletics (AA) *Primary position played*: Outfield *Game missed before streak*: May 21, 1885 (Philadelphia at Pittsburgh) *First game played of streak*: May 24, 1885 (Philadelphia at Cincinnati) *Last game played of streak*: August 13, 1887 (Philadelphia at New York) Game missed to end streak: August 15, 1887 (Brooklyn at Philadelphia)

Consecutive Game Streak's Statistical Totals:

Year	G	AB	R	H	2B	3B	HR	RBI	BB	SO	AVG	SLG	SB
1885	89	385	104	128	28	13	7	46	22	—	.332	.527	—
1886	139	565	133	180	36	16	2	74	59	—	.319	.450	32
1887	90	358	76	103	18	9	3	54	36	—	.288	.413	27
Total	318	1308	313	411	82	38	12	174	117	—	.314	.463	59

Henry Larkin played in the major leagues for 10 seasons from 1884 through 1893. He was used during a good portion of the first half of his playing career in the outfield, either in center or left field. His normal playing position became first base with the beginning of the 1888 season. He provided each of his teams with reliable, hard-hitting numbers that resulted in his retiring with a career batting average over the .300 level. He spent one year in organized ball with his hometown team in Reading, Pennsylvania, before graduating to the majors in 1884 with the Philadelphia Athletics of the American Association. He made his debut in the season opener on May 1, 1884, in Pittsburgh as the Athletics clubbed the Alleghenys 9–2. He appeared in close to 80 percent of the Athletics' games (a high majority of which he was in center field) and finished with a .276 average. He proved he had a bat with some power as he posted the second-highest number of doubles (behind Harry Stovey) in the club with 21 two-baggers along with nine triples.

Larkin started his playing streak five weeks into his second season when he appeared in the Athletics' lineup for the May 24, 1885, game in Cincinnati against the Reds. He had close to a career day a few weeks later when he went 6 for 6 with two doubles, a triple and a home run during the June 16 game as the Athletics bombed the Alleghenys in a 14–1 contest. His .329 batting paced the club along with his leading the league with 37 doubles and 59 extra-base hits. Additionally, he finished runner-up to the league leaders in runs batted in, on base percentage and runs scored. He also showed that he possessed a good throwing arm as he led all outfielders with nine double plays. There was no pennant race for Philadelphia and most other teams in the American Association for that matter as the St. Louis Browns ran away with the title and claimed the first-place prize by 16 games. Larkin's performance the following year (1886) proved to be the best the Athletics had to offer. His batting totals in every offensive category were team highs except for homers, walks and stolen bases. He led the league again with 36 doubles, edged Louisville's Pete Browning for second place by one percentage point for the on base percentage title (.390) and led all outfielders with 139 games played and 44 errors. He played the entire year without missing a game and extended his playing streak to 228 games. Philadelphia claimed a spot in the second division with a sixth-place finish. When the Dodgers' left-handed infielder Bill McClellan missed the June 7, 1887, contest against the Cleveland Blues, Larkin took over the major league's Iron Man title with a streak of 264 games. About 10 weeks later, Larkin injured an ankle while stealing a base in the game on August 13 against the New York Metros. The injury caused him to miss the Athletics' home game on August 15 against the Brooklyn Trolley Dodgers, thus ending both his Iron Man reign and his playing streak at 318 games. He finished with a .310 average and drove home 88 runs as Philadelphia finished in fifth place, 30 games behind the first-place St. Louis Browns, who won their third straight pennant.

Larkin made the shift from left field to first base permanent in 1888 due to the acquisition of Curt Welch from the Browns. Larkin played with the Athletics for two more seasons before abandoning the team in 1890 and jumping over to the renegade Players League, where he became a member of the Cleveland Infants. He was made the team's playing manager and guided the club to a 34–45 record before being replaced in July by the team's third baseman,

Patsy Tebeau. After one season, peace was agreed among the major leagues, the Players League was dissolved and Larkin was back in the American Association, manning first base for the Athletics. He batted .279 and attained a career high in homers with 10 round-trippers. When the American Association went out of business after the 1891 season, Larkin shifted over to the National League where he played for the Washington Senators (one of four teams left over from the American Association that made the changeover to the National League) over the next two years. He made his final appearance in a major league uniform on August 4, 1893, in a game against the Philadelphia Phillies. Soon after, he left the majors and played in the minor leagues through the 1895 season before retiring.

22. GEORGE PINKNEY

Born: January 11, 1862, Orange Prairie, Illinois *Died*: November 10, 1926, Peoria, Illinois *Bats*: Right *Throws*: Right *Height*: 5 feet, 7 inches *Weight*: 160 *Major league debut*: August 16, 1884 (Cleveland at Boston [NL]) *Last major league game*: September 29, 1893 (Baltimore at Louisville [NL])

Major league Iron Man from: August 15, 1887, to May 2, 1890 *Consecutive games played*: 577 *Games as major league Iron Man*: 334 (consecutive games 244 through 577) *Teams played for during streak*: Brooklyn Trolley Dodgers (AA) (1885–1887), Brooklyn Bridegrooms (AA) (1888–1889) and Brooklyn Bridegrooms (NL) (1890) *Primary position played*: Third base *Game missed before streak*: September 19, 1885 (Pittsburgh at Brooklyn) *First game played of streak*: September 21, 1885 (Cincinnati at Brooklyn) *Last game played of streak*: April 30, 1890 (Boston at Brooklyn) *Game missed to end streak*: May 2, 1890 (Boston at Brooklyn)

Consecutive Game Streak's Statistical Totals:

Year	G	AB	R	H	2B	3B	HR	RBI	BB	SO	AVG	SLG	SB
1885	10	36	6	8	0	0	0	1	7	—	.222	.222	—
1886	141	597	119	156	22	7	0	37	70	—	.261	.322	32
1887	138	580	133	155	26	6	3	69	61	—	.267	.348	59
1888	143	575	134	156	18	8	4	52	66	—	.271	.351	51
1889	138	545	103	134	25	7	4	82	59	43	.246	.339	47
1890	7	28	2	5	0	1	0	—	2	3	.179	.250	1
Total	577	2361	497	614	91	29	11	*241*	265	*46*	.260	.337	*190*

George Pinkney played for four teams in the major leagues in 10 seasons. He was a true professional, a very reliable fielding third baseman and a good contact hitter. Most of his time in the majors was played in relative obscurity (even though he was the third baseman on two consecutive pennant-winning teams in 1889 and 1890) although he is probably most noted today for putting together a streak of 577 consecutive games played. This was the longest streak in the majors during the 19th century and the all-time record until Everett Scott broke it with a 1,307-game streak compiled from 1916 to 1925 while playing in the American League with the Boston Red Sox and New York Yankees. Pinkney started his major league career in the National League with the Cleveland Blues on August 16, 1884, in Boston against the Beaneaters. He was used at either second base or shortstop his rookie year. In the abbreviated time he did play, he got into 36 games and had a .313 batting average.

Pinkney's time in Cleveland was short as he was sold to the Brooklyn Trolley Dodgers of the American Association in early January 1885. Upon his arrival in Brooklyn, he took over the team's second base position for the 1885 season, replacing Bill Greenwood. This plan stayed in place until July when Pinkney and third baseman Bill McClellan switched playing spots. This move was probably attributed to McClellan being left-handed and Pinkney being the better selection for the hot corner spot. Once this move was made permanent, he spent the rest of his career holding down the third base job wherever he played. He only missed two contests that year and one of those was the Dodgers' September 19, 1885, home game against the Pittsburgh Alleghenys. He started his playing streak in the team's next home game against the Cincinnati Reds on September 21 with just 10 games left on the schedule. He came in with a .277 average as the Dodgers finished fifth, tied with the Louisville Colonels. The following season, he hit for a solid .261 batting average as he appeared in every Dodgers game, and led the American Association with 597 at-bats and 70 walks (tied with teammate Ed Swartwood in this category). Pinkney's 141 games played at third base and his 184 putouts were also highs for the league's hot corner occupants. The year showed improvement in the team's performance as the Dodgers had a 23-game swing in their won-loss record and finished in third place, 16 games behind the front-running St. Louis Browns. Pinkney had played over 230 career games before connecting for his first ever major league home run on June 8, 1887. Later that season, he compiled a 244-game streak when he took over the Iron Man title on August 15, 1887, from Henry Larkin of the Philadelphia Athletics, who was recuperating from an ankle injury. Pinkney hit .267 and amassed team highs in at-bats, runs scored and total hits as the Dodgers dropped 14 games below .500 and fell to sixth place in the standings. He won his first third base fielding title with an .890 average along with posting the most assists at the position. He played his third straight season in 1888 without missing a game. He finished in a tie with Dave Foutz for the team lead in hits (156), had the league's second-highest total number of at-bats (575 — just one behind the leader, St. Louis' Charlie Comiskey), and had the league's highest marks with 134 runs scored and 234 times reaching base. At the hot corner, he led all third basemen in games played as he took in 143 contests. The 1888 season turned out to be the first year in major league history that there was just one Iron Man for the whole season with no changes. Brooklyn changed its name to the Bridegrooms before the start of the 1888 season. It may have brought the team good luck because they made great strides under the guidance of new manager Bill McGunnigle, finishing a strong second to the American Association champion Browns. Pinkney reached a couple of milestones in 1889 concerning his playing streak. On May 27, 1889, he passed Mike Hornung to establish a new major league record for consecutive games when his streak reached 465 straight contests. He became the first major leaguer to play 500 consecutive games, reaching that plateau on July 13, 1889. He drove in 82 runners (30 more than the previous season) even though his hitting fell to a .246 average. His main highlights were defensive though as he again led third basemen in fielding (.897) and games played (138). Brooklyn finally defeated the Browns for the league title by edging them by a couple of games. They faced the champions of the National League (the New York Giants) in the 1889 World's Series and were beaten 6–3 in a high-scoring best-of-11 affair. Pinkney collected eight hits and batted .258 in the losing effort. He rejoined the National League in 1890 after a five-year absence when the Bridegrooms divorced themselves from the American Association. A mere seven games into the 1890 season, his games-played streak ended at 577 contests because he suffered a spiking injury during a game against the Beaneaters. The game in which he was injured was rained out before it became an official contest. The injury was severe enough to cause him to miss the next game against the Beaneaters on May 2, 1890. Maybe the short duration of rest he received because of the injury had a positive effect. When the 1890 season closed out, Pinkney achieved career highs with a .309 batting average, nine triples, seven home runs, 80 walks and a .431 slugging average. The Bridegrooms won the National League crown by six games over the Chicago Colts and returned to the World Series in 1890 to face the Louisville Colonels. The Bridegrooms fought the Colonels to a seven-game stalemate (one game being a tie). The series was halted after seven games due to a combination of cold weather and lack of attendance. Pinkney played in just four of those seven games in the series (rotating with Oyster Burns) but finished second on the club with a .357 average (behind Patsy Donovan's .471 batting mark).

Pinkney played one more year in Brooklyn before leaving to join the St. Louis Browns. He played the most games at third base for the Browns in 1892, sharing the job mainly with Llewellyn Camp. Pinkney had an awful year at the plate, finishing with a career-low .172 average in 78 games. Due to his subpar performance, the Browns released him and he was picked up by the Colonels. He replaced the departed Charley Bassett at third base and capably handled the spot for the lowly Colonels. This turned out to be his final season as he closed out his big league career by hitting .235 and driving in 62 runners. He spent a short time in the minors, playing for Grand Rapids, before eventually retiring from the game and returning to his hometown of Peoria, Illinois.

23. SID FARRAR

Born: August 10, 1859, Paris Hill, Maine *Died*: May 7, 1935, New York, New York *Bats*: Unknown *Throws*: Right *Height*: 5 feet, 10 inches *Weight*: 185 *Major league debut*: May 1, 1883 (Providence at Philadelphia [NL]) *Last major league game*: October 4, 1890 (Philadelphia at Cleveland [PL])

Major league Iron Man from: May 2, 1890, to July 4, 1890 *Consecutive games played*: 403 *Games as major league Iron Man*: 53 (consecutive games 351 through 403) *Team played for during streak*: Philadelphia Quakers (NL) (1887–1889) and Philadelphia Quakers (PL) (1890) *Primary position played*: First base *Game missed before streak*: June 22, 1887 (Philadelphia at Chicago) *First game played of streak*: June 23, 1887 (Philadelphia at Chicago) *Last game played of streak*: July 3, 1890 (Philadelphia at Chicago) *Game missed to end streak*: July 4, 1890 (first game) (Philadelphia at Cleveland)

Consecutive Game Streak's Statistical Totals:

Year	G	AB	R	H	2B	3B	HR	RBI	BB	SO	AVG	SLG	SB
1887	82	313	60	79	11	8	4	—	31	22	.252	.377	16
1888	131	508	53	124	24	7	1	53	31	38	.244	.325	21
1889	130	477	70	128	22	2	3	58	52	36	.268	.342	28
1890	60	227	46	51	13	4	1	26	26	12	.225	.330	7
Total	403	1525	229	382	70	21	9	*137*	140	108	.250	.342	72

Sid Farrar was one of baseball's most durable players during his eight years in the big leagues. By playing in 943 out of a possible 963 games his teams participated in during his career, Farrar was in the lineup for 98 percent of those contests. His entire time in the majors was spent manning the first base position in Philadelphia. Until the 1883 season, Philadelphia had been without a National League franchise since the late stages of the 1876 season. After the 1882 season was completed, the National League wanted to have a new team in Philadelphia to compete against the rival American Association, which had established a base there with the Philadelphia Athletics during that league's first season of operation. The decision was made to transfer the Worcester Ruby Legs' franchise (which had finished dead last in 1882) to Philadelphia. Worcester's last first baseman was power-hitting Harry Stovey, who had jumped over to the American Association to play for the Athletics. With the new National League team in Philadelphia needing a first baseman, the team picked up Farrar. He made his debut at age 23 in the majors during the Quakers' season opener against the Providence Grays on May 1, 1883. He did not miss a single inning his rookie year and turned out to be the only Quaker to play every game. He finished with a .233 average but the team won only 17 games and finished at the bottom of the standings, 46 games behind the pennant-winning Boston Beaneaters.

Farrar showed slight improvement his second season as he added a dozen points to his batting average and led the league's first basemen with 42 assists. He also missed the first games of his career when he was replaced at first base for a couple of contests by pitcher-outfielder Jack Coleman, who would soon depart. The team also improved under new manager Harry Wright by more than doubling their previous win total as the Quakers finished with a 39–73 record, good enough to jump two spots in the standings and finish in sixth place. While he played another season in 1885 without missing a contest, he also showed his consistency with the bat by repeating his .245 batting average from the previous year. The club also continued to improve by coming in third place with a 56–54 record, even though they were still 30 games behind the first-place Chicago White Stockings when the season closed out. The Quakers dropped to fourth place the next year but the club proved they were playing tremendous ball by finishing with a 71–43 record. The league was much more competitive in 1886 as only 14 games separated the top four teams. Farrar maintained his role as a reliable player by hitting .248, smacking a career-best five homers, bringing home 50 runners and leading first basemen with a .980 fielding average. About a third of the way through the 1887 season, he started a playing streak on June 23 in a game in Chicago and wound up playing the final 82 games on the Quakers' schedule that year. He closed the year out by posting career highs with nine triples, 72 RBI and a .282 batting average while contributing to the Quakers' serious run at the National League title. The team came up just short as they claimed second place behind the Detroit Wolverines, who bested them by only three and a half games. Farrar played every game over the next two seasons (1888 and 1889) and extended his playing streak to 343, good for the second-longest streak in the big leagues, behind Brooklyn's George Pinkney. Philadelphia, in the meantime, finished in third and fourth places respectively over those two years but never quite got to the pinnacle of a first-place finish during Farrar's time with the club. With the end of the 1889 season, his time in the National League was over.

Farrar was one of many players who left the National League and defected to the new Players League for the 1890 season. Although he changed leagues, he stayed in Philadelphia and at first base, playing for his new team, who were also known as the Quakers. In the early stages of the year, long-time Iron Man Pinkney missed a couple of games in the first week of May thanks to a spiking injury. This resulted in Farrar's taking over the Iron Man role on May 2, 1890. A couple of months later, after not missing a single contest in over three years, Farrar's streak also came to a conclusion when he was rested during the Independence Day doubleheader in Cleveland on July 4, 1890. His time as Iron Man had come to an end after 53 games (and his playing streak after 403 games) when he sat out those contests. He finished the year batting .256 and driving home 69 runners as Philadelphia claimed fifth place in the Players League's first and only year of competition. After the season, a peace agreement was signed with the National League and the Players League closed. Farrar's last game turned out to be when the Quakers finished the year up in Cleveland on October 4, 1890. Soon after, his major league playing career was over. He spent some time in the minors before retiring. Although he was a decent and durable player in his time, Farrar is probably better known today as the father of the famous American opera singer Geraldine Farrar than as a ballplayer.

24. Dave Foutz

Born: September 7, 1856, Carroll County, Maryland *Died*: March 5, 1897, Waverly, Maryland *Bats*: Right *Throws*: Right *Height*: 6 feet, 2 inches *Weight*: 161 *Major league debut*: July 29, 1884 (St. Louis at Cincinnati [AA]) *Last major league game*: May 14, 1896 (Brooklyn at Cincinnati [NL])

Major league Iron Man from: July 4, 1890, to June 4, 1891 *Consecutive games played*: 398 *Games as major league Iron Man*: 106 (consecutive games 293 through 398) *Teams played for during streak*: Brooklyn Bridegrooms (AA) (1888–1889) and Brooklyn Bridegrooms (NL) (1890–1891) *Primary positions played*: First base and outfield *Game missed before streak*: June 16, 1888 (Brooklyn at Baltimore) *First game played of streak*: June 17, 1888 (Baltimore vs. Brooklyn at Ridgewood, NY) *Last game played of streak*: June 3, 1891 (Chicago at Brooklyn) *Game missed to end streak*: June 4, 1891 (Chicago at Brooklyn)

Consecutive Game Streak's Statistical Totals:

Year	G	AB	R	H	2B	3B	HR	RBI	BB	SO	AVG	SLG	SB
1888	96	386	60	100	10	9	1	63	24	—	.259	.339	30
1889	138	553	118	152	19	8	6	113	64	23	.275	.371	43
1890	129	509	106	154	25	13	5	98	52	25	.303	.432	42
1891	35	145	28	35	6	1	1	25	10	4	.241	.317	12
Total	398	1593	312	441	60	31	13	299	150	52	.277	.378	127

Dave Foutz had a varied career during his 13 years in the big leagues. He originally was a very effective pitcher who had a peculiar style of throwing the ball sidearm to the plate. An injury in his fourth season affected his pitching skills and ultimately he switched to playing first base and in the outfield. His quiet leadership skills were so impressive that he would eventually become a team captain and later a manager. He played for two seasons with the Bay City, Michigan, team of the Northwestern League. During that time, he established a reputation for being the best hurler in the minor leagues. His performance attracted representatives of several major league teams to take a serious look at this beanpole of a player with the unique delivery. When the Bay City team dissolved in the middle of the 1884 season, Foutz signed a contract to play in the American Association for the St. Louis Browns. By the end of July, he was in a Browns uniform and made an impressive start by going 15–6 with a 2.18 earned run average (tied for second place among league pitchers) along with a .227 batting average for the fourth-place Browns.

In his first full major league campaign, Foutz went 33–14 with a 2.63 ERA, led all league pitchers with 101 assists and also drove home 34 runners and hit .248 in 65 games. He teamed with fellow Browns' hurler Bob Caruthers to form a dominating pair of hurlers that put the Browns on top of the American Association. Between the two of them, they went 73–27 and easily helped the Browns coast to a league title by 16 games over the second-place Cincinnati Reds. The Browns faced the Chicago White Stockings in the 1885 World's Series, which ended in a stalemate after seven games. Each team had taken three games but game one had resulted in a tie because the contest was stopped due to darkness. Foutz went 2–2, winning games four and seven; he finished with the lowest ERA in the series with an anemic 0.61 mark and had two hits in 12 at-bats for a .167 average. Foutz had a year in 1886 that would have easily won him the league's best pitcher award if such an honor had existed. He had the most wins (41, tied with Pittsburgh's Ed Morris), the lowest earned run average (2.11), the best fielding percentage (.949) and the most putouts by a pitcher (57) in helping the Browns repeat as the American Association champions. Additionally, he performed well with the bat by hitting .280 and driving home 59 runners. Facing the White Stockings again in the World's Series, the Browns captured the world title by defeating Chicago in six games. Foutz had a win in two decisions and collected three hits for a .200 average. Although he had another superior year on the mound in 1887, a game in mid-August changed the direction of his playing career. He suffered a broken thumb during the August 14 contest. The injury caused his curveball not to work properly. Although he would still pitch, he just wasn't the same after that incident. He won only two more games the rest of the year as he went 25–12 but did lead the pitchers again with 44 putouts. Offensively he had one of his best years at the plate as he hit .357 and drove home 108 runners in 102 games played. The Browns won a third consecutive title and faced the Detroit Wolverines in a best of 15 series for the world championship. Detroit surprised most everyone by wrapping up the title by the 11th game and winning the overall series 10–5. Foutz was a major disappointment as he was clobbered in two of the three games he pitched. He finished 0–3 with a 3.46 ERA and a .169 batting average. Before the start of the next season, the Browns sold their star pitchers Foutz and Caruthers to the Brooklyn Trolley Dodgers. Brooklyn changed their name to the Bridegrooms with the start of the 1888 season. Although Foutz was still capable of pitching, his playing time in 1888 was divided more between the mound, first base and right field. His consecutive playing streak started on June 17, 1888, in a game against the Baltimore Orioles. His final stats that year showed that he led the Bridegrooms with 99 RBI and 13 triples along with having a .277 average. He also pitched the team to 12 victories in 19 decisions to help the Bridegrooms finish runner-up to the Browns in the final standings. Foutz became the team's starting first baseman in 1889, replacing Dave Orr who had left to join the Columbus Buckeyes. Foutz had a very productive year at the plate as he hit .275 and drove in 113 runs (a career high). His run production number was good enough for second place behind the Philadelphia Athletics' Harry Stovey's 119 RBI. Foutz also got some revenge on his former team as Brooklyn ended St. Louis' streak of four straight pennants when they edged the Browns by a couple of games to claim first place in the 1889 final standings. Facing the New York Giants, the Bridegrooms wound up on the losing end of a 6–3 decision in a best-of-11-game series. Foutz was the second-best offensive player on the Bridegrooms (behind Hub Collins) in the series as he went 10 for 35 for a .286 average and drove home nine runners. The 1889 season turned out to be the final year Brooklyn would compete in the American Association. When the 1890 campaign started up, the Bridegrooms had moved over to the National League. Playing with an Iron Man infield of Smith, Collins and Pinkney (this unit missed only three games all season and those were contests Pinkney sat out that ended his long playing streak), Foutz did not miss a single game for the second year running. He became the major league's most durable player with 293 consecutive games when he succeeded Philadelphia's Sid Farrar as Iron Man on July 4, 1890. He compiled a .303 batting average, led the team with 154 hits and brought home 98 runners as he helped Brooklyn to another pennant. He also stretched his consecutive games streak to 363 by season's end. The Bridegrooms faced the Louisville Colonels in the 1890 World's Series. This series turned out to be another stalemate as both teams won three games each and a tie (game three being the deadlock contest). Foutz hit an even .300 and collected a team-high nine hits. The following season, his playing streak was snapped on June 4, 1891, after playing 398 contests. He finished the year hitting .257 and driving home 73 runners. After two consecutive first-place finishes, the Bridegrooms fell to sixth place in the National League standings.

Foutz played only 61 games in 1892 because he lost his first base job to Dan Brouthers. He still was able to see some action at first, but the great majority of his appearances were on the mound or in the outfield. His hitting dropped off dramatically as he finished with a career-low .186 batting average. During the off-season, manager Monte Ward moved over to the crosstown New York Giants and Foutz was named the Bridegrooms' manager. In his first season (1893) as Brooklyn's manager, he included himself in all 130 games but this playing streak did not qualify him for the Iron Man title again because the length of this streak ended at 145 games. That season was also his last full season as a regular player because over the next three years he appeared in only 106 more games as a player. His tenure as manager was not successful because in four seasons at the Bridegrooms' helm, the best results he achieved were a couple of fifth-place finishes. When the 1896 Bridegrooms finished in a ninth-place tie with the Washington Senators, Foutz was dismissed as manager and replaced with Billy Barnie. It became obvious during that off-season that his health was not up to playing baseball anymore (this was fully evident by his playing just two games in 1896) and he retired. Within months, he was bedridden with asthma. He passed away from this illness at his mother's residence on March 5, 1897, less than six months after turning 40 years old.

25. HUB COLLINS

Born: April 15, 1864, Louisville, Kentucky *Died*: May 21, 1892, Brooklyn, New York *Bats*: Right *Throws*: Right *Height*: 5 feet, 8 inches *Weight*: 160 *Major league debut*: September 4, 1886 (St. Louis at Louisville [AA]) *Last major league game*: May 14, 1892 (Brooklyn at Boston [NL])

Major league Iron Man from: June 4, 1891, to July 21, 1891 *Consecutive games played*: 351 *Games as major league Iron Man*: 37 (consecutive games 315 through 351) *Teams played for during streak*: Brooklyn Bridegrooms (AA) (1888–1889) and Brooklyn Bridegrooms (NL) (1890–1891) *Primary position played*: Second base *Game missed before streak*: October 1, 1888 (Brooklyn at Cincinnati) *First game played of streak*: October 3, 1888 (Baltimore at Brooklyn) *Last game played of streak*: July 20, 1891 (New York at Brooklyn) *Game missed to end streak*: July 21, 1891 (New York at Brooklyn)

Consecutive Game Streak's Statistical Totals:

Year	G	AB	R	H	2B	3B	HR	RBI	BB	SO	AVG	SLG	SB
1888	12	42	16	13	5	1	0	3	9	—	.310	.476	9
1889	138	560	139	149	18	3	2	73	80	41	.266	.320	65
1890	129	510	148	142	32	7	3	69	85	47	.278	.386	85
1891	72	299	60	86	13	3	3	25	45	37	.288	.381	22
Total	351	1411	363	390	68	14	8	170	219	125	.276	.361	181

Hubert "Hub" Collins was the steady second baseman for Brooklyn Bridegrooms' championship teams of 1889 and 1890. In the seven seasons he played in the major leagues, he was a member of the Louisville Colonels from 1886 to 1888 and the Bridegrooms from 1888 to 1892. After playing for several amateur clubs, he turned professional in 1885 when he signed to play for the Columbus, Georgia, team of the Southern League. After one season, he stayed in the Southern League, but moved over to the Savannah team. Within months, his impressive performance was noticed by representatives of his hometown Louisville Colonels of the American Association. By the beginning of September, the Colonels had him under contract and he made his big league debut on September 4, 1886, in Louisville against the St. Louis Browns. Colonels' skipper Jim Hart decided to keep him in the daily lineup by using him in left field. Collins justified his presence on the club by hitting for a solid .287 average in 27 games.

Collins continued his outstanding performance the next season by slightly upping his batting average to .290 as he belted out 162 hits in 130 contests. He was performing well again during the 1888 campaign when he was sold to the Bridegrooms in late September of that year.

He didn't arrive in time to take in the Bridegrooms' October 1 game against the Cincinnati Red Stockings. The next game, October 3 against the Baltimore Orioles, Collins played in his first contest in a Brooklyn uniform. This game was also the beginning of his consecutive games played streak. Brooklyn had different plans for Collins as their manager, Bill McGunnigle, used him strictly as their new second baseman, replacing Jack Burdock in that role. Collins led the American Association with 31 doubles that season and again improved on his hitting as he came in with a .307 batting average. The next year, 1889, he played every Brooklyn game and led the league's second basemen with 138 games played. He suffered an off year at the plate by finishing with a career-low .266 batting average although he was still able to drive in 73 runners. Although the Bridegrooms were in the middle of the pack when it came to hitting, they had the skills, pitching and fortitude to capture the league's pennant as they edged the St. Louis Browns by two games. Brooklyn faced the National League champion New York Giants in the 1889 World's Series. The Bridegrooms came out on the short end of the affair as the Giants won six of the nine games to claim the world championship. Even though Brooklyn had gone down to defeat, Collins was one of several bright spots on the team during the series. His .371 average and 13 hits were team highs and he led all series players with 13 runs scored. The 1889 season turned out to be the last year that Brooklyn would play in the American Association. The next year the club jumped over to claim a spot in the National League. Collins took up where he left off from his post-season play by improving a dozen points in his hitting as he finished with a .278 average in 1890. Besides playing in every game for the second straight year, he also accomplished a unique feat by scoring more runs than he did hits. He scored a league-high 148 runs while amassing just 142 hits. He reached base 230 times and scored over 64 percent of the time. When the season came to an end, the Bridegrooms captured another pennant and faced Collins' hometown team, the Louisville Colonels, in the World's Series. Both teams won three games and tied one contest, and the 1890 World's Series ended in a stalemate because no further games were played due to cold weather and dwindling attendance figures. Collins again responded to the pressure of playing for the world championship as he went 9 for 29 for a .310 average and repeated as the player in the series with the most runs scored.

Collins became the Iron Man of baseball on June 4, 1891, when he succeeded his teammate, Dave Foutz, whose own 398-game streak had just ended. Collins' reign as Iron Man lasted only 37 games because less than two months later, he suffered a serious head injury after colliding with the team's right fielder, Oyster Burns, while running for a fly ball hit by the Giants' Roger Connor in the eighth inning of the July 20, 1891, game in Brooklyn. Both players were hurt but Collins' injury, a concussion, was much more serious. He was knocked out by the collision and for a time there was concern he might die. Eventually, Collins recovered and returned to play 35 more games before the 1891 season ended. The following season, he had completely recovered from that injury and had gotten off to a quick start with 17 runs driven home in just 21 games. Unfortunately, he came down with what he believed was a cold during a game against the Boston Beaneaters on May 14, 1892. Over the next seven days, his illness got progressively worse as the cold proved to be typhoid fever and he passed away May 21 at 28 years of age.

26. GERMANY SMITH

Born: April 21, 1863; Pittsburgh, Pennsylvania *Died*: December 1, 1927; Altoona, Pennsylvania *Bats*: Right *Throws*: Right *Height*: 6 feet *Weight*: 175 *Major league debut*: April 17, 1884 (Altoona at Cincinnati [UA]) *Last major league game*: October 9, 1898 (second game) (Cincinnati at Chicago [NL])

Germany Smith

Major league Iron Man from: July 21, 1891 to July 5, 1892 *Consecutive games played*: 433 *Games as major league Iron Man*: 130 (consecutive games 304 through 433) *Teams played for during streak*: Brooklyn Bridegrooms (AA) (1889), Brooklyn Bridegrooms (NL) (1890) and Cincinnati Reds (NL) (1891–1892) *Primary position played*: Shortstop *Game missed before streak*: June 3, 1889 (Kansas City at Brooklyn) *First game played of streak*: June 4, 1889 (Kansas City at Brooklyn) *Last game played of streak*: July 4, 1892 (second game) (Boston at Cincinnati) *Game missed to end streak*: July 5, 1892 (Philadelphia at Cincinnati)

Consecutive Game Streak's Statistical Totals:

Year	G	AB	R	H	2B	3B	HR	RBI	BB	SO	AVG	SLG	SB
1889	100	377	75	86	14	2	2	41	32	34	.228	.292	33
1890	129	481	76	92	6	5	1	47	42	23	.191	.231	24
1891	138	512	50	103	11	5	3	53	38	32	.201	.260	16
1892	66	255	29	59	7	3	5	39	19	19	.231	.341	9
Total	433	1625	230	340	38	15	11	180	131	108	.209	.271	82

Germany Smith was such an extremely reliable fielding shortstop that his normally weak hitting did not stop him from being a starting player during his time in the big leagues. He made the rounds with five teams in his 15-year career and was the shortstop on two pennant winners in Brooklyn. After putting in time with a semipro team, he became a major leaguer when he signed on to play for Altoona, which was granted a franchise in the new major league, the Union Association, in 1884. Making his major league debut on April 17, 1884, his time with the Altoona Mountain Citys was short as the team folded after just 25 games. Soon after, Smith joined the National League, playing for the Cleveland Blues. He finished his rookie season by compiling a .271 average in the 97 games he played with Altoona and Cleveland.

Before the start of his second season, Smith departed the National League when he was traded to the Brooklyn Trolley Dodgers of the American Association in January 1885. He replaced Billy Geer as the Dodgers' new shortstop. He kept busy at the position in 1885 when he had the most assists (and the most errors) at shortstop. In 1885, he also set a seasonal major league mark for shortstops that still stands today when he averaged 4.21 assists per game. The closest modern-day player to approach this record was San Diego's Ozzie Smith, who in 1980 averaged 3.93 assists per game. Over the next several years, Smith was firmly entrenched as the Dodgers' shortstop. Only on rare occasion would he be employed at another playing position. Although his spot in the lineup was guaranteed due to his superior fielding, his notoriously weak hitting at times brought surprising results. He missed 35 games during the 1887 season but he still led Brooklyn with a .294 average and 16 triples. That same year, he captured his first (of two) fielding titles when he led the league's shortstops with an .886 fielding percentage. The team changed their nickname from the Trolley Dodgers to the Bridegrooms with the startup of the 1888 season. While the Bridegrooms were having their best year in franchise history (finishing second to the St. Louis Browns with a .629 winning percentage), he was out of the lineup for nearly a third of the season. His hitting dramatically fell 80 points as he finished with just a .214 average. Up to this time in his career, Smith's durability was in question because he missed a good percentage of his team's games. This was soon to change as he started his consecutive playing streak on June 4, 1889, in a Bridegrooms' home game against the Kansas City Cowboys. Although his .231 batting average was lowest of all the team's starters, it was his spectacular play at shortstop that helped contribute to the Dodgers winning their first league pennant when they edged out the St. Louis Browns by a couple of games in the final standings. The Bridegrooms met the National League champion New York Giants in the 1889 World's Series. In what was a relatively high-scoring affair, the

Giants beat Brooklyn in six of the nine games and outscored them 73 to 52 in runs scored. Smith hit only .172 as he had five hits in 29 trips to the plate. Three of those hits were for extra bases. Before the start of the 1890 campaign, the Bridegrooms moved from the American Association over to the National League. During the 1890 season, the entire Brooklyn infield — consisting of Smith, first baseman Dave Foutz, second baseman Hub Collins and third baseman George Pinkney — missed just three games. Absent from those three contests was Pinkney, who had suffered an ankle injury that caused his record-setting 577 consecutive game run to end in early May. Smith, on the other hand, had an awful year with the bat as he hit just .191 (the lowest average among all league regulars), had a slugging percentage of only .231 and drove home 47 runners. Bridegrooms' skipper Bill McGunnigle still kept Smith in the daily lineup because his fielding skills were just too valuable to keep him on the bench. Brooklyn went on to win the National League pennant as they beat out the Chicago Colts by six games. The Bridegrooms contested against the American Association's Louisville Colonels in the 1890 World's Series. The series was tied 3–3 with one tie after seven games. The series did not come to a final conclusion because the weather was getting colder and the attendance was on a sharp decline (mainly due to the weather). Smith surprised many by hitting .276 and leading all Bridegroom players in the series with two triples and seven runs knocked in. The next season he transferred to the Cincinnati Reds when incoming Brooklyn manager Monte Ward took over the shortstop role for the Bridegrooms. Smith retained his shortstop role with the Reds as he replaced Oliver Beard at that position. Smith also became baseball's Iron Man later that year on July 21, 1891, when he replaced former Brooklyn teammate Hub Collins, who was seriously injured in a collision during the previous game while chasing a fly ball. Smith's troubles with the bat continued during 1891 as he hit .201 but he continued lengthening his playing streak along with leading the league's shortstops with 507 assists. This time his fielding couldn't help his new team much as the Reds placed well back in the pack with a seventh-place finish. The next season, his playing streak ended after 433 games when he missed a week's worth of action, starting on July 5, 1892. With a little rest, his hitting became more productive as he came in with a career-best eight homers, batted .243 and drove home 63 Red Leg runners. The Reds also showed improvement as the team jumped a couple of spots to fifth place in the standings and finished 20 games behind the pennant-winning Boston Beaneaters.

Smith spent four more years with the Reds before returning to Brooklyn through a trade in mid–November 1896. After just one year back with the Bridegrooms, he was sent packing to the St. Louis Browns, where he finished his major league career by hitting a very paltry .159 in just over 50 games for the last-place team. He played for three more seasons in the Western League, the American League (then a minor league) and the Western Association. After that, he did one stint of managing in the minors before leaving baseball.

27. Bid McPhee

Born: November 1, 1859, Massena, New York *Died*: January 3, 1943, San Diego, California *Bats*: Right *Throws*: Right *Height*: 5 feet, 8 inches *Weight*: 152 *Major league debut*: May 2, 1882 (Pittsburgh at Cincinnati [AA]) *Last major league game*: October 15, 1899 (second game) (Cleveland at Cincinnati [NL])

Major league Iron Man from: July 5, 1892, to September 25, 1892 *Consecutive games played*: 377 *Games as major league Iron Man*: 70 (consecutive games 308 through 377) *Team played for during streak*: Cincinnati Reds (NL) *Primary position played*: Second base *Game missed before streak*: May 31, 1890

Bid McPhee

(Cincinnati at New York) *First game played of streak*: June 2, 1890 (Cincinnati at Cleveland) *Last game played of streak*: September 24, 1892 (Cincinnati at St. Louis) *Game missed to end streak*: September 25, 1892 (first game) (Cincinnati at St. Louis)

Consecutive Game Streak's Statistical Totals:

Year	G	AB	R	H	2B	3B	HR	RBI	BB	SO	AVG	SLG	SB
1890	103	407	97	106	11	20	3	—	65	15	.260	.408	—
1891	138	562	107	144	14	16	6	38	74	35	.256	.370	33
1892	136	543	107	146	18	12	4	56	83	45	.269	.368	42
Total	377	1512	311	396	43	48	13	94	222	95	.262	.380	75

Bid McPhee is considered the best second baseman of the 19th century. He was also known as a very levelheaded player; during an 18-year major league career, he never once was fined or ejected from a game. He was such a reliable player that he played just one position (second base) for one team (the Cincinnati Reds, in the American Association from 1882 to 1889 and then the National League from 1890 to 1899) during his entire big league career. He was such a skilled defensive player that an overall perspective of his accomplishments at second base showed that he led players at that position in games played, putouts and fielding eight times each, most assists six times and double plays 11 times. Amazingly, he compiled all these statistics (except his last fielding championship in 1896) without wearing a glove. It wasn't until early in the 1896 season, 10 years after gloves starting making an appearance on the baseball diamond, that he finally relented and used one. Obviously, if the Gold Glove award had been in existence during McPhee's time, he would have been a perennial winner of this honor for many years running. He spent his first four years of organized ball playing for minor league teams in Davenport, Iowa, and Akron, Ohio. When the American Association was formed in November 1881, McPhee signed on to play for the Cincinnati Reds franchise. In his rookie season, he hit just .228 but helped lead the Reds to the league championship. This turned out to be the only occasion in McPhee's career that he was a member of a pennant-winning team. He settled in at second base and over the next several seasons led the position in numerous defensive categories. Some other of his achievements included leading the American Association with eight homers in 1886 and finishing in a tie with five other players for most triples hit (19) during the 1887 campaign. The 1889 season was the last year the Cincinnati franchise spent in the American Association. The team defected to the National League for the start of the 1890 campaign. McPhee started his playing streak on June 2, 1890, during a Reds' away game against the Cleveland Spiders and was in the Reds' lineup for the last 103 games that year. Three weeks after his streak commenced, he hit three triples in a 12–3 Reds victory over the New York Giants on June 28. In his first year in the National League, he hit .256, posted a team-high 125 runs scored and had the second-highest number of triples (22) in the league behind a teammate, first baseman Long John Reilly, who had 26 three-baggers. The change of leagues didn't affect the Reds' performance that much as they finished in fourth place for the third straight season. The 1891 season turned out to be just the second year (the other being 1884) that McPhee didn't miss a single contest in his long Hall of Fame playing career. In 138 games, he duplicated his previous season's .256 batting average and tied with Arlie Latham for most walks in the club with 74 free passes. After several seasons of being in the first division of the standings, the Reds plummeted to the lower depths as they finished in a tie for last place with the Pittsburgh Pirates. When teammate shortstop Germany Smith sat out the July 5, 1892, Reds' home game against the Philadelphia Phillies, McPhee became baseball's Iron Man with 308 consecutive games played. In the last weeks of the season, his 377-game streak came to an end on September 25 due to an illness that kept him out of the Reds' lineup for two weeks. With the club under new management (Charlie Comiskey, who left the St. Louis Browns to join the Reds), the team finished in fifth place out of a dozen teams.

McPhee played for seven more productive seasons at second base for the Reds. He had his best year at the plate in 1894 when he had career highs in hitting (.313), runs driven in (93) and slugging (.429). When a sore hand caused him to start wearing a glove in 1896, his fielding accuracy improved so dramatically that he ran away with the second base fielding title with a .978 average. During his final two playing years, 1898 and 1899, he was the oldest active player in major league baseball. He retired as a player once the 1899 season was completed. He returned to the club a couple of years later when he replaced Bob Allen as the Reds' manager in 1901. His short managerial career was not successful as Cincinnati finished in last place during his first season at the helm. The next year, he had the Reds playing at 10 games below .500 ball when he resigned on July 10, 1902. He moved to California after leaving the Reds and, except for occasional scouting for his old club, spent the rest of his life in retirement. It was not until 2000 that the Baseball Hall of Fame veterans' committee finally chose him for membership.

28. TOMMY MCCARTHY

Born: July 24, 1863, Boston, Massachusetts *Died*: August 5, 1922, Boston, Massachusetts *Bats*: Right *Throws*: Right *Height*: 5 feet, 7 inches *Weight*: 170 *Major league debut*: July 10, 1884 (Chicago at Boston [UA]) *Last major league game*: September 26, 1896 (Brooklyn at Philadelphia [NL])

Major league Iron Man from: September 25, 1892, to September 14, 1893 *Consecutive games played*: 392 *Games as major league Iron Man*: 133 (consecutive games 260 through 392) *Teams played for during streak*: St. Louis Browns (AA) (1891) and Boston Beaneaters (NL) (1892–1893) *Primary position played*: Outfield *Game missed before streak*: April 25, 1891 (St. Louis at Columbus) *First game played of streak*: April 26, 1891 (St. Louis at Columbus) *Last game played of streak*: September 13, 1893 (second game) (Boston at Chicago) *Game missed to end streak*: September 14, 1893 (Boston at Pittsburgh)

Consecutive Game Streak's Statistical Totals:

Year	G	AB	R	H	2B	3B	HR	RBI	BB	SO	AVG	SLG	SB
1891	124	526	120	166	18	5	8	85	45	18	.316	.414	37
1892	152	603	119	146	19	5	4	63	93	29	.242	.310	53
1893	116	462	107	160	28	6	5	111	64	10	.346	.465	46
Total	392	1591	346	472	65	16	17	259	202	57	.297	.390	136

Tommy McCarthy spent parts of 13 seasons in the major leagues with four clubs. He was exemplary in every aspect of his playing skills, whether he was playing defense, running the base paths or playing his innovative approaches to the game. He is credited with popularizing several baseball strategies that are used quite commonly today, including the fake bunt, the hit and run and the infield fly rule. Surprisingly, he did not craft his playing skills in the minor leagues before making it to the majors. He was playing sandlot baseball in the Boston area when he was discovered by a representative of the Boston Reds of the Union Association. By July 10, 1884, he was making his major league debut in a Reds' home game against the Chicago Browns. He started as an outfielder and pitcher but soon gave up pitching and concentrated solely on playing the outfield. He got into 53 games that first season and finished with an unimpressive .215 batting average.

Over the next three years, he had limited playing time with the Boston Beaneaters and Philadelphia Quakers in addition to some frequent stops in the minors. It wasn't until the 1888 season that he became a daily player with the St. Louis Browns of the American Association. He was inserted into the Browns' right field slot, replacing the previous season's rotating right field combo of Bob Caruthers and Dave Foutz. That first year in St. Louis saw McCarthy compile a .274 batting average and drive in 68 runners. He additionally led the league's outfielders in assists (44) and double plays (12). The Browns, under the guidance of Charlie Comiskey, won the American Association title for the fourth straight year as they edged the Brooklyn Bridegrooms by six and a half games. The Browns faced the National League titleholders, the New York Giants, in the 1888 World's Series. In a rather high-scoring affair, the Giants beat the Browns in 10 games to claim the world title. McCarthy played in all the games, went 10 for 41 for a .244 average and was tied with teammate Arlie Latham for most runs scored (10) in the series. The next year he played every game and showed some improvement as he upped his average to .291, along with topping the team with 136 runs scored, pacing the league with 604 at-bats and leading the outfielders with 140 games played and 11 double plays. For the first time in five seasons, the Browns did not finish atop the final standings; they ended the season in second place, edged out by the Brooklyn Bridegrooms by a couple of games. In 1890, McCarthy was chosen manager of the Browns but his time as skipper lasted just 27 games, from start of the season through May 18 and August 24 through 29, as the club went through five different managers that season. His managerial duties did not affect his playing at all as his hitting jumped nearly 60 points to a .350 average, good for third place in the league behind Louisville's Jimmy Wolf and Philadelphia's Denny Lyons. He also had league highs for stolen bases (83) and times on base (269) and finished second in runs (137), hits (192) and total bases (256). His consecutive playing streak that eventually achieved Iron Man status started very early the next season during the Browns' April 26, 1891, game at Columbus. Although he did not repeat his prior performance, he was one of three .300 hitters on the club as he came in with a .309 average. With Comiskey back at the Browns' helm after a one-year sabbatical, the club secured a solid second-place finish behind the first-place Boston Reds. The 1891 season turned out to be the 10th and final year of major league ball for the American Association as four of its teams were absorbed into the National League and the rest of the clubs disbanded. In 1892, McCarthy wound up playing right field for the Beaneaters as he replaced Harry Stovey in that position. It was also the year that he hooked up with the team's new center fielder, Hugh Duffy, to form the "heavenly twins" outfield. McCarthy inherited the Iron Man title late in the season when the Cincinnati Reds' Bid McPhee snapped his 377-game streak September 25, 1892. McCarthy didn't miss a single contest in that year but that might explain why he had his worst season as a regular player when he concluded the year with a .242 average (50 points below his career average) and brought home 63 runners. His off year had little effect on the team as Boston easily outpaced the Cleveland Spiders to capture the National League flag. In the 1892 World's Series, the Beaneaters faced those same Spiders and easily manhandled them by sweeping five of the six games (the other being a 0–0 tie in game one) and outscoring them 31 to 15 overall. McCarthy contributed eight hits and a couple of doubles for a .381 average. He moved to left field permanently starting with the 1893 campaign. With only 15 games left in that season, he suffered a season-ending injury when he broke a couple of toes while trying to steal third base in the nightcap of a double-header against the Chicago Colts on September 13, 1893. This injury caused him to miss the rest of the season. His streak officially ended after 392 games when he missed the Beaneaters' next game on September 14 at Pittsburgh. His 1893 final batting average rebounded to a .346 average (good for second place on the team behind Duffy) and he led the team in doubles and stolen bases. Boston won the pennant again by outlasting the Pittsburgh Pirates but there was no World's Series held at the end of the season to determine a world champion.

McCarthy put in two more solid years in Boston, including the 1894 season during which he achieved career highs in home runs (13) and runs batted in (126). After playing for the Beaneaters for four years, he was sold to the Brooklyn Bridegrooms in mid–November 1895. He spent just one season in Brooklyn before calling it a career after the 1896 season. He eventually returned to do some scouting for the Cincinnati Reds and Boston Beaneaters for several years. He also coached in the minors in 1918 before turning to coach baseball in the college ranks at Dartmouth, Holy Cross and Boston College. Although there are many players from his era who had better statistics and are not in baseball's Hall of Fame, McCarthy was selected to that revered place in 1946 due in no small part to the intellectual approach and impressive innovations he contributed to the game, in addition to his outstanding playing career.

29. JAKE BECKLEY

Born: August 4, 1867, Hannibal, Missouri *Died*: June 25, 1918, Kansas City, Missouri *Bats*: Left *Throws*: Left *Height*: 5 feet, 10 inches *Weight*: 200 *Major league debut*: June 20, 1888 (Pittsburgh at Chicago [NL]) *Last major league game*: June 15, 1907 (Boston at St. Louis [NL])

Major league Iron Man from: September 14, 1893, to July 18, 1894 *Consecutive games played*: 352 *Games as major league Iron Man*: 86 (consecutive games 267 through 352) *Team played for during streak*: Pittsburgh Pirates (NL) *Primary position played*: First base *Game missed before streak*: April 15, 1892 (Pittsburgh at St. Louis) *First game played of streak*: April 16, 1892 (Pittsburgh at St. Louis) *Last game played of streak*: July 17, 1894 (Pittsburgh at St. Louis) *Game missed to end streak*: July 18, 1894 (Pittsburgh at St. Louis)

Consecutive Game Streak's Statistical Totals:

Year	G	AB	R	H	2B	3B	HR	RBI	BB	SO	AVG	SLG	SB
1892	149	606	100	142	21	17	9	92	31	43	.234	.370	30
1893	131	542	108	164	32	19	5	106	54	26	.303	.459	15
1894	72	279	67	97	19	7	2	71	31	9	.348	.487	18
Total	352	1427	275	403	72	43	16	269	116	78	.282	.427	63

Jake Beckley put in 20 seasons in the major leagues with five teams. This left–handed slugger played his entire career at first base. Although he had a weak throwing arm, by the time he had retired Beckley established records for first basemen with the most games played, most total chances and most putouts recorded at the position. He spent the parts of three years in the minor leagues before being promoted to the Pittsburgh Alleghenys in June 1888. His debut game was in Chicago against the White Stockings on June 20, 1888. The club's manager was so impressed with Beckley's play that within a short time he became the team's regular first baseman. He played in 71 games his rookie season and achieved a .343 batting average. In his second year, he became the most offense-producing player on the club as he had team-high marks in just about every offensive category, including hitting nine homers and driving in 97 runners.

Like many of his contemporaries, Beckley left the National League in 1890 (because of the players' revolt) and signed on to play in the newly formed Players League for the Pittsburgh Burghers. He had another impressive year in 1890 as he led the team with a .324 average and 120 RBI along with finishing in second place with 38 doubles (only Cleveland's Pete Browning had more with 40 two-baggers) and having 69 extra base hits (the most in the league). The Players League dissolved after one season when the National League and the renegade players settled their differences. Beckley returned to the Pittsburgh franchise of the National League. The team also changed its name before the start of the 1891 season from the Alleghenys to the Pirates. Pittsburgh finished the year tied for last place but Beckley soothed the wounds the best he could by providing the offensive power to lead most of the team's hitting categories. He also was among the league leaders with 19 triples (one less than Boston's Harry Stovey) and 87 assists at first base (the highest total of all first basemen). The following year, he sat out only one contest and that was the third game of the season on April 15, 1892, in St. Louis. He began his consecutive games streak the next day as he played the last 149 on the Pirates' schedule. Although Beckley did post team highs in doubles, triples, homers and runs driven in, the 1892 season was actually his worst year with the bat as his batting average plummeted to a career low of .236 (a decrease of 56 points). Not all results were bad though as Beckley led the league's first basemen in assists and putouts and the Pirates won 25 more games than during the previous year and they improved two spots in the final standings with a sixth-place finish. With about a month left to play in the 1893 season, Beckley became baseball's leader of consecutive games played on September 14 when Boston Beaneaters outfielder Tommy McCarthy's playing streak came to a conclusion. Beckley became just the second left-hander batter to become baseball's Iron Man. His stats rebounded from the previous dreadful season when he batted .303 and brought home 106 runners with his clutch hitting. The Pirates had made such great improvement that they were in contention to win the league title before coming up short by five games by the close of the season. They finished second to the Beaneaters. Beckley's playing streak came to an end in the same place where it started—St. Louis. After 352 games, he was given a rest by Pirates manager Al Buckenberger on July 18, 1894. Ironically, this turned out to be the only game that he would miss the entire season. He finished the year with career highs in batting (.345) and runs batted in (122) as well as again leading the first basemen in putouts and assists. The Pirates unfortunately reverted to their mediocre ways as the club played only .500 ball and finished in seventh place, 25 games behind the pennant-winning Baltimore Orioles.

Jake Beckley: The Pittsburgh Pirates' Hall of Fame first baseman had an Iron Man run of 352 games in the mid–1890s.

Beckley remained in Pittsburgh until late July 1896 when he was traded to the New York Giants. His time in New York was short because by early in the 1897 campaign he was sent to the Cincinnati Reds. He took over the Reds' first base duties from Farmer Vaughn. He spent seven very productive years in Cincinnati before being sold to the St. Louis Cardinals in February 1904. Although his first year in

St. Louis was quite successful as he hit .325, his offensive numbers grew increasingly worse over the next three years. In his final big league year, 1907, he was hitting only .209 after 32 games when the Cardinals released him. He finished the year with Kansas City of the American Association and actually won that league's batting title. The next year, he took over as the club's playing manager and stayed through the 1909 season. He played two more years after that in the minors before retiring from playing in 1911. He passed away seven years later in 1918 of heart troubles. The veterans' committee of baseball's Hall of Fame selected Beckley for membership in 1971.

30. HUGH DUFFY

Born: November 26, 1866, Cranston, Rhode Island *Died*: October 19, 1954, Boston, Massachusetts *Bats*: Right *Throws*: Right *Height*: 5 feet, 7 inches *Weight*: 168 *Major league debut*: June 23, 1888 (Pittsburgh at Chicago [NL]) *Last major league game*: April 13, 1906 (New York at Philadelphia [NL])

Major league Iron Man from: July 18, 1894, to August 9, 1894 *Consecutive games played*: 225 *Games as major league Iron Man*: 18 (consecutive games 208 through 225) *Team played for during streak*: Boston Beaneaters (NL) *Primary position played*: Outfield *Game missed before streak*: October 8, 1892 (second game) (New York at Boston) *First game played of streak*: October 11, 1892 (first game) (Boston at Brooklyn) *Last game played of streak*: August 8, 1894 (Philadelphia at Boston) *Game missed to end streak*: August 9, 1894 (Philadelphia at Boston)

Consecutive Game Streak's Statistical Totals

Year	G	AB	R	H	2B	3B	HR	RBI	BB	SO	AVG	SLG	SB
1892	5	17	6	8	1	1	0	3	2	3	.471	.647	0
1893	131	560	147	203	23	7	6	118	50	13	.363	.461	44
1894	89	398	116	175	40	8	14	108	42	13	.440	.686	30
Total	225	975	269	386	64	16	20	229	94	29	.396	.556	74

Hugh Duffy was one of the top hitters in the 1890s and a member of six major league teams in a 17-year span between 1888 and 1906. His peak performance years were spent guarding the spots in either left or center field for the Boston Beaneaters. He spent his first season of organized ball in the minors in the New England leagues before being spotted by one of Cap Anson's scouts for the Chicago White Stockings. He was signed by Chicago and made his first appearance on a major league diamond on June 23, 1888. Soon after he replaced Bob Pettit as the team's right fielder. A little over a month after his debut and with just eight games of experience, he started proving his durability by playing the last 63 games on the White Stockings' schedule. He also proved his ability to handle major league pitching by batting .282 and hitting a surprising seven homers in just half a season.

In 1889, Duffy was firmly entrenched in right field for Chicago. He played every game, led the National League in games played and at-bats and finished the year with a .312 average (his first of nine straight years of hitting .300 or above), a dozen homers and 89 runs batted in. He was one of many big leaguers who left their National League or American Association teams and joined the renegade Players League for the 1890 season. Duffy signed on with the Chicago Pirates. The Pirates' playing manager, Charlie Comiskey, kept Duffy in his normal right field position. He turned in one of the better performances by hitting .320, driving in 82 runners and having league-high marks in at-bats, runs scored, base hits and games played by an outfielder. He also took in every contest and extended his playing streak to 337 games by the end of the year. This was good enough for second place overall and just behind Dave

Foutz of the National League Brooklyn Bridegrooms, who had a streak of 363 games. Duffy's chance to become the Iron Man ended, however, with the season opener of his new team, the Boston Reds of the American Association, on April 8, 1891. In the American Association's last year as a major league, the Reds seemed to be the team with the talent. Duffy helped lead them to a first-place finish by ending in a tie with teammate Duke Farrell for the most RBI (110) along with hitting .336. His batting average was good for second place in the league behind another teammate, Dan Brouthers, who finished with a .350 average. With the American Association's demise after the 1891 season, Duffy's services were acquired by the National League's Boston Beaneaters, which he would call his baseball home for the next nine seasons. Boston was already set in left field and new acquisition Tommy McCarthy was designated as the new right fielder. With the departure of future Iron Man Steve Brodie to St. Louis, the center field position was open, so Boston's skipper, Frank Selee, made Duffy the new center fielder and at the same time formed the outfield duo (Duffy and McCarthy) that became known as the "heavenly twins." During his initial year with the Beaneaters, Duffy started another playing streak with just five games left in the 1892 season, beginning October 11, 1892. He closed out the year batting .301 (a dip of 35 points) but still good enough to lead the team in that category and help the club to a league title. As a result of Boston's winning the league pennant, they faced the second-place Cleveland Spiders in the World's Series. The Spiders were no match for the more powerful Beaneaters as Boston completely dominated the series, winning five of six games with one contest ending in a tie. Duffy was the offensive star of the series. He had 12 hits in 26 at-bats for a series-high .462 average and another high mark of nine runs driven in. He would have easily run away with the MVP trophy for the series if one had existed. The next season saw his batting average dramatically improve by 62 percentage points in 1893 as he again led the team with a .363 average. He also drove in 118 runners in helping the Beaneaters repeat as National League champions. On July 18, 1894, he replaced Jake Beckley of the Pittsburgh Pirates as the new Iron Man. Three weeks later on August 9, a bothersome charley horse injury resulted in his missing two weeks' worth of action and ended his playing streak (and reign as Iron Man) at 225 games. Duffy's performance during the 1894 season was one of the greatest years put together by a major leaguer as he captured baseball's Triple Crown. He would have easily won the MVP voting that year too. He set an all-time single-season batting mark of .440 that still stands today (and most likely will never be matched) by amassing 237 hits in 539 at-bats. Besides the total number of hits, he also led with 18 homers. He actually hit 19 but his home run hit on June 20 was credited as a triple because of the sudden death rule of baseball at the time; credit was given only with the hit that would have scored the winning run. Duffy also led with 51 doubles, 374 total bases, 85 extra-base hits and 145 RBI. All of Duffy's accomplishments that year could not prevent the Beaneaters from finishing in third place, eight games behind the first-place Baltimore Orioles.

Duffy still had several years of quality playing time left in his career but since he is a two-time holder of the Iron Man title, the details of his other playing streak along with the rest of his playing career are addressed in a later portion of this book.

31. STEVE BRODIE

Born: September 11, 1868, Warrenton, Virginia *Died*: October 30, 1935, Baltimore, Maryland *Bats*: Left *Throws*: Right *Height*: 5 feet, 11 inches *Weight*: 180 *Major league debut*: April 21, 1890 (Brooklyn at Boston [NL]) *Last major league game*: October 4, 1902 (second game) (New York at Boston [NL])

STEVE BRODIE

Major league Iron Man from: August 9, 1894, to June 28, 1897 *Consecutive games played*: 574 *Games as major league Iron Man*: 355 (consecutive games 220 through 574) *Teams played for during streak*: St. Louis Browns (NL) (1893), Baltimore Orioles (NL) (1893–1896) and Pittsburgh Pirates (NL) (1897) *Primary position played*: Outfield *Game missed before streak*: October 15, 1892 (Chicago vs. St. Louis at Kansas City) *First game played of streak*: April 27, 1893 (Louisville at St. Louis) *Last game played of streak*: June 26, 1897 (St. Louis at Pittsburgh) *Game missed to end streak*: June 28, 1897 (Pittsburgh at Cleveland)

Consecutive Game Streak's Statistical Totals:

Year	G	AB	R	H	2B	3B	HR	RBI	BB	SO	AVG	SLG	SB
1893	132	566	89	184	23	10	2	98	45	18	.325	.412	49
1894	129	573	134	210	25	11	3	113	18	8	.366	.464	42
1895	131	528	85	184	27	10	2	134	26	15	.348	.449	35
1896	132	516	98	153	19	11	2	87	36	17	.297	.388	25
1897	50	198	28	58	6	8	2	35	12	—	.293	.434	6
Total	574	2381	434	789	100	50	11	467	137	58	.331	.429	157

Steve Brodie was one of the most durable players in the major leagues during the 1890s. This solidly built outfielder played for six teams in a big league career that lasted a dozen seasons. He turned pro in 1887 and played in the minor leagues for three seasons. With many established stars bolting the National League to play in the newly formed Players League, Brodie found a place in the National League as a member of the Boston Beaneaters in 1890. New Boston manager Frank Selee made him the everyday right fielder, replacing King Kelly who had crossed over to the Boston franchise of the Players League. Brodie's rookie year was quite impressive as he played in all but two of the Beaneaters' games, hit .296, led the team with 67 RBI (even though he didn't have a single home run) and was the top fielding outfielder in the league with a .953 percentage.

Beaneaters' skipper Selee shifted Brodie over to the center field in 1891 when the spot became open. Previous center fielder, old-timer Paul Hines (an early Iron Man), left the team to play in the American Association. Center field became Brodie's normal playing position and he stayed there for the remainder of his baseball career. Although his stats dropped off in that year as evidenced by a 36-point slippage in his batting average,

Steve Brodie: The Baltimore Orioles outfielder played in 574 consecutive games (just three short of the then-record 577 contests) in the 1890s. Because of a typo in his 1894 games played column which originally indicated 120 games (instead of the correct 129 games), his streak was not realized until years later.

he still helped the Beaneaters win the National League pennant. After the season was over, Boston sent him to the St. Louis Browns. He continued to show his durability in 1892 by playing in every game but one and even tried his hand at playing second and third bases for several games. The one game he sat out was the Browns' season finale on October 15, 1892, against the Chicago Colts. The Browns' season opener in 1893 occurred on April 27, 1893, against the Louisville Colonels. This was the date and game that started Brodie's playing streak that eventually became the second-longest playing streak achieved in 19th century major league baseball. Although he was having an excellent year at the plate with a .318 batting average and 79 runs driven in for the lowly Browns, the team traded him to the Baltimore Orioles in late August. He continued his torrid hitting by batting .361 the rest of the year for his new team and finished with an overall .325 hitting mark and driving in 98 runners. The following year, his playing streak stood at 220 games when he replaced Boston's Hugh Duffy as baseball's Iron Man on August 9, 1894. With this achievement, Brodie became just the third left-handed batter to be the sport's most durable contestant. He had another marvelous year with the bat as he finished third in hitting for the Orioles, behind teammates Joe Kelley and Willie Keeler, with a .366 average along with bringing home 113 runners; that is an amazing total considering he had just three homers the whole year. He also was busy with the glove as he made 310 putouts in center field. With the powerful squad that had been put together over the last few seasons, Baltimore won their first National League flag in 1894 and faced the second-place New York Giants in the first Temple Cup series. The Giants completely dominated the Orioles as Baltimore was swept in four games in addition to being outscored 33 to 11. Brodie was a complete no-show for this series as he didn't have a single hit in 15 at-bats and reached base only twice via walks which did eventually result in runs being scored. As his streak continued through the 1895 season, Brodie was still putting up big production numbers as he batted .348 and upped his RBI total to a team-high 134 runs, finishing tied on the team with Kelley. His efforts helped Baltimore repeat as league champs as they edged the Cleveland Spiders by three games for the title. Facing the Spiders in the 1895 Temple Cup, the Orioles wound up on the losing end again as they were beaten in five games. Brodie did go 4 for 20 for a .200 average but was basically a nonfactor again for the second year in a row in the championship round. In the latter portion of the following year, he became just the second major leaguer to play in 500 consecutive games when he accomplished this milestone on August 28, 1896. Although he was in the lineup every day, his final stats that year showed dramatic drops in his batting average (.297 — down 51 points) and RBI totals (87 — down 47 runs) although he did lead the league's outfielders with 320 putouts. His off year didn't seem to affect the Orioles much as the club won the National League for the third year running. The Orioles finally won the world championship when they swept the Spiders in four games in the 1896 Temple Cup series. Brodie had another awful series as he collected just a single in 15 at-bats for a .067 average. Team management was not too pleased with his overall performance and hooked up with the Pittsburgh Pirates in a trade in which they swapped their center fielders (Brodie for Jake Stenzel) in November 1896. Brodie was having an average year when a sore arm ended his streak in Cleveland on June 28, 1897, at 574 games. The Pirates decided to go on a road trip without him because of his lame arm. Later research showed that he was only four games away from breaking the then all-time record of 577 consecutive games held by George Pinkney. For many years, baseball records did not show that Brodie had such a long playing streak. A typo in the 1894 games played column indicated that Brodie played 120 contests instead of the actual 129 games he did play. Another interesting piece of information is that Brodie's streak would have been 731 straight games (and the overall record until Everett Scott's streak) if he had not sat out the final 1892

St. Louis Browns' game against the Colts. His streak was the National League record though because some of Pinkney's streak was accomplished in the American Association. Brodie's streak continued to be the senior circuit's record until it was surpassed in the 1920s by Eddie Brown. Brodie's offensive production continued to fall as he had a .292 batting average and drove in just 53 runners in 100 contests. He was still providing reliable defense as he led all outfielders for the second time in fielding with a .983 percentage.

Brodie's time in Pittsburgh proved short as he wound up back with the Orioles midway through the 1898 season. His second tour in Baltimore came to an end at the conclusion of the 1899 season. Soon after, he jumped over to the American League (considered a minor league at the time) to play for the Chicago White Stockings. He played two more years, the first with the American League version of the Baltimore Orioles in 1901 and returned to the National League for his final major league season (1902) and played with the New York Giants. He returned to the minor leagues and was always on the move as he played for a dozen teams in eight years before finally retiring as a player in 1910. With his playing days behind him, he took up coaching in the college ranks for about a dozen more years before giving up baseball altogether and returning to Baltimore to work for the city.

32. GEORGE VAN HALTREN

Born: March 30, 1866, St. Louis, Missouri *Died*: September 29, 1945, Oakland, California *Bats*: Left *Throws*: Left *Height*: 5 feet, 11 inches *Weight*: 170 *Major league debut*: June 27, 1887 (Boston at Chicago [NL]) *Last major league game*: September 26, 1903 (New York at Pittsburgh [NL])

Major league Iron Man from: June 28, 1897, to July 17, 1897 *Consecutive games played*: 324 *Games as major league Iron Man*: 17 (consecutive games 308 through 324) *Team played for during streak*: New York Giants (NL) *Primary position played*: Outfield *Game missed before streak*: May 3, 1895 (New York at Philadelphia) *First game played of streak*: May 4, 1895 (New York at Philadelphia) *Last game played of streak*: July 16, 1897 (second game) (New York at Louisville) *Game missed to end streak*: July 17, 1897 (first game) (New York at Louisville)

Consecutive Game Streak's Statistical Totals

Year	G	AB	R	H	2B	3B	HR	RBI	BB	SO	AVG	SLG	SB
1895	123	494	104	174	23	19	8	101	47	24	.352	.524	31
1896	133	562	136	197	18	21	5	74	55	36	.351	.484	39
1897	68	297	60	97	7	3	1	31	22	—	.327	.380	24
Total	324	1353	300	468	48	43	14	206	124	60	.346	.476	94

During the last decade of 19th century baseball, George Van Haltren was one of the more durable and reliable players. He stayed in the big leagues for 17 seasons with six teams but he had his most productive years during the latter portion of his career with the New York Giants, where he became a star. With less than 16 months of organized ball playing experience, he made his debut in a major league uniform as a pitcher on June 27, 1887, for the National League's Chicago White Stockings. He had trouble getting the ball across the plate that day and, as a result, tied a major league record by walking 16 batters in Chicago's 17–11 loss to Boston. He split his time in the lineup his first two seasons by either pitching (where he hurled a six-inning no-hitter in 1888) or playing in the outfield.

With the start of the 1889 season, Van Haltren gave up his career as a pitcher (except for the 1890 season and the rare cameo appearances after that) and took over the White Stockings' left field spot from Marty Sullivan, who had departed for the Indianapolis Hoosiers. By being in the lineup for just about every game, he proved he deserved his starting role by hitting .322, clubbing nine homers and driving home 81 runners. This turned out to be his last year with Chicago because of the players' revolt. He played in the Players League in 1890 for the Brooklyn Wonders where he served as the backup right fielder along with being third in the rotation of pitchers on the squad. He took in 92 games, hit .335 and went 15–10 on the mound for the second-place Wonders. He also proved he had some wildness left in his pitching because he led the league's pitchers with 19 hit batsmen. When the Players League expired after just one year of competition, Van Haltren shifted over to the Baltimore Orioles of the American Association. He split most of playing time in 1891 between shortstop and left field. The distraction of rotating between two distinctive positions did not seem to bother him as he played every game and was the team leader in at-bats, runs, hits, triples, hitting and slugging. With the demise of another major league (the American Association) after the 1891 campaign, the Orioles were absorbed into the National League. Van Haltren started out the 1892 season as playing manager for the Orioles. This lasted just 11 games when he was replaced by John Waltz. In the lineup, Van Haltren was used entirely in the outfield for the Orioles with the majority of the games evenly split between center and right fields. He also had a consecutive game streak of over 200 games running when he sat out the July 20 game. This streak, however, was entirely overlapped by the streak of Cincinnati Reds' second baseman Bid McPhee. With just a couple of weeks left in the season, the Orioles traded Van Haltren to the Pittsburgh Pirates on September 5, 1892. Even though he was no longer with Baltimore, that team's final stats revealed that he still led the club in runs, hits, RBI (tied with Wilbert Robinson), doubles (tied with Bill Shindle), homers, walks and stolen bases. In his only full season with the Pirates, Van Haltren played center field. He had his highest career batting average (up to that time) when he hit .338 (and his first of nine straight years of hitting above the .300 mark) and paced the team with 179 base hits. This performance did not prevent the Pirates from selling him to the New York Giants in November 1893. The good news was this would turn out to be his final major league move after having played only briefly with several other clubs in recent years. The Giants also had a new lead off hitter and permanent center fielder for the next decade in Van Haltren, after having rotated that position between General Stafford and Harry Lyons the previous year. Van Haltren responded to his new assign-

George Van Haltren: He was a two-time major league Iron Man for the New York Giants in the late 1890s and early 20th century.

ment by having another solid year with a .331 average, achieving a team-high 105 runs knocked in and leading the Giants to a second-place finish behind the Baltimore Orioles. Additionally, he played every one of the Giants' game and by the season's end was only a game or two behind the Orioles' Steve Brodie for the longest active playing streak. He began the year a dozen games behind Brodie but with the Giants having participated in 10 more contests that year than the Orioles, Van Haltren had shortened Brodie's lead to just a couple of games by the end of the 1894 season. The Giants finished in second place in the final standings and earned the privilege of meeting the Orioles in the first Temple Cup series that determined the sport's overall champion. The Giants stunned Baltimore by sweeping them in four games. Van Haltren turned out to be one of the more prominent players as he went 7 for 14 for a .500 average, which was the third-place batting average among the 1894 Temple Cup players.

The following season, his consecutive game streak of 267 contests came to an end just eight games in the year on May 3, 1895. At that time, he hadn't made up any ground on Brodie and still trailed him by two contests in consecutive games when his streak stopped. The missed game turned out to be the only one Van Haltren missed the entire year. The next day he commenced another playing streak that would finally earn him the Iron Man title after two previous close calls. Besides being the team's most durable player, he became one of their offensive forces. This was evident as he finished in third in the club in 1895 in the hitting and slugging categories along with having team highs in the hits and RBI totals. Unfortunately, the club's overall performance dropped off considerably from the previous second-place finish (and winning baseball's championship title in the Temple Cup) when they finished in ninth place (out of 12 clubs) with a 66–65 record. He kept up his consistent play in 1896 by hitting a career best .351, again leading the club in several statistics and having a league-high 21 triples (tied with Tom McCreery of the Louisville Colonels). Although the team's won-loss record actually receded slightly, they still improved two spots in the standings but were still in the second division. Van Haltren finally became baseball's Iron Man when Brodie's long playing streak ended on June 28, 1897. Van Haltren's first time as the Iron Man lasted just three weeks; his 324-game streak came to an end during the first game of a double-header on July 17, 1897. He would miss a week's worth of action before being returning to the lineup on a regular basis.

Eventually, Van Haltren would again become the Iron Man as the 20th century approached. The details of his next Iron Man streak and the rest of his playing career are contained in his later profile.

33. Kid Gleason

Born: October 26, 1866, Camden, New Jersey *Died*: January 2, 1933, Philadelphia, Pennsylvania *Bats*: Switch Hitter *Throws*: Right *Height*: 5 feet, 7 inches *Weight*: 158 *Major league debut*: April 20, 1888 (Boston at Philadelphia [NL]) *Last major league game*: August 27, 1912 (Chicago at Boston [AL])

Major league Iron Man from: July 17, 1897, to September 10, 1897 *Consecutive games played*: 335 *Games as major league Iron Man*: 51 (consecutive games 285 through 335) *Teams played for during streak*: Baltimore Orioles (NL) (1895) and New York Giants (NL) (1896–1897) *Primary position played*: Second base *Game missed before streak*: June 26, 1895 (New York at Baltimore) *First game played of streak*: June 28, 1895 (New York at Baltimore) *Last game played of streak*: September 9, 1897 (second game) (Pittsburgh at New York) *Game missed to end streak*: September 10, 1897 (Pittsburgh at New York)

Kid Gleason

Consecutive Game Streak's Statistical Totals

Year	G	AB	R	H	2B	3B	HR	RBI	BB	SO	AVG	SLG	SB
1895	83	337	71	101	7	7	0	55	26	13	.300	.362	15
1896	133	541	79	162	17	5	4	89	42	13	.299	.372	46
1897	119	493	76	155	15	4	1	97	23	—	.314	.367	37
Total	335	1371	226	418	39	16	5	241	91	26	.305	.368	98

Kid Gleason was definitely a career man when it came to baseball. He spent parts of 22 seasons as a player with seven teams. He started as a right-handed pitcher, switched to playing second base by his eighth year and then managed and coached after his playing career ended. After spending his first year of baseball in the minors, he got his chance to play in the majors with the Philadelphia Quakers and manager Harry Wright. He made his big league debut as the Quakers' starting pitcher in the team's season opener against the Boston Beaneaters on April 20, 1888. In his rookie year, he started 23 games, finished with a 7–16 win-loss record and had a rather impressive 2.84 earned run average.

Gleason mainly concentrated on pitching over the next seven seasons. He had an outstanding year on the mound in 1890, going 38–17, and had the second-highest totals in wins and winning percentage. Instead of divorcing himself from the National League in 1890 when many players bolted for the Players League, Gleason felt an obligation to manager Wright because the man had given him the opportunity to play in the majors. He felt he would be deserting the man that played such a vital role in his career. As a result, he stayed with Philadelphia for a couple of more years. He left the Quakers in 1892 when he moved on to the St. Louis Browns. He remained with the Browns for nearly three years before the Browns sold him in late June 1894 to the soon-to-be powerhouse Baltimore Orioles. The 1894 season turned out to be his last full season in which he was strictly used as a hurler. He went 15–5 for the Orioles and help lead Baltimore to the National League title. Facing the second-place New York Giants in the first Temple Cup series that determined baseball's world champion, the Orioles were thoroughly beaten, swept in four games and outscored by a 33–11 margin. Gleason pitched in games two and four of the series but was severely manhandled by the Giants' hitters. During the very early stages of the 1895 campaign, Orioles' manager Ned Hanlon was not pleased with Gleason as a pitcher and eventually assigned him to second base, replacing Heinie Reitz, who was relegated to backup duties. Soon after this shuffling of the Orioles' lineup, Gleason's consecutive playing streak commenced on June 28, 1895, during a home game against the New York Giants. He finished with a .309 average in his first season as an infielder. Baltimore repeated as league champs as they edged the Cleveland Spiders by three games. As in the previous Temple Cup series, the Orioles were again on the losing side as the Spiders trounced them in five games. Gleason had only two singles in 19 at-bats for a miserable .105 average. After the season, the Orioles sent him packing in a trade to the Giants in November 1895. The Giants made room for him at second base by moving previous second sacker General Stafford to the outfield. Gleason played all the Giants' games on the docket in 1896 as he led the team with 541 at-bats and extended his playing streak to 216 games. His efforts did not help the Giants much as they claimed seventh place in the overall standings. On July 17, 1897, he replaced teammate George Van Haltren as baseball's Iron Man. Gleason was the first switch hitter to become an Iron Man. He stretched his streak another 51 games until it came to closure after 335 contests when he sat out the Giants' home game on September 10 against the Pittsburgh Pirates. He finished the year with a .317 average and drove in 106 runs, an amazing total considering he had just one homer the whole year. However, he had a rough time at second base as he led the players at that position with 53 errors. The

Giants were in contention for the league title but finished in third place, nearly 10 games behind the first-place Beaneaters.

Gleason stayed on with the Giants through the 1900 season. He jumped over to the American League in 1901 and played for the Detroit Tigers for two years. In early March 1903, he was sent back to the Giants who further forwarded him to the Philadelphia Phillies. He was the starting second baseman for the Phillies for four seasons, after which he stayed on an additional two years in a limited playing role. He retired during the 1908 season but was kept on as a full-time coach through the 1911 season. The following year he went over to the Chicago White Sox as a coach but made one final appearance as a player on August 27. He was with the White Sox coaching staff for six seasons until he was named the White Sox manager, replacing Pants Rowland. While leading the White Sox to the World's Series in his first year as skipper, it was unfortunate that it also was the year of the Black Sox scandal, in which several players from his team took bribes to throw the 1919 World's Series. Gleason, a man of the highest integrity, was bitterly disappointed to learn that some of his players were in on the plan to throw the World's Series, in which the White Sox went down to defeat in eight games to the Cincinnati Reds. He stayed on for five years as manager before being released after the 1923 season. A few years later, he was back in uniform as a coach for Connie Mack and his Philadelphia Athletics. He stayed there for seven seasons before retiring permanently in 1932.

34. GENE DEMONTREVILLE

Born: March 26, 1874, St. Paul, Minnesota *Died*: February 18, 1935, Memphis, Tennessee *Bats*: Right *Throws*: Right *Height*: 5 feet 8 inches *Weight*: 165 *Major league debut*: August 20, 1894 (Pittsburgh at Baltimore [NL]) *Last major league game*: April 26, 1904 (St. Louis at Detroit [AL])

Major league Iron Man from: September 10, 1897, to August 5, 1898 *Consecutive games played*: 365 *Games as major league Iron Man*: 106 (consecutive games 260 through 365) *Teams played for during streak*: Washington Senators (NL) (1895–1897) and Baltimore Orioles (NL) (1898) *Primary positions played*: Shortstop and second base *Game missed before streak*: September 16, 1895 (second game) (Brooklyn at Washington) *First game played of streak*: September 17, 1895 (Brooklyn at Washington) *Last game played of streak*: August 4, 1898 (second game) (Baltimore at Chicago) *Game missed to end streak*: August 5, 1898 (first game) (Baltimore at Chicago)

Consecutive Game Streak's Statistical Totals:

Year	G	AB	R	H	2B	3B	HR	RBI	BB	SO	AVG	SLG	SB
1895	12	46	7	10	1	3	0	9	3	4	.217	.370	5
1896	133	533	94	183	24	5	8	77	29	27	.343	.452	28
1897	133	566	92	193	27	8	3	93	21	—	.341	.433	30
1898	87	337	56	112	7	1	0	53	34	—	.332	.359	29
Total	365	1482	249	498	59	17	11	232	87	31	.336	.421	92

Gene DeMontreville was a much-traveled infielder who put in 11 seasons in the major leagues with eight teams. He started his career as a shortstop but a few years later switched to playing second base. When he first came up to the big leagues, his name in the box scores appeared as Demont because his last name was so long that it took up too much space in the newspapers. He began his professional baseball career in 1894 by playing in the Eastern League, first with Binghamton and then Buffalo. He also got a brief call-up to the majors that same year with the Pittsburgh Pirates, appearing in a couple of games, including his debut game on August 20, 1894.

DeMontreville was still in the Eastern League the following season (1895), this time toiling for the Toronto team, when he returned to the majors with the Washington Senators. The team's shortstop position was quite unstable in 1895 as records show that 13 players filled it at various times. Frank Scheibeck came the closest to being called the regular shortstop with 44 games played at the position. On September 17, 1895, the Senators filled the spot with DeMontreville. He also started his consecutive playing streak during that same game when Washington played the Brooklyn Bridegrooms. The following year (1896), in his first full season, he hit a career-best .343 average and a team-high 183 hits. In fact, his batting average that year was the Senators' all-time top batting average in the history of the National League franchise (the club expired about a month before the start of the 1900 season). As for his defensive accomplishments, he did not miss a single game at shortstop and led the league at that position in games played, assists and errors committed. As for Washington, the Senators seemed a permanent fixture in the bottom section of the final standings. The 1896 season was no different as they tied with the Bridegrooms for ninth place while trailing the pennant-winning Baltimore Orioles by 33 games. DeMontreville became baseball's Iron Man, replacing Kid Gleason of the Orioles on September 10, 1897. While he went the whole season again taking in every contest, DeMontreville played about 20 percent of the games at second base. He had another outstanding year at the plate by hitting .341, posting a league-high 566 at-bats and leading the Senators with 193 hits and 93 runs driven in. He also repeated as the most error-prone shortstop in the game with 78 miscues. His offensive performance helped the Senators achieve their best result in years as they finished tied with the Bridegrooms again, only this time it was for sixth place. During the off-season, he was traded to the powerful Orioles in exchange for Heinie Reitz. DeMontreville took Reitz' place as the Orioles' new second baseman. His playing streak continued with his new team until he sat out a doubleheader in Chicago against the Orphans on August 5, 1898, thus ending his consecutive run of games at 365. He finished the year hitting .328 and driving in 86 runners. Additionally, he led the Orioles with 49 stolen bases, good for third in the league behind Philadelphia's Ed Delahanty and Boston's Billy Hamilton. DeMontreville also experienced being on a winning team for the first time as the Orioles finished with a 96–53 record that left them in second place, some six games behind the Boston Beaneaters.

Although DeMontreville had an outstanding year with the Orioles, a few months later he was on his way to the Orphans via a trade in January 1899. By midseason he was shipped back to the Orioles but his stay with Baltimore was nearly short lived because the next day he was shipped off in another transaction to the Brooklyn Superbas; however, the deal was canceled six days later. He finished the year with Baltimore and then resurfaced with the Superbas for the 1900 season. After one season with Brooklyn, he was sold to the Beaneaters in February 1901. He played in Boston for two years and then moved to Washington of the American League, where he made a dozen appearances in a Senators uniform. His final major league season (1904) was spent with the St. Louis Browns, where he played just four games. He made his final appearance on April 26 in a game against the Detroit Tigers. Soon after, he was back in the minors where he played for seven more seasons before retiring after the 1910 season.

35. DUFF COOLEY

Born: March 29, 1873, Leavenworth, Kansas *Died*: August 9, 1937, Dallas, Texas *Bats*: Left *Throws*: Right *Height*: 5 feet, 11 inches *Weight*: 158 *Major league debut*: July 27, 1893 (Cleveland at St. Louis [NL]) *Last major league game*: August 25, 1905 (Philadelphia at Detroit [AL])

Duff Cooley

Major league Iron Man from: August 5, 1898, to September 5, 1898 *Consecutive games played*: 309 *Games as major league Iron Man*: 24 (consecutive games 286 through 309) *Team played for during streak*: Philadelphia Phillies (NL) *Primary position played*: Outfield *Game missed before streak*: July 7, 1896 (Philadelphia at Cincinnati) *First game played of streak*: July 8, 1896 (Philadelphia at Cincinnati) *Last game played of streak*: September 5, 1898 (first game) (Baltimore at Philadelphia) *Game missed to end streak*: September 5, 1898 (second game) (Baltimore at Philadelphia)

Consecutive Game Streak's Statistical Totals:

Year	G	AB	R	H	2B	3B	HR	RBI	BB	SO	AVG	SLG	SB
1896	64	287	63	88	6	4	2	22	18	16	.307	.376	18
1897	133	566	124	186	14	13	4	40	51	—	.329	.420	31
1898	112	482	89	144	18	9	2	38	34	—	.299	.386	10
Total	309	1335	276	418	38	26	8	100	103	16	.313	.399	59

Duff Cooley played for the St. Louis Browns, Philadelphia Phillies, Pittsburgh Pirates, Boston Beaneaters and the Detroit Tigers in a 13-season major league career. Although a majority of the time he was used in the outfield, he was given the chance to show his dexterity by filling in occasionally at every playing position except pitcher. He first appeared in a big league game with the Browns on July 27, 1893, against the Cleveland Spiders. Through the rest of the 1893 season, he was used in 29 games as he filled in at catcher, shortstop or right field. In the limited opportunity that was given to him, he drove home 21 runs while hitting for a .346 average. He was kept in a backup role the following year (1894), as he mainly subbed in right field. He nearly doubled his number of games played (54), as he hit .296 and repeated his 21 RBI total from the previous season.

Cooley took over the left field on the Browns' roster in 1895 with the departure of Charlie Frank. Cooley thrived offensively with the additional playing time. He sat out just a couple of games all year as he finished with team highs in runs scored, hits, triples and batting average. He was hitting a solid .307 when the Browns traded him to the Phillies on June 28, 1896. It wasn't until the July 8 game in Cincinnati that his name appeared in a Phillies' lineup. This game was also the start of his consecutive playing streak. He played in 64 games (the majority of which were in center field) for Philadelphia and showed his consistency as he finished with the same .307 average that he had started with when the trade occurred. While Cooley was providing the team with the offense they were expecting, the team's overall on-field results were quite dismal as they finished in eighth place with no sign of being in contention for the pennant. The following year (1897), he returned as the squad's center fielder and had his third-best year at the plate by compiling a .329 average while playing every contest. Besides leading the team in runs scored and stolen bases, he also posted a league-high 566 at-bats. Unfortunately, the Phillies were still not a good team and finished in 10th place, 38 games out of first place. In the latter part of the next season, Cooley took over the Iron Man title from Baltimore Orioles' infielder Gene DeMontreville on August 5, 1898. His time as the Iron Man lasted exactly one month when the Phillies' manager, Bill Shettsline, rested Cooley during the second game of a twin bill on September 5. This snapped his playing streak at 309 games. That game turned out to be the only contest he didn't appear in all season. He hit .312 and drove in 55 runners by the end of the year while again topping all Phillies in at-bats and runs scored for the second straight year. Defensively, he was kept busy by amassing 352 putouts, tops among all National League outfielders. As for the Phillies, they showed some improvement and leapfrogged four spots to finish in the middle of the pack with a sixth-place showing.

In his final year (1899) with Philadelphia, Cooley switched over to first base, replacing

Klondike Douglass (who had become the team's backup catcher) as that position's regular occupant. Cooley took in only 94 contests and slumped badly enough that his batting average fell to .276. During the off-season, he was shipped off to the Pirates in a trade. In his one year with the Pirates, he shared the first base duties with Tom O'Brien. He batted a paltry .201 while appearing in only half of the scheduled games. Pittsburgh's management was not impressed with Cooley so they sold him off to the Beaneaters early the following year. After serving as a fourth outfielder in his first season in Boston, he made somewhat of a career comeback by taking over the left field spot in 1902 and putting together three solid offensive years. Although he had produced for the Beaneaters, the club decided to make some changes and waived him after the 1904 season. He played one more season with the Tigers, who had claimed him off waivers. He played 96 games and hit .247 while patrolling center field for Detroit during his final season in the majors.

36. HUGH DUFFY

Born: November 26, 1866, Cranston, Rhode Island *Died*: October 19, 1954, Boston, Massachusetts *Bats*: Right *Throws*: Right *Height*: 5 feet, 7 inches *Weight*: 168 *Major league debut*: June 23, 1888 (Pittsburgh at Chicago [NL]) *Last major league game*: April 13, 1906 (New York at Philadelphia [NL])

Major league Iron Man from: September 5, 1898, to August 17, 1899 *Consecutive games played*: 376 *Games as major league Iron Man*: 134 (consecutive games 243 through 376) *Team played for during streak*: Boston Beaneaters (NL) *Primary position played*: Outfield *Game missed before streak*: May 5, 1897 (Philadelphia at Boston) *First game played of streak*: May 6, 1897 (Washington at Boston) *Last game played of streak*: August 16, 1899 (second game) (Louisville at Boston) *Game missed to end streak*: August 17, 1899 (first game) (Louisville at Boston)

Consecutive Game Streak's Statistical Totals:

Year	G	AB	R	H	2B	3B	HR	RBI	BB	SO	AVG	SLG	SB
1897	124	508	122	171	24	9	11	122	50	—	.337	.484	36
1898	152	568	97	169	13	3	8	108	59	—	.298	.373	29
1899	100	411	74	123	22	6	5	77	23	—	.299	.418	17
Total	376	1487	293	463	59	18	24	307	132	—	.311	.424	82

To show how massive Duffy's numbers were in 1894 when he achieved the Triple Crown, his 1895 stats reveal that his batting average dropped nearly 100 points. He still had a solid year by coming in with a .353 average and driving in an even 100 runs. With the departure of McCarthy, who was sent to the Brooklyn Bridegrooms, a shuffling of the outfield positions was in order for the 1896 season. Billy Hamilton, who came from Philadelphia, was put in center and Duffy was moved over to left field. The position change did not seem to agree with Duffy's batting average as it dropped to .300, his lowest average since his rookie season in Chicago. That meant that in a matter of just two seasons, his batting average had fallen 140 points, from .440 to .300! The drop didn't affect his run production though as he still brought home an impressive 113 runners with his clutch hitting.

During the very early portion of the 1897 season, Duffy had missed several games but that was about to change. In a game in Boston against the Washington Senators, his second Iron Man streak commenced on May 6, 1897, when he played the last 124 games for the Beaneaters on that season's schedule. His hitting rebounded to a .340 average. He edged out George Davis of the New York Giants, 11 to 10, for the home run title and finished in third place in RBI with 129. In the race for the league title, it was a contest between Boston and the Baltimore Orioles. The Beaneaters edged them out by two games in the regular season to claim the league pennant. When the two teams met for the world title in the final Temple Cup series held in 1897, the teams switched places as the Orioles disposed of the Beaneaters in five games. This was no fault of Duffy's as he again performed in an exemplary fashion in the postseason. Leading Boston with a .524 average, 11 hits and seven RBI, he was one of the Beaneaters' main offensive providers in what turned out to be a losing effort in a high-scoring series. As the season was winding down in 1898, Duffy took another turn as baseball's Iron Man when Duff Cooley of the Philadelphia Phillies sat out the second game of a doubleheader on September 5. While Boston repeated as the league champs by edging the Orioles again (this time by six games), Duffy finished below the .300 hitting level for the first time since his rookie campaign, posting a .298 mark for the 1898 season. He was still producing runs with the bat as he went over the 100 RBI level for the sixth straight year by driving home 108 Boston runners. His time as baseball's Iron Man came to an end in the late summer of 1899 when his streak closed out at 376 contests. He was rested during the Beaneaters' doubleheader against the Louisville Colonels on August 17. His 1899 totals saw his average drop further to .279 while still driving in 102 runners. Boston came up short of winning a third consecutive title as they finished runner-up to Brooklyn in the final standings. The following year (1900), he got into only 55 games because of injuries that cut into his playing time. It was quite obvious his best years were behind him and that unless he did something first, Boston might release or trade him. Before that occurred, he decided to part ways after nine years in a Beaneaters uniform after the 1900 season and took an offer to manage the Milwaukee Brewers in the American League for the 1901 campaign.

His season as manager in Milwaukee was a complete failure on the field as the Brewers claimed the basement position with a 48–89 record. Besides managing the team, Duffy also played in 79 games and was able to hit .302 and drive in 45 runners. When the Brewers decided to move to St. Louis (and become the Browns) for the 1902 season, Duffy decided to remain in Milwaukee and serve as playing manager for the city's Western League franchise. After two seasons there, he returned to the major leagues as the new manager of the Philadelphia Phillies, replacing Chief Zimmer. Duffy stayed at the helm of the Phillies for three years with the best result being fourth-place finishes in 1905 and 1906. He also was able to get himself in the lineup for 34 games during that time including his final big league appearance on April 13, 1906, when he used himself as a pinch hitter. After his managerial tenure in Philadelphia came to an end with the closure of the 1906 season, he returned to managing in the minors for a few more years before resurrecting again as manager of the Chicago White Sox for the 1910 and 1911 seasons. It was then back to managing in the minors for some more years before taking one final tour of duty at managing a major league club with the Boston Red Sox in 1921 and 1922. After guiding the 1922 Red Sox to a dreadful last-place finish, he gave up managing for good and became a scout for the Red Sox organization. He lived to see his election to baseball's Hall of Fame in 1945. He was still scouting for Boston (and was approaching his 88th birthday) when he passed away on October 19, 1954.

37. GEORGE VAN HALTREN

Born: March 30, 1866, St. Louis, Missouri *Died*: September 29, 1945, Oakland, California *Bats*: Left *Throws*: Left *Height*: 5 feet, 11 inches *Weight*: 170 *Major league debut*: June 27, 1887 (Boston at Chicago [NL]) *Last major league game*: September 26, 1903 (New York at Pittsburgh [NL])

George Van Haltren

Major league Iron Man from: August 17, 1899, to May 8, 1901 *Consecutive games played*: 462 *Games as major league Iron Man*: 206 (consecutive games 257 through 462) *Team played for during streak*: New York Giants (NL) *Primary position played*: Outfield *Game missed before streak*: September 27, 1897 (Washington at New York) *First game played of streak*: September 29, 1897 (Philadelphia at New York) *Last game played of streak*: May 7, 1901 (Philadelphia at New York) *Game missed to end streak*: May 8, 1901 (Philadelphia at New York)

Consecutive Game Streak's Statistical Totals:

Year	G	AB	R	H	2B	3B	HR	RBI	BB	SO	AVG	SLG	SB
1897	3	13	4	6	0	0	0	0	0	—	.462	.462	1
1898	156	654	129	204	28	16	2	68	59	—	.312	.413	36
1899	152	607	118	183	22	3	2	58	75	—	.301	.357	31
1900	141	571	114	180	30	7	1	51	50	—	.315	.398	45
1901	10	33	5	11	2	1	0	6	4	—	.333	.455	2
Total	462	1878	370	584	82	27	5	183	188	—	.311	.391	115

Although his first Iron Man streak had ended earlier in the year, Van Haltren started his second Iron Man streak late in the New York Giants' 1897 schedule with just three contests left. The first game of this streak occurred on September 29 in a Giants' home game against the Philadelphia Phillies. He checked out with another decent year with a .329 average along with having the most hits on the National League's third-place Giants. He also led the league's outfielders in assists by nabbing 31 runners on the base paths. He was becoming the most consistent offensive player on the team. This was proven when in 1898 he was the team leader under every hitting column except homers, RBI and base on balls. In fact, his closest competitor in the club was nearly 40 runs and over 50 hits behind Van Haltren. The Giants, unfortunately, were just above a .500 club and were never in serious contention for the league title as they came in seventh place. The following year, Van Haltren became a two-time Iron Man when he succeeded Boston's Hugh Duffy as baseball's most durable player on August 17, 1899, with a 257-consecutive-game stretch actively running. Although he again repeated as the team's leader in several statistics, Van Haltren had his lowest batting average (.301) since the 1892 season. The Giants also were nothing to brag about as they finished deeply entrenched in 10th place out of 12 teams. Van Haltren rebounded from his off-year in 1899 by improving his batting average to .315 in 1900 along with extending his Iron Man streak to 452 games by the end of the year. Additionally, he led all National League outfielders for the second time with 28 assists. As for the Giants, they finished in the cellar (eighth place) of the newly downsized National League. Van Haltren's playing streak finally ended just 10 games into the 1901 season. He suffered a shoulder injury during the first inning of the May 7 game against the Phillies, which caused his 462-game playing streak to end the next day. The injury kept him out of the Giants' lineup for 10 days. Upon his return, there seemed to be no residual effects of this injury as he finished his ninth straight season with a batting average above .300 (with a .335 average). His run production number of 47 RBI was his lowest total in that department since the 1888 campaign. He again repeated as the outfield assists leader as he eliminated 23 runners from the base paths.

After years of rarely missing a game, Van Haltren suffered a broken ankle a month into the 1902 season. Not only did he miss the duration of that season, but the injury also played a prominent role in shortening his major league playing career. He returned to the Giants in 1903 but he wasn't the same player. His playing time was limited to just 84 contests in his last major league season. His final batting average (.257) and slugging percentage (.286) were his lowest performance marks since his rookie season. As the season was closing out in late September 1903, Van Haltren made his final appearance in the majors in a Giants' game in

Pittsburgh against the Pirates. He spent the next six seasons applying his trade in the Pacific Coast League with Seattle in 1904 and then his hometown team in Oakland from 1905–1909. He also worked as an umpire in the minors for a couple of seasons and coached and scouted for the Pirates for a few years. His final major league stats confirm he had 2,544 hits and a .316 batting average along with a durability record that showed he missed very few games in a 10-year period between 1891 and 1900. Although he has not been elected to baseball's Hall of Fame, there is still a chance he might achieve that distinction considering that another outstanding player from his era, Bid McPhee, was selected to membership in 2000.

38. Jimmy Slagle

Born: July 11, 1873, Worthville, Pennsylvania *Died*: May 10, 1956, Chicago, Illinois *Bats*: Left *Throws*: Right *Height*: 5 feet, 7 inches *Weight*: 144 *Major league debut*: April 17, 1899 (Washington at Philadelphia [NL]) *Last major league game*: October 3, 1908 (Chicago at Cincinnati [NL])

Major league Iron Man from: May 8, 1901, to June 22, 1901 *Consecutive games played*: 326 *Games as major league Iron Man*: 34 (consecutive games 293 through 326) *Teams played for during streak*: Washington Senators (NL) (1899) and Philadelphia Phillies (NL) (1900–1901) *Primary position played*: Outfield *Game missed before streak*: May 6, 1899 (Washington at New York) *First game played of streak*: May 8, 1899 (Washington at New York) *Last game played of streak*: June 21, 1901 (St. Louis at Philadelphia) *Game missed to end streak*: June 22, 1901 (Cincinnati at Philadelphia)

Consecutive Game Streak's Statistical Totals

Year	G	AB	R	H	2B	3B	HR	RBI	BB	SO	AVG	SLG	SB
1899	137	565	89	156	14	8	0	37	51	—	.276	.329	20
1900	141	574	115	165	16	9	0	45	60	—	.287	.347	34
1901	48	183	20	37	6	2	1	20	16	—	.202	.273	5
Total	326	1322	224	358	36	19	1	102	127	—	.271	.329	59

Jimmy Slagle was a career outfielder who put in 10 seasons with four National League clubs. He gained a reputation for basically being a singles hitter and having great speed on the base paths. During the entire scope of his playing days, he maintained his status as an everyday player. When he joined the Washington Senators' roster for the 1899 season, he essentially replaced the previous season's center fielder, John Anderson, in the lineup. Anderson had been sent back to the Brooklyn Superbas just before the closure of the 1898 season. While the Senators were getting trounced by the Philadelphia Phillies by an 11-to-4 score, Slagle was making his debut in a major league lineup as a pinch hitter on April 17, 1899.

Just over three weeks after his first appearance in a big league uniform and with only 10 games of major league experience, Slagle commenced his playing streak on May 8, 1899, and played the final 137 games on the Senators' 1899 season schedule. He put up very respectable numbers for a rookie as he hit .272 and brought home 41 Senator runners. He was also busy in the outfield as he caught 407 fly balls to lead all outfielders in that defensive category. This did not translate into much success for the Senators as they finished near the bottom of the National League standings with a 54–98 record. With the Senators being forced out of the league (along with three other teams), Slagle found himself assigned to the Philadelphia Phillies for the 1900 campaign. With the acquisition of Slagle, Phillies' skipper Bill Shettsline decided to increase his team's speed in the outfield by putting him in left field and bringing batting champion Ed Delahanty in from the outfield to play first base. While playing every contest that year, Slagle showed slight improvement in nearly every offensive column. He led all players with 27 sacrifice hits and finished with the second-best league at-bat totals (trailing Boston's Jimmy Collins) as well as in runs scored (behind teammate Roy Thomas). His defensive record shows a league-high 141 games in the outfield while also making a league-high 29 miscues by an outfielder. The Phillies, in the meantime, were repeating their third-place finish from the season before as they closed out the year just eight games behind the league champion Superbas. Early the next season, while he was achieving the second anniversary of not missing a contest, Slagle became the majors' most durable player on May 8, 1901, when the New York Giants' George Van Haltren missed a game after injuring his shoulder the previous day. Slagle's reign as Iron Man was relatively short; just six weeks later, the streak came to an end after 326 games when the Phillies decided to release him from their playing roster. A short time later, the Boston Beaneaters agreed to accept Slagle as the compensation from a pending transaction in which the Phillies had earlier acquired second baseman Shad Barry. Slagle spent the rest of the 1901 trying his hand in the Beaneaters' right field slot. He proved he had an accurate arm by leading the league's outfielders with 23 assists.

Slagle was on the move again after less than one year in Boston when he was sent to the Chicago Cubs for the 1902 season. Although he missed over two dozen games that season, he actually turned in his best seasonal performance with the bat. He hit a career-high .315 and led the fifth-place Cubs with 146 hits and 66 runs along with 41 stolen bases. He would go on to play for six more years with the Cubs. During the 1903 and 1905 seasons, he proved he was still durable by playing every game during those years, even though those streaks did not come close to being long enough to qualify for another turn at the Iron Man title. In his last three years, from 1906 through 1908, the Cubs won the National League title each year. Unfortunately, Cubs skipper Frank Chance used Slagle in only the 1907 World's Series against the Detroit Tigers. In his only World's Series appearances, he took full advantage of the opportunity by being the Cubs' offensive star as he went 6 for 22 for a .273 average and led both squads with four RBI and six stolen bases. His last season (1908), he appeared in only 104 contests and hit for a lowly .222 batting average (more than 45 points below his career average). His final major league game was in Cincinnati on October 3, 1908.

39. JESSE BURKETT

Born: December 4, 1868, Wheeling, West Virginia *Died*: May 27, 1953, Worcester, Massachusetts *Bats*: Left *Throws*: Left *Height*: 5 feet, 8 inches *Weight*: 155 *Major league debut*: April 22, 1890 (Philadelphia at New York [NL]) *Last major league game*: October 7, 1905 (second game) (New York at Boston [AL])

Major league Iron Man from: June 22, 1901, to June 14, 1902 *Consecutive games played*: 428 *Games as major league Iron Man*: 133 (consecutive games 296 through 428) *Teams played for during streak*: St. Louis Perfectos (NL) (1899), St. Louis Cardinals (NL) (1900–1901) and St. Louis Browns (AL) (1902) *Primary position played*: Outfield *Game missed before streak*: June 17, 1899 (St. Louis at Louisville) *First game played of streak*: June 18, 1899 (Washington at St. Louis) *Last game played of streak*: June 13, 1902 (Washington at St. Louis) *Game missed to end streak*: June 14, 1902 (Washington at St. Louis)

Consecutive Game Streak's Statistical Totals:

Year	G	AB	R	H	2B	3B	HR	RBI	BB	SO	AVG	SLG	SB
1899	103	401	87	165	16	7	6	61	51	—	.411	.531	21
1900	141	559	88	203	11	15	7	68	62	—	.363	.474	32
1901	142	601	142	226	20	15	10	75	59	—	.376	.509	27
1902	42	173	24	51	10	5	1	23	16	—	.295	.428	8
Total	428	1734	341	645	57	42	24	227	188	—	.372	.495	88

JESSE BURKETT

Jesse Burkett has to be ranked right up there with some of the greatest hitters in baseball history. During a major league playing career that lasted 16 seasons, he was known for his ability to hit solid line drive base hits along with producing a .340 average or better for nine straight years. He also acquired the nickname of "Crab" because of his reputation of always complaining to umpires or not getting along with the fans, his opponents or his teammates. This didn't seem to affect his play because his abilities were always at the highest standards. He also had two seasons where he finished above the .400 level. The only other major leaguers to achieve this feat were Ed Delahanty, Ty Cobb and Rogers Hornsby. Spending just two seasons in the minor leagues, he started his major league career with the New York Giants as a pitcher on April 22, 1890. While he was a disappointment as a major league hurler because he finished with a 3–10 record, he proved he was very talented with the bat as he hit .309 and drove in 60 runs.

Before the start of the 1891 season, the Giants made what would turn out to be a major mistake when they sold Burkett to the Cleveland Spiders. He was immediately farmed out to the minors until his recall to the parent club in the middle of August. He stayed with Cleveland for the rest of the 1891 campaign and got into 40 games but batted only .269. From this point on in his major league career, Burkett remained a regular player until his departure from the big leagues after the 1905 season. The following year (1892), he took over the Spiders' left field position from Jimmy McAleer and manned the spot in Cleveland's lineup over the next seven seasons. In his first full season in Cleveland, he hit for a .275 average and led the team with six homers as the Spiders came in second place behind the Boston Beaneaters. This resulted in Boston and Cleveland's meeting in the 1892 World's Series to determine a champion. Boston won five of six games with the other contest resulting in a tie. Although he was on the losing team, Burkett held up his end by going 8 for 25 for a .320 batting average along with leading all players from both teams with four stolen bases. His hitting improved immensely over the next two seasons as he finished with averages of .348 (1893) and .358 (1894). He followed up these performances by leading the National League in hitting in 1895 with an incredible .405 average. In addition, he didn't miss a single game that season and amassed league-high marks with 225 hits and reaching base 307 times. His amazing hitting performance helped the Spiders finish just three games behind the first-place Baltimore Orioles. Their second-place finish qualified them to meet the Orioles in the 1895 Temple Cup series. The winner of this series would be recognized as baseball's world champion. Burkett had a tremendous series again as he went 9 for 20, had the most hits and led all the participants with a .450 batting average. This time, Cleveland completely dominated their opponent (Orioles) and claimed the world title by beating Baltimore in five games. In what might be difficult to believe, Burkett further elevated his statistics in 1896. This resulted in his leading the National League with 586 at-bats, 160 runs scored, 240 hits, and 317 total bases along with repeating as the National League hitting champ with another truly amazing .410 average. His efforts helped Cleveland repeat as runner-up to the Orioles in the final standings. Meeting for the second consecutive time in the Temple Cup, the Orioles exacted revenge on the Spiders by sweeping Cleveland in four games. The problem for the Spiders was that their offense was completely dominated by the Orioles' pitching combination of Joe Corbett and Bill Hoffer, who held the Spiders to just five runs scored in the four contests. Burkett was one of the few bright spots on the Spiders' squad as he led the team with a .333 average and contributed five hits to the cause. He stayed in Cleveland for two more years during which his batting average dropped off considerably from his 1895 and 1896 seasons but was still high enough to easily lead the team in hitting. In late March 1899, Burkett was permanently assigned to play for the St. Louis Perfectos because the owners of the Spiders and the Perfectos decided to consolidate their forces (since several individuals had ownership in both teams) and fill one team with their best players and the other team with lower-echelon players. After being out of the Perfectos' lineup for 10 days in mid–June, Burkett returned to the lineup and started his playing streak on June 18, 1899, in a game against the Washington Senators. When the season came to a conclusion, he just missed out on hitting .400 for the third time as he led the club with a .396 average. His batting average and total hits were good for second place on the league's leader board behind Philadelphia's Ed Delahanty in both categories. As the team finished in fifth place, it was quite evident that St. Louis had made great improvements from the 1898 season. This was due to the addition of several major players the club had received from the Spiders. In 1900, Burkett's .363 average was a downward turn but his overall season performance was still good enough to lead the team in many hitting categories. On the defensive side of the ledger, he had the most putouts and played the most games for an outfielder. Although the newly named Cardinals had another fifth-place finish in 1900, the team had nearly 20 fewer wins than during the previous season. A couple of months into the following campaign, Burkett took over the Iron Man title from Jimmy Slagle on June 22, 1901, when Slagle was released from the Phillies' roster. By the end of the year, Burkett had stretched his playing streak to 386 games. He won his third National League batting title in 1901 with a .376 average along with leading the league in at-bats, runs scored, hits, times on base, total bases and on base percentage. All his offensive achievements didn't help St. Louis as far as the standings were concerned. They finished right in the middle of the pack, in fourth place, nearly 15 games behind the champion Pittsburgh Pirates. During the off-season, Burkett decided he was going to stay in St. Louis but not in a Cardinals uniform. He made the decision to jump over to the St. Louis Browns of the American League for the 1902 season. That first season with the Browns saw his 428-consecutive-game playing streak come to an end when he sat out the Browns' home game against the Washington Senators on June 14, 1902. The next day he was back at his normal position in left field. He finished the year hitting .306 (this was the last time he would hit above .300 in the majors) and helped the team edge out the Boston Americans for second place (the Philadelphia Athletics took first place) in the league's final standings.

Burkett put in two more good years in a Browns uniform before being shipped off to the Boston Americans in January 1905. In the final season of his big league career, Boston used him as their everyday left fielder during the 1905 campaign. Although he held his own, the batting average (.257) and on base percentage (.339) he produced were career lows for the future Hall of Famer. Despite knowing his time as a major leaguer was nearing an end, he still wanted to be active in the game. He asked Boston for his release so he could purchase the Worcester club of the New England League. There he served as owner and playing manager for eight years and another two years after that as just the owner and manager. He kept managing in the minors for several more years after that along with a few years handling coaching duties at the college level. He returned to the majors one last time in 1921 and served as a coach with that year's World's Series winner, the New York Giants, and their manager, John McGraw. He kept active in the game in various capacities for several more years until finally retiring for good in the early 1930s. His career numbers fully justified his membership in baseball's Hall of Fame and his selection was approved by the veterans' committee in 1946.

40. Jimmy Collins

Born: January 16, 1870, Buffalo, New York *Died*: March 6, 1943, Buffalo, New York *Bats*: Right *Throws*: Right *Height*: 5 feet, 9 inches *Weight*: 178 *Major league debut*: April 19, 1895 (Washington at Boston [NL]) *Last major league game*: August 29, 1908 (second game) (Detroit at Philadelphia [AL])

Major league Iron Man from: June 14, 1902, to July 1, 1902 *Consecutive games played*: 338 *Games as major league Iron Man*: 14 (consecutive games 325 through 338) *Teams played for during streak*: Boston Beaneaters (NL) (1900) and Boston Americans (AL) (1901–1902) *Primary position played*: Third base *Game missed before streak*: October 14, 1899 (Philadelphia at Boston) *First game played of streak*: April 19, 1900 (Philadelphia at Boston) *Last game played of streak*: June 28, 1902 (Boston at Baltimore) *Game missed to end streak*: July 1, 1902 (Washington at Boston)

Consecutive Game Streak's Statistical Totals:

Year	G	AB	R	H	2B	3B	HR	RBI	BB	SO	AVG	SLG	SB
1900	142	586	104	178	25	5	6	95	34	—	.304	.394	23
1901	138	564	108	187	42	16	6	94	34	—	.332	.495	19
1902	58	233	45	75	12	7	4	38	16	—	.322	.485	9
Total	338	1383	257	440	79	28	16	227	84	—	.318	.450	51

Jimmy Collins put in 14 solid years of performance in the big leagues. He played most of his career in Boston, either with the National League Beaneaters or the junior circuit's Americans (which eventually became known as the Red Sox). If baseball experts put together a team of the greatest players at each position during the first 50 years of major league ball, Jimmy Collins would be the choice at third base. Not until the emergence of Pie Traynor in the 1920s had anyone seen a player master the hot corner position like Collins. He is credited with having third basemen decide on how to play in certain situations and not just remain stationary near the bag. As a result, Collins became an expert at fielding bunts barehanded and easily throwing out the runners. After playing his first two seasons of pro ball in his hometown of Buffalo (of the Eastern League), he made his major league debut with the Beaneaters on April 19, 1895 (opening day). Although he didn't impress anyone with his play in right field, the team didn't want to give up on him too quickly. Boston made arrangements to loan Collins to the lowly Louisville Colonels for the rest of the 1895 season. Colonels manager John McCloskey used Collins at third base, where he would remain for the rest of his playing career. When the curtain finally closed on the season, he justified his presence in the majors by batting .273, hitting seven homers and driving in 57 runners in 107 contests.

Boston was so impressed with Collins' performance with Louisville that when he was returned to Boston after the 1895 season, the team traded their long-time third baseman, Billy Nash, to the Philadelphia Phillies to open up the third base slot for him. Although he was in only 84 contests in 1896, he still was able to provide some offensive support by hitting .296. The following year (1897), he displayed his potential offensive and durability capabilities by playing in every game except the season finale on October 2, batting .346 and producing 132 RBI, a total good for second place behind the New York Giants' George Davis, who had 136 RBI. Collins also led all third basemen in games played, putouts, assists and double plays. The Beaneaters' performance that season earned them the league pennant as they edged out the Baltimore Orioles by a couple of games. In the fourth (and last) Temple Cup series that determined the world champion, Boston squared off against those same second-place Orioles. Unfortunately, Boston's fortunes were reversed as the Orioles defeated the Beaneaters in five games. Collins was a big disappointment in this championship round as he went only 4 for 22 for a measly .182 average. Although his batting average dipped nearly 20 points in 1898, the Beaneaters were more than satisfied with his performance on the field as he took in every game, topped the league both in homers (he had 15 clouts, which was a career high) and total bases (286) along with pacing the team in numerous other categories. He also was runner-up in slugging percentage (.479) and RBI (111). Defensively, he again led the hot corner occupants in games played and putouts. His performance directly contributed to Boston's repeating as the National League champ as they again edged out the Orioles (this time by a half dozen games). He had an off year in 1899 as all his offensive totals were down and he batted only .277 but did drive in 92 runners. He missed only two contests, the first game of a double-header on September 14 and the season finale on October 14. If he hadn't been rested in the last game of 1897, he would have become the league Iron Man when teammate Hugh Duffy's consecutive streak ended on August 17. That decision a couple of years earlier resulted in the Giants' George Van Haltren having a slight edge (less than a 10-game lead) in consecutive games played when Duffy's streak closed out. Collins stayed in close competition with Van Haltren until he sat out the September 14 game. Eventually, Collins would still one day become the major league Iron Man. His streak started with the season opener in Boston against the Philadelphia Phillies on April 19, 1900. The 1900 campaign would also be his last season in the National League. He hit for a .304 average and produced 95 runs in leading the Beaneaters to a fourth-place finish behind the Brooklyn Superbas. He had the league's top mark in at-bats along with most putouts, assists, double plays and games played by third base-

1903 Boston Americans team photo: The 1903 Boston Americans (winners of the first modern-day World's Series) had four players on their roster who became Iron Men during their careers: Jimmy Collins (manager and third baseman) center; Candy LaChance (first baseman) top row, second from left; Freddy Parent (shortstop) top row, second from right; Buck Freeman (right fielder) fourth row, first from left).

men. During the off-season, an offer was made for him to jump over to the Boston Americans of the American League to serve as playing manager. He took the offer and became a member and manager of the Boston Americans in March 1901. In his first year with the Americans, he hit .332, drove in 94 runners and led the club to a second-place finish, just four games behind the Chicago White Sox. He also finished in second place behind the Philadelphia Athletics' Nap Lajoie in total bases and extra-base hits. His consecutive playing streak was extended to 280 games as he played his second straight season without missing a contest. On June 14, 1902, Jesse Burkett of the St. Louis Browns had his participation streak come to an end. This resulted in Collins taking over the Iron Man title. His time as the Iron Man was short because just over two weeks later he was suspended by league president Ban Johnson for three games as a result of an altercation Collins had with umpire Bob Caruthers. When he sat out the first game of the suspension on July 1, 1902, his playing streak officially ended after 338 games. Although he did hit .322 for the year, he still had one of his worst seasons in run production with only 61 RBI in 108 games. In his managerial capacity, he led the team to a third-place finish in the tightly contested American League.

Collins guided Boston to the league title in 1903. This resulted in the Americans becoming the first participants, along with the Pittsburgh Pirates, in the first modern World's Series. Boston went on to defeat Pittsburgh in eight games to claim the world title as Collins led all players in at-bats and went 9 for 36 for a .250 average. The following year, Boston again was the American League titleholder, only this time the National League champs, New York Giants, refused to play them in any series because the Giants' leadership did not recognize the American League as a major league. Collins would remain as the playing manager well into the 1906 season when he was relieved of his managerial duties in August as a result of his taking some time off without the permission of the team's hierarchy. His dismissal resulted in his being replaced by teammate Chick Stahl as the team's manager. The following year (1907), Collins was traded to the Athletics in the first week of June for a player and some cash. He would serve with Philadelphia through the end of the 1908 season. Although his major league playing career was over with the finish of the 1908 campaign, he did some managing and playing in the minor leagues for three more years before calling it a career in 1911. He left the game and returned to Buffalo, where he lived out the rest of his time in his hometown until his passing in March 1943. One of his great disappointments was that he was not seriously considered for inclusion in baseball's Hall of Fame. This situation was rectified a couple of years after his death when the veterans' committee selected him for membership in 1945.

41. JIMMY BARRETT

Born: March 28, 1875, Athol, Massachusetts *Died*: October 24, 1921, Detroit, Michigan *Bats*: Left *Throws*: Right *Height*: 5 feet, 9 inches *Weight*: 170 *Major league debut*: September 13, 1899 (first game) (Cincinnati at Washington [NL]) *Last major league game*: May 13, 1908 (Detroit at Boston [AL])

Major league Iron Man from: July 1, 1902, to August 26, 1902 *Consecutive games played*: 352 *Games as major league Iron Man*: 48 (consecutive games 305 through 352) *Teams played for during streak*: Cincinnati Reds (NL) (1900) and Detroit Tigers (AL) (1901–1902) *Primary position played*: Outfield *Game missed before streak*: May 26, 1900 (Boston at Cincinnati) *First game played of streak*: May 27, 1900 (Pittsburgh at Cincinnati) *Last game played of streak*: August 25, 1902 (second game) (Detroit at Washington) *Game missed to end streak*: August 26, 1902 (Detroit at Washington)

Consecutive Game Streak's Statistical Totals

Year	G	AB	R	H	2B	3B	HR	RBI	BB	SO	AVG	SLG	SB
1900	115	450	91	140	11	6	4	30	60	—	.311	.389	36
1901	135	542	110	159	16	9	4	65	76	—	.293	.378	26
1902	102	391	69	119	15	5	3	31	54	—	.304	.391	18
Total	352	1383	270	418	42	20	11	126	190	—	.302	.385	80

Jimmy Barrett had a relatively short career in the major leagues. Playing parts of just 10 seasons, he manned outfield positions for the Cincinnati Reds (two tours), the Detroit Tigers and the Boston Red Sox between 1899 and 1908. During the first portion of his career, he proved extremely durable as he rarely missed a game. This trend reversed itself in the latter stages of his career when in three of his last four years in the major leagues his games-played totals were drastically reduced. He made his major league debut with the Reds in the first game of a double-header against the Washington Senators on September 13, 1899. Suiting up for the rest of the Reds' games on the 1899 schedule and playing most often in right field, he justified his presence in the lineup by hitting a remarkable .370 in 26 contests.

Barrett returned as the Reds' right fielder at the beginning of the 1900 campaign. He filled this role until just before his consecutive games played streak began. In the first game of his streak, May 27, 1900, Reds' manager Bob Allen moved Barrett over to center field. He would not play another position until he took in some games in right field for the Reds during the 1906 season. He finished the 1900 season hitting .316 along with pacing the Reds in runs scored, walks and stolen bases. His 114 runs scored total were good for a third-place tie (he shared this position with the New York Giants' two-time Iron Man George Van Haltren) in the league behind Philadelphia Phillies' teammates Roy Thomas and Jimmy Slagle. The Reds, however, were at the lower end of the scale when it came to results. Cincinnati escaped being the National League's doormat by just barely edging out the New York Giants for seventh place. After the season, Barrett left the Reds and joined the Detroit Tigers of the American League for the 1901 season. He had a .293 batting average that year and also topped the Tigers with 110 runs, 159 hits and 76 walks. He proved the strength of his arm by throwing out 31 runners as he led the league outfielders in assists. The race for the American League pennant during the league's first season in the major leagues was quite competitive. The Tigers finished in third place, just eight and a half games behind the first-place Chicago White Sox. When the Boston Americans' playing manager, Jimmy Collins, was out due to a suspension, Barrett took over the active role of Iron Man on July 1, 1902, by virtue of having appeared in 305 straight contests. His hold on the Iron Man title lasted nearly two months (and 48 games). His streak ended after 352 games when he sat out the Tigers' August 26 game in Washington. That would be the only game Barrett would miss all year. The only full-time Tiger to hit above .300 (he batted .303), he led the Tigers in every major offensive statistic except triples and RBI. He also was busy in center field catching 326 fly balls, which was a league high among outfielders. Although Barrett was the main producing player on the club, this had little effect as Detroit plummeted in the standings, falling from third to seventh position in one year.

Missing just one contest in 1903, he hit .315 to finish in second place in the Detroit club behind Sam Crawford. Additionally, he led the American League in walks (74) and on-base percentage (.407) along with having a league-high 19 assists in the outfield. He continued to show durability by playing all the Tigers' games in the 1904 season. While his batting average fell nearly 50 points (.268), it was still good enough to top the team's hitters. He also posted a league-high 79 walks and again led the league's outfielders with 339 putouts and 29 assists. He played one more season (1905) with the Tigers before being released. The following February, his old team, the Reds, claimed him off waivers. He took in several games with the Reds in 1906 before catching on with the Red Sox. Although he returned to being a full-time player in 1907, he suffered a major knee injury that drastically shortened his career. When he returned the following year, he participated in just three games for Boston before retiring from the game by midseason.

42. Topsy Hartsel

Born: June 26, 1874, Polk, Ohio *Died*: October 14, 1944, Toledo, Ohio *Bats*: Left *Throws*: Left *Height*: 5 feet, 5 inches *Weight*: 155 *Major league debut*: September 14, 1898 (Louisville at Brooklyn [NL]) *Last major league game*: September 30, 1911 (second game) (Cleveland at Philadelphia [AL])
Major league Iron Man from: August 26, 1902, to May 12, 1903 *Consecutive games played*: 314 *Games as major league Iron Man*: 55 (consecutive games 260 through 314) *Teams played for during streak*: Cincinnati Reds (NL) (1900), Chicago Orphans (NL) (1901) and Philadelphia Athletics (AL) (1902–1903) *Primary position played*: Outfield *Game missed before streak*: September 19, 1900 (Cincinnati at Philadelphia) *First game played of streak*: September 21, 1900 (Chicago at Cincinnati) *Last game played of streak*: May 11, 1903 (Philadelphia at Chicago) *Game missed to end streak*: May 12, 1903 (Philadelphia at Chicago)

Consecutive Game Streak's Statistical Totals:

Year	G	AB	R	H	2B	3B	HR	RBI	BB	SO	AVG	SLG	SB
1900	18	64	10	21	2	1	2	5	8	—	.328	.484	7
1901	140	558	111	187	25	16	7	54	74	—	.335	.475	41
1902	137	545	109	154	20	12	5	58	87	—	.283	.391	47
1903	19	80	13	21	7	4	1	6	7	—	.263	.488	5
Total	314	1247	243	383	54	33	15	123	176	—	.307	.439	100

Although Topsy Hartsel was one of baseball's smallest players during his playing era, most of the pitchers of his time would testify that Hartsel made them work to get him out. He played for 14 years with four major league clubs but spent the majority of his career (10 seasons) in the American League patrolling the left field spot for the Philadelphia Athletics. He made his big league debut in the National League with the Louisville Colonels in a game against the home team Brooklyn Bridegrooms on September 14, 1898. In the 22 contests he was able to appear in that season, he hit an impressive .324 average. That was the only year he spent exclusively in right field. During the rest of his playing career he was a left fielder except for 68 games that he played in center or right field.

Hartsel played in the minors with an Indianapolis team except for 30 games with the Colonels. He started the 1900 season in the American League (the only season the league was not considered a major league) with the Indianapolis Hoosiers where he played over 100 games and produced a .300 average before transferring to the Cincinnati Reds. His consecutive playing streak started with his promotion to the Reds on September 21, 1900, in a Reds' home game against the Chicago Orphans. Taking over left field in the Reds' lineup, he played the last 18 contests on the 1900 schedule and finished with a .328 average. Just before the beginning of the 1901 season, the Reds sold him to the Chicago Orphans where he replaced Jack McCarthy in left field. Hitting .335 and driving in 54 runs, he surprised everyone by leading the Orphans in every offensive category except RBI (Charlie Dexter paced the club with 66 RBI). Additionally, Hartsel had high totals in walks, stolen bases and times on base that were good enough for second place among the league leaders. Although the Orphans welcomed his productive bat to their lineup, it didn't result in many wins as the club finished in sixth place with a 53–86 record, some 37 games behind the league champion Pittsburgh Pirates. With the season completed,

Hartsel was on the move again. This time he joined the powerful Athletics' lineup, replacing Matty McIntyre in left field. Late in the 1902 season, he took over the major league lead with his 260th consecutive game played on August 26 when Detroit's Jimmy Barrett ended his Iron Man playing streak. When the season closed out, Hartsel had finished with a very solid .283 batting average, but it was the second lowest of the team's regulars. He displayed his ability to get on base and make things happen by leading the American League with 87 walks, 47 stolen bases and coming in in a dead heat in runs with teammate Dave Fultz with 109 scores. In the last year before the start of the World Series, the Athletics won their first league crown, five games ahead of the St. Louis Browns. Three weeks into the following campaign, Hartsel was injured in a game against the Chicago White Sox on May 11, 1903. This mishap caused his Iron Man run to end on May 12 after 314 games. He didn't return full time to Philadelphia's lineup until May 20. Limited to 93 games that year, he hit .311, had a team-high 14 triples and finished second in the league behind the Tigers' Barrett in on base percentage.

After his playing streak had concluded, Hartsel spent eight more seasons with the Athletics. He led the league in walks four more times, inclusively from 1905 through 1908. His base on balls total directly led to his having league highs in on base percentage in 1905 and 1907. He saw action in two World's Series in the coming years. In 1905, after edging the Chicago White Sox by two games for the American League title, Philadelphia lost in five contests to the New York Giants in the World's Series. Although on the losing end of the series, Hartsel had the second-best batting average among all players when he went 5 for 17 for a .294 average. Five years later, Connie Mack and his Athletics were back in the World's Series against the Chicago Cubs. This time there was no stopping Philadelphia as they defeated the Cubs in five games. By now, Hartsel was no longer a regular player on the squad. He was in only one contest and went 1 for 5 but did score two runs. His time in the majors was nearing an end. He put in one last season in Philadelphia, making his final appearances during a double-header in Philadelphia on September 30, 1911, against the Cleveland Broncos. About 10 weeks later, Philadelphia sold his playing contract to Toledo of the American Association. He spent parts of four seasons in the minors before calling it quits in August 1915.

43. FREDDY PARENT

Born: November 25, 1875, Biddeford, Maine *Died*: November 2, 1972, Sanford, Maine *Bats*: Right *Throws*: Right *Height*: 5 feet, 7 inches *Weight*: 154 *Major league debut*: July 14, 1899 (St. Louis at New York [NL]) *Last major league game*: April 30, 1911 (St. Louis at Chicago [AL])

Major league Iron Man from: May 12, 1903, to September 26, 1903 *Consecutive games played*: 413 *Games as major league Iron Man*: 119 (consecutive games 295 through 413) *Team played for during streak*: Boston Americans (AL) *Primary position played*: Shortstop *Game missed before streak*: (Did not play any major league games during 1900 season) *First game played of streak*: April 26, 1901 (Boston at Baltimore) *Last game played of streak*: September 25, 1903 (Detroit at Boston) *Game missed to end streak*: September 26, 1903 (first game) (St. Louis at Boston)

Consecutive Game Streak's Statistical Totals:

Year	G	AB	R	H	2B	3B	HR	RBI	BB	SO	AVG	SLG	SB
1901	138	517	87	158	23	9	4	59	41	—	.306	.408	16
1902	138	567	91	156	31	8	3	62	24	—	.275	.374	16
1903	137	551	82	165	31	17	4	76	13	—	.299	.445	22
Total	413	1635	260	479	85	34	11	197	78	—	.293	.407	54

Freddy Parent played in the major leagues for 12 seasons. He made his big league debut with the St. Louis Perfectos of the National League on July 14, 1899. He appeared in only one other game that season and in both contests was used at second base. Except for this brief time with the Perfectos, he would spend the rest of his baseball career in the American League with the Boston Americans (Red Sox) and Chicago White Sox. When Boston was given a franchise in the new major league (American League) in 1901, the steady Parent was selected by the team's manager, Jimmy Collins, to man the shortstop position.

In the 1901 season opener on April 26 in Baltimore, Parent took up his new position at short and also started a consecutive playing streak. In his first full major league season, he hit for a career high .306 batting average and drove in 59 runners as Boston finished in second place, just four games behind the front-running Chicago White Sox. While Parent played all 138 contests for Boston that season, it should be noted that the Americans' infielders were quite durable as the entire unit played the last 63 games of the season together and for the season missed just nine contests. First baseman Buck Freeman was the only infielder on the club to miss any games during the 1901 season. During the early years of the American League, Boston had more than their fair share of Iron Men. Besides Parent, other Boston teammates who accomplished Iron Man streaks were playing manager Jimmy Collins, first baseman Candy LaChance and outfielder Buck Freeman. Parent also finished the 1901 season playing more games at shortstop than any other league player. In 1902, Parent again played in every contest on the Americans' schedule. While his hitting percentage fell to a .275 average, he posted a league high 567 at-bats and improved his RBI total by three as he drove home 62 Americans runners. He provided reliability at shortstop by again leading the position in games played and amassing a league-high 492 assists. On May 12 of the following year (1903), Parent became the Iron Man of major league baseball when the Philadelphia Athletics' Topsy Hartsel sat out Philadelphia's game in Chicago. Parent came very close to completing a third year without sitting out a contest but his 413-game playing streak was snapped when he was rested (in preparation for the upcoming World's Series) during a double-header in Boston on September 26, 1903, against St. Louis. His batting average rebounded to a solid .304 mark, he led the American League shortstops in games played for the third straight season and helped the Americans win the league championship by nearly 15 games over their closest competitor. He also was third in the league in total hits with 170 base knocks, behind teammate Patsy Dougherty, who led the league with 195 hits, and the Detroit Tigers' Sam Crawford, who was runner-up with 184 hits.

The Americans faced the Pittsburgh Pirates in the first modern-day World's Series in October 1903. Parent played all eight contests at shortstop and went 9 for 32 for a .281 average, hit three triples and led all series players with eight runs scored. Boston was down three games to one game in the series but came back and won the last four games of the world championship to claim the title. It is also noteworthy to mention that when Parent passed away in early November 1972 (as he was approaching his 97th birthday), he was the last surviving participant of the first modern World's Series played. Even though Parent's long playing streak had come to a conclusion in September 1903, he would start another streak the following year that would make him a two-time holder of the Iron Man title. Additionally, he was at the beginning of his baseball career and still had eight more years of playing in the major leagues left in him. Because Parent is one of the few players to become a two-time major league Iron Man, additional facts and statistics about his second streak and the rest of his playing career are included in a later profile.

44. CANDY LaCHANCE

Born: February 14, 1870, Putnam, Connecticut *Died*: August 18, 1932, Waterville, Connecticut *Bats*: Switch Hitter *Throws*: Right *Height*: 6 feet, 1 inch *Weight*: 183 *Major league debut*: August 15, 1893 (New York at Brooklyn [NL]) *Last major league game*: April 28, 1905 (Washington at Boston [AL])

Major league Iron Man from: September 26, 1903, to April 29, 1905 *Consecutive games played*: 539 *Games as major league Iron Man*: 173 (consecutive games 367 through 539) *Teams played for during streak*: Cleveland Blues (AL) (1901) and Boston Americans (AL) (1902–1905) *Primary position played*: First base *Game missed before streak*: June 22, 1901 (Cleveland at Boston) *First game played of streak*: June 24, 1901 (Cleveland at Boston) *Last game played of streak*: April 28, 1905 (Washington at Boston) *Game missed to end streak*: April 29, 1905 (Washington at Boston)

Consecutive Game Streak's Statistical Totals:

Year	G	AB	R	H	2B	3B	HR	RBI	BB	SO	AVG	SLG	SB
1901	91	377	49	110	12	7	1	46	1	—	.292	.369	5
1902	138	541	60	151	13	4	6	56	18	—	.279	.351	8
1903	141	522	60	134	22	6	1	53	28	—	.257	.328	12
1904	157	573	55	130	19	5	1	47	23	—	.227	.283	7
1905	12	41	1	6	1	0	0	5	6	—	.146	.171	0
Total	539	2054	225	531	67	22	9	207	76	—	.259	.326	32

Candy LaChance was a big, strapping, reliable first baseman who toiled in the majors for a dozen years. He also was one of around two dozen switch hitters to play in the majors during the 19th century. After spending his initial three years of professional ball in the minors, his big league career started in the National League with the Brooklyn Bridegrooms. Making his debut in a Brooklyn home game against the New York Giants on August 15, 1893, he was used in the team's lineup during that season as either a catcher or an outfielder. He took part in only 11 contests and went 6 for 35 for a .171 average.

LaChance's playing opportunities increased the following season (1894) when Brooklyn manager and first baseman Dave Foutz used him quite often as his backup at first base. He took in 69 games, batted .318 and drove in 52 runners in his limited playing time. In 1895, Foutz decided to concentrate more time on managing and did not play as much. This decision gave LaChance the opportunity to take over Brooklyn's first base position. Missing just a handful of contests that year, he led the Bridegrooms with 111 RBI and 37 stolen bases while finishing with a solid .314 batting average. In 1896, his batting average (.284) and RBI (58) totals fell off quite a bit as he missed about a third of Brooklyn's games. After batting .308 and producing a team-high 16 triples in 126 games during 1897, he slumped badly again in 1898 as evidenced by his 61-point drop in his batting average, although he did lead the 10th-place Bridegrooms in homers and doubles. During the off-season, LaChance was sent to the Baltimore Orioles in a transaction that saw Brooklyn and Baltimore transfer several players, including their respective first basemen, LaChance and Dan McGann. In his one year with Baltimore (1899), LaChance brought his batting average back to .307 along with bringing home 75 runners. He jumped to the Cleveland Spiders of the new American League (formed by Ban Johnson) in 1900. With the National League dropping four franchises after the 1899 campaign, Cleveland was without a professional ball club. The American League leadership chose Cleveland as a member. Although it was not considered a major league at the time, LaChance still decided to play in the new league. He made the most of this chance with the Spiders by hitting .302 and pacing the team with 29 stolen bases. During the off-season, Cleveland changed its name to the Blues and the American League was recognized for the first time as a major league. LaChance started his playing streak on June 24, 1901, with the Blues while the club was in Boston for a game against the Americans. Being the reliable player he was noted for, LaChance came through again by finishing the year with .303 batting average and driving home 75 Cleveland runners. His performance didn't help the Blues, though, as the team finished with a 55–82 record that placed them in next to last place in the final standings. Just before the start of the 1902 campaign, the Boston Americans acquired LaChance from Cleveland. He replaced fellow Iron Man Buck Freeman (who was made the new right fielder) as the team's regular first baseman. His first year in Boston did not prove very impressive. Although he did provide the team with reliable defense at first base by leading the American Leaguers at that position with 138 games played and 1,544 putouts, his offensive output was somewhat disappointing. His hitting average was down nearly 25 points and his RBI total fell off by 20 runs although he did hit six homers (five more than during the previous season). The Americans finished in third place in the final outcome of a closely contested pennant race. LaChance's consecutive game streak was still running when his teammate and baseball's Iron Man, shortstop Freddy Parent, was rested during a double-header on September 26, 1903. LaChance at this point took over as the major league Iron Man with a 367-game mark actively running. His final 1903 stats were nearly the same as in 1902. He also repeated as the leader of games played and putouts by first basemen. The final American League results in 1903 saw the Americans claim their first league flag by nearly 15 games over their closest competitor, the Philadelphia Athletics. The first modern-day World's Series included three other past or future Iron Men (Collins, Parent and Freeman) in their lineup besides LaChance. Boston defeated the Pittsburgh Pirates in eight games to win the world title. In the series, LaChance hit for only a .222 average but he did drive home four runs in contributing to the Americans' championship. During the latter stages of the 1904 season, during the first game of a double-header on September 14, LaChance became only the third player (the others being George Pinkney and Steve Brodie) in baseball history to reach the 500 consecutive game pinnacle. It was obvious from his performances over the last several years that his better playing days were behind him. This was even more evident when he finished the 1904 season by hitting just .227 and contributed only 47 RBI in 157 games. Despite no longer producing with the bat, his glove was as reliable as ever as he led the league's first basemen in games played and putouts for the third straight year and added the fielding title and most double plays to his credit. The conclusion of the 1904 campaign saw the Americans repeat as American League champs as they edged the New York Highlanders by a game and a half in the final outcome. The Americans didn't have the chance to defend their world title because the National League pennant winners, the New York Giants, refused to play Boston in a World's Series. This came about because the Giants' owner and especially their manager, John McGraw, refused to accept the American League as their equal when it came to competing on the field. As a result, no World's Series was contested and Boston claimed the world title by default.

Due to his lackluster hitting at the beginning of the 1905 season, LaChance was benched by manager Collins on April 29 after playing 539 straight games. Many baseball references show that LaChance's streak was 540 games. The research conducted on this subject concludes that his streak was actually 539 contests. It is also noted that he didn't sit out a single inning in the last 424 games of his streak (stretching back to May 1902). Soon after his streak ended, he was sold by Boston to Montreal of the Eastern League. He would spend what time he had left (nearly four seasons) playing minor league ball until his retirement in 1908.

45. BUCK FREEMAN

Born: October 30, 1871, Catasauqua, Pennsylvania *Died*: June 25, 1949, Wilkes-Barre, Pennsylvania *Bats*: Left *Throws*: Left *Height*: 5 feet, 9 inches *Weight*: 169 *Major league debut*: June 27, 1891 (Philadelphia at Washington [AA]) *Last major league game*: April 20, 1907 (Boston at New York [AL])

Major league Iron Man from: April 29, 1905, to June 7, 1905 *Consecutive games played*: 536 *Games as major league Iron Man*: 25 (consecutive games 512 through 536) *Team played for during streak*: Boston Americans (AL) *Primary positions played*: Outfield and first base *Game missed before streak*: July 26, 1901 (Boston at Milwaukee) *First game played of streak*: July 27, 1901 (Boston at Chicago) *Last game played of streak*: June 5, 1905 (Boston at New York) *Game missed to end streak*: June 7, 1905 (St. Louis at Boston)

Consecutive Game Streak's Statistical Totals:

Year	G	AB	R	H	2B	3B	HR	RBI	BB	SO	AVG	SLG	SB
1901	63	244	38	77	13	5	3	38	25	—	.316	.447	9
1902	138	564	75	174	38	19	11	121	32	—	.309	.502	17
1903	141	567	74	163	39	20	13	104	30	—	.287	.496	5
1904	157	597	64	167	20	19	7	84	32	—	.280	.412	7
1905	37	130	16	29	4	3	1	—	—	—	.223	.323	3
Total	536	2102	267	610	114	66	35	*347*	*119*	—	.290	.457	41

Buck Freeman was one of baseball's most feared power hitters during the early portions of the deadball era. It is ironic that this home run hitter started as a pitcher. This was the position he played when he made his major league debut on June 27, 1891, with the Washington Senators of the American Association. He got into five games (four of them as the starting pitcher), finished with a 3–2 win-loss record, had an earned run average of 3.29 and a batting average of .222. His performance did not seem to impress anyone though and, as a result, he was sent to the minor leagues. Seven seasons would pass before he would make it back to the major league level.

Freeman returned to the big leagues with the Senators (now a member of the National League) in 1898. He participated in 29 contests in right field, hit a solid .364 and drove in 21 runs in the abbreviated time he was in the lineup. Freeman's career year occurred the following season, his first full season in the majors. He did not miss a single game in right field in 1899 and had a monster year at the plate. Only two National Leaguers hit more than 10 homers that season: Freeman and St. Louis' infielder Bobby Wallace, who had a dozen clouts. Freeman on the other hand, completely ran away with the home run title by more than doubling Wallace's total and finishing with a career-high 25 homers in 155 games played. While he came in with a .318 batting average, he also posted career highs in runs (107), triples (25) and RBI (122). In addition, he was runner-up to Ed Delahanty of the Philadelphia Phillies in slugging percentage, total bases, extra-base hits and RBI. His triples total was also good for second place in the league behind the Pittsburgh Pirates' Jimmy Williams, who had 27 three-baggers. Even with all this production from one player, the Senators finished a dismal 11th place in the final standings. The only team they finished ahead of was the pathetic Cleveland Spiders, who went 20–134 and set a new major league standard for lowest winning percentage. In February 1900, the Senators sold Freeman to the Boston Beaneaters. In his one year with Boston's National League team, Freeman's numbers dropped off dramatically as his batting average fell to .301 and his homer and RBI totals plummeted. He decided to switch leagues and teams but not leave the city. Following Beaneaters teammates Jimmy Collins and Chick Stahl over to the American League for the 1901 season, Freeman joined the Boston Americans as their newly crowned first baseman. On July 27, 1901, he started a playing streak that would continue well into the 1905 season. He rebounded from his 1900 performance doldrums by hitting a dozen homers, batting .339 and bringing home 114 runners. His stats in these categories were all team-high marks as well as the second-best league totals for homers and RBI behind the Triple Crown winner, Cleveland's Nap Lajoie. Freeman was the team's offensive leader and helped lead Boston to a second-place finish, trailing the Chicago White Sox by just four games. In the off-season, the Americans acquired first baseman Candy LaChance from the Cleveland Blues. When the 1902 season opened, manager Jimmy Collins inserted LaChance at first base and moved Freeman back to right field. Of course, Collins' decision to replace Freeman with LaChance at first base was quite easy due to the fact that Freeman led the league's first basemen with 36 errors during the 1901 campaign. While his batting average dropped down to a .309 mark, he still led the league in 1902 with 68 extra-base hits and 121 runners driven in. He also had the team's top marks in home runs (11), hits (174), doubles (38), triples (19) and slugging percentage (.504). Boston stayed in contention for the top spot in the standings all season but at the end came up short by a half dozen games to the Philadelphia Athletics. One of the highlights for Freeman during the 1903 season was when he hit for the cycle in Boston's 12–7 victory over Cleveland on June 21. By the end of the year, his hitting average had continued its downward trend as he checked out of 1903 with a .287 mark. This did not stop him, though, from leading the league with 13 homers and repeating as the RBI king with 104. He also was the league leader in total bases, extra-base hits and games played by an outfielder. Freeman had extended his playing streak to 342 by the end of the 1903 season. This was good for second place in the majors for the second-longest active streak, just behind teammate Candy LaChance, who had a 28-game edge over him. As the team's offensive leader, Freeman took great pride in helping Boston run away with the league championship by nearly 15 games. In the first modern World's Series, the Americans defeated the Pittsburgh Pirates in eight games. Freeman went 9 for 32 for a .281 average and contributed three triples and four RBI to the cause. Although he again led the Americans in homers and RBI during the 1904 season, many of his numbers continued to diminish. After years of being among the league leaders, the only category in which he retained his prowess was RBI, earning second place, finishing 18 RBI behind Cleveland's Lajoie. As for the team, Boston repeated as league champs and claimed the world championship by default when the New York Giants (thanks to their owner and manager) refused to participate in the World's Series. In Boston's 1905 season opener on April 14, Freeman became just the fourth player in major league history to reach the 500 consecutive games plateau. As the end of April was approaching and just a dozen games into the new season, Freeman took over the Iron Man title from teammate and first baseman LaChance whose own streak ended when he was benched on April 29, 1905. Just over five weeks later, Freeman's streak of 536 games ended on June 7 when he sat out a home game against the St. Louis Browns as the result of an injury. This injury kept him out of the Americans' lineup for nearly three weeks (except for three brief appearances through the first week of July). Many baseball reference books have listed Freeman's consecutive games streak at 535 games. A game-by-game analysis has revealed that his actual consecutive run was 536 games (one game more than he is credited for having achieved). Except for the first game of his streak, he participated in every inning of the last 535 games during this consecutive run of contests.

Upon his full-time return to the team's lineup on July 5, 1905, manager Collins started rotating Freeman between first base and right field, depending on the situation, for the rest of the year. He had his worst showing as a major leaguer that season as he batted only .240, hit just three homers and drove in 49 runners. He played only one more full season and the beginning of another. Relegated to bench-warming duties, he made his final bow on April 20, 1907, when he pinch-hit for catcher Lou Criger in the ninth inning of an 8–1 loss to the New York Highlanders. Soon after, Freeman asked for his release from the Red Sox. The team granted his request and he quite rapidly was signed to a contract by the Washington Senators. Ironically, the Senators never used him in any of their games and sent him to the minors where he finished his playing career.

46. Bill Bradley

Born: February 13, 1878, Cleveland, Ohio *Died*: March 11, 1954, Cleveland, Ohio *Bats*: Right *Throws*: Right *Height*: 6 feet *Weight*: 185 *Major league debut*: August 26, 1899 (Brooklyn at Chicago [NL]) *Last major league game*: September 28, 1915 (Baltimore at Kansas City [FL])

Major league Iron Man from: June 7, 1905, to August 29, 1905 *Consecutive games played*: 320 *Games as major league Iron Man*: 74 (consecutive games 247 through 320) *Team played for during streak*: Cleveland Naps (AL) *Primary position played*: Third base *Game missed before streak*: July 31, 1903 (Cleveland at Chicago) *First game played of streak*: August 1, 1903 (Cleveland at Chicago) *Last game played of streak*: August 28, 1905 (New York at Cleveland) *Game missed to end streak*: August 29, 1905 (first game) (Philadelphia at Cleveland)

Consecutive Game Streak's Statistical Totals:

Year	G	AB	R	H	2B	3B	HR	RBI	BB	SO	AVG	SLG	SB
1903	56	220	39	74	19	10	3	31	13	—	.336	.555	8
1904	154	609	94	183	32	8	6	83	26	—	.300	.409	23
1905	110	405	54	112	27	2	0	—	—	—	.277	.353	17
Total	320	1234	187	369	78	20	9	*114*	*39*	—	.299	.417	48

Playing for 14 seasons in the major leagues, Bill Bradley established a reputation of being one of the most reliable players in the game during the infancy years of the American League. He started out his big league career with the National League's Chicago Orphans, making his major league debut in Chicago's loss to Brooklyn on August 26, 1899. The 21-year-old impressed the team management as he hit .310 in 35 contests. In the opening days of the 1900 season, Bradley took over the third base job when the Orphans decided to trade regular third baseman Harry Wolverton to the Philadelphia Phillies. Playing in 122 games, Bradley finished with a .282 batting average and posted a team-high eight triples.

With the American League gaining major league status, Bradley decided to switch to the junior circuit and joined his hometown team, the Cleveland Blues, for the 1901 season. Missing just a handful of games at third base, he hit .293, drove in 55 runners and led the team with 28 doubles and 13 triples. On the defensive side of the ledger, he led the league's third basemen with a .930 fielding percentage and 25 double plays. The following season (1902), the team changed their name to the Broncos. Bradley turned out to be the only player on the squad to play in all 137 contests during the 1902 campaign. He turned in a MVP performance by achieving team highs in several major offensive categories and putting together the longest hitting streak (29 games) in the majors that season. The year also saw his hitting increase 48 points to a career-best .340 average, while he smacked 11 homers and drove in 77 runners. He finished in a tie in the runner-up position for both homers and total bases and also came in third to Boston's Buck Freeman in extra-base hits. He also was the third base leader in games played (137) and putouts (188). His playing streak commenced the following year during a game in Chicago on August 1, 1903. When the season concluded, his hitting dropped to .313 in 1903, but the mark was still good for second place in the team as he again led in runs and triples. While the team outlasted the New York Highlanders to finish in third place, they were still 15 games behind the first-place Boston Americans. Cleveland changed their nickname for the third time in three years. Now being called the Naps (after manager Nap Lajoie), this name stayed with the team until they finally settled on the Indians in 1915. In 1904, Bradley again appeared in all the Naps' games and extended his playing run to 210 games. He again hit the .300 level in batting and led the American League's hot corner occupants in fielding with a .955 percentage. His performance kept the Naps in contention for the league crown but they came up just short with a fourth-place finish in the hotly contested race. The 1905 season saw several long playing streaks come to an end early in the campaign: Candy LaChance (539), Lave Cross (447) and Buck Freeman (536). Finally when Freeman's streak ended on June 7, 1905, Bradley took over the active leadership of the Iron Man title and also ended a streak of Boston American players who were successive Iron Men. His time as Iron Man lasted another three months before closing out at 320 straight games. A minor injury that kept him out of the Naps' lineup for a week ended his streak on August 29, 1905. His batting average sunk for the third straight year as it plummeted 32 points to a .268 mark. He gained some managerial experience in 1905 by filling in for Lajoie in 41 games as the Naps' skipper. As for the team, they also regressed to fifth place and came in 19 games behind the flag-winning pace.

Bradley experienced the first major injury of his career in 1906 when he suffered a broken wrist which limited his service to just 82 games. After this season, he stayed with the Naps for four more years. He departed the Cleveland scene after the 1910 season only to reappear in Brooklyn in 1914 where he served as the playing manager (mainly for pinch-hitting appearances) for the city's Tip-Tops of the Federal League. He guided the team to a .500 winning percentage and a fifth-place finish. His last year of major league ball (1915) was spent with the Federal League's Kansas City Packers. He was used strictly as a backup to third baseman George Perring. Bradley got into 66 contests but hit for only a .187 average. With this lackluster performance and the folding of the Federal League after two years of big league play, he realized the time was ripe to retire from the game.

47. LEE TANNEHILL

Born: October 26, 1880, Dayton, Kentucky *Died*: February 16, 1938, Live Oak, Florida *Bats*: Right *Throws*: Right *Height*: 5 feet, 11 inches *Weight*: 170 *Major league debut*: April 22, 1903 (Chicago at St. Louis [AL]) *Last major league game*: May 8, 1912 (Chicago at Washington [AL])

Major league Iron Man from: August 29, 1905, to September 17, 1905 *Consecutive games played*: 265 *Games as major league Iron Man*: 20 (consecutive games 246 through 265) *Team played for during streak*: Chicago White Sox (AL) *Primary position played*: Third base *Game missed before streak*: May 11, 1904 (Chicago at Philadelphia) *First game played of streak*: May 12, 1904 (Chicago at Philadelphia) *Last game played of streak*: September 16, 1905 (St. Louis at Chicago) *Game missed to end streak*: September 17, 1905 (Cleveland at Chicago)

Consecutive Game Streak's Statistical Totals

Year	G	AB	R	H	2B	3B	HR	RBI	BB	SO	AVG	SLG	SB
1904	133	476	41	107	27	2	0	52	16	—	.225	.290	12
1905	132	442	34	86	16	2	0	—	—	—	.195	.240	8
Total	265	918	75	193	43	4	0	*52*	*16*	—	.210	.266	20

Lee Tannehill

Lee Tannehill was the Chicago White Sox third baseman for most of his 10-year major league career, from 1903 through to the 1912 season. He was the second member of his family to make the major leagues. Older brother Jesse was a pitcher who spent the majority of his 15-year big league baseball career with the Pittsburgh Pirates and Boston Americans. Lee made his debut in the majors on April 22, 1903, in a White Sox contest in St. Louis. He had taken over the White Sox's shortstop position as a rookie from longtime veteran George Davis, who had left the team to play in the National League for the New York franchise. This situation didn't last long because White Sox president Charles Comiskey went to court to prevent Davis from playing with any team except the White Sox during the 1903 season. Although Tannehill couldn't replace Davis' offensive presence on the team, he proved he could field the position. In fact, he led the league's shortstops with 58 double plays that season. Even though not a lot of production was expected from his hitting, he hit for a .225 average and drove in 50 runners, which was the fourth-highest total in the team (behind outfielder Danny Green, first baseman Frank Isbell and playing manager-third baseman Nixey Callahan).

With Davis returning to his old position at shortstop for the 1904 season, White Sox skipper Callahan decided to switch Tannehill to third base and moved himself from third base to the outfield. Except for filling in at shortstop on the rare occasion, the hot corner would be Tannehill's permanent spot on the White Sox roster for the next six seasons. After missing three games in the early part of May, his consecutive playing streak started on May 12, 1904, when the White Sox were in Philadelphia to take on the Athletics. He played the last 133 games of the 1904 season at third base. It should be noted that while playing a game in Boston against the Americans on August 17, Tannehill was in the White Sox's lineup that day when a no-hitter was pitched by the Boston pitcher (his big brother Jesse) in a 6–0 Americans' victory. He checked in with a final batting average of .229 and led the team in games played and doubles. In

Lee Tannehill: The Chicago White Sox third baseman compiled a 259-game mark during the 1904–1905 seasons. He was one of only two players to attain the Iron Man title without having played a complete season with perfect attendance. The other player was also from a Chicago team, the Cubs' Phil Cavarretta, who put his Iron Man streak together in the mid-1940s.

fact, his 31 doubles were good for fourth place in the American League. On the defensive side of the ledger, he had league-high marks for third basemen in assists (369) and double plays (22). His performance that year also helped the White Sox improve from a seventh-place finish in 1903 to a third-place outcome in 1904 as they finished only six games behind the league champion Americans. Late in the following year, Tannehill would claim the Iron Man title on August 29, 1905, when Cleveland third baseman Bill Bradley's streak ended on that date. Tannehill's time as Iron Man would end 20 games later when his 265 games played streak ended on September 17. Although he was the majors' most durable player for just over two weeks, Tannehill is one of only two major leaguers to achieve the Iron Man status by putting a playing streak together that did not include at least a full season of not missing a contest. The only other player with this distinction was the Chicago Cubs' Phil Cavarretta, who put a 259-game streak together over two partial seasons in 1943 and 1944. Tannehill's 1905 production was not too impressive as he had only a .200 average and brought just 39 runners home all year. Although he did lead the third basemen again with 358 assists, even his defense suffered as he made 39 miscues with the glove to lead the league's hot corner occupants in errors. The bright spot of the year was that Chicago was in very close contention with the Athletics for the American League crown, but the White Sox fell two games short of their goal as they finished in second place.

After a couple of near miss years, the White Sox won the pennant in 1906 by three games over the New York Highlanders. Tannehill had finished the season with an anemic .183 batting average (the lowest mark of any American Leaguer that year who was considered a regular player). Facing the crosstown rivals, the Chicago Cubs, for the 1906 world title, the White Sox surprised the skeptics by winning the series in six games with a .198 team batting average. Tannehill didn't surprise anybody with the bat as he managed but one hit in nine tries for a .111 average. After winning the World's Series, Tannehill played just six more years with the White Sox. Of these, he missed a great majority of three of them (1907, 1910 and 1912) while recuperating from injuries. Early in the 1912 season, his throwing arm was broken by a pitched ball thrown by the Washington Senators' Walter Johnson. This injury affected his ability to throw the ball and, as a result, prematurely ended his ballplaying career.

48. Freddy Parent

Born: November 25, 1875, Biddeford, Maine *Died*: November 2, 1972, Sanford, Maine *Bats*: Right *Throws*: Right *Height*: 5 feet, 7 inches *Weight*: 154 *Major league debut*: July 14, 1899 (St. Louis at New York [NL]) *Last major league game*: April 30, 1911 (St. Louis at Chicago [AL])

Major league Iron Man from: September 17, 1905, to September 5, 1906 *Consecutive games played*: 408 *Games as major league Iron Man*: 152 (consecutive games 257 through 408) *Team played for during streak*: Boston Americans (AL) *Primary position played*: Shortstop *Game missed before streak*: May 21, 1904 (St. Louis at Boston) *First game played of streak*: May 23, 1904 (St. Louis at Boston) *Last game played of streak*: September 4, 1906 (second game) (New York at Boston) *Game missed to end streak*: September 5, 1906 (New York at Boston)

Consecutive Game Streak's Statistical Totals:

Year	G	AB	R	H	2B	3B	HR	RBI	BB	SO	AVG	SLG	SB
1904	130	503	74	146	21	7	5	69	20	—	.290	.390	18
1905	153	602	55	141	16	5	0	33	47	—	.234	.277	25
1906	125	510	60	124	12	8	0	—	—	—	.243	.298	15
Total	408	1615	189	411	49	20	5	*102*	*67*	—	.254	.319	58

After missing two contests in the third week of May 1904, Freddy Parent returned to the Americans' lineup on May 23 to start his second Iron Man streak. A few months later, while in Cleveland during the first of August, Parent and several of his teammates were staying in a hotel that caught fire. The players helped many hotel guests evacuate the structure and, as a result, were honored as heroes. Parent finished the year hitting .291, driving in 77 runners and leading the team with 20 stolen bases. During the 1904 season, he played more games at shortstop than any other American Leaguer for the fourth consecutive season, but he must have had a hole in his glove because he led the position with 63 errors. His presence was definitely needed in the lineup as Boston was in a dogfight for the league pennant. The Americans prevailed and won their second league title when they edged the New York Highlanders by a game and a half. Unfortunately, there was no World's Series in 1904. The National League titleholder New York Giants refused to play the American League winners because the Giants' team owner and manager both thought the junior circuit was a minor league. Since a World's Series competition did not occur, the Boston Americans claimed the world title by default. Late the following season, Parent became baseball's Iron Man (with a 257-game streak) for the second time when Chicago White Sox third baseman Lee Tannehill sat out a contest on September 17, 1905.

Even though Parent didn't miss a single inning during the course of the 1905 season, it was his worst year since turning pro. His offensive production fell off dramatically as he hit for only a .234 average (a falloff of 57 points), scored 55 runs (a decline of 30 runs) and drove in 33 runners (down 44 RBI). The only categories he led the Americans in were his at-bats total and the 25 bases he swiped. He also repeated as the American League shortstop's error leader with 66 miscues. Parent's off-year had a residual effect on the team as Boston finished in fourth place, 16 games behind the new American League champion, the Philadelphia Athletics. As for his consecutive games streak, he held onto the Iron Man title for nearly a year before injuring one of his legs in a home game against the Highlanders on September 4, 1906. This injury kept him out of Boston's lineup for about a week. It was around the time of Parent's injury that longtime Boston manager and captain Jimmy Collins gave up the managerial reigns to Chick Stahl. The reasoning for this move was obvious; the mighty Boston team had fallen on hard times. Just two years after winning their second league title, the Americans were no longer one of the powerhouse teams as they finished deep in the basement with a 49–105 record. Parent's numbers with the bat did not improve that dramatically but he did lead the team in a couple of statistical categories.

Parent played only one more year in Boston. During his last season (1907) with the Americans, he was used at various positions in a utility man's role since he was replaced at shortstop by Heinie Wagner. While playing in 114 games (his lowest total since becoming a regular), Parent's batting average experienced a 40-point improvement but he just wasn't providing the team with the offense that was previously expected of him. Just after the 1907 season was completed, Boston traded Parent to the Chicago White Sox. He replaced veteran George Davis (who was moved over to second base) as the White Sox' new shortstop. Although he missed a few weeks with a knee injury, Parent was still able to take in 119 games but he finished with a measly .207 batting average. He put in two more full seasons and a fraction of a third with Chicago before leaving the major leagues. He would go on to lead a long life as he passed away on November 2, 1972, just three weeks short of his 97th birthday. Not only was he the last surviving player from the 1903 World's Series, he also was the oldest living World's Series participant (replacing the "no-hit wonder" Chicago White Sox catcher Billy Sullivan), a title he held from January 28, 1965, to his death.

49. Sherry Magee

Born: August 6, 1884, Clarendon, Pennsylvania *Died*: March 13, 1929, Philadelphia, Pennsylvania *Bats*: Right *Throws*: Right *Height*: 5 feet, 11 inches *Weight*: 179 *Major league debut*: June 29, 1904 (Brooklyn at Philadelphia [NL]) *Last major league game*: September 27, 1919 (Chicago at Cincinnati [NL])

Major league Iron Man from: September 5, 1906, to July 1, 1907 *Consecutive games played*: 447 *Games as major league Iron Man*: 88 (consecutive games 360 through 447) *Team played for during streak*: Philadelphia Phillies (NL) *Primary position played*: Outfield *Game missed before streak*: July 21, 1904 (Philadelphia at St. Louis) *First game played of streak*: July 22, 1904 (Philadelphia at St. Louis) *Last game played of streak*: June 28, 1907 (New York at Philadelphia) *Game missed to end streak*: July 1, 1907 (first game) (New York at Philadelphia)

Consecutive Game Streak's Statistical Totals

Year	G	AB	R	H	2B	3B	HR	RBI	BB	SO	AVG	SLG	SB
1904	79	304	49	85	9	12	3	—	—	—	.280	.418	10
1905	155	603	100	180	24	17	5	98	44	—	.299	.420	48
1906	154	563	77	159	36	8	6	67	52	—	.282	.407	55
1907	59	221	34	72	13	5	2	—	—	—	.326	.457	23
Total	447	1691	260	496	82	42	16	*165*	*96*	—	.293	.420	136

Although the deadball era of baseball had many great stars, Sherry Magee is up there with the best of them. He had all the ballplaying tools a manager could ask for in a player. In fact, he was so skilled that soon after baseball scouts first noticed him he went from playing for a local team to becoming a major leaguer. He made his debut with Philadelphia Phillies on June 29, 1904, against the Brooklyn Superbas. Magee stayed in the majors for 16 seasons and played for three National League teams (the Phillies, Boston Braves and Cincinnati Reds). His appearance in the Phillies' lineup was expedited because one of the team's other outfielders was injured. As a result, he took over the right field position in the Phillies' outfield.

Less than a month after his big league debut, Magee's consecutive-games-played streak started on July 22, 1904, when the Phillies were in St. Louis to play the Cardinals. Although he did not start until the last days of June, he still participated in 95 contests and came in with a .277 batting aver-

Sherry Magee: This Philadelphia Phillie was one of the more dominating players of the deadball era. He had a streak of 447 games very early in his playing career which he compiled from July 1904 to June 1907.

age along with 57 RBI. Quite remarkable (since he played in just over 60 percent of the season) was that he had a team-high 12 triples and his closest competitor in the club had six. During this era, the Phillies were a permanent fixture in the second division of the final standings. The 1904 season was no different as they finished in last place and were well over 50 games behind the first-place New York Giants. With the start of the 1905 campaign, Phillies' skipper Hugh Duffy inserted Magee into left field, replacing John Titus, who went over to the right field spot. With a full season of experience, Magee proved that he was one of the more valuable Phillies as he took in all 155 games and just missed hitting .300. Additionally, he led the team in several statistics, including home runs and RBI. The team also improved a great deal as they escaped the second division by coming in fourth place, although they were still over 20 games behind the league leaders. On September 5, 1906, Boston Americans' shortstop Freddy Parent's long playing streak stopped due to a leg injury. Magee took over the active lead in consecutive games with a 360-game streak running. When the season concluded it revealed that many of his production numbers had dropped off. His batting average alone fell nearly 20 points. Even with these lower numbers, he still led the team in every major offensive category with the exception of runs scored and walks. The Phillies experienced the same drop off as Magee. The only category they improved on from the 1905 season was the number of doubles the team hit. This situation did not affect the team in the standings as they repeated their fourth place but were not in contention as they came in 22 games behind the third-place Pittsburgh Pirates. Three months into the following season, Magee finally missed a game when he sat out the double-header against the New York Giants on July 1, 1907. His streak was over after 447 consecutive contests played and his Iron Man reign ended after 88 games. Although his run was over that did not stop Magee from having one of his better years with the bat. He hit .328, led the National League with 85 RBI and again was the team's offensive leader in just about every major category. If it was not for the Pirates' Honus Wagner, he would have been a serious candidate for Most Valuable Player honors (if the award had existed back then). He finished second to Wagner in hitting, on base percentage, slugging, doubles, triples, extra-base hits and stolen bases. Although the team was never in contention to win the league title, they did finish in third place. It is just that the Chicago Cubs ran away with the National League championship that season.

Magee played for a dozen more years in the majors. He won the National League batting title in 1910 and paced the league in RBI three more times (1910, 1914 and 1918). Although he would be one of the National League's premier stars as the deadball era was coming to a close, there was one incident that left a black mark on his career. In July 1911, he knocked out umpire Bill Finneran after being ejected from a game for throwing his bat after being called out on strikes. The league president suspended Magee for the rest of the season, although the suspension was lifted after 30 games. He stayed with the Phillies through the 1914 season before being sent in a trade to the Boston Braves in February 1915. Midway through his third year with Boston, the Braves put him on waivers. The Cincinnati Reds promptly claimed him. He spent his last couple of seasons in the majors with the Reds. In his last season he finally realized his goal of being on a league champion team. The Reds won the National League title in 1919 and faced the Chicago White Sox in the World's Series. The Reds stunned the baseball world by defeating the favored White Sox in eight games. Magee only made two pinch-hitting appearances in the series. In the third game, he hit for pitcher Ray Fisher in the eighth inning and flew out to right field; then, in what would turn out to be his last major league at-bat, he singled in the seventh inning of the seventh game while hitting for pitcher Dolf Luque. Although the Reds won the series, soon after some of the luster was taken out of winning the world title. This was the year of the famous "Black Sox" scandal in which several

White Sox players took bribes from a gambler to throw some of the games and ensure a Reds' victory. Eventually, the baseball commissioner position was created and the players involved were given lifetime bans from the sport. It also marked the end of baseball's deadball era. Soon after, a player named Babe Ruth would forever change the great game of baseball. As for Magee, although he never played in the minors coming up, he did see action in the minors as his big league career ended. He played in the minor leagues for seven seasons (most of them in the American Association) before hanging up his spikes after the 1926 campaign. Ironically, he took up umpiring (considering he decked an ump back in 1911) and wound up being named a National League umpire for the 1928 season. He would umpire for only one season because during the following off-season, he contacted pneumonia and passed away at 44 years old on March 13, 1929. It is puzzling why Magee has never been seriously considered for membership in baseball's Hall of Fame because his hitting numbers proved he was one of the more dominating players of his time.

50. GEORGE STONE

Born: September 3, 1877, Lost Nation, Iowa *Died*: January 3, 1945, Clinton, Iowa *Bats*: Left *Throws*: Left *Height*: 5 feet, 9 inches *Weight*: 175 *Major league debut*: April 20, 1903 (second game) (Philadelphia at Boston [AL]) *Last major league game*: October 9, 1910 (second game) (Cleveland at St. Louis [AL])

Major league Iron Man from: July 1, 1907, to June 21, 1908 *Consecutive games played*: 425 *Games as major league Iron Man*: 146 (consecutive games 280 through 425) *Team played for during streak*: St. Louis Browns (AL) *Primary position played*: Outfield *Game missed before streak*: August 12, 1905 (St. Louis at Philadelphia) *First game played of streak*: August 14, 1905 (St. Louis at Philadelphia) *Last game played of streak*: June 20, 1908 (New York at St. Louis) *Game missed to end streak*: June 21, 1908 (New York at St. Louis)

Consecutive Game Streak's Statistical Totals

Year	G	AB	R	H	2B	3B	HR	RBI	BB	SO	AVG	SLG	SB
1905	60	247	25	59	11	2	2	—	—	—	.239	.324	9
1906	154	581	91	208	25	20	6	71	52	—	.358	.501	35
1907	155	596	77	191	13	11	4	59	59	—	.320	.399	23
1908	56	217	35	65	11	3	1	—	—	—	.300	.392	8
Total	425	1641	228	523	60	36	13	*130*	*111*	—	.319	.423	75

Although George Stone's big league career was quite short in length (just seven seasons), he took full advantage of his chance to be in the major leagues by serving as a regular player for just about his entire career (with the exception of his extremely abbreviated time in a Boston Americans uniform). Although he made his major league debut in Boston during the dawning of the 1903 season, that year he was used only as a pinch hitter on two occasions. Spending the rest of the season in the minors, Boston sold Stone to the Washington Senators organization in January 1904. After one season with Senators' system, he was sent back to Boston on January 16, 1905, and was immediately shipped off to the St. Louis Browns. It was with the Browns that he spent the remainder of his big league career.

The Browns had big plans for Stone. With the left field position being vacant thanks to Jesse Burkett being sent to Boston in the trade that brought Stone to the Browns, manager Jimmy McAleer immediately inserted Stone into the position. In 1905 (his rookie season), Stone had a year that would have easily garnered rookie of the year honors (if the award had been in existence). Besides leading the Browns in every offensive category except RBI and base on balls, he led the American League in at-bats (632), hits (187), total bases (259) and games played by an outfielder (154). Additionally, he finished second to the Philadelphia Athletics' Harry Davis in home runs and runner-up to the Athletics' Topsy Hartsel in times reaching base. The 1905 season was also eventful because on August 14, 1905, he started his consecutive playing streak with 60 contests left on the Browns' schedule. All the production Stone achieved that season had little effect on where the Browns finished as the team easily captured the basement position in the standings. He followed up his rookie performance by having another enormous year at the plate in 1906. This season, he did even better by capturing all the team's statistical honors and proved he was one of the top hitters in the game as he led the league in hitting, slugging percentage, on base percentage, total bases and times reaching base. Additionally, he had the American League's second-best mark in hits and triples and as the season closed out extended his playing streak to 214 contests. Stone's Most Valuable Player-caliber performance was a contributing factor to the Browns' improving as they finished in fifth place with a 76–73 record (the team's best year since 1902 when the club finished in second place). Midway through the following season, he took over baseball's Iron Man title when Philadelphia's Sherry Magee sat out a game on July 1, 1907. For the third straight season, Stone put up numbers that were quite impressive as he hit a team-leading .320 average (good enough for third in the league behind Detroit Tigers Ty Cobb and Sam Crawford). He paced the league in times on base and finished runner-up in hits and on base percentage. After one season of finishing above .500 in winning percentage, the Browns reverted to their losing ways as they came in in sixth place with a 69–83 record. In the latter part of June 1908, Stone missed a week's worth of action. As a result, when he missed the Browns' home game against the New York Highlanders on June 21, 1908, his playing streak came to an end after 425 consecutive contests. After three straight seasons of impressive offensive numbers, Stone started a downward trend in his performance. His average dropped off nearly 40 points as he hit .281 and had just 31 runs knocked in during the entire 1908 campaign. Despite his statistical subpar year, the Browns had one of their best years in their history as they finished with an 83–69 record and only six and a half games behind the pennant-winning Tigers when the season ended.

After going four seasons and rarely missing a contest, Stone suffered an ankle injury that curtailed his playing time in 1909 to just 83 games. The 1910 season was his last in the majors as he finished with a career worst .256 average. He played parts of two years with Milwaukee of the American Association before hanging up his spikes as a player. He eventually stayed in the game by becoming a minor league owner and then a league president.

51. JIGGS DONAHUE

Born: July 13, 1879, Springfield, Ohio *Died*: July 19, 1913, Columbus, Ohio *Bats*: Left *Throws*: Left *Height*: 6 feet, 1 inch *Weight*: 178 *Major league debut*: September 10, 1900 (Pittsburgh at Brooklyn [NL]) *Last major league game*: October 2, 1909 (second game) (Washington at Philadelphia [AL])

Major league Iron Man from: June 21, 1908, to June 24, 1908 *Consecutive games played*: 413 *Games as major league Iron Man*: 3 (consecutive games 411 through 413) *Team played for during streak*: Chicago White Sox (AL) *Primary position played*: First base *Game missed before streak*: August 30, 1905 (Washington at Chicago) *First game played of streak*: August 31, 1905 (Washington at Chicago) *Last game played of streak*: June 23, 1908 (Chicago at Detroit) *Game missed to end streak*: June 24, 1908 (Chicago at Cleveland)

Consecutive Game Streak's Statistical Totals

Year	G	AB	R	H	2B	3B	HR	RBI	BB	SO	AVG	SLG	SB
1905	44	151	24	52	12	1	0	—	—	—	.344	.437	15
1906	154	556	70	143	17	7	1	57	48	—	.257	.318	36
1907	157	609	75	158	16	4	0	68	28	—	.259	.299	27
1908	58	211	19	48	7	2	0	—	—	—	.227	.280	12
Total	413	1527	188	401	52	14	1	*125*	*76*	—	.263	.317	90

Jiggs Donahue was a rather weak hitting but exemplary fielding first baseman whose major league career lasted just nine seasons. His first appearance in the big leagues was in the National League with the Pittsburgh Pirates in a game at Brooklyn on September 10, 1900. When he first made it to the majors, he was being used as a left-handed catcher. Although this experiment did not last long because he was a dismal failure at this position, he holds the 20th century record for most games caught (45) by a left-handed catcher. His career with the Pirates lasted but five games between 1900 and 1901, before Pittsburgh sold him to the American League's Milwaukee Brewers in April 1901. It wasn't until the first week of July, though, that he signed a contract to play for them. When he got into the Brewers' lineup, he split his time between catching and covering first base. In 37 contests, he proved he could handle major league pitching by hitting .318 and slugging at a .439 clip. The franchise moved to St. Louis for the 1902 season and became the Browns. Browns manager McAleer had Donahue mainly riding the bench and used him only as a backup catcher. After the season, St. Louis released him. The next year, he went back to Milwaukee and played in the minors with their American Association team. A year later, he won a spot on the Chicago White Sox's roster for the 1904 campaign. Originally signed as a backup to starting first baseman Frank Isbell, he was groomed to take over the role as the season progressed.

White Sox manager Fielder Jones decided to make Donahue the permanent first baseman with the commencement of the 1905 season. On the last day of August that year, his Iron Man playing streak started during a White Sox home game against the Washington Senators. When the season closed out, the 26-year-old first sacker had proved his worth by having team-high marks in RBI and stolen bases and being tied with teammate George Davis for most hits in the club with 153 base knocks. He also led the American League first basemen in putouts, assists, double plays and fielding average. Although the White Sox ended in last place in home runs with only 11 clouts, they fell just a couple of games short of winning the American League title from the Philadelphia Athletics. Donahue became such a stabilizing presence at first base that in 1906 he did not miss a single game the entire season. Although he did not top the team in any offensive department except for at-bats, he produced a .257 average and drove home 57 runners in helping the White Sox win the American League pennant by three games over the New York Highlanders. Defensively, he captured the fielding Triple Crown for first basemen by leading in fielding, putouts and assists along with most games played at the position. It was remarkable that the White Sox had made it to the world championship series because the team had an overall anemic batting average of .230. Because of this stat, they were nicknamed "the hitless wonders." In the World's Series against the crosstown rival Chicago Cubs, the Sox pitchers dominated the Cubs in the six-game series as the White Sox won their first championship. Even though Donahue had the reputation of being a weak hitter, he stepped up to the task by going 6 for 18 for a .333 average. And being tied with teammate shortstop George Rohe for the highest batting average in the series. Donahue repeated his true Iron Man performance by playing every inning of all the White Sox's games in 1907 along with accomplishing the league lead in at-bats and having club season marks in hits and RBI. For the third straight campaign, he performed magic with the glove that would have easily earned him a Gold Glove as he paced the first sackers in every major fielding category. In addition, he extended his playing streak to 355 games, good for second place in the majors just behind the Browns' left fielder George Stone. The White Sox did not repeat as champions but finished a solid third as the Detroit Tigers claimed the league crown. On June 21, 1908, Stone's consecutive playing string finally came to an end. On that date, Donahue took over the Iron Man role but his reign was very short because just three games later, on June 24 in a game at Cleveland, skipper Jones decided to rest Donahue due to his batting average being about 30 points lower then normal. This resulted in his games played streak being snapped after 413 contests. He ended the year appearing in just 93 contests and came in with a career low .204 batting average.

By the start of the 1909 season, Donahue had relinquished the first base job to Isbell. He appeared in only two games for the White Sox before being sent in a trade on May 16, 1909, to the Washington Senators. He finished the year out with the Senators by manning their first base position for 81 games. Although he did not know it at the time, when he played in the season finale on October 2, this turned out to be his final appearance in a major league uniform. Over the next couple of years, he returned to the Chicago area to play in a semipro circuit and also dabble in running several area bowling alleys. When the occasion presented itself, he was always trying to make the White Sox roster but this never came to fruition. Eventually, he began a mental deterioration and wound up being placed in an asylum. The cause was paresis (syphilis) and this eventually caused his premature death on July 19, 1913, just six days past his 34th birthday.

52. TOM JONES

Born: January 22, 1877, Honesdale, Pennsylvania *Died*: June 19, 1923, Danville, Pennsylvania *Bats* Right *Throws*: Right *Height*: 6 feet, 1 inch *Weight*: 195 *Major league debut*: August 25, 1902 (Chicago at Baltimore [AL]) *Last major league game*: October 9, 1910 (Detroit at Chicago [AL])

Major league Iron Man from: June 24, 1908, to May 20, 1909 *Consecutive games played*: 451 *Games as major league Iron Man*: 122 (consecutive games 330 through 451) *Team played for during streak*: St. Louis Browns (AL) *Primary position played*: First base *Game missed before streak*: May 30, 1906 (second game) (St. Louis at Cleveland) *First game played of streak*: May 31, 1906 (St. Louis at Cleveland) *Last game played of streak*: May 19, 1909 (New York at St. Louis) *Game missed to end streak*: May 20, 1909 (New York at St. Louis)

Consecutive Game Streak's Statistical Totals:

Year	G	AB	R	H	2B	3B	HR	RBI	BB	SO	AVG	SLG	SB
1906	116	437	41	106	20	3	0	—	—	—	.243	.302	22
1907	155	549	52	137	17	3	0	34	34	—	.250	.291	24
1908	155	549	43	135	14	2	1	50	30	—	.246	.284	18
1909	25	87	7	18	1	0	0	—	—	—	.207	.218	1
Total	451	1622	143	396	52	8	1	84	64	—	.244	.288	65

Tom Jones was a decent fielding first baseman who had a relatively brief career (eight seasons) with three American League teams. His power hitting was on the very weak side; in over 4,000 plate appearances, he hit only four homers. These numbers reflect one of the lowest homer ratios in major league history. Even with his lack of power, Jones was a regular starter his entire career in the big leagues with the exception of his rookie season with the Baltimore Orioles in 1902. He made his major league debut against the Chicago White Sox on August 25, 1902. Playing in 37 games, he was a pleasant surprise for Baltimore as he came in with a .283 batting average. With the Orioles moving over to New York for the 1903 season, Jones was out of a job as the club decided to go with John Ganzel at first base.

Jones spent a year out of the major leagues before returning to the St. Louis Browns for the 1904 season. With the Browns' previous first baseman, John Anderson, going over to the New York Highlanders, St. Louis was looking for a new player to fill the position. Jones took over the job and appeared in all of the Browns' games that year. He hit .243 and led the team with 625 at-bats and tied with outfielder Snags Heidrick for the most triples. Jones followed that up with another decent year in 1905 but it did not help the cellar-dwelling club much as they were over 40 games behind the league champion Philadelphia Athletics. The next year, he had missed nearly half of the Browns' games up to May 31, 1906, when he started a playing streak in a contest at Cleveland. A couple of weeks earlier, he set an American League record for most putouts by a first baseman in a nine-inning game. During the May 11 game, he had 22 putouts out of a possible 27 chances. The other five putouts were two strikeouts, two fly balls to the outfield and a putout by the second baseman. Although he drove home only 30 runners for the entire year, he helped the Browns improve to fifth place in the league standings. In the 1907 season, he extended his playing streak to 271 by the year's conclusion. He hit a consistent .250 and with 24 base swipes edged out teammate George Stone, the team's left fielder, for the club's stolen base crown. The Browns also showed their consistency (in a negative way) by finishing in the bottom half of the standings for a fifth straight season. In the following campaign (1908), Jones had the third-longest major league playing streak as June was starting to wind down. In a matter of just three days, he went from third to first when he inherited the Iron Man title on June 24, 1908, as teammate Stone and the White Sox's first baseman, Jiggs Donahue, saw their long playing streaks end. A few weeks after becoming the Iron Man, he hit an inside-the-park home run against Washington Senator rookie pitcher Eli Cates. This was his first homer since the 1904 season. He finished with a .246 batting average and drove home an even 50 runs. He also led the league's first basemen in games played, putouts and double plays. The Browns finally made it out of the second division by having a solid fourth-place finish in the final results. Early the next season, as his streak was nearing the 500-game milestone, it came to an sudden end when after appearing in 451 straight games he was benched (along with second baseman Jimmy Williams) for the May 20, 1909, contest against the New York Highlanders by Browns' manager Jimmy McAleer. The Browns' skipper hoped to add some speed and youth to the team's lineup, in addition to trying to end the club's losing streak. Jones was replaced in the box score that day at first base by Ham Patterson. The lineup changes seemed to help as the Browns ended their losing streak by beating the Highlanders 2–1. Within days, Jones was back in the lineup at his normal first base position.

While Stone was still the everyday first baseman, his time with the Browns (after six years) was coming to a close. Two months after his playing streak ended, St. Louis and the Detroit Tigers decided to swap first basemen. In return for Jones, the Browns got Claude Rossman from the Tigers. With the Browns being out of the pennant race, the team decided to make changes and Jones was made expendable. The Tigers acquired Jones for their stretch run for the 1909 American League flag. He responded by hitting an impressive .281 in the 44 contests he was in the Tigers' lineup. In the end, the Tigers outlasted the Philadelphia Athletics for the league championship. In the hotly contested series for the world championship, the Tigers gave it their best but were defeated by the Pittsburgh Pirates in seven games. Finally making it to a World's Series, Jones played in all seven contests and contributed a .250 hitting average as he went 6 for 24. Additionally, he provided Detroit with the steady defense that was expected of him at the premier sack. The following season, his final major league season, he hit .255 and drove in 45 Tigers runners in 135 contests. He played his final major league contest on October 9, 1910, in the season closer at Chicago.

53. ED KONETCHY

Born: September 3, 1885, LaCrosse, Wisconsin *Died*: May 27, 1947, Fort Worth, Texas *Bats*: Right *Throws*: Right *Height*: 6 feet, 2½ inches *Weight*: 195 *Major league debut*: June 29, 1907 (St. Louis at Cincinnati [NL]) *Last major league game*: October 1, 1921 (second game) (New York at Philadelphia [NL])

Major league Iron Man from: May 20, 1909, to July 28, 1909 *Consecutive games played*: 327 *Games as major league Iron Man*: 51 (consecutive games 277 through 327) *Team played for during streak*: St. Louis Cardinals (NL) *Primary position played*: First base *Game missed before streak*: June 27, 1907 (St. Louis at Cincinnati) *First game played of streak*: June 29, 1907 (St. Louis at Cincinnati) *Last game played of streak*: July 27, 1909 (Chicago at St. Louis) *Game missed to end streak*: July 28, 1909 (first game) (Chicago at St. Louis)

Consecutive Game Streak's Statistical Totals:

Year	G	AB	R	H	2B	3B	HR	RBI	BB	SO	AVG	SLG	SB
1907	91	331	34	83	11	9	2	30	26	—	.251	.356	13
1908	154	545	46	135	19	12	5	50	38	—	.248	.354	16
1909	82	308	46	80	12	9	2	—	—	—	.260	.377	15
Total	327	1184	126	298	42	30	9	*80*	*64*	—	.252	.361	44

Ed Konetchy played all but one season of his 15-year major league career in the National League. He established a reputation as the league's best fielding first baseman. He paced all National League first basemen in fielding percentage seven times. Undoubtedly, he would have received many Gold Glove honors if this award had existed during his playing days. He put in tours of duty with the St. Louis Cardinals, Pittsburgh Pirates, Pittsburgh Rebels (of the Federal League), Boston Braves, Brooklyn Robins and the Philadelphia Phillies. Discovered by a Cardinals' scout while playing with a minor league team, he was purchased by St. Louis and signed to a big league contract. With the Cardinals searching for a permanent first baseman to replace Jake Beckley, whom the team released in May of that year, Konetchy was the perfect fit and immediately took over the job.

Konetchy put together two playing streaks long enough to attain the major league Iron Man honor. These streaks could very easily have gone unnoticed because his name was listed in a great number of the box scores at the time as Koney. His first streak started with his debut in a major league uniform on June 29, 1907, while the Cardinals were paying a visit to Cincinnati to play the Reds. He competed in 91 contests and hit for a .251 batting average when the 1907 season concluded. During this era, the Cardinals were consistent occupants of the second division of the standings. The 1907 season was no different as they were over 55 games behind the first-place Chicago Cubs and claimed the bottom spot in the standings. The following year, while the Cardinals were repeating as titleholders of the worst record in the National League, Konetchy appeared in every game in 1908 as their first baseman. He led his playing position with 122 assists along with landing second place in putouts. He put in another consistent performance at the plate by hitting .248 that year. Less than two months into the following campaign, he succeeded the St. Louis Browns' first baseman, Tom Jones, as baseball's Iron Man on May 20, 1909. Konetchy stretched his consecutive-games-played streak to 327 before missing the first contests of his major league career by sitting out a double-header against the Cubs in St. Louis on July 28, 1909. These were the only two contests he missed the entire season. This 327-game Iron Man streak set a mark for most consecutive games played by a National Leaguer at the start of a big league career, a record that is now held by the Cubs' Ernie Banks with 424 games established in 1956. Konetchy's final batting statistics that season showed that he was the team's major offensive leader as he led all Cardinals players in every category except walks. He also finished in a tie for second place in the National League in both triples and times reaching base. Defensively, he had enough putouts and assists in 1909 to lead the National League's first basemen in both these departments. As for the Cardinals, they finally escaped the cellar in 1909 but still finished in the second division with a 54–98 record, good enough for a seventh-place showing.

Although Konetchy's first Iron Man streak came to an end in the middle of the 1909 season, there were still many seasons left in this dedicated ballplayer's career. He achieved another playing streak a little later in his career that made him a two-time major league Iron Man in the early stages of the 1912 season. Details about this second Iron Man streak and the duration of his big league career are included in a later profile.

54. JOHN HUMMEL

Born: April 4, 1883, Bloomsburg, Pennsylvania *Died*: May 18, 1959, Springfield, Massachusetts *Bats*: Right *Throws*: Right *Height*: 5 feet, 11 inches *Weight*: 160 *Major league debut*: September 12, 1905 (first game) (Brooklyn at New York [NL]) *Last major league game*: September 2, 1918 (second game) (Boston at New York [AL])

Major league Iron Man from: July 28, 1909, to August 7, 1909 *Consecutive games played*: 285 *Games as major league Iron Man*: 9 (consecutive games 277 through 285) *Team played for during streak*: Brooklyn Superbas (NL) *Primary positions played*: First base, shortstop, third base and outfield *Game missed before streak*: August 27, 1907 (Chicago at Brooklyn) *First game played of streak*: August 28, 1907 (Chicago at Brooklyn) *Last game played of streak*: August 6, 1909 (Brooklyn at Pittsburgh) *Game missed to end streak*: August 7, 1909 (Brooklyn at Chicago)

Consecutive Game Streak's Statistical Totals

Year	G	AB	R	H	2B	3B	HR	RBI	BB	SO	AVG	SLG	SB
1907	36	127	13	24	4	1	0	—	—	—	.189	.236	2
1908	154	594	51	143	11	12	4	41	34	—	.241	.320	20
1909	95	355	37	104	9	8	3	—	—	—	.293	.389	8
Total	285	1076	101	271	24	21	7	41	34	—	.252	.333	30

John Hummel was a versatile career utility player who played for a dozen seasons in the major leagues for the Brooklyn Superbas (Robins) and New York Yankees. He was in his first year of playing organized ball when in the late summer, the Superbas purchased his contract. Within a few days, he made his major league debut on September 12, 1905, against the New York Giants. He immediately took over Brooklyn's second base job from Charlie Malay and held the position for the rest of the season. Hummel played in 30 games and hit .266 in the short time he was in the lineup. Because the team finished in the basement with a dreadful 48–104 record, the 1905 season turned out to be the final year for longtime Brooklyn manager Ned Hanlon. Patsy Donovan took over the team in 1906 and he used Hummel more as a utility player. This caused Hummel to be replaced at second base by rookie Whitey Alperman. Hummel got into 97 contests that year and shared backup duties at second base, first base and left field. He hit only a .199 average but connected for his first career homer in July 1906. Even though the Superbas finished 50 games behind in the win column, the team showed great improvement by winning 18 more games than during the previous season (1905) and jumped three spots to claim fifth place.

The following year, Hummel retained his status as a utility player. It seems that whenever Donovan wanted to give one of his regular players a day off, he easily penciled in Hummel for the position that was open. On August 28, 1907, Hummel commenced a playing streak in Brooklyn against the Chicago Cubs that would continue for nearly two years. His final 1907 batting average jumped 35 points as he hit .234 that season. The Superbas almost duplicated their 1906 performance and repeated their fifth-place showing. By playing games at first base, second base, shortstop and a clear majority in left field, Hummel did not miss a single contest in the 154 games played in 1908. His batting average just slightly improved and he achieved team highs in at-bats, hits, triples (tied with Harry Lumley) and finished second with 20 stolen bases. His at-bats total (594) was the second highest in the league, trailing only Philadelphia's Eddie Grant. Brooklyn started getting close to the basement as the club finished seventh, just four games ahead of the last-place St. Louis Cardinals. Starting another year in his utility man role, Hummel amazingly was keeping his playing streak alive as he shifted back and forth between first base, second base, shortstop and the outfield. He had just passed 275 games played when he took over the sport's Iron Man role from the Cardinals' first baseman, Ed Konetchy. Hummel held onto the durability title for only nine games as his streak ended in Chicago on August 7, 1909, after 285 straight contests. Being in the lineup every day seemed to improve his performance as he was hitting .293 when his streak ended. He eventually came in with a .280 average (his best year to date) and was the Brooklyn player who drove in the most runners (52) in 1909. Outfielder Lumley took over the club from Donovan but the move had no effect as the Superbas spent another season in the second division.

Another managerial change occurred in 1910 as Bill Dahlen took the helm from Lumley. One of his first moves was to let Hummel have his old job back as the starting second baseman, replacing Alperman. Hummel again led the team in RBI but also took the league's strikeout crown by whiffing 81 times during the course of the year. Defensively, he led the second basemen in games played and fielding average. He retained his infield job for a second season and reinforced the notion that he could handle the job by again leading the second basemen with a .972 fielding accuracy. In 1912, he returned to his utility role for the rest of his major league playing career. He left the Dodgers after the 1915 season and chose to play in the minor leagues for three seasons. He returned for one more year in the big leagues by signing on with the New York Yankees, who were shorthanded during the 1918 season because of World War I. He made his final appearance on September 2 in a Yankees' home game against the Boston Red Sox. With his big league career at an end, Hummel returned to the minors to play, coach and even have time to manage a half dozen teams in 10 years before deciding to hang up his baseball uniform for good.

55. GEORGE McBRIDE

Born: November 20, 1880, Milwaukee, Wisconsin *Died*: July 2, 1973, Milwaukee, Wisconsin *Bats*: Right *Throws*: Right *Height*: 5 feet, 11 inches *Weight*: 170 *Major league debut*: September 12, 1901 (first game) (Chicago at Milwaukee [AL]) *Last major league game*: July 29, 1920 (second game) (Washington at Detroit [AL])

Major league Iron Man from: August 7, 1909, to May 6, 1910 *Consecutive games played*: 330 *Games as major league Iron Man*: 72 (consecutive games 259 through 330) *Team played for during streak*: Washington Senators (AL) *Primary position played*: Shortstop *Game missed before streak*: (did not play any major league games in 1907) *First game played of streak*: April 14, 1908 (Washington at Boston) *Last game played of streak*: May 5, 1910 (Washington at Philadelphia) *Game missed to end streak*: May 6, 1910 (Washington at Philadelphia)

Consecutive Game Streak's Statistical Totals

Year	G	AB	R	H	2B	3B	HR	RBI	BB	SO	AVG	SLG	SB
1908	155	518	47	120	10	6	0	34	41	—	.232	.274	12
1909	156	504	38	118	16	0	0	34	36	—	.234	.266	17
1910	19	65	3	10	3	1	0	—	—	—	.154	.231	1
Total	330	1087	88	248	29	7	0	68	77	—	.228	.268	30

George McBride spent time with four major league teams during a 16-year career, most of which were in a Washington Senators uniform. He was a very weak hitter and it was his defensive capabilities that kept him in the big leagues for so many years. In fact, during his era, many baseball historians consider McBride the best defensive fielding shortstop in the American League. Making his debut on September 12, 1901, he played only three contests that year for the Milwaukee Brewers. He would not make it back to the majors until the 1905 season when he played for the Pittsburgh Pirates and then served strictly as a backup third baseman until he was traded to the St. Louis Cardinals in early July of that season.

The Cardinals were hoping that they had found a new shortstop in McBride. They had been in the midst of trying to find a replacement for their previous regular shortstop, Danny Shay, who was out due to his finger being amputated. McBride played 80 games at shortstop after his acquisition from Pittsburgh but hit only .217 during this chance. The next season, he played in 90 games but his batting numbers sunk even further as he finished with an extremely low .169 average. This was not conducive to being on a major league team's roster, no matter how effective a player was defensively. As a result, he was out of the majors for the 1907 season before signing up to play for the Washington Senators. Washington's manager, Joe Cantillon, immediately put McBride into the regular lineup as the team's shortstop, replacing Dave Altizer (who was relegated to being a utility infielder). With his arrival in Washington, McBride finally found a permanent home. In the Senators' season opener in Boston on April 14, 1908, McBride's consecutive-games-played streak started. Not missing a single game at short that season, he led the league's shortstops with 155 games played and 58 double plays. Although he hit only .232 for the season, it was one of his better years at the plate. During most of this era, the Senators usually found themselves in a battle to keep from finishing at the bottom of the final standings. This year was no different as they achieved a seventh-place final result, finishing just ahead of the New York Highlanders. The 1909 season results saw McBride having another decent year with the bat for this weak hitting shortstop. He hit .234 and led the Senators in numerous offensive categories. Although McBride was one of the most mild-mannered players of his time, there was one game in 1909 that he was ejected for arguing a call when umpire Fred Perrine tossed him from a contest in the first inning of the second game of a double-header in Boston on July 3. The situation did not affect his playing streak because no suspension was handed out by the American League president and therefore McBride did not miss any games. By the next game, McBride was back at his normal playing position at shortstop. Just over a month later, he inherited the major league Iron Man title (with a streak of 259 games played) from the Brooklyn Superbas' utility infielder, John Hummel, on August 7, 1909. By season's end, this streak stood at 311 games as McBride played the full slate of 156 games at short and led the American League's shortstops in putouts, double plays and fielding average. As for the team, the Senators' performance on the diamond was just atrocious as they came in with a 42–110 record and were so deeply entrenched in the basement position that they were 20 games from their closest competitors, the seventh-place St. Louis Browns. Early the following year, McBride suffered a minor injury in the May 5, 1910, game at Philadelphia. The next day, his playing streak was snapped at 330 games when he was not in the Senators' lineup. In addition, he missed two additional games after that before starting up another playing streak that eventually made him the Iron Man a second time.

McBride still had many more years left at manning the shortstop position for the Senators. Because he is one of the few players to become a two-time major league Iron Man, additional facts and information about his second streak and the rest of his playing days are contained in a later profile of his performance.

56. Eddie Grant

Born: May 21, 1883, Franklin, Massachusetts *Died*: October 5, 1918, Argonne Forest, France *Bats*: Left *Throws*: Right *Height*: 5 feet, 11½ inches *Weight*: 168 *Major league debut*: August 4, 1905 (Cleveland at Boston [AL]) *Last major league game*: October 6, 1915 (second game) (New York at Boston [NL])

Major league Iron Man from: May 6, 1910, to June 29, 1910 *Consecutive games played*: 324 *Games as major league Iron Man*: 43 (consecutive games 282 through 324) *Team played for during streak*: Philadelphia Phillies (NL) *Primary position played*: Third base *Game missed before streak*: June 12, 1908 (St. Louis at Philadelphia) *First game played of streak*: June 13, 1908 (Chicago at Philadelphia) *Last game played of streak*: June 28, 1910 (Philadelphia at New York) *Game missed to end streak*: June 29, 1910 (Philadelphia at New York)

Consecutive Game Streak's Statistical Totals

Year	G	AB	R	H	2B	3B	HR	RBI	BB	SO	AVG	SLG	SB
1908	113	472	55	116	10	7	0	—	—	—	.246	.297	19
1909	154	631	75	170	18	4	1	37	35	—	.269	.315	28
1910	57	222	29	61	3	1	1	—	18	24	.275	.311	16
Total	324	1325	159	347	31	12	2	37	53	24	.262	.308	63

Although Eddie Grant played in the major league for parts of 10 seasons (four of which were as a regular player), he is mostly noted in baseball circles as the most prominent major leaguer killed in combat during World War I. He was college educated when he started playing baseball and further expanded his education while playing to get a law degree so he could eventually become a practicing attorney. He had played some college and semipro ball, but had no organized ball experience before making his major league debut as an emergency replacement player for the Cleveland Indians in a game against the Boston Americans on August 4, 1905. His first taste of big league experience lasted only two games because the Indians no longer needed his services. He spent the next year in the minors fine tuning his ballplaying skills. The following year (1907), the Philadelphia Phillies decided to take a chance on him. That season, he shared the team's third base duties with Ernie Courtney. In 74 contests, he hit .243 and drove home 19 runners.

Phillies' manager Billy Murray had been so impressed with Grant's play the previous season that with the beginning of the 1908 season, he named Grant the team's permanent third baseman and relegated Courtney to a backup and utility infielder role. A little more than two months into his first season as a regular, Grant commenced his consecutive-games-played streak on June 13, 1908, in a game against the Chicago Cubs. Most of the last 113 consecutive games he played on the 1908 schedule were at third base, but on about a dozen occasions Murray used him to fill in at shortstop when regular shortstop Mickey Doolan needed a rest. Grant finished the year with a .244 batting average and had more at-bats (598) than any other major leaguer that season. He also paced the league's third sackers with 22 double plays and (on a negative note) 35 errors. Grant's efforts contributed to a solid fourth-place finish for the Phillies. The following year (1909), he didn't miss a single inning as he played all 154 games at third base. In addition to leading the majors again in at-bats (631), he came in second (behind the New York Giants' Larry Doyle) in base hits and also registered another team high in runs scored along with hitting .269. The Phillies, unfortunately, fell into the second division by finishing in fifth place. A month into the following campaign, Grant achieved Iron Man status by becoming the active leader in consecutive games played on May 6, 1910, when the streak of Washington Senators' shortstop George McBride ended. Grant's reign as Iron Man would last only 43 more games, coming to an abrupt halt. In consecutive game 324, he got into an argument with the umpire in the June 28, game at New York against the Giants. In what was the standard practice at the time, any verbal disagreements with umpires were immediately reviewed by the league president. In this case, National League president Lynch decided to suspend Grant for a couple of games. Upon his return to the lineup after the suspension, Grant went on to have a solid year both offensively and defensively as he hit .268, drove home 67 Phillies, and led the league's third basemen with 152 games played and 193 putouts.

Eddie Grant: As the Phillies' third baseman, he put together a run of 324 games that ended in late June 1910. He was the most prominent major leaguer to lose his life while serving in France during World War I.

The 1910 season turned out to be Grant's last year with Philadelphia. He was traded in February 1911 to the Cincinnati Reds for Hans Lobert and Dode Paskert. In his first season with the Reds, he replaced Lobert as the new third baseman. He hit only .223 for the 1911 season and, as a result, was relegated to a utility infielder role for the rest of his time with the Reds. Early in the 1913 season, the Reds put Grant on the move by trading him to the New York Giants. He was used so rarely that from the time he arrived in New York in May to the end of the year, he participated in only 27 contests for the Giants. He finally wound up on a winner as the Giants had won the National League pennant that season. While the Giants were losing the World's Series to the Philadelphia Athletics in five games, Grant made only two appearances. In the second game of the series, he pinch-ran for catcher Larry McLean in the 10th inning and scored the game's first run in the Giants' only victory over Philadelphia.

In the fourth game, he pinch-hit for pitcher Rube Marquard and popped out in foul territory. He put in two more years with New York as a backup player before retiring from the game just before the start of the 1916 season. Although he intended to start a new career as a lawyer, his plans changed a year later when the United States got involved in World War I. He enlisted in the army and soon after became a commissioned officer. He eventually was sent to France and was killed in action in the Argonne Forest on October 5, 1918.

57. Eddie Collins

Born: May 2, 1887, Millerton, New York *Died*: March 25, 1951, Boston, Massachusetts *Bats*: Left *Throws*: Right *Height*: 5 feet, 9 inches *Weight*: 175 *Major league debut*: September 17, 1906 (Philadelphia at Chicago [AL]) *Last major league game*: August 2, 1930 (second game) (Boston at Philadelphia [AL])

Major league Iron Man from: June 29, 1910, to October 5, 1910 *Consecutive games played*: 308 *Games as major league Iron Man*: 93 (consecutive games 216 through 308) *Team played for during streak*: Philadelphia Athletics (AL) *Primary position played*: Second base *Game missed before streak*: October 6, 1908 (Philadelphia at Washington) *First game played of streak*: October 7, 1908 (first game) (Philadelphia at Boston) *Last game played of streak*: October 4, 1910 (Boston at Philadelphia) *Game missed to end streak*: October 5, 1910 (New York at Philadelphia)

Consecutive Game Streak's Statistical Totals

Year	G	AB	R	H	2B	3B	HR	RBI	BB	SO	AVG	SLG	SB
1908	2	6	1	1	1	0	0	—	—	—	.167	.333	0
1909	153	571	104	198	30	10	3	56	62	—	.347	.450	63
1910	153	581	81	188	16	15	3	81	49	—	.324	.418	81
Total	308	1158	186	387	47	25	6	*137*	*111*	—	.334	.434	144

During a good portion of his playing career, Eddie "Cocky" Collins was one of baseball's best players. He maintained this status through the end of the deadball era and before Babe Ruth became the dominant player in the 1920s. His nickname came from his confidence in his baseball playing skills, not from his attitude. In his 25 years in the major leagues, Collins played for only the Philadelphia Athletics and the Chicago White Sox. He is one of just a few players to put together long playing streaks to qualify as baseball's Iron Man on two occasions. After attending Columbia University, he made his big league debut late in the 1906 season. He got into only a total of 20 games his first two seasons before securing a spot on the 1908 Athletics' roster as a utility infielder.

Collins was rotated between second base and shortstop in 1908 in addition to an occasional appearance in the outfield. With only two games remaining in the 1908 season, he started his run of consecutive games on October 7 in Boston. He finished the year with what would be a career-low .273 average (yet it was still the team high) for him as Connie Mack's Athletics finished sixth in the American League standings. With the arrival of the 1909 season, the 22-year-old Collins was made the team's starting second baseman. It was one of the wisest decisions Mack ever made. If it wasn't for Ty Cobb's great performance for Detroit that year, Collins would have led the league's hitters in several offensive categories. While posting team highs in several categories, he also finished runner-up to Cobb in hits, on base percentage and batting average. In forming a dazzling defensive trio (along with shortstop Jack Barry and third baseman Frank Baker), he had what would have been a Gold Glove year at second, as he led all the league's second sackers in every statistical category except errors committed. By securing the infield and putting up the offensive numbers, Collins was the team's Most Valuable Player as Philadelphia finished a close second to the repeating American League champions (Detroit Tigers) when the season ended. The following year on June 29, 1910, Collins became the Iron Man of the sport when the reigning Iron Man, the Philadelphia Phillies' Eddie Grant, was suspended because of an argument with an umpire in a previous game. Collins didn't miss a game all year until the very end of the 1910 season. The Athletics coasted to the league title, with the closest team being nearly 15 games in the rear, and Mack rested several of his regulars in preparation for the World's Series. Collins was one of those players and as a result his run of consecutive game appearances ended after 308 contests. In the World's Series against the Chicago Cubs, he showed off his playing skills by leading all series players with a .429 batting average, nine hits and four doubles as he, along with Baker and outfielder Danny Murphy, helped lead the Athletics' offensive charge that resulted in a five-game series victory over the Cubs.

Eddie Collins: He was a Hall of Fame second baseman for the Philadelphia Athletics and Chicago White Sox. He had two streaks that qualified him to be the Iron Man. The second streak ran for 478 games and was a record for second basemen. The mark would later be broken in the late 1950s by Nellie Fox of the White Sox.

With all of the infield back the following year (except first baseman Harry Davis, who was replaced by Stuffy McInnis), Collins had another solid year on the diamond by hitting .365 as the Athletics again took the American League flag in 1911. He had a below-average performance (for him) in the World's Series as he produced just six hits for a .286 average, but Philadelphia still repeated as champions by besting the New York Giants in six games. The 1912 season was an off year for the team as they dropped to third place in the standings and came up 15 games short of winning another title. Collins led the Athletics in hitting for the fifth straight season as he edged teammate Baker by just one point along with leading the American League with 137 runs scored. In 1913, the Athletics took the lead in the American League by the end of the first month of play and never fell out of first place as they claimed their third league title in four years. Collins again had another superior year at the plate by repeating as the runs scored leader in the American League plus having team highs in batting (.345) and triples (13). In the World's Series, he went 8 for 19 for a .421 average with five runs scored and two triples. Philadelphia won another championship as they conquered the Giants in five contests. Due to Collins being a two-time major league Iron Man, more information about his second streak and other aspects of his outstanding Hall of Fame career are contained in a later profile.

58. Zack Wheat

Born: May 23, 1888, Hamilton, Missouri *Died*: March 11, 1972, Sedalia, Missouri *Bats*: Left *Throws*: Right *Height*: 5 feet, 10 inches *Weight*: 170 *Major league debut*: September 11, 1909 (first game) (Brooklyn at New York [NL]) *Last major league game*: September 21, 1927 (Cleveland at Philadelphia [AL])
Major league Iron Man from: October 5, 1910, to August 16, 1911 *Consecutive games played*: 287 *Games as major league Iron Man*: 110 (consecutive games 178 through 287) *Team played for during streak*: Brooklyn Superbas (NL) *Primary position played*: Outfield *Game missed before streak*: September 9, 1909 (Brooklyn at New York) *First game played of streak*: September 11, 1909 (first game) (Brooklyn at New York) *Last game played of streak*: August 15, 1911 (Brooklyn at Boston) *Game missed to end streak*: August 16, 1911 (Pittsburgh at Brooklyn)

Consecutive Game Streak's Statistical Totals

Year	G	AB	R	H	2B	3B	HR	RBI	BB	SO	AVG	SLG	SB
1909	26	102	15	31	7	3	0	4	6	—	.304	.431	1
1910	156	606	78	172	36	15	2	55	47	80	.284	.403	16
1911	105	407	44	114	18	12	4	—	26	49	.280	.413	15
Total	287	1115	137	317	61	30	6	59	79	129	.284	.409	32

From his debut in September 1909 through the end of the 1926 season when he departed the Brooklyn scene, Zack Wheat was stationed in left field for the Brooklyn Superbas (Robins). A quiet player who was very popular with the local fans, he gained a reputation as one of the best curveball hitters in the game. National League pitchers dreaded having to pitch to him because he was one of the hardest players to get out. He spent the majority of his first two seasons of professional baseball in the minors with Shreveport and Mobile. In the middle of July 1909, the Superbas purchased his playing contract from Mobile. Within two months, he was making his major league debut at the age of 21 during the first game of a twin bill against the New York Giants where he replaced Wally Clement in left field. During that game on September 11, 1909, he also started his consecutive-games-played streak that would eventually earn him the Iron Man of baseball distinction. Playing the final 26 games of Brooklyn's 1909 schedule, he collected 31 hits and hit .304 in this short time.

Wheat played his first full year in the majors in 1910 and took in all 156 games that season. While finishing with a solid .284 batting average, he also had a high strikeout total and came in with 80 whiffs. This total was the second most strikeouts in the league behind only teammate John Hummel, who fanned 81 times. Additionally, by leading the Superbas in many offensive categories, he took over as the most effective offensive threat the team had on its roster. In the waning days of the 1910 season, Wheat took over from the Philadelphia Athletics' Eddie Collins (who was being rested in preparations for the World's Series) as baseball's new Iron Man with only 178 games played. The final standings for the 1910 season saw the Superbas finish in sixth place for the second straight season. The club was well off the pennant-winning pace of the Chicago Cubs as they were 40 games behind the league champions. Wheat's reign as the most durable player in baseball lasted 110 games and ended when a minor injury resulted in his sitting out a home game on August 16, 1911, against the Pittsburgh Pirates.

Wheat finished the season with a .287 average along with again pacing the Brooklyn team in numerous categories. Although the Superbas had another disappointing conclusion by finishing in seventh place in the final results, the bright side was the team had their best won-loss record (64–86) since the 1907 campaign. Wheat finished the 1912 season with a .305

average as he knocked in 65 runners and smacked a team-high eight homers, all while missing 30 games because of an ankle injury. He hit over .300 the next two seasons and the team started to show improvement under its new manager, Wilbert Robinson. In fact, the team became so associated with Robinson that the team's nickname was changed from the Superbas to the Robins commencing with the 1914 season. After having his worst year at the plate in 1915 with a .258 average, Wheat never again hit below .290 in a season. He was the offensive leader of the Robins as he helped drive them to the National League pennant in 1916 by leading the league in slugging percentage (.461) and total bases (262) and also compiling a team record 29-game hitting streak that would not be broken until the 1969 season. Winning the pennant meant that Brooklyn was making their first post-season appearance of any kind since the 1890 campaign. Although most of the games were closely contested, the results of the World's Series were disappointing as the Boston Red Sox beat the Robins in five games. Wheat went only 4 for 19 (for a .211 average) and was, for the most part, a nonfactor in the series. Two years later, he led the National League hitters with a .335 average. A couple of years after that, Brooklyn won the league pennant again and found themselves facing the Cleveland Indians in the 1920 World's Series. Although the Robins came out on the short end by losing the series in seven games, Wheat led all players in at-bats and base hits along with finishing in a three-way tie with Cleveland's Steve O'Neill and Charlie Jamieson for the series' best average (.333). After this series, Wheat played six more seasons with the Robins. Most impressive during this time were the .375 batting averages he compiled in both 1923 and 1924. Although these were career bests for him, the hitting numbers the St. Louis Cardinals' Rogers Hornsby put up during those years easily claimed the batting titles. After the 1926 season, the Robins no longer required Wheat's services and, because of his longtime faithful service to the Brooklyn team, was given his outright release. Soon after, he was signed by the Philadelphia Athletics but that team used him only as a part-time player. After his major league career ended when the 1927 season concluded, he played one year in the minors with the American Association before retiring. His statistics easily qualified him for Hall of Fame status, but it was not until 1959 that the veterans' committee wisely selected him for membership.

59. GEORGE MCBRIDE

Born: November 20, 1880, Milwaukee, Wisconsin *Died*: July 2, 1973, Milwaukee, Wisconsin *Bats*: Right *Throws*: Right *Height*: 5 feet, 11 inches *Weight*: 170 *Major league debut*: September 12, 1901 (first game) (Chicago at Milwaukee [AL]) *Last major league game*: July 29, 1920 (second game) (Washington at Detroit [AL])

Major league Iron Man from: August 16, 1911, to April 23, 1912 *Consecutive games played*: 295 *Games as major league Iron Man*: 50 (consecutive games 246 through 295) *Team played for during streak*: Washington Senators (AL) *Primary position played*: Shortstop *Game missed before streak*: May 9, 1910 (Washington at Philadelphia) *First game played of streak*: May 10, 1910 (Chicago at Washington) *Last game played of streak*: April 20, 1912 (Philadelphia at Washington) *Game missed to end streak*: April 23, 1912 (Washington at Boston)

Consecutive Game Streak's Statistical Totals

Year	G	AB	R	H	2B	3B	HR	RBI	BB	SO	AVG	SLG	SB
1910	135	449	51	108	16	3	1	—	—	—	.241	.296	10
1911	154	557	58	131	11	4	0	59	52	—	.235	.269	15
1912	6	21	4	4	0	0	0	—	2	—	.190	.190	0
Total	295	1027	113	243	27	7	1	59	54	—	.237	.279	25

The weak hitting but superb fielding Washington Senator shortstop had just ended a 330 game streak a few days before when he picked up where he left off by continuing to display his durability. He missed three straight Senators games between May 6 and May 9, 1910, when he commenced his second Iron Man streak in a game against the Chicago White Sox on May 10 in the nation's capital. Not missing a turn at shortstop the rest of the season, which consisted of 135 contests, he impressed the team's management by hitting .241 upon his return to the lineup and actually had a team-high 55 RBI when the final stats were issued. He also led the league's shortstops in every defensive category except errors and fielding percentage. The Senators were trying to find their way out of the lower part of the standings but still finished a dreadful seventh out of eight teams for the league championship.

In 1911, McBride regained the Iron Man title from Brooklyn left fielder Zack Wheat, whose 287-game streak stopped on August 16. McBride's streak had amounted to only 246 games when he took back baseball's durability title. For the third time in four years, McBride played the full slate of Senators games at shortstop and further extended his playing streak to 289 games when the 1911 season closed. He finished the year by having his best year at the plate with a .235 batting average and driving in 59 runners. Additionally, he again repeated as the shortstop leader in games played and double plays. Although the Senators repeated their seventh-place finish from the year before with a 64–90 record, they were comfortably ahead of the last-place St. Louis Browns in the final results. Just into the second week of the 1912 season, McBride's 295-game playing streak and second reign as baseball's Iron Man came to an abrupt end when he had a run-in with umpire Fred Westervelt during the seventh inning of the April 20, 1912, game against Philadelphia. The case immediately went before the American League president. McBride stated he did not use abusive language toward the umpire, but the league czar, Ban Johnson, still decided to suspend McBride for two games even after reviewing the case. These were the only games that McBride missed that season or his playing streak would have gone into the 1913 season.

Although McBride's second streak had ended, the Senators were responding to their new manager's way of doing things. Clark Griffith had taken over the team starting with the 1912 season and immediate results were accomplished when the team, which for so long had resided at or near the bottom of the standings, finished with an outstanding 91–61 record, good for second place in the junior circuit behind only the league champion Boston Red Sox by 14 games. While the Senators would stay in the standing's first division for several more years, McBride would hold down the team's shortstop position and be Washington's most durable player through the 1916 season. Starting with the 1917 campaign, McBride was relegated to being the backup shortstop behind his replacement, Howard Shanks. The 1917 season would be his last to get into any reasonable number of games. His playing career would continue another three seasons but his playing time was very sporadic. He made his final playing appearance in a Senators uniform in a game at Detroit on July 29, 1920. With Griffith taking a more active role as the team's president, he handed the managerial reins of the club over to McBride for the 1921 season. In his only season as a manager, McBride guided the Senators to an 80–73 record, good enough for fourth place in the final American League standings. In spring training the following year, he was injured during batting practice and this incident caused him to give up his role as the Senators' skipper. Although he never returned to managing, he did serve as a coach for several years with the Detroit Tigers in the mid- to late 1920s. He returned to his hometown of Milwaukee, Wisconsin, and lived into his 93rd year before passing away in the summer of 1973.

60. Ed Konetchy

Born: September 3, 1885, LaCrosse, Wisconsin *Died*: May 27, 1947, Fort Worth, Texas *Bats*: Right *Throws*: Right *Height*: 6 feet, 2½ inches *Weight*: 195 *Major league debut*: June 29, 1907 (St. Louis at Cincinnati [NL]) *Last major league game*: October 1, 1921 (second game) (New York at Philadelphia [NL])

Major league Iron Man from: April 23, 1912, to July 4, 1912 *Consecutive games played*: 279 *Games as major league Iron Man*: 61 (consecutive games 219 through 279) *Team played for during streak*: St. Louis Cardinals (NL) *Primary position played*: First base *Game missed before streak*: August 13, 1910 (second game) (St. Louis at Philadelphia) *First game played of streak*: August 15, 1910 (first game) (St. Louis at Boston) *Last game played of streak*: July 1, 1912 (St. Louis at Cincinnati) *Game missed to end streak*: July 4, 1912 (first game) (Chicago at St. Louis)

Consecutive Game Streak's Statistical Totals

Year	G	AB	R	H	2B	3B	HR	RBI	BB	SO	AVG	SLG	SB
1910	51	180	39	65	6	9	2	—	32	24	.361	.528	9
1911	158	571	90	165	38	13	6	88	81	63	.289	.433	27
1912	70	266	49	94	11	9	4	—	33	40	.353	.508	13
Total	279	1017	178	324	55	31	12	88	146	127	.319	.469	49

Konetchy's consecutive-games-played streak that resulted in his becoming the major league Iron Man a second time started in the first game of a double-header on August 15, 1910, in Boston, where the Cardinals were taking on the Doves. With this playing streak being less than 15 games old, he also commenced a hitting streak on August 27 until he was held hitless on September 23. The total length of this streak lasted 20 games and was the longest hitting streak in the major leagues for the 1910 season. When the season ended, he had hit over .300 for the first time in his big league career with a .302 batting average. Additionally, he led the league's first basemen in putouts, assists and fielding average along with handling more total chances that year than any first baseman. It was unfortunate that he was playing with the lowly Cardinals because he was not receiving much attention except from other managers in the league who were quite impressed with his attitude and style while playing. As for the Cardinals, the team again finished in seventh place, 10 games ahead of the last-place Doves.

Although his batting average dipped slightly to .289 in 1911, Konetchy still had a very good year. He was the Cardinals' team leader in several offensive categories that included at-bats, hits, doubles, triples (tied with Steve Evans), home runs, RBI and slugging percentage. Additionally, his 38 doubles were enough to lead the National League. In the field, he repeated as the best defensive first baseman with a .991 fielding percentage along with leading the position in games played and putouts. His performance helped the team achieve an above .500 won-loss record for the first time in many years. In fact, the Cardinals got off to a great start and were in a race for first place in mid–August when disaster struck. The team was traveling by train from Philadelphia to Boston when an accident killed a dozen passengers and injured nearly 50 others. Fortunately, no players were injured and in fact many of the Cardinals (including Konetchy) helped to rescue passengers and carry them to safety. Although the Cardinals were fortunate none of their players were hurt, the incident seemed to take the enthusiasm out of their play. They came in just barely above .500 with a 75–74 record, but finished in fifth place and 22 games behind the New York Giants' pennant-winning pace. Early in the 1912 season, Konetchy claimed his second Iron Man designation when the Washington Senators' shortstop, George McBride, was suspended for arguing with an umpire.

Konetchy's streak was only 219 games long when he became the Iron Man on April 23, 1912. His reign lasted only till July 4, 1912, when his appearance streak ended after 279 contests because he was not in the Cardinals' lineup for that day's double-header.

Konetchy had another great year in 1912 as he was the major offensive force for the lowly Cardinals. He led the team in every offensive category, which included a career-best .314 average, except stolen bases. Unfortunately, the Cardinals reverted to a below .500 winning percentage, finishing in sixth place with a 63–90 record. Konetchy played only one more season in a St. Louis uniform and was shipped off to the Pittsburgh Pirates in December 1913. After playing for the Pirates for just one season, team management refused his request for a raise and he jumped over to the Pittsburgh Rebels of the Federal League. His tour with the Rebels was also short because the league folded after the 1915 season. In February 1916, the Rebels sold him to the Boston Braves. He stayed with the Braves for three seasons before getting sold again, this time to the Brooklyn Robins. In his second of three years with the Robins, Konetchy finally made it to the World's Series in 1920 when the Robins won the National League pennant by seven games over the New York Giants. He went 4 for 23 for a .174 average with a couple of RBI as Brooklyn lost the series to the Cleveland Indians by a 5–2 margin. About halfway through the following season, Brooklyn released him and he was claimed off waivers by the Philadelphia Phillies. In his limited time with the Phillies, he showed he still had the skills to be productive by hitting .321 and knocking out eight homers in just half a season. The 1921 season turned out to be his last in the big leagues. After departing the majors, he spent many more years playing and managing in the minor leagues before leaving baseball entirely in the early 1940s.

61. CLYDE MILAN

Born: March 25, 1887, Linden, Tennessee *Died*: March 3, 1953, Orlando, Florida *Bats*: Left *Throws*: Right *Height*: 5 feet, 9 inches *Weight*: 168 *Major league debut*: August 19, 1907 (Washington at Chicago [AL]) *Last major league game*: September 22, 1922 (Washington at Chicago [AL])

Major league Iron Man from: July 4, 1912, to October 4, 1913 *Consecutive games played*: 511 *Games as major league Iron Man*: 236 (consecutive games 276 through 511) *Team played for during streak*: Washington Senators (AL) *Primary position played*: Outfield *Game missed before streak*: August 11, 1910 (second game) (Washington at Cleveland) *First game played of streak*: August 12, 1910 (Washington at Cleveland) *Last game played of streak*: October 3, 1913 (second game) (Boston at Washington) *Game missed to end streak*: October 4, 1913 (Boston at Washington)

Consecutive Game Streak's Statistical Totals

Year	G	AB	R	H	2B	3B	HR	RBI	BB	SO	AVG	SLG	SB
1910	49	192	31	56	6	3	0	—	—	—	.292	.354	23
1911	154	616	109	194	24	8	3	35	74	—	.315	.394	58
1912	154	601	105	184	19	11	1	79	63	—	.306	.379	88
1913	154	579	92	174	18	9	3	54	58	25	.301	.378	75
Total	511	1988	337	608	67	31	7	*168*	*195*	25	.306	.381	244

Clyde Milan played most of his 16-year major league career filling the center field spot for the Washington Senators. He was nicknamed "Deerfoot" because of his speed on the base paths and his capability of tracking down long flies in the outfield. After spending part of two seasons in the minors with Wichita, he received the call-up to the Senators in August 1907 and made his debut in Chicago during the Senators' lopsided 16–2 loss to the White

Sox on August 19. He got into 48 games (rotating between center and right fields) by the end of the season and hit a respectable .279 in those contests.

Senators manager Joe Cantillon made Milan the team's permanent center fielder with the start of the 1908 season. Milan stayed in this capacity until the 1921 season. The results of his second year in the big leagues showed his batting fall to a .239 average but he did lead the team with a dozen triples. The 1909 season was somewhat of a failure at the plate for Milan as he managed but 80 hits in 130 games and finished with one of the lowest batting averages in the league (.200). It also did not help that Washington finished dead last, some 20 games behind the seventh-place St. Louis Browns. On August 12, 1910 (with 49 games left in the season), Milan initialed his consecutive games streak in a Senators game in Cleveland against the Indians. He rebounded from his 1909 subpar performance by lifting his batting average back to .279. His at-bats, runs scored and base hit totals led the Senators in addition to having the second-most bases on balls in the league behind the Detroit Tigers' Donie Bush. The 30 assists and 10 double plays he accumulated in 1910 led the American League's outfielders. Washington escaped the basement by reversing places with the Browns in the final standings. In fact, it was the Browns that were behind the Senators by 20 games when the season concluded. The succeeding year, the 25-year-old center fielder appeared in Washington's lineup for all 154 games in 1911 as he was again the Senators' leader in many statistical categories. His hitting made tremendous progress as he batted .315, had the most at-bats of all American League batters and the second-highest totals in walks and stolen bases. His run production, however, was a disappointment as he drove in only 35 runners the entire year. The team placed seventh in the final standings and was never in any position to contend for the league title. During the off-season, there was a change in managers as the Senators hired Clark Griffith to take over the reins of the club. Milan inherited the Iron Man title on July 4, 1912, when the playing streak of the St. Louis Cardinals' Ed Konetchy ended. Milan completed the year without missing a contest for the second season in a row. He hit over .300 again, more than doubled his RBI total by bringing home 79 runners and set an all-time American League record with 88 stolen bases. This record lasted only a few years before the Tigers' Ty Cobb broke the mark with 96 swipes in 1915. With a new skipper at the helm, the Senators vastly improved by winning nearly 30 more games than the 1911 Senators did and finishing runner-up (and 14 games behind) to the American League champion Boston Red Sox. On September 19, 1913, Milan became just the fifth player in major league history to cross over the 500-consecutive-game barrier. It also looked like he was going to finish another season without missing a game until Griffith decided to rest him on the very last day of the season (October 4, 1913) in a game against the Red Sox. This ended his streak after playing 511 straight contests in center field for the Senators. He hit .300 again when he finished with a .301 average. He also repeated as the league's stolen base king by swiping 75 bases. Washington nearly duplicated their 1912 won-loss record as the club again finished in second place in the standings. This time it was the Philadelphia Athletics that claimed the American League crown.

After his playing streak came to a close, Milan continued playing for the Senators and had many solid performances over the course of the next nine seasons. His last season of active playing (1922), he was chosen the team's manager, replacing former Senator shortstop (and two-time Iron Man) George McBride. Milan served only one year and guided the team to a sixth-place finish with a 69–85 record. He left the Senators and became a playing manager for a couple of minor league clubs over the next four seasons and then served as a manager only for several more teams in the minor league system. He returned to Washington for the 1928 and 1929 seasons as a coach and then scouted for them during the 1937 season. In 1938, he returned to the Senators for another tour as one of their coaches. He was still serving in this capacity when he suffered a fatal heart attack at the Senators' 1953 spring training camp.

62. Owen "Chief" Wilson

Born: August 21, 1883, Austin, Texas *Died*: February 22, 1954, Bertram, Texas *Bats*: Left *Throws*: Right *Height*: 6 feet, 2 inches *Weight*: 185 *Major league debut*: April 15, 1908 (Pittsburgh at St. Louis [NL]) *Last major league game*: October 1, 1916 (St. Louis at Chicago [NL])

Major league Iron Man from: October 4, 1913, to October 4, 1914 *Consecutive games played*: 484 *Games as major league Iron Man*: 156 (consecutive games 329 through 484) *Teams played for during streak*: Pittsburgh Pirates (NL) (1911–1913) and St. Louis Cardinals (NL) (1914) *Primary position played*: Outfield *Game missed before streak*: September 9, 1911 (second game) (Pittsburgh at St. Louis) *First game played of streak*: September 10, 1911 (Pittsburgh at St. Louis) *Last game played of streak*: October 3, 1914 (second game) (Chicago at St. Louis) *Game missed to end streak*: October 4, 1914 (first game) (Chicago at St. Louis)

Consecutive Game Streak's Statistical Totals

Year	G	AB	R	H	2B	3B	HR	RBI	BB	SO	AVG	SLG	SB
1911	23	82	10	23	5	2	1	12	6	7	.280	.427	1
1912	152	583	80	175	19	36	11	95	35	67	.300	.513	16
1913	155	580	71	154	12	14	10	73	32	62	.266	.386	9
1914	154	580	64	150	27	12	9	73	32	66	.259	.393	14
Total	484	1825	225	502	63	64	31	253	105	202	.275	.431	40

Owen "Chief" Wilson had a relatively short career in the major leagues. A powerfully built player who had the capability to stroke the ball over many an outfielders' heads, he played for only nine seasons in the National League, from 1908 through 1916. He is prominently known in historical baseball circles as the player who hit an amazing 36 triples during the 1912 season. This figure established an all-time triples record that still stands. He first got into organized ball in 1905 and spent the first three years in the minors.

Signed to a contract with the Pittsburgh Pirates before the 1908 season, he took over the right field spot on the roster, replacing Goat Anderson. Wilson made his debut in the season opener on April 15 in St. Louis. The final results of his first year were not that impressive as he batted only .227 along with achieving one of the lowest on base percentages (.260) in the league. Pirates manager Fred Clarke had faith in him and used him in every Pirates game in 1909. Wilson responded by lifting his average to .272. A bonus was that Pittsburgh won the National League flag by nearly seven games over the Chicago Cubs. In what would be his only appearance in a World's Series, Wilson went only 4 for 26 for a minuscule .154 average but the team still took home the world championship by beating the Detroit Tigers in seven games. In 1910, his batting average slightly improved to .276 as he led all Pirates players in triples with 13 three-baggers. The 1911 season turned out to be a career year for Wilson. He posted career highs in doubles (34), homers (12), RBI (107), walks (41) and batting average (.300). His RBI total also tied for the league high with the Chicago Cubs' Wildfire Schulte. With only 23 games left on the schedule, Wilson started his consecutive game streak when he received a base on balls while pinch hitting for Pirate pitcher Claude Hendrix in the eighth inning of a game in St. Louis against the Cardinals. The Pirates repeated their third-place finish from the previous year by trailing nearly 15 games off the New York Giants' pennant-winning pace. In 1912, Pirates skipper Clarke decided to shuttle Wilson between center and right field on a consistent basis. He actually played nearly 20 more games in center field that season. He was the only player in the National League to not miss a single contest that year. It also was the season that he smacked his incredible 36 triples. The reason for Wilson to have so many triples was not that he was a speed demon but that he played in the vast Forbes Field, where hitting a triple was probably easier than hitting a home run. His final stats that year showed he duplicated his career-best .300 average along with being the Pirates home run leader (in addition to having the league high in triples). Additionally, he came in in second place among all league players in total bases and extra-base hits, where he finished up behind the Cubs' Heinie Zimmerman. Although the team improved to second place in the standings, they still were 10 games behind the first-place Giants when the year closed out. There was no more shifting back between center and right in 1913. He played only three times in center field while spending the rest of the year in right field. For the second straight year, Wilson was the only National Leaguer not to miss a single contest. With just a game left until the closing of the baseball season, the Washington Senators' Clyde Milan sat out his team's finale and ended a 511-game streak on October 4, 1913. Wilson's 329-games-played streak was long enough to succeed Milan as the Iron Man of baseball. While Wilson was taking over the durability title, the Pirates fell to fourth place in the standings with a 78–71 record. The Pirates front office soon after decided to clean house and Wilson was one of those players to depart Pittsburgh when he was traded to the St. Louis Cardinals in mid–December. He found himself working under Cardinals manager Miller Huggins (a future New York Yankees manager), who inserted Wilson as the team's regular right fielder. He responded to his new surroundings by hitting a solid .259 and finishing in a tie for second place with a dozen triples (the Pirates' Max Carey had 17 three-baggers). He also had his best year defensively when he led the league outfielders in games played (for the fourth time), assists, double plays and fielding percentage. During the last week of the 1914 season, he had extended his consecutive games to 484 contests when he voluntarily ended his streak on October 4, 1914, while the Cardinals were playing host to the Cubs. He elected to sit out the last few contests of the regular season so could he could rest up for the upcoming city series with the American League's St. Louis Browns. This series was conducted after the regular season ended. It should be noted that 1914 turned out to be the first season in National League history that not a single player in the league took part in all of his team's games.

Wilson played for only two more years with the Cardinals. His last year in the majors, his batting, slugging and on base percentage averages reflected levels that hadn't occurred since his rookie year in 1908. He last stepped on a major league diamond on October 1, 1916, when the Cardinals were visiting the Cubs at Wrigley Field. The following year, he appeared in about two dozen games for a minor league club before deciding to call it a career.

63. SAM CRAWFORD

Born: April 18, 1880, Wahoo, Nebraska *Died*: June 15, 1968, Hollywood, California *Bats*: Left *Throws*: Left *Height*: 6 feet *Weight*: 190 *Major league debut*: September 10, 1899 (first game) (Cleveland at Cincinnati [NL]) *Last major league game*: September 16, 1917 (Cleveland at Detroit [AL])

Major league Iron Man from: October 4, 1914, to April 18, 1916 *Consecutive games played*: 472 *Games as major league Iron Man*: 163 (consecutive games 310 through 472) *Team played for during streak*: Detroit Tigers (AL) *Primary position played*: Outfield *Game missed before streak*: October 6, 1912 (Chicago at Detroit) *First game played of streak*: April 10, 1913 (Detroit at St. Louis) *Last game*

Sam Crawford

played of streak: April 17, 1916 (Detroit at Cleveland) *Game missed to end streak*: April 18, 1916 (Detroit at Cleveland)

Consecutive Game Streak's Statistical Totals

Year	G	AB	R	H	2B	3B	HR	RBI	BB	SO	AVG	SLG	SB
1913	153	609	78	193	32	23	9	83	52	28	.317	.489	13
1914	157	582	74	183	22	26	8	104	69	31	.314	.483	25
1915	156	612	81	183	31	19	4	112	66	29	.299	.431	24
1916	6	22	1	6	0	0	0	—	3	0	.273	.273	0
Total	472	1825	234	565	85	68	21	*299*	190	88	.310	.465	62

During the deadball era, "Wahoo Sam" Crawford was one of the most feared left-handed hitters. He had the capability to hit a lot of extra-base hits. He played for 19 seasons in the major leagues with the Cincinnati Reds (1899–1902) and the Detroit Tigers (1903–1917). For many years, Crawford and his Detroit teammate Ty Cobb formed one of the most productive duos in early 20th century baseball. Crawford would have won two batting and three slugging titles but his peak years occurred at the same time Cobb was running off with these titles for several seasons. Crawford was in his first year of professional ball with just over 100 games of experience when he got the call to join the Reds. Making his debut in September 1899, he got into 31 games mainly playing in center field (although by the 1901 season he manned the right field spot for the Reds for the remainder of his time with Cincinnati) and contributed a .307 batting average before the close of the season.

Crawford spent three more seasons in the National League with the Reds, highlighted by the 16 homers he hit in 1901 to lead the majors in that category. In his last year (1902) with Cincinnati, he led the National League with 22 triples and 256 total bases along with finishing runner-up to the batting title (behind Pittsburgh's Ginger Beaumont) and slugging title (behind Pittsburgh's Honus Wagner). The following year he made the switch to the American League and landed in Detroit with the Tigers. This turned out to be his only move as he spent the rest of his career in a Tigers uniform. His first year with the Tigers, he

Sam Crawford: This Hall of Famer is baseball's all-time record holder for most triples (309). He played in 472 contests for the Detroit Tigers from April 1913 to April 1916.

made the change to occupying right field in the lineup. The 1903 season also was his first of five seasons where he took in all of the Tigers' games. For the second straight year, he had a league high among hitters with 25 triples and posted a second-place finish in the batting championship with a .335 average; only Nap Lajoie of Cleveland had a higher average with a .344 mark. After having a career low in hitting average in 1904, he bounced back with a good performance over the next two seasons. With the Tigers finishing in sixth place in 1906, a change was needed for the upcoming season so Detroit hired Hughie Jennings as their new skipper. One of his first acts was to move Crawford over to center field. When the curtain closed on the 1907 season, Detroit had claimed their first American League pennant by edging the Philadelphia Athletics for the title. In the World's Series, the Tigers' bats went silent. The team that had led the entire major league in runs scored during the season scored but six runs in the five games against the Chicago Cubs. They went down to defeat to the Cubs 4–0 with one tie. Although Crawford hit only .238 for the series, he drove in three of the six runs that the Tigers scored. The next year was the same result — winning the American League title with the slightest of margins (only this time it was Cleveland) and then losing the World's Series to the Cubs in five games. Crawford even repeated his .238 World's Series average from the year before. Detroit won the league flag for a third year running in 1909 but this time faced the Pittsburgh Pirates for the world title. The result was the same, a Tigers loss, but at least the series went the full seven games as Crawford hit .250, had a homer and tied for the team high with four RBI. Jennings shifted Crawford back to right field for the 1910 season. That season saw Crawford hit 19 triples and drive in 120 runners (both league-leading marks) while hitting .289 as Detroit finished out of first place for the first time since the 1906 season. While he did not lead the Tigers in any statistical columns in 1911, he had a career year at the plate. Finishing with 217 hits and 115 RBI, he hit an amazing .378 for the season. The only problem was that his fellow Tiger teammate, Ty Cobb, led the league in every major offensive category you could think of except homers. Even with all this offensive might, Detroit still finished second, some 13½ games behind the pennant-winning Athletics. The following year, the Tigers fell into the second division (and a sixth-place finish) in 1912 but Crawford had another excellent year, hitting .325 and leading the team with 109 RBI. When he sat out the season finale in Detroit against the Chicago White Sox on October 6, 1912, this turned out to be the last game Crawford would sit until the early portions of the 1916 season.

In the 1913 season opener in St. Louis on April 10, Crawford started his consecutive-games-played streak. Crawford was one of just two American Leaguers to play the full slate of games that year (the St. Louis Browns' Del Pratt was the other player). Although several baseball references indicate that Crawford's teammate Donie Bush also played every game in 1913, it was discovered during this research that Bush sat out the season finale in Detroit on October 5, 1913. Baldy Louden filled in at shortstop for Bush during that game. If Bush had played in that contest, he would have been in a tie with Crawford for most consecutive games and been an Iron Man along with Crawford until early on in the 1915 season. As for Crawford, he played most of the games in right field but shifted over to first base for 13 games in 1913. He also had another strong year with the bat as he put together team highs in several categories along with league highs in at-bats and triples. Detroit finished with close to the same win-loss record as the year before in addition to repeating their sixth-place finish in the final standings. Crawford continued his impressive performance in 1914 and came in in second place as the league's Most Valuable Player (behind the Athletics' Eddie Collins). His average stayed over .300 for the fourth straight year as he hit .314, repeated as the triples leader, was the top RBI man with 104 and led league outfielders in games played. When the St. Louis Cardinals' Owen Wilson ended his long streak of games on October 4, 1914, Crawford inherited the Iron Man title from him with an active streak of 310 games. The Tigers jumped up a couple of places in the 1914 standings but still finished nearly 20 games off the pace of the first-place Athletics. Crawford continued his streak through the 1915 season as he appeared in right field for all 156 Tigers games. He hit .299, had a league-high 54 extra-base hits and for the third straight season led the American League in triples. Additionally, he repeated as the RBI champion along with playing more games than any other league outfielder for the second year running. He just missed making it back to the World's Series as the Tigers were edged out by the Boston Red Sox for the league pennant. Early in the 1916, a severe cold caused Crawford to miss the April 18 game in Cleveland, thus ending his games-played streak at 472 consecutive contests. By season's end, he took in only 100 games (his lowest total since his rookie year in 1899) and posted his lowest batting average (.286) since the 1904 season.

Crawford had his worst season as a professional his last season in the major leagues as he hit only .173 in 61 games (he was primarily used as a pinch hitter). He kept playing baseball by signing on with Los Angeles of the Pacific Coast League (PCL) and put in four years with that club. After his playing days were over, he umpired in the PCL for four seasons. When he had left the majors, he was less than 40 hits short of the 3,000 hits plateau, held the American League record for career homers (70) which was demolished a few years later by Babe Ruth, and to this day still holds the all-time record of most triples in a career with 309 three-baggers to his credit. Although his statistical accomplishments on the baseball diamond justified his selection to baseball immortality, it was not until 1957 that he was selected for membership into baseball's Hall of Fame.

64. GEORGE CUTSHAW

Born: July 29, 1886, Wilmington, Illinois *Died*: August 22, 1973, San Diego, California *Bats*: Right *Throws*: Right *Height*: 5 feet, 9 inches *Weight*: 160 *Major league debut*: April 25, 1912 (Boston at Brooklyn [NL]) *Last major league game*: July 5, 1923 (Detroit at Cleveland [AL])

Major league Iron Man from: April 18, 1916, to April 24, 1916; April 24, 1916, to April 25, 1916 (tied with Ray Chapman); April 27, 1916, to June 19, 1916 *Consecutive games played*: 309 *Games as major league Iron Man*: 42 (consecutive games 267 and 268, consecutive game 269 [tied with Chapman], consecutive games 271 through 309) *Team played for during streak*: Brooklyn Robins (NL) *Primary position played*: Second base *Game missed before streak*: June 12, 1914 (St. Louis at Brooklyn) *First game played of streak*: June 13, 1914 (St. Louis at Brooklyn) *Last game played of streak*: June 17, 1916 (Chicago at Brooklyn) *Game missed to end streak*: June 19, 1916 (Philadelphia at Brooklyn)

Consecutive Game Streak's Statistical Totals

Year	G	AB	R	H	2B	3B	HR	RBI	BB	SO	AVG	SLG	SB
1914	110	421	49	116	14	11	2	—	16	25	.276	.375	27
1915	154	566	68	139	18	9	0	62	34	35	.246	.309	28
1916	45	169	15	44	8	1	1	—	5	9	.260	.337	5
Total	309	1156	132	299	40	21	3	62	55	69	.259	.337	60

George Cutshaw was one of the National League's most durable and best fielding second basemen of his era. He had tours in the National League with Brooklyn and Pittsburgh before finishing his playing days in the American League with the Detroit Tigers. Although his playing career lasted just 12 seasons, in every one of those years (except his last season) he was his team's starting second baseman. He was nearly 26 years old when he finally made his major league debut for the Brooklyn Superbas in a home game on April 25, 1912, against the

Boston Braves. A couple of months into the season, he displaced former Iron Man John Hummel as the club's second baseman. While Cutshaw's run production was on the low side (28 RBI in 102 games), he hit a solid .280 during his rookie season. In 147 contests the next year (1913), his hitting dropped off slightly (down 13 points) but he pleasantly surprised the club by posting team highs with 592 at-bats, 13 triples, seven homers (tied with teammates Zack Wheat and Casey Stengel) and driving in 80 runners. Defensively, he led the league's second basemen with 402 putouts and 79 double plays.

During the off-season, changes occurred in Brooklyn. Club management decided that four years was long enough for Bill Dahlen to spend as Brooklyn's manager. Longtime major league catcher Wilbert Robinson was chosen as the team's new skipper. A change in the team's nickname was also made when the term Superbas was dropped in favor of Robins. In 1914, Cutshaw missed just one contest. That game was in Brooklyn on June 12 against the St. Louis Cardinals. The following day, his consecutive playing streak commenced in the same series versus St. Louis on June 13, 1914. He finished the year playing the final 110 games on the Robins' schedule. While his batting average fell slightly to .257, he repeated as the club's triples leader with a dozen three-baggers. This total was good for a tie for second place (with the Cardinals' Owen Wilson and the Cubs' Heinie Zimmerman) in the league's totals trailing only the 17 three-baggers hit by the Pittsburgh Pirates' Max Carey. Cutshaw also took first place in putouts, assists, double plays and games played by National League second basemen. As for the performance of the team, the Robins won 10 more games than the previous year and finished fifth (one place higher in the standings than in 1913). While Cutshaw played all the Robins' games in 1915 (and extended his playing streak to 264 games), the team acquired Ivy Olson from the Cincinnati Reds to use him as an occasional defensive replacement for the team's infielders. This included Cutshaw, whom Olson supplanted during the year so he could get the needed rest. It seems the rest was necessary because Cutshaw's batting average went south again for the third straight year when he hit only .246. The only offensive mark that he posted a team high in was his 28 stolen bases. With the glove, he led the second basemen in fielding for the first of two times with a .971 percentage along with repeating as the position's leader in games played, putouts and assists. The Robins continued to improve as they finished third, just 10 games back of the National League champion Philadelphia Phillies. Trailing only Sam Crawford of the Detroit Tigers in consecutive games at the commencement of the 1916 season, Cutshaw became the majors' Iron Man on April 18 when Crawford was grounded due to a bad cold. Within a week (April 24) and due to several Robins' postponements, Ray Chapman of the Cleveland Indians had caught up to Cutshaw in the number of consecutive games played. Chapman actually took the Iron Man title from him the very next day. A couple of days later (April 27), the Iron Man title was back in Cutshaw's hands when Chapman suffered a knee injury. About eight weeks later, on June 17, 1916, in the fifth inning of a home game against the Chicago Cubs, Cutshaw suffered an injury when he was running out an infield hit and collided with Cubs' pitcher Hippo Vaughn near first base. The injury caused Cutshaw to be taken out of the game. In the next game, two days later, he was not in the Robins' lineup and his playing streak ended after 309 games. His 1916 stats finally showed improvement in his hitting as he batted .260, again claimed the team's base-stealing crown with 27 thefts, and repeated as the leader of putouts, assists and games played by the second basemen of the National League. The climb was complete for the Robins as the franchise captured its first league title since the 1900 season by edging the defending league title-holding Phillies by a couple of games. The Robins, unfortunately, were no match for the American League champion Boston Red Sox as they went down to defeat in five games. Cutshaw had but two hits in 19 at bats for a very paltry .105 batting average, along with a couple of runs driven in.

Cutshaw spent one more year manning second base for the Robins before being shipped off to the Pirates in January 1918. Upon his arrival in Pittsburgh, he replaced Jake Pitler as the Buccaneers' second baseman. In his first two seasons with the Pirates, he did not miss a single contest and had compiled another lengthy playing streak. He did not, however, qualify for the Iron Man title because during this time Everett Scott was in the midst of putting his own 1,307-game streak together. Cutshaw stayed in the Steel City for two additional seasons. Overall highlights of his employment with Pittsburgh included finishing second in RBI in 1918 to the Phillies' Sherry Magee with 68 and being the major league's toughest batter to strike out in 1920 with just 10 whiffs in 488 at-bats. He was released by Pittsburgh after the 1921 season and claimed on waivers by the Tigers in late December 1921. He played in Detroit for two years before leaving the majors. The last season was somewhat of a washout; due to illness, he played in only 45 contests.

65. RAY CHAPMAN

Born: January 15, 1891, Beaver Dam, Kentucky *Died*: August 17, 1920, New York, New York *Bats*: Right *Throws*: Right *Height*: 5 feet, 10 inches *Weight*: 170 *Major league debut*: August 30, 1912 (Chicago at Cleveland [AL]) *Last major league game*: August 16, 1920 (Cleveland at New York [AL])

Major league Iron Man from: April 24 to April 25, 1916 (tied with George Cutshaw); April 25, 1916, to April 27, 1916 *Consecutive games played*: 271 *Games as major league Iron Man*: 3 (consecutive game 269 [tied with Cutshaw], consecutive games 270 and 271) *Teams played for during streak*: Cleveland Naps (AL) (1914) and Cleveland Indians (AL) (1915–1916) *Primary position played*: Shortstop *Game missed before streak*: June 14, 1914 (Washington at Cleveland) *First game played of streak*: June 15, 1914 (Washington at Cleveland) *Last game played of streak*: April 26, 1916 (Chicago at Cleveland) *Game missed to end streak*: April 27, 1916 (Chicago at Cleveland)

Consecutive Game Streak's Statistical Totals

Year	G	AB	R	H	2B	3B	HR	RBI	BB	SO	AVG	SLG	SB
1914	105	374	59	103	16	10	2	42	48	47	.275	.388	24
1915	154	570	101	154	14	17	3	67	70	82	.270	.370	36
1916	12	46	8	10	1	0	0	—	4	6	.217	.239	2
Total	271	990	168	267	31	27	5	*109*	122	135	.270	.371	62

Ray Chapman played in the major leagues for only nine seasons with the Cleveland Indians as their reliable shortstop. During his brief time in the big leagues, Chapman established himself as the best shortstop the American League had to offer. He was well on his way to a Hall of Fame career before his life was tragically shortened; he was hit in the head by a ball that New York Yankees pitcher Carl Mays threw in a game on August 16, 1920. His place in the annals of baseball history is ensured as he is (up to the present time) the only major leaguer to die as a result of injuries suffered on the field of play. His time with the Indians started with a game in Cleveland against the Chicago White Sox on August 30, 1912. That year the Indians started the season with Ivy Olson at short but Roger Peckinpaugh was also used quite often before Chapman took over the position permanently upon his arrival. His performance at the plate and in the field showed that Cleveland made the right decision by hiring Chapman. In the 31 games he played that rookie year, he hit .312, drove home 19 runners and showed his speed by swiping 10 bases.

Settling in at shortstop his first full year, Chapman played in 140 contests, hit .258 and led the league with 45 sacrifice hits. He also was the top base stealer on the team that led the majors by a far margin in that category. The next year, a leg injury in spring training kept him out of the Indians' lineup until mid–June. On June 15, 1914, he made it back into the lineup on a permanent basis and his name appeared in every Cleveland box score for the rest of the season. Although he mostly played at short, Indians' manager Joe Birmingham got him into a good portion of games at second base. Chapman repeated as the team's leading base stealer with 24 swipes even though he missed a third of the 1914 campaign. He came in with a solid .275 average but because the Indians were without his talents for quite a while at the start of the season, the team never recovered. They finished deep in the cellar by nearly 20 games with a 51–102 record. During the 1915 season, the club kept him at shortstop for all 154 contests as Chapman again led the team in numerous categories. In addition, he led all league shortstops with 378 putouts and finished second in strikeouts (82) to St. Louis Brown shortstop Doc Lavan's 83 whiffs. Cleveland still had not recovered from the previous year's debacle as they finished in seventh place. At the start of the 1916 season, Chapman was trailing George Cutshaw of the Brooklyn Robins by just five contests for the second-longest playing streak actively running. Sam Crawford had the lead but had his streak snapped at the end of the first week of action (April 18). Cutshaw took over the longest streak on that date but by April 24 Chapman pulled into a tie with him. The next day, with the Robins having another day off, Chapman took over the lead to become the new Iron Man of baseball. His reign ended just a couple of games later when he badly twisted his knee while tagging out a runner who was coming into second base. The injury ended his streak at 271 games and landed him in the hospital for a couple of weeks to recuperate. After his prolonged absence, he returned to the Indians' lineup to appear in 109 games by season's end. Cleveland stayed in the second division with a sixth-place finish and Chapman had a .231 average, which turned out to be his worst career year at the plate.

Ray Chapman: The Cleveland Indians' shortstop had a very short reign as Iron Man in 1916. Four years later he became the only major leaguer to die as a result of an on-field injury (he was hit in the head by a pitch from New York Yankees pitcher Carl Mays).

Chapman continued to hold down his role as the Indians' shortstop over the next four seasons. The club had started showing improvement in the annual standings and came very close to winning the American League title a couple of times. With the startup of the 1920 season, there was speculation that this was going to be Cleveland's year. Chapman had one of his worst games in the field (in Cleveland) during a 7–1 Yankees victory on June 14, 1920, when in just the fifth inning alone he committed four errors. Later in the year, with about six weeks left in the campaign, the Indians were in a battle for the league pennant with the defending American League titleholders, the Chicago White Sox. Leading by just a half a game on August 20, the Indians were in New York playing the Yankees. Chapman was hit by Mays' pitch in the fifth inning. While Cleveland won the game by a 4–3 score, no one was celebrating on either team because everyone was concerned about Cleveland's popular shortstop. Falling unconscious soon after the incident, Chapman passed away 12 hours after being hit in the head. A few weeks before the end of the year, future Iron Man Joe Sewell took Chapman's place on the roster. After the tragedy, Cleveland skipper Tris Speaker's leadership helped instill the confidence that was needed in his players. This directly contributed in helping the Indians win their first World's Series championship in 1920.

66. Del Pratt

Born: January 10, 1888, Walhalla, South Carolina *Died*: September 30, 1977, Texas City, Texas *Bats*: Right *Throws*: Right *Height*: 5 feet, 11 inches *Weight*: 175 *Major league debut*: April 11, 1912 (St. Louis at Chicago [AL]) *Last major league game*: September 29, 1924 (Detroit at Chicago [AL])

Major league Iron Man from: June 19, 1916, to April 30, 1917 *Consecutive games played*: 363 *Games as major league Iron Man*: 118 (consecutive games 246 through 363) *Team played for during streak*: St. Louis Browns (AL) *Primary position played*: Second base *Game missed before streak*: September 2, 1914 (second game) (St. Louis at Boston) *First game played of streak*: September 4, 1914 (St. Louis at Detroit) *Last game played of streak*: April 29, 1917 (St. Louis at Cleveland) *Game missed to end streak*: April 30, 1917 (St. Louis at Cleveland)

Consecutive Game Streak's Statistical Totals

Year	G	AB	R	H	2B	3B	HR	RBI	BB	SO	AVG	SLG	SB
1914	32	116	19	34	6	3	1	—	11	9	.293	.422	12
1915	159	602	61	175	31	11	3	78	26	43	.291	.394	32
1916	158	596	64	159	35	12	5	103	54	56	.267	.391	26
1917	14	55	5	17	2	1	0	—	3	5	.309	.382	4
Total	363	1369	149	385	74	27	9	*181*	94	113	.281	.394	74

Del Pratt was a hard-hitting second baseman who played in the American League from 1912 through 1924 with the St. Louis Browns, New York Yankees, Boston Red Sox and Detroit Tigers. Unfortunately, the teams he played for usually finished in the second division of the standings. Additionally, if it was not for Eddie Collins and his skills, Pratt would have seriously been considered the best at the second base position during his era of play. He started his major league career in a Browns uniform in Chicago on April 11, 1912 (Opening Day), against the White Sox. For the first half of the 1912 season, Pratt shared the second base job with Frank LaPorte. In July, the Browns' management decided the club did not need two full-time players at second, so LaPorte was sold to the Washington Senators. With a year that would have easily made him the American League's rookie of the year, he became the weak-hitting Browns' offensive leader by achieving team highs in hits, doubles, triples, homers, RBI and slugging average.

The following year (1913), as the Browns were claiming the role of basement dwellers, there was no sophomore jinx for Pratt. Although his batting average had dropped off a few points, he was still the team's run-producing king as evidenced by his driving in over 20 percent of his team's runs with 87 RBI. Defensively, he did not help the team much with his glove as he had a league-high 41 miscues at second, although he did pace the position with 364 putouts. Pratt continued his role as the team's second baseman in 1914, but would occasionally take chances in the outfield. He missed only one game that year when he sat out the nightcap of a double-header in Boston on September 2. The following Browns' game in Detroit on September 4 was the initial game of Pratt's consecutive playing streak as he played the final 32 games of the 1914 season. Thanks to outfielder Tilly Walker's offensive output that season, Pratt was not looked upon as the sole source of the Browns' offense. Pratt did lead the team, however, in hits and doubles along with batting .283 as he helped lift St. Louis to fifth place in the standings. He did sit out one game at second base in 1915 although he did make it into the lineup as his modest playing streak was stretched to 191 games by the conclusion of the year. Pratt reclaimed his distinction as the Browns' threat at the plate by claiming team leads in most offensive categories. The Browns were no threat to the more powerful teams, though, as they wound up in sixth place, nearly 40 games off the pennant-winning pace. A couple of months into the 1916 season, Pratt became the major league's Iron Man when Brooklyn's George Cutshaw had a 309-game streak stopped on June 19. Pratt finished the year by appearing in every contest at second base as his streak was lengthened to 349 games. Although he had his second-lowest hitting average in his career (.267) in 1916, he made the most of his 159 hits by reaching a career-high 103 RBI (which also led the American League). For the fourth straight year, he led the league's second basemen in putouts and for the third consecutive season in games played. Although St. Louis finished in fifth place by the end of the year, they were only a dozen games behind the Boston Red Sox in the closely contested 1916 pennant race. Just 14 games into the 1917 season, Pratt suffered a cracked wrist bone which kept him out of the Browns' lineup for three weeks. His consecutive-games-played streak ended at 363 games in Cleveland on April 30, 1917. Playing every day did not negatively affect his stats as he had his best years both offensively and defensively during his playing streak.

When the 1917 season ended, Pratt had turned in the worst year of his 13-season career. Playing in just 123 contests, he had only 111 hits and a .247 batting average. St. Louis barely escaped the cellar, finishing just ahead of the Philadelphia Athletics. The 1917 season turned out to be Pratt's last year in a Browns uniform. Earlier that year, he had wound up in court involving a controversial statement the Browns owner had made against some of the team's players. Being the prideful man that he was, Pratt took exception to the statement and sued the Browns team owner. Although Pratt won the case, he was traded in January 1918 to the New York Yankees. He performed solidly for three seasons as the Yankees' second baseman before another controversy involving money send him northward to Boston in December 1920 to play for the Red Sox. He stayed in Boston for two years before being shipped out again, this time to the Detroit Tigers, a few weeks after the close of the 1922 season. He played in Detroit for two more years and finished his major league career when he played his last game on September 29, 1924, when the Tigers were visiting the Chicago White Sox. When the 1924 season concluded, he retired from baseball.

67. EDDIE COLLINS

Born: May 2, 1887, Millerton, New York *Died*: March 25, 1951, Boston, Massachusetts *Bats*: Left *Throws*: Right *Height*: 5 feet, 9 inches *Weight*: 175 *Major league debut*: September 17, 1906 (Philadelphia at Chicago [AL]) *Last major league game*: August 2, 1930 (second game) (Boston at Philadelphia [AL])

Major league Iron Man from: April 30, 1917, to May 3, 1918 *Consecutive games played*: 478 *Games as major league Iron Man*: 149 (consecutive games 330 through 478) *Teams played for during streak*: Philadelphia Athletics (AL) (1914) and Chicago White Sox (AL) (1915–1918) *Primary position played*: Second base *Game missed before streak*: October 3, 1914 (Washington at Philadelphia) *First game played of streak*: October 5, 1914 (New York at Philadelphia) *Last game played of streak*: May 2, 1918 (Chicago at Detroit) *Game missed to end streak*: May 3, 1918 (Chicago at Detroit)

Consecutive Game Streak's Statistical Totals:

Year	G	AB	R	H	2B	3B	HR	RBI	BB	SO	AVG	SLG	SB
1914	3	7	3	2	0	0	0	—	3	0	.286	.286	2
1915	155	521	118	173	22	10	4	77	119	27	.332	.436	46
1916	155	545	87	168	14	17	0	52	86	36	.308	.396	40
1917	156	564	91	163	18	12	0	67	89	16	.289	.363	53
1918	9	31	4	9	1	0	0	—	8	0	.290	.323	1
Total	478	1668	303	515	55	39	4	*196*	305	79	.309	.396	142

Collins had one of his best years in 1914 as most of his stats were near the top of the leader board. As a result of having another outstanding year and leading Philadelphia to their fourth pennant in five years, he was chosen the American League's Most Valuable Player. The consecutive game streak that made him the Iron Man for a second time started as the 1914 season was winding down in Philadelphia against the New York Yankees on October 5 with just three games left in the season. In attempting to capture their fourth world championship in five years, the Athletics hit only .172 for the series and were swept in four straight games by the Boston Braves, whose pitchers allowed only six runs. Collins had but three singles in the four games for a lowly .214 average. After the 1914 season, Philadelphia owner-manager Connie Mack was having trouble trying to meet the demand for higher salaries that some players wanted. This was the main reason why Collins was sold to the Chicago White Sox in December 1914.

With the arrival of Collins in Chicago in 1915, first-year White Sox manager Pants Rowland moved second baseman Lena Blackburne over to third base to make room for one of the game's best players. Collins hit over .300 for the seventh consecutive season when he topped all White Sox players with a .332 average. He led the league with 119 walks and finished second to Ty Cobb in runs scored and on base percentage. In the field, he didn't miss a game all year at second and claimed his fourth fielding title at that position with a .974 percentage along with a top mark of 487 assists. Collins' presence in the lineup helped the White Sox jump from a sixth-place finish in 1914 to a solid third place in 1915. The 1916 season saw a downward slide in his offensive numbers as he ended up with his lowest batting average (.308) since the 1908 season, although he still had the best fielding percentage for the league's second basemen. Playing another full docket of games in 1916, he extended his playing streak to 313 games by end of the year. The White Sox just missed going to the World's Series as they were edged out by the Boston Red Sox for the American League title. In 1917, his batting numbers fell close to another 20 points as he finished below the .300 hitting plateau for the first time in nearly ten years. The only statistical category he led in that season was defensively as he had the most assists, and he also played more games than any other league second baseman. Still, with his presence in the lineup every day bolstering the team's confidence, the White Sox won their second junior circuit title by a healthy nine games over the defending world champion Boston Red Sox. Leading the team with nine hits and a .409 average, Collins helped lead the White Sox to the world title as Chicago whipped the New York Giants in a well-fought six-game series. This was the fourth and final time in his illustrious career that Collins would be on the winning side in World's Series competition. His second tenure as Iron Man came to an end early in the 1918 season. He was suffering from the flu but was determined to keep the streak going. On May 2 he was out of the starting lineup for the first time since the 1914 season but got into the game as a pinch hitter, contributing a single. The next day, his illness made it too difficult for him to play so he ended his games-played streak at 478 when he sat out the May 3 game in Detroit. Although he still put up some good offensive figures, it seems that during his second playing streak, his offensive numbers were not at the level that was expected of him.

When the 1918 season came to a close, the White Sox dropped to sixth place in the final standings. This outcome resulted in a change at the managerial level. Kid Gleason replaced Rowland, who had led them to the 1917 championship. The season saw Collins finished with a near-career-low batting average (.276), plus he saw action in only 97 games (the lowest figure since he became a full-time player). Both Collins and the White Sox rebounded in 1919. Collins played every game and improved his batting average to .319. The White Sox edged out the Cleveland Indians by a few games to win the American League pennant. Chicago was heavily favored to beat the Cincinnati Reds in the World's Series. In this affair, Collins went 7 for 31 for only a .226 average and the Sox were stunned when the Reds defeated them. The next year, it was discovered several members of the 1919 White Sox had been bribed by gamblers to throw the World's Series. Those players were banned from ever playing organized baseball again. Collins was discovered to be one of the honest players. He loved the game of baseball and the competition it presented. Plus, he took great pride in performing his best at all times while on the baseball diamond. He stayed on with the White Sox through the 1926 season (the last two as the White Sox player-manager) when he rejoined Connie Mack in 1927 as his key assistant in Philadelphia. He filled in when necessary but during the last couple of years was used in a pinch-hitting role on the occasional rare appearance. He made his last appearance as an active player on August 2, 1930, in Philadelphia. By the time his career had come to an end, he was at the top of several career statistical categories and held many second baseman records. He stayed on to coach the Athletics for two more years before leaving to join the Boston Red Sox front office in 1933 as their general manager. In 1939, he was easily chosen for membership in baseball's Hall of Fame.

68. Fred Luderus

Born: September 12, 1885, Milwaukee, Wisconsin *Died*: January 5, 1961, Three Lakes, Wisconsin *Bats*: Left *Throws*: Right *Height*: 5 feet, 11½ inches *Weight*: 185 *Major league debut*: September 23, 1909 (second game) (Brooklyn at Chicago [NL]) *Last major league game*: June 23, 1920 (Cincinnati at Philadelphia [NL])

Major league Iron Man from: May 3, 1918, to April 14, 1920 *Consecutive games played*: 533 *Games as major league Iron Man*: 250 (consecutive games 284 through 533) *Team played for during streak*: Philadelphia Phillies (NL) *Primary position played*: First base *Game missed before streak*: June 1, 1916 (New York at Philadelphia) *First game played of streak*: June 2, 1916 (St. Louis at Philadelphia) *Last game played of streak*: September 28, 1919 (second game) (Philadelphia at New York) *Game missed to end streak*: April 14, 1920 (Philadelphia at Brooklyn)

Consecutive Game Streak's Statistical Totals

Year	G	AB	R	H	2B	3B	HR	RBI	BB	SO	AVG	SLG	SB
1916	116	408	40	124	20	2	4	—	27	22	.304	.392	7
1917	154	522	57	136	24	4	5	72	65	35	.261	.351	5
1918	125	468	54	135	23	2	5	67	42	33	.288	.378	4
1919	138	509	60	149	30	6	5	49	54	48	.293	.405	6
Total	533	1907	211	544	97	14	19	*188*	188	138	.285	.381	22

Fred Luderus was one of the leading slugging first basemen during the latter days of baseball's deadball era. He played in the National League for the Chicago Cubs and Philadelphia Phillies between 1909 and 1920. His major league career started when the Cubs signed him to a contract after recruiting him from the minors. Soon after, he made his major league debut in Chicago on September 23, 1909, against the Brooklyn Superbas. He filled in at first base for the remainder of the season in place of the ailing Frank Chance. He responded by hitting .297, drilling a homer and driving in nine runners in just 11 games.

The next season, with Chance back at his normal position, Luderus was used less frequently and appeared in only 24 contests when the Cubs traded him to the Phillies in the summer of 1910. He spent the remainder of that year as the occasional backup to the Phillies' regular first baseman, Kitty Bransfield. At the Phillies' training camp in 1911, Luderus impressed manager Red Dooin, who then decided to give Luderus the first baseman job permanently, replacing Bransfield. Luderus performed so well with the bat that the Phillies soon after released Bransfield. Dooin's choice made him look like a genius as Luderus went on to hit .301 and lead the team with 166 hits, 11 triples and 16 homers. Except for Wildfire Schulte of the Cubs (who had 21 clouts), no one else had more homers in the majors than Luderus. In 1912, Luderus was joined with new teammate Gavvy Cravath and between them combined to form a one-two power punch in the Phillies' lineup over the next several seasons. Of course, it didn't hurt to play your home games at Philadelphia's Baker Bowl, which was noted for having a short right field fence. Luderus' hitting numbers dropped off some in 1912 but he did lead the first basemen in putouts and assists for the first time. The following year (1913), his career-best 18 homers, 254 total bases and 57 extra-base hits were good enough to finish second in the league in those categories behind teammate Cravath as they both helped the Phillies finish in second place behind the National League champion New York Giants. Luderus came in with a career-low .248 batting average in 1914 along with a dozen circuit clouts and only 55 RBI. Before the next season opened, Dooin was replaced by Pat Moran as the Phillies' manager in 1915. One of the moves Moran made was to select Luderus as the team's new captain. He responded by hitting a career-high .315 as he led the Phillies and putting him in second place in the league behind

Fred Luderus: He was a Philadelphia Phillies first baseman during the 1910's. He succeeded Eddie Collins as Iron Man in May 1918. His 533-game streak ended when he sat out the Phillies' season opener in April 1920 because of a bad case of lumbago.

the New York Giants' Larry Doyle's .320 leading mark. Luderus also posted team highs in hits and doubles (and finished second in the National League to Doyle's 40 two-baggers) and was an offensive force along with Cravath in helping lead the Phillies to the 1915 National League pennant. Although Philadelphia came out on the short end of the five-game World's Series to the Boston Red Sox, Luderus was the one bright spot on the team. Taking full advantage of the only time he ever played in a World's Series, he amassed a team-leading .438 average and led all players in the series with two doubles and six RBI.

Starting with the 1916 season, his power stroke left him, but what he lacked in power he gained in durability. He commenced his consecutive playing streak on June 2, 1916, in Philadelphia and completed the last 116 games on the schedule that year. At the end of the season, he finished with a .281 batting average. Philadelphia came close to repeating as National League champs, but were edged out by the Brooklyn Robins. Luderus's name appeared in the Phillies' lineup each game at first base in 1917 and Philadelphia repeated as league runner-up, only this time it was the Giants who took the senior circuit's flag. Relatively early in the war-shortened 1918 campaign, Luderus claimed the Iron Man title (with 284 consecutive games played) on May 3 as Eddie Collins' streak came to an end when he was sidelined with the flu. The Phillies' final performance saw them plummeted to sixth place in the final standings. Luderus continued putting up good numbers as he again led the team in hits, RBI and batting average. Additionally, he led the league's first basemen with 98 assists and 74 double plays. In his last full year in the majors (1919), he was honored with his own day at the tail end of the season in the 525th game of his playing streak. He finished the year hitting .293 and leading the team in doubles. Philadelphia's downward free fall was complete as they won only 47 games and claimed the bottom spot in the final standings. His streak was terminated on April 14, 1920, when he missed the Phillies' season opener because he was suffering from a severe case of lumbago. The condition made it nearly impossible for him to play. In fact, it was so serious that he played only 16 more major league games in the rest of his big league career. When Luderus compiled his 533-game playing streak, most baseball sources thought this was the new all-time record when (after some in-depth research was completed) his streak was factually determined to be the fifth longest (up to that time) behind George Pinkney (577), Steve Brodie (574), Candy LaChance (539) and Buck Freeman (536). After leaving the majors for good after the 1920 season, he spent the rest of his time in organized baseball playing and serving as a player-manager in the minors until leaving the game for good in the mid–1930s.

69. Everett Scott

Born: November 19, 1892, Bluffton, Indiana *Died*: November 2, 1960, Fort Wayne, Indiana *Bats*: Right *Throws*: Right *Height*: 5 feet, 8 inches *Weight*: 148 *Major league debut*: April 14, 1914 (Washington at Boston [AL]) *Last major league game*: July 27, 1926 (first game) (Cincinnati at Brooklyn [NL])

Major league Iron Man from: April 14, 1920, to May 6, 1925 *Consecutive games played*: 1307 *Games as major league Iron Man*: 783 (consecutive games 525 through 1307) *Teams played for during streak*: Boston Red Sox (AL) (1916–1921) and New York Yankees (AL) (1922–1925) *Primary position played*: Shortstop *Game missed before streak*: June 18, 1916 (Boston at Chicago) *First game played of streak*: June 20, 1916 (New York at Boston) *Last game played of streak*: May 5, 1925 (Philadelphia at New York) *Game missed to end streak*: May 6, 1925 (Philadelphia at New York)

Everett Scott

Consecutive Game Streak's Statistical Totals:

Year	G	AB	R	H	2B	3B	HR	RBI	BB	SO	AVG	SLG	SB
1916	103	313	34	77	17	2	0	—	22	21	.246	.313	7
1917	157	528	40	127	24	7	0	50	20	46	.241	.313	12
1918	126	443	40	98	11	5	0	43	12	16	.221	.269	11
1919	138	507	41	141	19	0	0	38	19	26	.278	.316	8
1920	154	569	41	153	21	12	4	61	21	15	.269	.369	4
1921	154	576	65	151	21	9	1	62	27	21	.262	.335	5
1922	154	557	64	150	23	5	3	45	23	22	.269	.345	2
1923	152	533	48	131	16	4	6	60	13	19	.246	.325	1
1924	153	548	56	137	12	6	4	64	21	15	.250	.316	3
1925	16	53	3	11	0	0	0	3	2	2	.208	.208	0
Total	1307	4627	432	1176	164	50	18	*426*	180	203	.254	.323	53

Everett "Deacon" Scott played in the majors for 13 seasons, mostly with the Boston Red Sox and New York Yankees. During his era (1910s and 1920s), there was no better fielding shortstop in the American League than Scott. He led that position in fielding percentage eight straight seasons from 1916 through 1923. By the time he was 21 years old, he had made the Red Sox roster in 1914, replacing the Red Sox's long-time shortstop, Heinie Wagner. In his rookie season, Scott appeared in 144 games and finished with a .239 average. The following season (1915), he hit only .201 but it was his fielding that secured his place in the lineup as he helped the Red Sox edge the Detroit Tigers for the American League pennant. While Boston went on to defeat the Philadelphia Phillies in five games in the World's Series, Scott contributed but one single in 18 at-bats for an anemic .056 average.

About two months into the 1916 season, Scott's consecutive games streak started on June 20 in Boston against the Yankees. Although he was rather weak at the plate, he still anchored the infield that led the Red Sox to another pennant as they edged the Chicago White Sox by a couple of games. During this time, Boston was one of the powerhouse teams in baseball and proved it by repeating as World's Series champs in 1916 as

Everett Scott: He was the first major leaguer to cross over the 1,000-consecutive-game barrier. This Boston Red Sox and New York Yankees shortstop stretched the record to 1,307 until his benching in May 1925. His all-time record was broken in August 1933 by the Yankees' Lou Gehrig.

they defeated the Brooklyn Robins in five games. Scott had another dismal performance at the plate by going 2 for 16 for a .125 average. One of his hits, though, was a triple early in the second game. He eventually scored on a base hit by Babe Ruth as the Red Sox went on to win that contest in extra innings 2–1. As the Red Sox returned to defend their title in 1917, Scott stayed at shortstop while the team replaced manager Bill Carrigan with second baseman Jack Berry, who filled the role as player-manager. While Scott was winning his second fielding title at his position, the Red Sox recorded nearly the same win-loss mark as the previous year but wound up as second-place finishers behind the White Sox. The next year (1918), he recorded one of the team's lowest batting averages (.221) but stayed in the lineup as he extended his playing streak to 386 games by the conclusion of the war-shortened season. Boston (now under the guidance of new manager Ed Barrow) won another American League flag, just beating out the Cleveland Indians. Although Scott was having another miserable time offensively, going 2 for 21 (.095), he became a member of the World Championship team for the third time in four years as the Red Sox beat the National League's Chicago Cubs in six games. This turned out to be the Red Sox's last World's Series title until their 2004 championship run (a span of 86 seasons). Scott surprised many by posting a career-high .278 average during the 1919 season. Earlier in the year, he passed the 500-straight-game level in the second game of a double-header on August 28. As for the team, they went in the other direction as Boston fell to sixth place in the standings, well behind the first-place White Sox. Scott entered the 1920 season with 524 straight games and was in a close race with the Phillies' Fred Luderus for the Iron Man title. Luderus' streak ended when he missed Philadelphia's opener on April 14 because of a lumbago problem. Scott, who at the time was only eight games behind Luderus in consecutive games, assumed the role as baseball's new reigning Iron Man. A couple of months later, on June 21, 1920, he set the major league all-time consecutive game record when he played his 578th straight contest, eclipsing Brooklyn's George Pinkney's record of 577 games. When this record was set, little media coverage occurred because the subject was not covered much at the time. Additionally, most baseball folks were not sure if this was the record. In the early years of baseball, records were not kept accurately. This situation resulted in some sources having a streak of 731 games by Steve Brodie as the record. Years later, researchers discovered Brodie actually sat out the last game of the 1892 season. This resulted in Brodie's streak being 574 (not 731) games and that Pinkney's streak of 577 was the confirmed record.

After setting the new Iron Man mark, Scott would stay in Boston for only two more seasons to stretch his playing streak to 832 games. Boston's time as one of the top teams in the sport had ended as the team finished in fifth place the next two seasons (1920 and 1921). In December 1921, the Red Sox traded their long-time shortstop to the Yankees. Scott replaced another long-tenured player with the Yankees, Roger Peckinpaugh, as their new shortstop. The Yankees also had replaced the Red Sox as the new power in the American League. Showing how much respect the team had for Scott, he was named the Yankees' captain upon his arrival in New York. Playing all the Yankees' games in 1922, Scott contributed to another American League pennant by pacing all the league's shortstops in fielding (for the seventh straight year) and hitting a better-than-expected .269 average as the Bronx Bombers edged the St. Louis Browns by one game. Meeting one of their cross-town rivals, the New York Giants, the Yankees were swept 4–0 in a five-game series (one game was a tie as a result of being called because of darkness). Scott, never one to hit well in the World's Series, provided a couple of singles in 14 at-bats for a .143 average. In early May of the following year, he became the first major leaguer to appear in 1,000 consecutive contests. Although his final 1923 batting average dropped to .246, the Yankees were happy just to have him in their lineup for his fielding. He led shortstops again in fielding for a remarkable eighth straight year, further stretched his playing streak to 1,138 games and helped New York capture their third American League flag in a row. In his final World's Series appearance, he finally responded by hitting .318 (7 for 22) as the Yankees again met the Giants for the world title. The Yankees invoked some revenge on the Giants by vanquishing the National Leaguers in six games. Scott kept his playing streak going through the 1924 season as the Yankees' string of league pennants came to an end as they finished behind the Washington Senators by two games. On May 6, 1925, after 1,307 consecutive games at shortstop, Scott's knees were starting to give out. Because of that and his lack of productive hitting he was benched by Yankees manager Miller Huggins. His playing streak stood as the all-time record until the Yankees first baseman Lou Gehrig topped it in August 1933.

Just weeks after his streak ended, Scott was released by the Yankees and picked up by the Senators. Serving primarily as a utility player, he stayed with the Senators until his release at the end of the 1925 season. He was acquired by the White Sox just before the start of the 1926 season. By midseason, Chicago let him go and he wound up in the National League with the Cincinnati Reds in early July. Three weeks later, he played his final game in the majors on July 27, 1926.

70. JOE SEWELL

Born: October 9, 1898, Titus, Alabama *Died*: March 6, 1990, Mobile, Alabama *Bats*: Left *Throws*: Right *Height*: 5 feet, 6½ inches *Weight*: 155 *Major league debut*: September 10, 1920 (New York at Cleveland [AL]) *Last major league game*: September 24, 1933 (New York at Boston [AL])

Major league Iron Man from: May 6, 1925, to May 2, 1930 *Consecutive games played*: 1103 *Games as major league Iron Man*: 764 (consecutive games 340 through 1103) *Team played for during streak*: Cleveland Indians (AL) *Primary positions played*: Shortstop and third base *Game missed before streak*: September 12, 1922 (Cleveland at Chicago) *First game played of streak*: September 13, 1922 (Washington at Cleveland) *Last game played of streak*: April 30, 1930 (Cleveland at St. Louis) *Game missed to end streak*: May 2, 1930 (Cleveland at Boston)

Consecutive Game Streak's Statistical Totals

Year	G	AB	R	H	2B	3B	HR	RBI	BB	SO	AVG	SLG	SB
1922	16	51	6	13	2	1	0	6	5	1	.255	.333	3
1923	153	553	98	195	41	10	3	109	98	12	.353	.479	9
1924	153	594	99	188	45	5	4	106	67	13	.316	.429	3
1925	155	608	78	204	37	7	1	98	64	4	.336	.424	7
1926	154	578	91	187	41	5	4	85	65	6	.324	.433	17
1927	153	569	83	180	48	5	1	92	51	7	.316	424	3
1928	155	588	79	190	40	2	4	70	58	9	.323	.418	7
1929	152	578	90	182	38	3	7	73	48	4	.315	.427	6
1930	12	41	4	9	1	1	0	2	4	0	.220	.293	1
Total	1103	4160	628	1348	293	39	24	641	460	56	.324	.431	56

Joe Sewell played for the Cleveland Indians and New York Yankees during a 14-year career that was started under very tragic circumstances. He was playing his first season of pro ball in New Orleans (with less than 100 games' experience) when he became Cleveland's starting shortstop a few weeks after Ray Chapman's fatal beaning in 1920 at the hands of the Yankees' Carl Mays. He started out at shortstop but eventually made the switch to third base beginning with the 1929 season. He was one of baseball's great contact hitters. He was extremely difficult to strike out as evidenced by his fanning only 114 times in 7,132 at-bats during his major league career. He led the American League as the most difficult player to strike out every season from 1925 through 1933. In fact, the numbers prove that he was the most difficult player to strike out in major league history.

Upon his call-up to the Indians in September 1920, Sewell contributed to Cleveland's winning the league pennant as the Tribe edged out the Chicago White Sox. In the abbreviated time he had on the club that year, Sewell proved his abilities by going 23 for 70 for a .329 batting average. Less than a month after making his big league debut on September 10, he was playing shortstop for the Indians in the 1920 World's Series against the Brooklyn Robins. At the plate, he contributed but four singles in seven games but provided steady fielding as the Indians won the series 5–2 and their first baseball world championship. The next year (1921), in his first full year in the majors, Sewell led the league's shortstops in games played by not missing a single game all year and having a .318 batting average and 93 RBI to show

Joe Sewell: He was the toughest batter to strike out in the history of the major leagues. This Hall of Famer and long-time Cleveland Indians shortstop threatened Scott's all-time record until a virus knocked him out of the lineup after 1,103 games on May 2, 1930.

for it. In 1922, he had a streak that was over 300 games when Indians manager Tris Speaker rested him for a couple of games. Speaker did not believe that much in playing streaks and when he realized that Sewell was starting to compile a long streak, he put an end to it by resting Sewell. At this time, Boston's Everett Scott had a much longer playing streak running so Sewell was never in contention to become the Iron Man when the Indians' manager decided to rest him. Late in this season, though, he started his consecutive playing streak that eventually earned him the Iron Man title when he was used as a pinch hitter against Washington in the September 13 game in Cleveland. The next day, Speaker had done some managerial maneuvering and put Sewell at second and regular second baseman Bill Wambsganss at shortstop. This experiment ended after 12 games and Sewell was back at his normal position with the September 24 game. His final 1922 statistics showed that he experienced a nearly 20-point drop in hitting (.299), but he was still productive with the bat by bringing home 83 runners. The succeeding season, his batting average rebounded quite impressively as he posted career highs in hitting (.353 average) and RBI (109). He played the full slate of games in 1923 at shortstop with the exception of two contests in which he was used only as a pinch hitter. Cleveland came in a distant third that year behind the Yankees and Detroit Tigers for the American League title. Although Sewell's hitting dropped to a .316 average in 1924, he was still able to lead the league with 45 doubles and pace the Tribe with 99 runs scored and 106

RBI. Additionally, he led all American League shortstops in putouts and assists. The Indians, meanwhile, had plummeted to sixth place in the final standings, just one game from occupying the cellar position. On May 6, 1925, baseball had a new Iron Man; Sewell inherited the title when the Yankees' Scott was benched after 1,307 consecutive contests. Upon assumption of the honor, Sewell's streak stood at 340 games. Except for a couple of occasions in which he played second base, he took in every game again at shortstop during the 1925 season. Although he had only one homer for the whole year, he repeated as the Tribe's RBI leader with 98 runs knocked in. Besides leading shortstops again in games played, putouts and assists, he topped all players at that position in fielding average for the first time. His efforts could not help Cleveland, though, as the 1925 team repeated their sixth-place finish from the previous year. Early in the 1926 season (on May 8), he became just the ninth player in major league history to play in 500 consecutive games. He finished another year without missing a game at shortstop and hit over .300 for the fourth straight year (.324). As for the Indians, they improved immensely by coming in second place and finishing just three games behind the American League champion Yankees in what turned out to be long-time Cleveland manager Tris Speaker's last season as the Tribe's skipper. Sewell continued his consistent performance in 1927 by having team highs in hits and RBI as he finished with a .316 average and extended his playing streak to 784 games. Unfortunately, under the guidance of new manager Jack McCallister, the Tribe retreated to sixth place in the standings. With the 1928 season upon them, Cleveland replaced McCallister with Roger Peckinpaugh. Although Peckinpaugh kept Sewell at shortstop for most of the year, the Cleveland skipper did some switching around of the infield positions and eventually shifted Sewell to third base. With this maneuvering, Sewell was still able to keep his games streak active. He finished the year with a .323 average but had his lowest RBI total (70) for a full season since his promotion to the majors. The team barely escaped from finishing in the basement by coming in in seventh position, nearly 40 games off the Yankees' pennant-winning rate. The following season (1929) saw his permanent switch to third base. On June 26, 1929, he crossed the 1,000-consecutive-game plateau, just the second player (the other one being Everett Scott) to achieve this milestone. Although his run production wasn't what it had been, he still came in with a .315 batting average and fanned only four times in over 630 plate appearances. Cleveland showed big improvements by finishing in third place, but it was still 24 games off the Philadelphia Athletics' flag-winning performance. Sewell was hoping he could maintain his health, be injury free and set a new major league consecutive-games-played record. This was not to be because just a dozen games into the 1930 season, his streak came to an end when he was rested (due to a virus) on May 2 after 1,103 straight games. In the last couple of games (April 29 and 30) of the streak, he was battling the virus and got in only one at-bat in each of these last contests just to keep the streak going. With the streak over, it made Peckinpaugh's decision to rest Sewell easier. While Cleveland came in fourth place, 21 games off the league lead, Sewell took in only 109 contests and had only 48 RBI and a .289 batting average.

As a result of his performance in 1930, he was released by Cleveland after the season. He was picked up by the Yankees in January 1931. New York shifted Ben Chapman, who had manned the third base position in 1930, to the outfield and inserted Sewell at third base. He put in three quality years at that position for the Bombers. In fact, in 1932 he made it back in the World's Series for the first time since his initial season in 1920 with the Indians. He went 5 for 15 for a .333 average as the Yankees swept the Chicago Cubs in four straight games to win baseball's crown. Sewell retired as an active player after the 1933 season and served as a Yankees coach for the next couple of seasons. He went on to scout for the Indians for 10 years and for a season with the New York Mets in their expansion year. He also did some coaching in the college ranks for several years. He was elected to the baseball's Hall of Fame by its veterans' committee in 1977.

71. Lou Gehrig

Born: June 19, 1903, New York, New York *Died*: June 2, 1941, Riverdale, New York *Bats*: Left *Throws*: Left *Height*: 6 feet *Weight*: 200 *Major league debut*: June 15, 1923 (St. Louis at New York [AL]) *Last major league game*: April 30, 1939 (Washington at New York [AL])

Major league Iron Man from: May 2, 1930, to May 2, 1939 *Consecutive games played*: 2130 *Games as major league Iron Man*: 1386 (consecutive games 745 through 2130) *Team played for during streak*: New York Yankees (AL) *Primary position played*: First base *Game missed before streak*: May 31, 1925 (Boston at New York) *First game played of streak*: June 1, 1925 (Washington at New York) *Last game played of streak*: April 30, 1939 (Washington at New York) *Game missed to end streak*: May 2, 1939 (New York at Detroit)

Consecutive Game Streak's Statistical Totals

Year	G	AB	R	H	2B	3B	HR	RBI	BB	SO	AVG	SLG	SB
1925	115	414	70	125	21	10	20	68	43	44	.302	.546	6
1926	155	572	135	179	47	20	16	112	105	73	.313	.549	6
1927	155	584	149	218	52	18	47	175	109	84	.373	.765	10
1928	154	562	139	210	47	13	27	142	95	69	.374	.648	4
1929	154	553	127	166	32	10	35	126	122	68	.300	.584	4
1930	154	581	143	220	42	17	41	174	101	63	.379	.721	12
1931	155	619	163	211	31	15	46	184	117	56	.341	.662	17
1932	156	596	138	208	42	9	34	151	108	38	.349	.621	4
1933	152	593	138	198	41	12	32	139	92	42	.334	.605	9
1934	154	579	128	210	40	6	49	165	109	31	.363	.706	9
1935	149	535	125	176	26	10	30	119	132	38	.329	.583	8
1936	155	579	167	205	37	7	49	152	130	46	.354	.696	3
1937	157	569	138	200	37	9	37	159	127	49	.351	.643	4
1938	157	576	115	170	32	6	29	114	107	75	.295	.523	6
1939	8	28	2	4	0	0	0	1	5	1	.143	.143	0
Total	2130	7940	1877	2700	527	162	492	1981	1502	777	.340	.633	102

Lou Gehrig was one of the most popular and greatest ballplayers in major league baseball history. It was quite ironic that he played for the Yankees at the same time as the great Babe Ruth. Many baseball experts' opinion is that Ruth is the greatest of all time. Gehrig started out playing pro baseball for a Yankees farm team in Hartford of the Eastern League, spending most of the 1921, 1923 and 1924 seasons there fine-tuning his baseball skills. He was out of organized baseball in 1922. Gehrig made his major league debut on June 15, 1923, when the Yankees played host to St. Louis and shut the Browns out 10–0. He got into only 13 games in 1923 and 10 games in 1924 for the Yankees. The 1925 season was Gehrig's first full season as a regular player but longtime Yankees player Wally Pipp was still the starting first baseman. Gehrig's consecutive game streak started on June 1, 1925, when he pinch-hit for shortstop Peewee Wanninger. Ironically, Wanninger had earlier replaced Everett Scott as the Yankees' shortstop on May 6, 1925, thereby ending Scott's consecutive-games-played streak at 1,307 games. The next day during batting practice, Pipp was hit in the head by a pitch and nearly knocked unconscious. Yankees manager Miller Huggins decided to replace Pipp with Gehrig at first base. For the next 885 games Gehrig played first base. At the start of the 1930 season, Cleveland's Joe Sewell was major league baseball's Iron Man. On May 2 of that year, Sewell missed a game, ending his 1,103-game streak. This is the date that Gehrig took over the Iron Man title. On September 28, 1930, his first baseman streak ended when he played the entire game in left field with Harry Rice playing first. This was because of a late-season managerial maneuver in which Babe Ruth pitched a complete game to beat the Red Sox 9–3 and Gehrig took Ruth's place in the outfield. On August 17, 1933, in St. Louis, Gehrig broke Scott's record. During the 1934 season, there were a couple of times Gehrig's streak might have come to an end. In late June, he was hit in the head by a pitched ball during an exhibition game played in Norfolk, Virginia. Fans were very surprised to see him at his normal position the next day in Washington. He showed no negative effects of the beaning when he hit three triples in four and a half innings before the game was rained out. The most serious threat to his streak occurred on July 13, 1934, when he came down with a severe case of lumbago while running to first base after hitting a single. The next day in Detroit, Yankees manager Joe McCarthy put Gehrig in the lineup batting lead-off and slotted to play shortstop. As the first man up, Gehrig singled and was immediately replaced by Red Rolfe as a pinch runner. Rolfe played the rest of the game at shortstop and Jack Saltzgaver played Gehrig's normal position at first base. After this game, the condition cleared up and the next day he was back in the lineup as if nothing had happened. As the seasons passed, the streak continued. Early in the 1939 season, it was obvious that something was wrong with Gehrig. He had a terrible exhibition season with a batting average around .100. He was not himself. Through the first eight games of the regular season, he was batting .143 and had driven in only one run. Gehrig himself realized something was not right and told manager McCarthy to leave him out of the Yankees' lineup on May 2, 1939, at Detroit. The streak ended with this decision. The last game of his streak was on April 30 when the Yanks hosted the Washington Senators. The Senators beat the Yanks that day 3–2. The ending of the streak was also the ending of an Iron Man era. From the beginning of the 1920 season through May 2, 1939, baseball had only three iron men: Scott, Sewell and Gehrig. Gehrig would never play another game. A few weeks later he was checked out by the Mayo Clinic and the news was not good. He was suffering from

Lou Gehrig: One of the greatest players to step onto a baseball diamond, this Hall of Fame first baseman played in 2,130 consecutive contests from 1925 to 1939 while wearing the uniform of the New York Yankees. A rare and fatal disease which now bears his name brought his playing streak, and soon after his life, to an early end.

amyotrophic lateral sclerosis, a rare and fatal illness. Today, the world knows it as Lou Gehrig's disease. In July 1939 during Lou Gehrig Appreciation Day, he gave the famous "Luckiest Man on the face of the Earth" speech. On this occasion, the Yankees retired uniform number 4, the number Gehrig wore for so many years with the Yanks. He kept as busy as possible after his retirement by working for the New York City Parole Commission. He was appointed to this position in 1939 by New York City's mayor LaGuardia. Within two years after leaving major league baseball, the great Lou Gehrig was dead at the young age of 37.

Gehrig's 2,130-game streak was one of the most notable records in baseball history. Because of his streak, he was nicknamed "The Iron Horse." The streak spanned nearly his entire career. He played in a grand total of 2,164 regular season games from 1923 to 1939. That means he played only 34 games outside of the streak. During his streak, he left 66 games for either a minor injury, pinch runner, pinch hitter or defensive replacement. The 1931 season was the only season during the streak that Gehrig played every inning of every game. His streak was brought to the forefront in 1995 when Cal Ripken broke the record in September 1995. Ripken went on to play 2,632 consecutive games before sitting out a contest against the Yankees on September 20, 1998. Year after year, Gehrig produced massive offensive numbers that most players could only dream about. He also was considered a manager's dream player. He was quiet and unassuming and all business when he was on the field of play. During the years of his streak, the Yankees achieved great success on the ball field and became a dynasty.

During Gehrig's streak, the Yankees won seven American League pennants, played in seven World's Series and won six of those. With Gehrig's bat in their lineup every day, the Yankees led the major leagues in runs scored every year from 1925 through 1938, except for the 1925, 1929, 1934 and 1935 seasons. The 1925 season was the Yankees' worst showing during Gehrig's time with the club. They finished in seventh place and compiled a dismal 69–85 record. The next season the team had a great turnaround. They finished in first place by three games over Cleveland but were beaten in the World's Series by the St. Louis Cardinals in a seven-game series. Next came the 1927 Yankees. This team is considered the greatest team of all time by numerous baseball experts. The Yanks took the American League pennant that season by 19 games over the Philadelphia Athletics. They also swept the series from the Pirates by outscoring them 23–10 in the four games. Another pennant followed the next season and the Athletics were again the bridesmaid by finishing two and a half games behind the Yankees. The Yanks again dominated the World's Series in 1928 by sweeping the National League champs, the St. Louis Cardinals, in four games. Philadelphia put a stop to the Yankees' string of pennants by taking the next three American League championships in 1929, 1930 and 1931. It should be noted that long time Yankees manager Miller Huggins died late in the 1929 season and was replaced by Yankees coach Art Fletcher for the remaining portion of the season. Bob Shawkey managed the Yanks for one season during the 1930 campaign. By 1931, the Yankees hired Joe McCarthy to take the managerial reins. McCarthy would be Gehrig's manager the rest of the Iron Horse's career. The 1932 season found the Yankees back on top of the American League standings by 13 games over the Athletics. The 1932 World's Series resulted in yet another Yankees sweep. This time it was the Chicago Cubs being outscored 37–19 in the four games. The next three seasons drew a blank for any Yankees titles when the team finished in second place each season. At the start of the 1935 season (after Babe Ruth had left the team and moved on to the Boston Braves of the National League), Gehrig was named team captain. He would retain this title through the end of the 1939 season. In 1936, the Yankees far outpaced the competition by taking the American League pennant by 19½ games over the Tigers. The Yanks met the New York Giants, one of their city rivals, that year in the World

Series. The outcome was another championship for the Yankees when they beat the Giants 4–2 and outscored them 43–23 in runs. The 1937 season was another repeat performance for the Yanks as they outpaced the Tigers again by 13 games for the American League pennant. They met the Giants again in the series and the outcome was the same, with the Yankees winning 4–1 and outscoring the Giants 28–12. In Gehrig's last full season, the Yanks won their third straight pennant by besting the Red Sox by nine and a half games and their third straight World Series title by sweeping the Chicago Cubs 4–0 along with outscoring them 22–9. During the seven World Series that Gehrig played in, he had a .361 batting average along with 10 home runs and 35 RBI. He also played in all the annual major league All-Star games from 1933 through 1938. His batting average in those six contests was .222 (4 for 18) along with a couple of home runs and five RBI.

During his spectacular career with the Yankees, Gehrig led the American League in many seasonal statistics categories. These included runs scored in 1931, 1933, 1935, and 1936; hits in 1931; doubles in 1927 and 1928; triples in 1926; home runs in 1931, 1934, and 1936; RBI in 1927, 1928, 1930, 1931, and 1934; batting average in 1934; walks in 1935, 1936, and 1937; on base percentage in 1928, 1934, 1935, 1936, and 1937; and slugging percentage in 1934 and 1936. He also led the American League's first basemen in several fielding statistics. Those categories were: games played in 1926, 1927, 1928, 1932, 1936, 1937 and 1938; putouts in 1927 and 1928; assists in 1930; double plays in 1938; and errors in 1928 and 1937. It should be noted that although he was not noted for his speed on the base paths (he had a career total of 102 stolen bases), Gehrig stole home 15 times. To this day, he still holds some major league and American League records. These include: major league record for most grand slams in a career (23), American League record for most RBI in a season (184 during the 1931 season), and tied a record for most home runs in a game (four) on June 3, 1932. He was chosen the American League's Most Valuable Player in 1927 and 1936. He also won the Triple Crown in 1934 by leading the American League in hitting, home runs and RBI. Because Gehrig had to retire as a result of his fatal illness, the waiting period for eligibility to be voted into baseball's Hall of Fame was waived and he was unanimously elected into the hall in late 1939.

72. PETE FOX

Born: March 8, 1909, Evansville, Indiana *Died*: July 5, 1966, Detroit, Michigan *Bats*: Right *Throws*: Right *Height*: 5 feet, 11 inches *Weight*: 165 *Major league debut*: April 12, 1933 (Cleveland at Detroit [AL]) *Last major league game*: September 23, 1945 (second game) (New York at Boston [AL])

Major league Iron Man from: May 2, 1939, to May 7, 1939 *Consecutive games played*: 306 *Games as major league Iron Man*: 5 (consecutive games 302 through 306) *Team played for during streak*: Detroit Tigers (AL) *Primary position played*: Outfield *Game missed before streak*: May 15, 1937 (Detroit at St. Louis) *First game played of streak*: May 16, 1937 (Detroit at St. Louis) *Last game played of streak*: May 6, 1939 (Boston at Detroit) *Game missed to end streak*: May 7, 1939 (Philadelphia at Detroit)

Consecutive Game Streak's Statistical Totals

Year	G	AB	R	H	2B	3B	HR	RBI	BB	SO	AVG	SLG	SB
1937	135	591	114	196	38	7	12	75	39	38	.332	.481	12
1938	155	634	91	186	35	10	7	96	31	39	.293	.413	16
1939	16	68	4	21	0	0	0	7	5	5	.309	.309	0
Total	306	1293	209	403	73	17	19	178	75	82	.312	.439	28

Pete Fox played in the majors for 13 seasons with two teams, the Detroit Tigers and the Boston Red Sox. His career started with the Tigers where he spent eight seasons patrolling the outfield. He made his major league debut on April 12, 1933, when the Tigers hosted the Cleveland Indians. He became a starter his rookie year by playing in 128 games and batting .288. He led all American League outfielders with four double plays. The Tigers finished in fifth place with a 75–79 record. The next year was different. He played in the same number of game as the previous year and batted .285 as he helped lead the Tigers to the American League pennant by seven games over the New York Yankees. That October found Fox and the Tigers in the World's Series against the St. Louis Cardinals. The series was very exciting as it went down to a seventh game. Unfortunately for the Tigers, the Cardinals pitched Dizzy Dean in the finale and he shut out them out as the Cards won the game 11–0 to claim baseball's world championship. Fox did his part by batting .286 and leading all series hitters with six doubles. The Tigers claimed another pennant in 1935 by again beating the Yanks by three games. Fox had a great year with a .321 batting average in 131 games. He also put together a 29-game hitting streak that ended on July 11, 1935. In the World's Series that year, the Tigers beat the Chicago Cubs in six games to win the world championship. Fox was the Tigers' best player in this series as he was the top hitter with a .385 average and also led all series players in at-bats (26) and hits (10), and tied in doubles (three) and triples (one). If the World's Series Most Valuable Player award had been in existence back then, there is a good shot Fox would have deserved it. The Tigers' string of championships ended in 1936 when they finished second to the Yankees by 19½ games. Although he participated in only 73 games, he had another plus .300 batting average (.305). In 1937, the Tigers again missed out on a league pennant by finishing runner-up to the Yankees by 13 games. Fox's season started slowly because he missed seven of the first 20 games. His playing streak commenced with Detroit's 21st game that year on May 16 at St. Louis. He wound up playing 148 games with a .331 batting average, good for only fourth place with the Tigers (Charlie Gehringer led the team with a .371 average). The Tigers finished the next year in the middle of the pack with an 84–70 record. Manager Mickey Cochrane was let go by the club with a little over 50 games left in the season. He was in his fifth year at the helm of the Tigers and was replaced by Del Baker. Fox played in all the Tigers' games that season and extended his streak to 290 consecutive games by year's end. He also led all American League outfielders with a .994 fielding average.

The 1939 Tigers finished in fifth place that season. Fox had another consistent year with a .295 batting average. He became the major league Iron Man the day Gehrig's 2,130-consecutive-game streak came to a close in Detroit. On that day (May 2, 1939), the new active leader (Fox) of consecutive games played was in the same ballpark along with the next active leader — the Yankees' Frankie Crosetti. Fox had just recently played his 300th consecutive game. He was the Iron Man for less than a week when his streak came to an end on May 7, 1939, in Detroit at 306 games. In comparing his stats over both his entire career and his streak, Fox maintained a steady performance throughout his career. His career batting average was .298 while his streak average was a little bit higher where he batted at a .312 clip. It should also be noted that from April 1920 through May 1939, major league baseball had only three iron men (Scott, Sewell and Gehrig) yet in less than a week, two active streaks ended (Gehrig and Fox) and baseball had three iron men during this short time (Gehrig, Fox and Crosetti). In Fox's final year with Detroit, the Tigers won the pennant by edging the Cleveland Indians by just one game. Fox got into only 93 contests but still batted a very respectable .289 for the season. In October, Detroit was involved in another close series but they lost in seven games to the Cincinnati Reds. Fox, by this time, was not a regular player with the team. In the series, he made only one pinch-hit appearance. His time with the Tigers came to a close when he was sold to the Boston Red Sox on December 12, 1940.

In his first season with the Red Sox, Fox played in only 73 games and batted .302. The Red Sox finished in second, behind the Yankees by 17 games. In 1942, Boston again played second fiddle to the Yankees by finishing nine games behind in the pennant race. Fox spent another season as a substitute outfielder by getting into 77 games. With the war raging in both Europe and the Pacific, many major league players joined the service. The Red Sox lost several key players to the military, most notably Ted Williams, Bobby Doerr and Dom DiMaggio. With these openings, Fox became a regular outfielder during the 1943 and 1944 seasons. In 1943, Boston finished near the bottom of the standings with a 68–84 record. Fox played in 127 contests and led the Red Sox team with a .288 batting average. The next season Boston climbed to a .500 winning percentage but still finished in fourth place, 12 games behind the first-place St. Louis Browns. Fox had a decent year, hitting .315 in 121 contests. His final season (1945) found him back as a substitute outfielder even though the Sox star players were still in the military. He played in only 66 games and had a .245 batting average. He played his final major league game in the second game of a double-header on September 23, 1945, against the Yankees.

73. Frankie Crosetti

Born: October 4, 1910, San Francisco, California *Died*: February 11, 2002, Stockton, California *Bats*: Right *Throws*: Right *Height*: 5 feet, 10 inches *Weight*: 165 *Major league debut*: April 12, 1932 (New York at Philadelphia [AL]) *Last major league game*: October 3, 1948 (New York at Boston [AL])

Major league Iron Man from: May 7, 1939, to May 11, 1940 *Consecutive games played*: 418 *Games as major league Iron Man*: 158 (consecutive games 261 through 418) *Team played for during streak*: New York Yankees (AL) *Primary position played*: Shortstop *Game missed before streak*: July 5, 1937 (second game) (Boston at New York) *First game played of streak*: July 9, 1937 (Washington at New York) *Last game played of streak*: May 10, 1940 (Boston at New York) *Game missed to end streak*: May 11, 1940 (Boston at New York)

Consecutive Game Streak's Statistical Totals

Year	G	AB	R	H	2B	3B	HR	RBI	BB	SO	AVG	SLG	SB
1937	90	371	81	82	17	3	5	30	48	60	.221	.323	6
1938	157	631	113	166	35	3	9	55	106	97	.263	.371	27
1939	152	656	109	153	25	5	10	56	65	81	.233	.332	11
1940	19	73	10	11	0	1	0	5	16	7	.151	.178	1
Total	418	1731	313	412	77	12	24	146	235	245	.238	.338	45

One of the more underrated players on the great New York Yankees teams of the 1930s and 1940s was their shortstop, Frankie Crosetti. At various times during his playing career he had among his teammates Babe Ruth, Lou Gehrig, Joe DiMaggio and Yogi Berra. A tough and intense competitor, he played his entire major league career (17 seasons) for the Yankees, eight of which resulted in world championships. He was a master of the hidden ball trick and had a knack for getting hit by pitches, leading the American League in that category eight times between 1934 and 1945. He became a member of the Yankees organization when his playing contract was acquired from a Pacific Coast League team in 1929. He stayed in the minors until making the parent team for the 1932 season.

During his rookie season, Crosetti took over the shortstop position from Lyn Lary. He batted .241 and drove in 57 runners that first season. With the Yankees winning the American League pennant in 1932, he found himself, at the age of 21, the team's shortstop in the World's Series. Although Crosetti had only two hits in 15 at-bats, the Yankees easily dispatched the Chicago Cubs in four games to claim the title of world champion. While Crosetti started anchoring New York's infield, the team would go the next three years without a league title as they came in second each of those seasons in the standings. It wasn't until 1936 that the Yankees broke through to another league championship. Crosetti had a solid year for what shortstops produced back then. He hit .288 (only Tony Lazzeri had a lower average among the regular Yankees) and contributed 15 homers and 78 RBI. In the World Series, the powerhouse Yankees defeated the New York Giants in six games and outscored them 43–23 in runs scored. He went 7 for 26 for a .269 average along with five runs scored. The following season (1937), he started his consecutive game streak on July 9 in a game in New York versus the Washington Senators. He finished the rest of the 90 games on the 1937 Yankees schedule and the team easily repeated as league champs. Although the Yankees also won the World Series again, vanquishing the Giants (only this time the task was accomplished in five games), Crosetti couldn't buy a hit as he contributed a lonely single to the team's offense in the five-game series. He toiled at his shortstop position for all 157 Yankee games in 1938 as he extended his playing streak to 247 games by the season's conclusion. There were only three games that he didn't finish and in those contests he was relieved by Bill Knickerbocker. Offensively, he led the league in stolen bases (27) and strikeouts (97) as he helped the team cruise to a third consecutive American League title. The Yankees had no problem in sweeping the Cubs in four games during the 1938 World's Series. Crosetti had a much better time in this series as he hit .250 and led all series players in doubles and RBI (he actually was tied with teammate Joe Gordon in both categories). Early in 1939, Gehrig's record streak ended and less than a week after his great teammate took himself out of the lineup, Crosetti became baseball's new reigning Iron Man, replacing the Detroit Tigers' Pete Fox. Crosetti completed his second straight year without missing a contest. Among the regular Yankees players, Crosetti had the lowest average (.233) and home run output (10) for the 1939 American League champions. He did pace the league shortstops in fielding with a .968 average along with position highs in games played, putouts and double plays. The World Series that year resulted in another four-game sweep for the Bombers, only on this occasion it was the Cincinnati Reds. He hit a lowly .063 for the series as he went 1 for 16 with a couple of runs scored. Just 20 games into the 1940 campaign, Crosetti's streak came to an end after 418 games when he was benched by Yankees manager Joe McCarthy in favor of backup infielder Knickerbocker. Crosetti's benching was the result of a prolonged batting slump which showed him hitting just .151 for the new season. His slump continued for the rest of the season as he finished with a .194 average, the lowest total among all regular players in the major leagues. From looking at his stats during his streak, you can tell that Crosetti was in the New York lineup for his steadiness in the field with his reliable glove and his ability to get on base, not for his productive bat.

After the 1940 season, Crosetti was replaced at shortstop by future Yankees great Phil Rizzuto and would remain for the rest of his major league career a backup infielder at short or third base (except for the 1943 and 1945 seasons when he was back at shortstop because Rizzuto was in the military during World War II). Although his playing career came to a permanent end after the 1948 season, he continued to wear the uniform of the Yankees for many more years. He served as the Yankees third base coach for 20 seasons before retiring after the 1968 season. By the time of his retirement, he had worn the Yankees uniform longer (from 1932 through 1968) than any previous player, coach or manager.

74. STAN HACK

Born: December 6, 1909, Sacramento, California *Died*: December 15, 1979, Dixon, Illinois *Bats*: Left *Throws*: Right *Height*: 6 feet *Weight*: 170 *Major league debut*: April 12, 1932 (Chicago at Cincinnati [NL]) *Last major league game*: September 24, 1947 (Chicago at Cincinnati [NL])

Major league Iron Man from: May 11, 1940, to May 18, 1940 *Consecutive games played*: 332 *Games as major league Iron Man*: 5 (consecutive games 328 through 332) *Team played for during streak*: Chicago Cubs (NL) *Primary position played*: Third base *Game missed before streak*: April 21, 1938 (Chicago at Cincinnati) *First game played of streak*: April 22, 1938 (St. Louis at Chicago) *Last game played of streak*: May 17, 1940 (Chicago at New York) *Game missed to end streak*: May 18, 1940 (Chicago at New York)

Consecutive Game Streak's Statistical Totals

Year	G	AB	R	H	2B	3B	HR	RBI	BB	SO	AVG	SLG	SB
1938	151	606	108	193	34	11	4	67	93	39	.318	.431	16
1939	156	641	112	191	28	6	8	56	65	35	.298	.398	17
1940	25	94	15	24	6	1	0	4	14	1	.255	.340	2
Total	332	1341	235	408	68	18	12	127	172	75	.304	.409	35

Stan Hack was one of the most popular Chicago Cubs in the history of the team until Ernie Banks arrived on the scene. Hack played his entire 16-year major league career in a Cubs uniform. During a great majority of this time, he was the team's regular third baseman. After spending one year in the Pacific Coast League with Sacramento, he made the Cubs' roster for the 1932 season. That year he was the backup to regular hot corner occupant Woody English, but he did get into 72 contests and had a .236 batting average. The Cubs won the National League title that year but were swept by the New York Yankees in the World's Series in four games. Hack got into only one contest as a pinch runner.

The following season, he spent most of 1933 back in the minors, playing for Albany of the International League, but he returned to the Cubs for a 20-game stint. This time he took better advantage of his chance with the Cubs by averaging over a hit a game and finishing with a .350 average. In 1934, Cubs skipper Charlie Grimm decided to make Hack the third baseman and have English rotate between third and short, spelling Hack and shortstop Billy Jurges whenever either player was out of the lineup. His first year as the Cubs third baseman, Hack was in the lineup for 111 games and hit at a .289 clip as the team came in third place, just eight games behind the St. Louis Cardinals. In 1935, he knocked in 64 runners and improved his batting 22 points by finishing with a .311 average in 124 contests. Chicago claimed their second National League pennant in four years as they edged the Cards by four games. The Cubs met the Detroit Tigers in the World Series but were defeated in six games. Playing in all six contests, Hack went 5 for 27 with two runs scored, a double, a triple and a .227 average. The following two seasons, he missed only a handful of games and had a batting average that hovered near the .300 mark. The 1937 season saw Hack lead the league's third basemen in games played (150), putouts (151) and double plays (25). The team finished in second place both years, just behind the New York Giants. After missing two of the first three games of the 1938 season, Hack started his consecutive games streak on April 22 in Chicago against the Cards. He did not miss another game the rest of the season as he played the final 151 games. In the statistical column, he had much to be proud of as he led the Cubs with 195 hits and a .320 batting average. Additionally, he paced the National League in stolen bases and times on base along with repeating as the third base leader in games played, putouts and double plays for a second straight year. Because of his outstanding year on the diamond, Hack deserves credit for leading the Cubs to another National League championship. In the 1938 World's Series, they had the dubious pleasure of facing the Yankees again for baseball's ultimate prize. As in 1932, the Cubs were swept in four games by the mighty Bronx Bombers. The next year (1939), Hack played all 156 games at third base as he hit .298 and repeated as the league's stolen base king (tied with Pittsburgh Pirate Lee Handley with 17 swipes) along with games played and putouts by third basemen. The Cubs had their worst showing that season since 1927. They fell to fourth place, 13 games behind the first-place Reds. On May 11, 1940, reigning Iron Man Frankie Crosetti's streak ended and Hack became the new Iron Man of baseball. Although his streak started a few games later than that of the Reds' Frank McCormick, Hack actually passed him in the total number of consecutive games played by this time. He was baseball's Iron Man for only a week when his 332-games-played streak (all of which were played at third base) came to an abrupt end when he was struck by a foul line drive off the bat of teammate Hank Leiber during the first inning of the May 17, 1940, game at New York. He had been the runner at third base and in foul territory when he was injured by the batted ball. The concussion caused him to miss a week's worth of action. The injury had no long lasting effects as he finished among the league's batting leaders with a .317 average. He finished in a tie for most hits with his successor as Iron Man (McCormick) with 191 base hits and topped all players by reaching base 269 times. His accomplishments on the field couldn't help the Cubs as they went 75–79 and finished in fifth place.

Hack played for seven more productive years in Chicago. He had retired after the 1943 season due to a dispute with Cubs manager Jimmy Wilson. With the firing of Wilson early in the 1944 campaign (and the rehiring of his old skipper, Charlie Grimm), Hack was back in a Cubs uniform by June. The next year (1945), he proved he was not done just yet by posting a career-best .323 average, leading the team with 191 hits and contributing to yet another league title. In the struggle for the world championship with the Detroit Tigers in 1945, the Cubs put up a great fight but came out on the losing end of the seven-game series. Hack had a great series by going 11 for 30, finishing with a .367 average and finishing in a tie with teammate Phil Cavarretta and the Tigers' Doc Cramer for most hits. Hack played two more years before retiring after the 1947 season. With his playing days over, he went into managing in the minors for several seasons before returning to the Cubs as their manager for three years (1954–1956). Upon leaving the Cubs, he coached for the Cardinals for two years (including 10 games at the end of the year as interim manager in 1958). Once he left the Cards, he went back to managing in the minors for another 10 years.

75. Frank McCormick

Born: June 9, 1911, New York, New York *Died*: November 21, 1982, Manhassett, New York *Bats*: Right *Throws*: Right *Height*: 6 feet, 4 inches *Weight*: 205 *Major league debut*: September 11, 1934 (Cincinnati at Brooklyn [NL]) *Last major league game*: October 3, 1948 (Boston at New York [NL])

Major league Iron Man from: May 18, 1940, to May 25, 1942 *Consecutive games played*: 652 *Games as major league Iron Man*: 322 (consecutive games 331 through 652) *Team played for during streak*: Cincinnati Reds (NL) *Primary position played*: First base *Game missed before streak*: October 3, 1937 (second game) (Cincinnati at Pittsburgh) *First game played of streak*: April 19, 1938 (Chicago at Cincinnati) *Last game played of streak*: May 24, 1942 (second game) (Cincinnati at St. Louis) *Game missed to end streak*: May 25, 1942 (Pittsburgh at Cincinnati)

Consecutive Game Streak's Statistical Totals

Year	G	AB	R	H	2B	3B	HR	RBI	BB	SO	AVG	SLG	SB
1938	151	640	89	209	40	4	5	106	18	17	.327	.425	1
1939	156	630	99	209	41	4	18	128	40	16	.332	.495	1
1940	155	618	93	191	44	3	19	127	52	26	.309	.482	2
1941	154	603	77	162	31	5	17	97	40	13	.269	.421	2
1942	36	148	20	40	6	0	7	29	6	1	.270	.453	0
Total	652	2639	378	811	162	16	66	487	156	73	.307	.456	6

Frank McCormick was a great offensive first baseman with a superb glove who starred for the Cincinnati Reds in the '30s and '40s. Native to New York City, he first tried out with the New York Giants but the team decided not to sign him to a contract. He finally got his call to the big leagues with the Reds and made his debut late in the 1934 season. He made it into the lineup for only a dozen games and finished with a .313 average. Nearly three more years passed before Cincinnati gave him another opportunity to show off his talent. This time (1937), he played in two dozen contests and compiled a .325 average. After he sat out the last game of the 1937 season, McCormick would not miss another game in over four years.

When the 1938 season opened in Cincinnati on April 19 against the Chicago Cubs, McCormick was the Reds' new regular first baseman. This contest also was the start of his consecutive-games-played streak. The statistics he achieved his first full year in the majors proved beyond any doubt that he was right where he belonged. He compiled a .327 batting average, drove in 106 runners, led the National League with 209 hits and 640 at-bats along with helping to improve the Reds' performance in the standings. The team won 26 more games

Frank McCormick: The longtime Cincinnati Reds first baseman held the Iron Man title for over two years until his streak ended after 652 games in May 1942.

than during the previous season and jumped from the basement to fourth place. By posting league highs in hits (209) and RBI (128) in 1939, McCormick helped lead the Reds to their first National League pennant in 20 years by hitting .332. His batting average was good for a second-place tie with the Cards' Ducky Medwick. Medwick's Cardinals teammate Johnny Mize led the league with a .349 batting mark. Defensively, McCormick led first basemen in fielding average, putouts, and double plays. In the 1939 World Series, Cincinnati had the pleasure of facing the mighty New York Yankees. It was not a contest as the Yankees easily handled the Reds and took the championship in a four-game sweep. McCormick was one of the few bright spots for Cincinnati as he led the Reds with a .400 average (6 for 15). The 1940 season was extraordinary for McCormick. He was in close competition for the Iron Man title with the Cubs' Stan Hack. Even though Hack's streak started after his, McCormick trailed Hack by a few games. On May 18, McCormick became baseball's Iron Man when Hack missed that day's game because of a concussion after being hit by a foul ball. With the stats showing that he led the league in at-bats, hits (for the third straight season), and doubles along with finishing second in total bases, extra-base hits and RBI, McCormick was chosen the National League's Most Valuable Player. The Reds repeated as league champs and faced the Detroit Tigers in the 1940 World Series. Although McCormick hit only .214, the Reds won the World Championship by edging the Tigers in the series-deciding seventh game 2–1. The following year (1941), McCormick and the team suffered letdowns as his batting dropped 40 points and the team fell to third place after winning the National League flag the two previous seasons. In a game on May 28, 1941, he became just the 17th player in major league history to achieve appearances in 500 consecutive contests. Although he had an off year offensively, he was still doing well with the glove as he led the league's first basemen in every major fielding stat except assists and his fielding percentage led all the league's first basemen for the third consecutive year. It should also be noted that in 1941 he was the toughest major league hitter to strike out as he fanned only 13 times in over 600 at-bats (once every 46 times at the plate). The following year on May 25, 1942, a pulled muscle forced him to sit out the Reds' game against the Pittsburgh Pirates. After more than two years as the sport's Iron Man, his streak was finished after 652 games. He played every game of this streak at first base and set the National League mark that still stands today for most consecutive games played at that position. His .307 batting average during his streak is slightly better than his career mark.

After the 1942 season ended, McCormick played in a Reds uniform for three more years. He maintained a consistent pattern in most of his offensive stats although his run-producing numbers started a slow decline. After playing for the Reds for 10 seasons, he was sold to the Philadelphia Phillies. He stayed in Philly for just over one season before landing in Boston with the Braves early in 1947. In Boston, he got into games only as a pinch hitter or when regular first baseman Earl Torgeson needed a rest. His last year he was with the Braves as the team won the National League flag and faced the Cleveland Indians in the 1948 World Series. McCormick did get into a few games but was a nonfactor as Boston went down to defeat in six games to the Tribe. He retired after the series and went into scouting, coaching, broadcasting and even managing in the minors for the Reds' organization.

76. Rudy York

Born: August 17, 1913, Ragland, Alabama *Died*: February 5, 1970, Rome, Georgia *Bats*: Right *Throws*: Right *Height*: 6 feet, 1 inch *Weight*: 209 *Major league debut*: August 22, 1934 (Detroit at Washington [AL]) *Last major league game*: September 20, 1948 (Philadelphia at Cleveland [AL])

Rudy York

Major league Iron Man from: May 25, 1942, to July 31, 1942 *Consecutive games played*: 413 *Games as major league Iron Man*: 63 (consecutive games 351 through 413) *Team played for during streak*: Detroit Tigers (AL) *Primary position played*: First base *Game missed before streak*: October 1, 1939 (second game) (Cleveland at Detroit) *First game played of streak*: April 16, 1940 (St. Louis at Detroit) *Last game played of streak*: July 30, 1942 (second game) (Philadelphia at Detroit) *Game missed to end streak*: July 31, 1942 (Boston at Detroit)

Consecutive Game Streak's Statistical Totals

Year	G	AB	R	H	2B	3B	HR	RBI	BB	SO	AVG	SLG	SB
1940	155	588	105	186	46	6	33	134	89	88	.316	.583	3
1941	155	590	91	153	29	3	27	111	92	88	.259	.456	3
1942	103	392	57	100	13	3	15	56	48	50	.255	.418	1
Total	413	1570	253	439	88	12	75	301	229	226	.280	.494	7

One of the most feared players at the plate in the late 1930s and 1940s was Rudy York. Although he played with four major league teams during his 13-year big league career, his most productive years were spent in a Detroit Tigers uniform. He also was one of the more durable players in the 1940s as he played in at least 150 or more games for eight straight years from 1940 through 1947. His first four years of professional ball were spent in the minors although he had a brief call-up to the Tigers in the latter part of the 1934 season. He made his debut when the Tigers visited the nation's capital to face the Washington Senators on August 22, 1934. His stint that season was so brief that he was in only three contests.

York made it to the majors permanently with the arrival of the 1937 season. He was used as the catcher but also filled in at third base on occasion. In his rookie year, he made quite an impression. In August, he set records for most home runs and RBI in a month when he knocked 18 pitches out of the park and drove home 49 runners. He completed the season with 35 homers, 103 RBI and a solid .307 average. Not bad for a rookie; in fact, if the Rookie of the Year award had been in existence back in 1937, he definitely would have won it for the American League. He proved his first year was no fluke when in 1938 he clubbed 33 home runs, drove home 127 runners and batted .298 in 135 games. He also made his first of seven all-star game appearances that season. In 1939, he was out a good portion of the year but managed to hit .307 and knocked out 20 pitches in 102 contests. In the spring of 1940, the Tigers' manager, Del Baker, decided to relieve York of his catching duties and install him at first base and shifted the team's superstar, Hank Greenberg, to left field. Besides manning first base at the start of the new season, York also began his consecutive games streak in the season opener on April 16 in Detroit against the St. Louis Browns. Playing every game that year at first, he rebounded from his previous year's totals by belting 33 pitches over the fence and driving home 134 runners as he and Greenberg provided the firepower that helped the Tigers edge the Cleveland Indians by one game for the American League pennant. The 1940 World Series against the Cincinnati Reds turned out to be a classic as it went the full seven games. Unfortunately for the Tigers, Detroit came out on the short end as they lost the deciding seventh game 2–1. York had a mediocre series as he went 6 for 26 for a .231 average with a homer and a couple of runs knocked in. With the departure of Greenberg for most of the 1941 season, the Tigers heavily relied upon York to provide the power to guide the Tigers to another pennant. Although he didn't miss a game all season and led the team in doubles (29), homers (27) and RBI (111), Detroit still missed Greenberg's bat in the lineup. As a result, the Tigers fell below .500 baseball, finishing 75–79, good enough for only a fourth-place tie with the Cleveland Indians. Just over a month into the 1942 season, York became the

Iron Man of major league baseball when the Reds' durable first baseman, Frank McCormick, suffered a muscle injury. York's reign as Iron Man lasted another 63 games before he was benched (due to his lack of home run power) by Baker for a series that was starting against the Boston Red Sox. In nearly two months of action before his benching, York had hit only three homers. He was replaced at first base by Rip Radcliff. York's streak was over after 413 straight games (all of which were played at first base). Detroit had another below-average year as the team sunk into the second division with a fifth-place finish. Although York barely made the 20 homer plateau with 21 clouts, that stat along with his 90 RBI were the team's highs.

In 1943, his power production numbers rebounded as he led the American League with 34 homers, 118 RBI and a .527 slugging average. He took third place in the league MVP voting, behind New York Yankees pitcher Spud Chandler and Chicago White Sox great Luke Appling. As for the team, Baker was let go as manager and replaced by Steve O'Neill. The change really had no effect as Detroit again finished in fifth place. York's career would continue in Detroit until his trade to the Boston Red Sox in January 1946. He had made it back to the World Series with the Tigers in 1945. They beat the Chicago Cubs in seven games to claim the Tigers' second World Championship. York's .179 series average (five hits in 28 at-bats) did not provide much influence in the Tigers' championship triumph. The next year (1946), he was back in the World Series, only this time in a Red Sox uniform. Boston lost the closely contested series to the St. Louis Cardinals in seven games. Although he hit only .261 by going 6 for 23, he led the series players with six runs, a triple and two homers. He was traded the next year in midseason to the White Sox. After the 1947 season, he was released by Chicago and picked up by the Philadelphia Athletics. He got into only 31 games that year by pinch hitting or filling in at first base for the A's regular first baseman, Ferris Fain. He played his final major league game in Cleveland on September 20, 1948. He hung around in the minors for a few years before calling it a career after the 1951 season. He did some coaching and managing in the minors before returning to the Red Sox in 1959 as a coach. That first season, he even got to manage the Red Sox for one game between the firing of Pinky Higgins and the hiring of Billy Jurges as Boston's manager.

77. Danny Litwhiler

Born: August 31, 1916, Ringtown, Pennsylvania *Bats*: Right *Throws*: Right *Height*: 5 feet, 10½ inches *Weight*: 198 *Major league debut*: April 25, 1940 (Brooklyn at Philadelphia [NL]) *Last major league game*: September 25, 1951 (St. Louis at Cincinnati [NL])

Major league Iron Man from: July 31, 1942, to June 3, 1943 *Consecutive games played*: 325 *Games as major league Iron Man*: 92 (consecutive games 234 through 325) *Teams played for during streak*: Philadelphia Phillies (NL) (1941–1943) and St. Louis Cardinals (NL) (1943) *Primary position played*: Outfield *Game missed before streak*: May 3, 1941 (St. Louis at Philadelphia) *First game played of streak*: May 4, 1941 (Cincinnati at Philadelphia) *Last game played of streak*: June 2, 1943 (Brooklyn at St. Louis) *Game missed to end streak*: June 3, 1943 (Philadelphia at St. Louis)

Consecutive Game Streak's Statistical Totals

Year	G	AB	R	H	2B	3B	HR	RBI	BB	SO	AVG	SLG	SB
1941	137	536	65	169	27	6	17	58	35	41	.315	.483	1
1942	151	591	59	160	25	9	9	56	27	42	.271	.389	2
1943	37	143	23	37	6	0	5	17	11	14	.259	.406	1
Total	325	1270	147	366	58	15	31	131	73	97	.288	.431	4

Danny Litwhiler

A reliable fielding outfielder, Danny Litwhiler played in the National League for 11 seasons with four major league ball clubs. He began his career with the Philadelphia Phillies in April 1940. Although he played in only 36 games his rookie year, he made quite the impression by putting together a 21-game hitting streak that was stopped on September 17. He completed the year with a .345 average by going 49 for 142 along with contributing five homers and 17 RBI in limited action.

Litwhiler's consecutive game streak started on May 4, 1941, in Philadelphia against the Cincinnati Reds as he participated in the last 137 games of the season. He took over the Phillies' left field position, replacing Johnny Rizzo who was moved over to right field. Although Philadelphia finished a dreadful 57 games behind the first-place Brooklyn Dodgers in the 1941 final National League standings with a 43–111 record, Litwhiler was one of the few bright spots on the club as he hit .305 and led the team with 590 at-bats, 180 hits, 29 doubles, 18 homers and a .466 slugging percentage in 151 games played. His final hit total was good for third place in the league behind the Reds' Stan Hack and the Dodgers' Pete Reiser. He also led the National League outfielders with 393 putouts and 15 miscues. Not missing a single game the following year, he became the offensive force on a team that only scored 394 runs the entire season. He led the team in every major category including a minuscule nine home runs and a .271 batting average. He had 317 total chances out in left field and, amazingly, did not make a single error for a 1.000 fielding percentage. He took part in his only all-star game that year. He had played only 234 consecutive games when he took over baseball's Iron Man title on July 31, 1942, from the Detroit Tigers' Rudy York. Philadelphia had changed managers, naming old-time ballplayer Hans Lobert as the new skipper. The move had no effect as the team finished in the basement for the fifth straight season with another dreary won-loss record of 42–109. Early in that season, Litwhiler suffered a minor injury in the third game of the year on April 27. Over the next two games, he was used as a pinch hitter to keep his streak going. He returned to the lineup and the streak was still running when he was traded to the pennant-contending St. Louis Cardinals on June 1, 1943. After playing just one game in a Cards uniform, Litwhiler was not in the team's lineup on June 3. This brought his playing streak to a conclusion after 325 contests. He finished the year with a .272 average and helped lead the Cards to the league flag by a healthy 18 games over the second-place Reds. Facing the New York Yankees in the World Series, he went 4 for 15 for a .267 average in a five-game series loss to the Bronx Bombers.

Litwhiler took in 136 games in left field in 1944 and put in a solid season which included driving in 82 runners as the Cards repeated as National League champs. The Cardinals faced their cross-town rival St. Louis Browns in the World Series. The Cards went on to defeat the Browns in six games to lay claim to the world championship of baseball. Although he hit a solo homer off the Browns' Denny Galehouse in the fifth game of a 2–0 Cards' win, Litwhiler did not influence the outcome as he produced only four hits and a .200 average. He missed the entire 1945 season due to his military service in World War II. Upon his return to the major league scene in 1946, he took his place on the Cardinals' roster but played only six games before he was traded on June 9 to the Boston Braves. He stayed with the Braves for a couple of years and then left the club via another trade to the Reds in May 1948. He spent the last four seasons of his major league baseball career in Cincinnati, playing in right field when he was given the chance to participate. His last quality performance year was 1949 when he hit .291 in 102 games. He was used mainly as a platoon player the last two years. Knee problems that he had endured his entire career left him unable to do the job anymore. He last appeared in a major league box score on September 25, 1951, in Cincinnati against one of his old teams, the St. Louis Cardinals.

78. MICKEY VERNON

Born: April 22, 1918, Marcus Hook, Pennsylvania *Bats*: Left *Throws*: Left *Height*: 6 feet, 2 inches *Weight*: 170 *Major league debut*: July 8, 1939 (first game) (Washington at Philadelphia [AL]) *Last major league game*: September 27, 1960 (Cincinnati at Pittsburgh [NL])

Major league Iron Man from: June 3, 1943, to June 7, 1943; June 7, 1943, to June 9, 1943 (tied with Billy Herman); June 9, 1943, to June 24, 1943; June 24, 1943, to June 30, 1943 (tied with Billy Herman); July 7, 1943 to July 15, 1943 (tied with Billy Herman); July 15, 1943, to July 21, 1943; July 21, 1943, to July 22, 1943 (tied with Billy Herman); July 22, 1943, to September 4, 1943 *Consecutive games played*: 292 *Games as major league Iron Man*: 83 (consecutive games 202 through 205, consecutive game 206 [tied with Herman], consecutive games 207 through 221, consecutive game 222 through 227 [tied with Herman], consecutive games 236 through 241 [tied with Herman], consecutive games 242 through 246, consecutive games 247 and 248 [tied with Herman], consecutive games 249 through 292) *Team played for during streak*: Washington Senators (AL) *Primary position played*: First base *Game missed before streak*: September 15, 1941 (Detroit at Washington) *First game played of streak*: September 16, 1941 (Detroit at Washington) *Last game played of streak*: September 3, 1943 (Washington at New York) *Game missed to end streak*: September 4, 1943 (Washington at New York)

Consecutive Game Streak's Statistical Totals:

Year	G	AB	R	H	2B	3B	HR	RBI	BB	SO	AVG	SLG	SB
1941	13	46	8	13	2	1	0	5	4	4	.283	.370	1
1942	151	621	76	168	34	6	9	86	59	63	.271	.388	25
1943	128	497	81	129	25	5	7	65	61	52	.260	.372	23
Total	292	1164	165	310	61	12	16	156	124	119	.266	.381	49

Mickey Vernon played in the majors for 20 seasons, mostly for second-division teams. Most of his career was spent in the American League with the Washington Senators (1939–1943, 1946–1948, and 1950–1955), Cleveland Indians (1949–1950, 1958), and Boston Red Sox (1956–1957), but he gave his farewell tour as a player in the National League where he played two seasons with the Milwaukee Braves (1959) and Pittsburgh Pirates (1960). He was a smooth fielding first baseman who was a regular player most of his career except for his first two and final two seasons in the majors and the time he spent in the armed forces during World War II (1944–1945). This quiet player is one of the better players never elected to baseball's Hall of Fame.

Vernon was 21 years old when he made his major league debut with the Washington Senators on July 8, 1939, in the first game of a double-header in Philadelphia against the Athletics. He pinch-ran for first baseman Sammy West in the ninth inning of a 6–5 loss. In the nightcap, he made his first start at first and had one single in five at-bats. That rookie season he got into 76 games and soon after took over the job as the Senators' first baseman. Although the Senators finished in sixth place that year, Vernon proved he could play in the big leagues by hitting for a respectable .257 average. In 1940, he was in the minors with Jersey City of the International League. He received a call-up to the Senators but played in only five games and had a .158 batting average. The 1941 season found Vernon back as the regular first baseman. He started his consecutive playing streak on September 16, 1941, in a Senators' home game against the Detroit Tigers. He hit for a .299 average, drove in 93 runs and led all American League first sackers in double plays with 122. Washington, as was the norm in that era, finished near the bottom of the standings. The next season (1942), Vernon played every game, finishing with a .271 average, leading the Senators with 34 doubles and all American League first basemen in errors with 26 miscues. It was another poor showing for the Senators as they finished in seventh place, several games ahead of the cellar-finishing Philadelphia Athletics. During the off-season, the Senators let manager Bucky Harris go and replaced him with longtime Senator player Ossie Bluege. The Senators responded to change by having their best season since 1933. They finished runner-up in the standings to the Yankees by 13½ games. Vernon, in the meantime, had a decent year, batting .268 in 145 games played. He also led the league in being hit by pitches by being plunked 10 times by opposing pitchers. On June 3, 1943, Vernon became the major league's Iron Man when Danny Litwhiler of the St. Louis Cardinals sat out a game. During this time, Vernon was in close competition for the Iron Man title with the Dodgers' Billy Herman. In fact, between June 7 and July 22, Vernon and Herman were tied for the consecutive games lead on four occasions and from June 30 to July 7, Herman took over the lead from Vernon. On July 22, Vernon retook the lead for good and held the Iron Man title through September 4, when he was forced to miss a game in New York against the

Mickey Vernon: He was a Washington Senators first baseman and their most reliable hitter in the 1940s and 1950s era. This two-time American League batting champion had streaks of 292 and 369 games in the 1940s that were long enough to qualify him to be the big league's Iron Man on two occasions.

Yankees due to being injured by a pitch during an exhibition game earlier in the week. The injury, a bruised hand, caused him to miss several games. He was replaced in the Senators' lineup by Bob Johnson. His playing streak ended at 292 games.

After the 1943 season was completed, Vernon answered his country's call to arms and entered the military. He would miss two years while fighting in World War II. After the war ended, he rejoined the Senators for the 1946 season and resumed his position as their first baseman. Vernon would go on to play in the majors through the 1960 season. Since he was a two-time major league Iron Man, information about the rest of his career is addressed in a later profile.

79. Billy Herman

Born: July 7, 1909, New Albany, Indiana *Died*: September 5, 1992, West Palm Beach, Florida *Bats*: Right *Throws*: Right *Height*: 5 feet, 11 inches *Weight*: 180 *Major league debut*: August 29, 1931 (Cincinnati at Chicago [NL]) *Last major league game*: August 1, 1947 (New York at Pittsburgh [NL])

Major league Iron Man from: June 7, 1943, to June 9, 1943 (tied with Mickey Vernon); June 24, 1943, to June 30, 1943 (tied with Mickey Vernon); June 30, 1943, to July 7, 1943; July 7, 1943, to July 15, 1943 (tied with Mickey Vernon); July 21, 1943, to July 22, 1943 (tied with Mickey Vernon); September 4, 1943, to April 18, 1944 *Consecutive games played*: 313 *Games as major league Iron Man*: 50 (consecutive game 206 [tied with Vernon], consecutive games 222 through 227 [tied with Vernon], consecutive games 228 through 235, consecutive games 236 through 241 [tied with Vernon], consecutive games 247 and 248 [tied with Vernon], consecutive games 287 through 313) *Team played for during streak*: Brooklyn Dodgers (NL) *Primary positions played*: Second base and third base *Game missed before streak*: September 21, 1941 (second game) (Brooklyn at Philadelphia) *First game played of streak*: September 22, 1941 (Brooklyn at Philadelphia) *Last game played of streak*: October 3, 1943 (Brooklyn at Cincinnati) *Game missed to end streak*: April 18, 1944 (Brooklyn at Philadelphia)

Consecutive Game Streak's Statistical Totals

Year	G	AB	R	H	2B	3B	HR	RBI	BB	SO	AVG	SLG	SB
1941	5	16	1	2	1	0	0	0	1	2	.125	.188	0
1942	155	571	76	146	34	2	2	65	72	52	.256	.333	6
1943	153	585	76	193	41	2	2	100	66	26	.330	.417	4
Total	313	1172	153	341	76	4	4	165	139	80	.291	.373	10

Billy Herman was definitely in the top echelon of the best defensive second basemen the game of baseball has ever witnessed. This was evident by his leading National League second basemen in games played (seven times), putouts (seven times), assists (three times), double plays (four times) and fielding (three times). He would go on to spend 15 seasons in the major leagues with the Chicago Cubs (1931–1941), Brooklyn Dodgers (1941–1943 and 1946), Boston Braves (1946) and Pittsburgh Pirates (1947). He played in the minors (mostly in the American Association) for five years before his call-up to the Cubs in late August 1931. He made his debut on August 29 at Wrigley Field against the Cincinnati Reds. Playing in 25 contests, he impressed Cubs' management by hitting .327 (32 hits in 98 at bats) and knocking in 16 runs in this limited action.

When the 1932 season opened, Herman was the Cubs' regular second baseman. While playing in every team game his first full year in the majors, he proved management was correct to put him in the daily lineup as he lead the Cubs in at-bats (656), runs (102) and hits (206). He also was a direct force in leading the Cubs to the National League flag as the team won the league championship by four games over the Pittsburgh Pirates. In the 1932 World's Series, the Cubs were swept in four games by the mighty New York Yankees. Herman went 4 for 18 for a .222 average and scored five of the 19 runs the Cubs plated in the series. After a couple of third-place finishes in 1933 and 1934, Herman was one of the Cubs' key players as the team won the league title again by outlasting the St. Louis Cardinals by four games. He had just an awesome year as he finished with a .341 average and led the league with 227 hits, 57 doubles and 24 sacrifice hits. Although the Cubs put up a valiant effort in a closely contested World's Series, they lost the championship to the Detroit Tigers in six games. Herman gave it his best effort as he belted a homer, went 8 for 24 (.333) and led all series contestants with six RBI. He put together two more rock-solid seasons in 1936 and 1937 (with batting averages of .334 and .335), but the Cubs played bridesmaid each year by coming in second place to the New York Giants. Although his batting average dropped a dramatic 58 points in 1938, it did not matter much to Herman because his team found its way to the summit of the National League by taking the league title again, this time by two games over the Pirates. Unfortunately, the Cubs' opponent in the World's Series that year happened to be the Yankees. The Yankees completely dominated Chicago, outscoring them 22–9 and sweeping them again in four games. Herman played with the Cubs for just over two more years, but after being the team's second baseman for nearly a decade, he was traded to the Brooklyn Dodgers in May 1941.

Herman immediately replaced Pete Coscarart as the Dodgers' second baseman and went on to take in 133 contests for the Bums and contributed with a .291 average. The start of his consecutive playing streak began with just five games left in the season as the Dodgers visited the Philadelphia Phillies on September 22, 1941. Winning had a habit of following Herman as the Dodgers won the league crown in 1941 as they edged the Cardinals by two and a half games. In his fourth World Series in 10 years, he wound up facing the Yankees for a third time. The Bronx Bombers won another title by besting the Dodgers in five games. Herman's influence was minimal as he had only one hit in eight tries at the plate. The next year, he hit for a .256 average, took in all Dodgers games at second in 1942 except for a couple of opportunities in which he played first base. The Dodgers came close to winning a second straight pennant, but came up short by taking second place.

The 1943 season saw Herman take frequent turns at third base because the team had no permanent player for the position and this caused several players to be rotated at the hot corner. In early June 1943, Herman was only a couple of games behind Mickey Vernon of the Washington Senators for the Iron Man title. He pulled into a tie with Vernon several times between June 7 and July 22 as the Iron Man. In fact, there was a eight-game span from June 30 to July 7 that Herman actually had the consecutive game lead over Vernon. When Vernon missed a game in early September 1943, Herman took over as the new leader in consecutive games. He completed the year with a 313-consecutive-game streak intact. Although the Dodgers finished well behind the Cardinals again for the league championship, Herman rebounded from his previous year's numbers by hitting a team-high .330 average. He also led the team in hits (193), doubles (41) and RBI (100). His 313 game streak and Iron Man reign ended at the beginning of the 1944 season because during the off-season Herman decided to join the war effort by enlisting in the armed forces.

After the war ended, Herman returned to the Dodgers for the 1946 season. Three months into the season, Brooklyn traded him to the Boston Braves on June 15, 1946. Boston's main use for him was as a utility infielder. He responded by hitting .306 for the time he spent with the Braves. Right after the season concluded, he was sent packing again, this time to the Pittsburgh Pirates. The Pirates then hired him to manage the team. He still wanted to play and put himself into 15 contests during the course of the 1947 season. By the time he was done as Pirates manager (near the end of the year), the team was fighting to stay out of last place with the Philadelphia Phillies. That year also turned out to be his final major league season as a player. He put in a couple of years managing in the minors in addition to playing two of the next three years. After his playing days ended, he managed several more minor league clubs. At the big league level, he scouted and coached for at least five teams and even took another crack at managing by taking the Boston Red Sox job for a short time in the mid–1960s, where he had very little success. In 1975, the veterans' committee of the National Baseball Hall of Fame selected Herman for membership.

80. BILL NICHOLSON

Born: December 11, 1914, Chestertown, Maryland *Died*: March 8, 1996, Chestertown, Maryland *Bats*: Left *Throws*: Right *Height*: 6 feet *Weight*: 205 *Major league debut*: June 13, 1936 (second game) (Cleveland at Philadelphia [AL]) *Last major league game*: September 19, 1953 (Philadelphia at Brooklyn [NL])

Major league Iron Man from: April 18, 1944, to July 13, 1944 *Consecutive games played*: 348 *Games as major league Iron Man*: 72 (consecutive games 277 through 348) *Team played for during streak*: Chicago Cubs (NL) *Primary position played*: Outfield *Game missed before streak*: May 19, 1942 (Chicago at Brooklyn) *First game played of streak*: May 20, 1942 (Chicago at New York) *Last game played of streak*: July 9, 1944 (second game) (New York at Chicago) *Game missed to end streak*: July 13, 1944 (Pittsburgh at Chicago)

Consecutive Game Streak's Statistical Totals

Year	G	AB	R	H	2B	3B	HR	RBI	BB	SO	AVG	SLG	SB
1942	122	467	69	141	18	9	17	63	63	57	.302	.488	7
1943	154	608	95	188	30	9	29	128	71	86	.309	.531	4
1944	72	268	51	77	16	4	15	51	40	36	.287	.545	0
Total	348	1343	215	406	64	22	61	242	174	179	.302	.519	11

In the 1940s, the Chicago Cubs relied upon their right fielder, Bill Nicholson, to provide the power during this homer-starved era and drive in runs for the club. Originally signed to a contract by the Philadelphia Athletics of the American League, he had a big league career that spanned 16 years. A great majority of that time was spent in the senior circuit with the Cubs and the Philadelphia Phillies. He made his debut for the Athletics on July 13, 1936, against the Cleveland Indians. He appeared in less than a dozen games and was still looking for his first major league hit when the season closed. He spent much of the next three years toiling in the minor leagues. Nicholson was sold to the Cubs in late June 1939. He finally made it back to the majors with the Cubs soon after his acquisition. Although he got into only 58 games, he showed he could handle major league caliber pitching by hitting .295 and driving in 38 runners during those contests.

In his first season as a regular in 1940, Nicholson played in 135 contests, hit for a .297 average and wound up leading the Cubs with 25 homers and 98 RBI. He finished in second place in the National League, behind the St. Louis Cardinals' Johnny Mize, with a .534 slugging percentage and played in his first of four all-star games. The next year, he again led the team in home runs (26) and RBI (98) but his hitting dropped 43 points to a .254 average. The following season, he started his consecutive game streak on May 20, 1942, in New York against the Giants as he played the final 122 games on the 1942 schedule. For the third consecutive season, Nicholson was the Cubs' home run (21) and RBI (78) leader but he also paced the team in at-bats (588) and hits (173) along with leading all league batters in being hit by pitches with eight beanings. His presence in the starting lineup every day did not prevent the Cubs from finishing in sixth place for the second straight year with a 68–86 record. In 1943, as the Cubs were occupying their customary spot in the standings (somewhere in National League's second division), Nicholson led the team in every major offensive category except triples and batting average. He also posted league highs in homers (29) and RBI (128, a career high) and finished runner-up in the slugging department to the Cards' Stan Musial. Additionally, he extended his playing streak to 276 games by being at his right field assignment for all 154 games on the 1943 schedule. When the new season commenced (1944), Nicholson took over the Iron Man title from the Dodgers' Billy Herman, who had left for military service during the off-season. Nicholson was having another great year as the all-star game approached. The last game before the all-star break, he suffered an injured thumb and bruised forearm when he was hit by a pitch from the Giants' Ace Adams. He lost the pitch in the background of the white-shirted fans in the stands at Wrigley Field and when he picked up the ball, it was almost on top of him. He threw up both arms to protect his face, but the ball struck his thumb and arm. Ironically, between being hit by this pitch and missing a regular season game, Nicholson batted in the all-star game and provided a key double for the National Leaguers in their 7–1 victory in the 1944 game. His streak ended after 348 games when he sat out the July 13, 1944, contest at Wrigley against the Pittsburgh Pirates. That was the only game he missed during the 1944 season. He finished the year repeating as the National League home run king with 33 clouts plus posting other league highs in runs (116) and total bases (317). Additionally, for the third time, he came in second in slugging behind Musial (.548) with a .545 percentage. While the Cubs improved to fourth place, Nicholson just missed being named the league's Most Valuable Player by the narrowest of margins, losing to the Cards' Marty Marion by just one point (190 to 189).

Playing every day agreed with Nicholson. Many of the statistics he achieved during his streak were career highs but once his streak had ended, Nicholson's performance took a downward turn. In 1945, as the Cubs were winning the National League championship, his offensive numbers dropped off dramatically. He hit only 13 homers (this total still led the team), drove in 88 runners and hit .243 (a drop of 44 percentage points). In the series, the Cubs went the distance with the Detroit Tigers but ended up losing in the seven-game set. Since this World Series loss, the Cubs have not made an appearance in the Fall Classic. Although Nicholson went only 6 for 28 for a lowly .214 average, his hits were timely as he finished with eight RBI, which topped all 1945 series players. He spent three more seasons with the Cubs, achieving modest results when he was traded to the Phillies right after the closing of the 1948 season. Except for his first season in Philadelphia, he served most of his time there (five years) either filling in at right field or appearing as the occasional pinch hitter. The lowly numbers he produced were indicative of a player at the tail end of a ballplaying career. He made his final appearance as a player on a professional baseball diamond September 19, 1953, where the Phillies lost 5–4 to the Brooklyn Dodgers.

81. BOBBY DOERR

Born: April 7, 1918, Los Angeles, California *Bats*: Right *Throws*: Right *Height*: 5 feet, 11 inches *Weight*: 175 *Major league debut*: April 20, 1937 (Boston at Philadelphia [AL]) *Last major league game*: September 7, 1951 (first game) (Boston at Philadelphia [AL])

Major league Iron Man from: July 13, 1944, to August 25, 1944 *Consecutive games played*: 344 *Games as major league Iron Man*: 44 (consecutive games 301 through 344) *Team played for during streak*: Boston Red Sox (AL) *Primary position played*: Second base *Game missed before streak*: July 17, 1942 (Chicago at Boston) *First game played of streak*: July 19, 1942 (first game) (Cleveland at Boston) *Last game played of streak*: August 25, 1944 (first game) (Boston at Philadelphia) *Game missed to end streak*: August 25, 1944 (second game) (Boston at Philadelphia)

Consecutive Game Streak's Statistical Totals

Year	G	AB	R	H	2B	3B	HR	RBI	BB	SO	AVG	SLG	SB
1942	67	242	33	57	4	3	4	41	41	22	.236	.326	1
1943	155	604	78	163	32	3	16	75	62	59	.270	.412	8
1944	122	456	93	148	30	9	15	80	57	27	.325	.529	5
Total	344	1302	204	368	66	15	35	196	160	108	.283	.437	14

During a great portion of the Ted Williams' era in Boston, Bobby Doerr was the steady fielding second baseman for the Red Sox. Doerr spent his first three seasons of pro ball in the Pacific Coast League before making the Red Sox roster for the 1937 season. He made his debut in the 1937 season opener at Philadelphia. He was the second-youngest player in the league that season behind the Cleveland Indians' pitcher, Bob Feller. The Red Sox were looking for Doerr to replace the veteran Oscar Melillo at the second base position but were aware that the rookie would need to be broken in slowly. Because of this, Eric McNair played more games then Doerr at second that season but Doerr was able to take in 55 games and bat .224 his rookie season. The next season, Red Sox skipper Joe Cronin knew the time was right to make Doerr the Red Sox starting shortstop. Except for the 1945 season, when he fought in World War II, Doerr would keep that job until his retirement after the 1951 season.

In his first season as a regular player (and still the club's youngest player), Doerr was an important part of the team that helped Boston finish as runner-up to the New York Yankees for the American League championship. He sat out just five games, hit an impressive .289, drove in 80 runners and had a league high among second basemen with 118 double plays. The Red Sox repeated their second-place finish the following season as

Bobby Doerr: A Hall of Fame second baseman for the Boston Red Sox, he was the major league's Iron Man until his streak ended just before he entered the military in 1944 to serve in World War II (Transcendental Graphics/ruckerarchive.com).

Doerr improved his batting average nearly 30 points by hitting .318 and driving home 73 runs. He also led his position in fielding for the first time out of five occasions with a .976 average. With the arrival of Ted Williams on the scene in Boston in 1939, Doerr relinquished his title as youngest Red Sox to the future baseball immortal. The Red Sox came close to winning the league title during the next couple of seasons but came up short, thanks to the Detroit Tigers in 1940 and the Yankees in 1941. This was no fault of Doerr's as he had two solid years at the plate and in the field. The following year, his consecutive game streak started during the first game of a double header on July 19, 1942, in Boston against the Cleveland Indians. He was used as a pinch hitter in the game. He played the final 67 games on the 1942 schedule but hit a disappointing .236 during that stretch. He finished 1942 by batting .290 and driving in 102 runs, a total what was good for second place in the club behind Ted Williams' 137 RBI. For the fourth time in five seasons, the Red Sox finished in second place in the junior circuit's final standings. On this occasion, they finished nine games behind the Yankees. With World War II raging in Europe and the Pacific, many major league players left for military service. The Red Sox were especially hit hard by these circumstances as stars Ted Williams, Johnny Pesky and Dom DiMaggio left the team and didn't return until after the war ended in 1945. With these key players gone, the Red Sox regressed 25 games in the win column and finished a very disappointing seventh place with a 68–84 record. Doerr was one of three regular players returning for the 1943 season and he responded by hitting .270 as he played all 155 games at second base. He led the team in runs scored (78), hits (163), doubles (32), homers (16) and slugging percentage (.412). Just after participating in his third career all-star game, Doerr took over the major league Iron Man role when the streak of the Chicago Cubs' Bill Nicholson ended on July 13, 1944. Doerr's time as the Iron Man was relatively short (44 games); his streak ended after 344 straight games on August 25, 1944, when he missed the twilight game of a double-header at Philadelphia. In the opener, he suffered torn ligaments near the base of his spine and wound up missing several games. Upon his return to the lineup, he informed the Red Sox that he would be leaving for military service with the U.S. Army after the September 3 game. He played only three more games after returning from his injury and then left for the military. He finished the year with a .325 batting average and had the league's best slugging percentage (.528). Boston played .500 ball but still finished fourth, a dozen games behind the league champion St. Louis Browns.

Missing the 1945 season because of his military commitment, he returned to the Red Sox lineup in 1946. His first season back, he helped the Red Sox win their first pennant in years as he drove in 116 runners and finished third in the MVP voting behind teammate Ted Williams and Detroit Tigers pitcher Hal Newhouser. Additionally, he led the league's second basemen in games played (151), putouts (420), assists (483), double plays (129) and fielding average (.986). Facing the St. Louis Cardinals for the World Championship, the final result came down to a seventh game that was clinched when the Cards' Enos Slaughter scored the deciding run in the bottom of the eighth by hustling around the bases from first base on a hard hit double to left field. His boldness stunned the Red Sox players and by the time the relay man, Red Sox shortstop Pesky, reacted to Slaughter's aggressiveness on the base paths, the throw was too late and the Cardinals had the lead late in the game, and soon after the title. Doerr led all series players as he went 9 for 22 for a .409 average along with a homer and three runs batted in. He played five more productive years in the Red Sox lineup and consistently produced around 20 homers and over 100 RBI each season. In 1950, he had his last great season with the bat when he hit .294, clobbered 27 homers, hit a league-high 11 triples and produced a career-best 120 RBI. Boston claimed third place, just four games back of the ever-powerful New York Yankees. In the field, he showed he could still perform the job by pacing the American League's second basemen with 443 putouts and leading in fielding percentage (.988) for the fifth time in his career. If the Gold Glove awards were in existence back then, Doerr would have surely won a few because he was one of the better fielding second basemen of his era. He suffered severe back problems in 1951 that caused his early retirement, at the relatively young age of 33, from the game after only 14 seasons in the big leagues. After his retirement, he spent time scouting and coaching in the Red Sox and Toronto Blue Jays organizations. In 1986, he was selected for membership into baseball Hall of Fame by its veterans committee. When the Red Sox won the 2004 World Series, Doerr finally got to see his old team win a world championship.

82. STAN MUSIAL

Born: November 21, 1920, Donora, Pennsylvania *Bats*: Left *Throws*: Left *Height*: 6 feet *Weight*: 175 *Major league debut*: September 17, 1941 (second game) (Boston at St. Louis) (NL) *Last major league game*: September 29, 1963 (Cincinnati at St. Louis) (NL)

Major league Iron Man from: August 25, 1944, to September 12, 1944 *Consecutive games played*: 314 *Games as major league Iron Man*: 16 (consecutive games 299 through 314) *Team played for during*

Stan Musial

streak: St. Louis Cardinals (NL) *Primary position played*: Outfield *Game missed before streak*: September 3, 1942 (New York at St. Louis) *First game played of streak*: September 4, 1942 (St. Louis at Cincinnati) *Last game played of streak*: September 10, 1944 (second game) (Chicago at St. Louis) *Game missed to end streak*: September 12, 1944 (first game) (Pittsburgh at St. Louis)

Consecutive Game Streak's Statistical Totals

Year	G	AB	R	H	2B	3B	HR	RBI	BB	SO	AVG	SLG	SB
1942	22	82	11	26	7	3	1	17	8	2	.317	.512	0
1943	157	617	108	220	48	20	13	81	72	18	.357	.562	9
1944	135	520	103	181	48	14	10	87	86	26	.348	.552	7
Total	314	1219	222	427	103	37	24	185	166	46	.350	.555	16

Stan "the Man" Musial was one of the greatest hitters the game has ever witnessed. He also was very popular with the fans, sports writers and fellow ballplayers. He played for only one team his entire 22-year career: the St. Louis Cardinals. Signed as a free agent in 1938, he originally started out as a pitcher in the Cards' farm system but then switched over to playing the outfield. He was in his fourth year in the minors when he was called up to the parent club and never spent another day in the minors. He made his major league debut in mid–September 1941 during a Cardinals home game against the Boston Braves. He got into a dozen games and had 20 hits in 47 at-bats for a .426 average. This performance was an indication of hitting achievements to come as this great player would go on to become a two-time major league baseball Iron Man title holder.

As the 1942 season approached, the Cardinals knew they had a potentially great player on their team in Musial so the decision was made to shift left fielder Johnny Hopp to first base to make room for Musial in the outfield. In his first full season, he helped lead the team to the National League pennant by hitting .315 with 10 homers and 72 RBI. He started his first Iron Man streak by playing the final 22 regular season games commencing with the September 4, 1942, game in Cincinnati. In that year's World Series, the Cardinals defeated the Yankees in five games to capture the world championship. Musial played all five series games but batted only .222 with a couple of runs knocked in. The next season proved he was the real thing as he led the league in seven major offensive categories (hits, doubles, triples, batting average, on base percentage, total bases and slugging average) and helped St. Louis win their second consecutive league title. His performance that year garnered the National League MVP honor. He also played all 157 Cardinals games and extended his game streak to 179 games by the end of the season. In the World

Stan Musial: He was the greatest player ever to wear a St. Louis Cardinals uniform. A two-time Iron Man, this Hall of Famer's second Iron Man streak set a National League record for consecutive games (895) in 1957 (which was later surpassed by Chicago's Billy Williams).

Series that October, the Yankees returned the favor from the previous year by beating the Cards in five games. Musial had five hits and batted .278.

The Cardinals made it a hat trick in 1944 as the team won their third straight title by finishing 14½ games ahead of the Pittsburgh Pirates. Musial continued putting up the big offensive numbers by hitting .347 and again topped the league in hits, doubles, on base percentage and slugging average. When Red Sox second baseman Bobby Doerr missed a game on August 25, 1944, Musial became the new major league Iron Man. Less than three weeks later, however, he was injured in a collision with teammate Debs Garms in the third inning of the second game of a double-header on September 10, 1944, at home against the Cubs. On September 12, the injury ended his streak when he missed the game against the Pirates. He was out of action for several games but was back in the Cards' lineup in time for the World Series. The Cards went on to win their second world championship in three years as they beat their crosstown rival, the St. Louis Browns, in six games. Musial batted .304 and contributed two doubles, a homer and a couple of RBI. He missed the entire 1945 season due to military service in World War II. It is quite obvious from looking at Musial's stats that he really thrived on work by hitting an amazing .350 during the 314-game stretch. Since Musial was a two-time major league Iron Man, his second streak and other aspects of his career are addressed later in the book.

83. Phil Cavarretta

Born: July 19, 1916, Chicago, Illinois *Bats*: Left *Throws*: Left *Height*: 5 feet, 11½ inches *Weight*: 175 *Major league debut*: September 16, 1934 (first game) (Chicago at Brooklyn [NL]) *Last major league game*: May 8, 1955 (first game) (Detroit at Chicago [AL])

Major league Iron Man from: September 12, 1944, to September 14, 1944 *Consecutive games played*: 259 *Games as major league Iron Man*: 3 (consecutive games 257 through 259) *Team played for during streak*: Chicago Cubs (NL) *Primary position played*: First base *Game missed before streak*: May 28, 1943 (New York at Chicago) *First game played of streak*: May 29, 1943 (Boston at Chicago) *Last game played of streak*: September 14, 1944 (first game) (Cincinnati at Chicago) *Game missed to end streak*: September 14, 1944 (second game) (Cincinnati at Chicago)

Consecutive Game Streak's Statistical Totals

Year	G	AB	R	H	2B	3B	HR	RBI	BB	SO	AVG	SLG	SB
1943	123	457	89	139	24	8	8	64	69	34	.304	.444	3
1944	136	546	91	167	32	10	4	68	61	39	.306	.423	3
Total	259	1003	180	306	56	18	12	132	130	73	.305	.433	6

A good-hitting first baseman who on occasion would play in the outfield, Phil Cavarretta toiled in the majors for 22 seasons, never leaving his native Chicago (except, of course, for road games). Most of his career was spent with the National League Chicago Cubs but at the tail end of his playing days he became a member of the crosstown rival Chicago White Sox in the American League. In his first season of pro ball, he played in the minors with Peoria and Reading before being promoted to the Cubs at the tender age of 18. Making his major league debut on September 16, 1934, he got into seven games before the season ended, going 8 for 21 (for a .381 average), hitting a homer and driving in six runs.

The following season (while still a rookie) (1935), he took over the first base job from long-time Cubs first sacker Charlie Grimm. The youngest player in the league, Cavarretta played 146 games in the field as he contributed to the Cubs winning the National League pennant by hitting .275, driving in 82 runs and leading the team with 12 triples. Although he made 20 miscues (a league high for first basemen) that first season, he participated in more double plays (129) than any other first basemen. Chicago edged the St. Louis Cardinals by four games to qualify to face the Detroit Tigers for the 1935 World Championship. In the World's Series, Cavarretta hit .125 (3 for 24) and banged out only three singles and a run scored as the Cubs came out on the losing end in six games against the Tigers. After one more year at first base in 1936, he lost his job to Ripper Collins the following season. Serving as a backup at first base on occasion during the next couple of seasons, he also had playing time in the outfield. In 1938, the Cubs won the league pennant again by edging the Pittsburgh Pirates by a couple of games. In the World's Series, the Cubs were swept in four games by the powerhouse New York Yankees. Although the outcome was not good for the Cubs, Cavarretta was definitely one of Chicago's better players. Playing in all four games, he scored a run, had five singles and a double and went 6 for 13, good enough for a .462 average. The next two years (1939 and 1940), Cavarretta did not get into much action because he suffered ankle injuries relatively early in each season that caused him to miss much of each campaign. After the 1940 season, the Cubs replaced manager Gabby Hartnett with Jimmie Wilson. For the 1941 and 1942 seasons, Wilson continued the practice of rotating Cavarretta between first and the outfield to get him into as many games as possible. After playing only 61 contests at first base in 1942, Cavarretta took over the first sacker job on a regular basis in 1943. Taking in 134 games, he started his consecutive playing streak on May 29, 1943, in Chicago against the Boston Braves. He played the last 123 contests on the 1943 schedule. The Cubs went on to finish in fifth place, well behind the first-place St. Louis Cardinals. The 1944 season was one of Cavarretta's best. He got used to being in the starting lineup every day and seemed to thrive on the work. Playing in his first all-star game that year, he reached base a record five times in helping lead the National League squad to a 7–1 victory over the American Leaguers. When the Cards' Stan Musial missed a game on September 12, Cavarretta become the new big league Iron Man. His reign was only three games long as the Cubs' manager rested him in the nightcap of a twin bill on September 14 against the Cincinnati Reds. While his streak was over after 259 straight games, it is noted that Cavarretta is one of only two players to attain the title of major league Iron Man without having played a completed season during their streaks. The other player was Lee Tannehill of the Chicago White Sox who put together a 265-game streak in the early 1900s. The Cubs improved to fourth place in 1944, but still finished 30 games behind the Cards for the league flag. The team's finish was no fault of Cavarretta as he tied with Musial for most hits (197) in the league along with leading the Cubs in at-bats (614), triples (15) and batting average (.321). He followed up that performance by being the league's top hitter in 1945 with a .355 batting average and .449 on base percentage. His achievements directly helped the Cubs win the 1945 National League championship by three games over those pesky Cardinals. He continued his exemplary play in the World Series by going 11 for 26 for a series-high .423 average among all 1945 series participants. Although the Cubs lost the series in seven games to the Tigers, Cavarretta likely would have won the World Series MVP if that honor had been around at the time. To soothe the wounds from losing the World Series, he was later selected the regular season MVP.

Cavarretta would go on to play for portions of eight more seasons with the Cubs. In midseason of 1951, he became the team's player-manager, replacing Frankie Frisch. Over the next two and a half years, his playing time was somewhat limited as he concentrated on his managerial duties. During the 1954 training camp, the Cubs ownership decided a change was needed and replaced him as manager with former Cubs player (and former major league Iron

Man) Stan Hack. Cavarretta hooked up with the White Sox after being fired by the Cubs. Seeing limited action, he hit a surprising .316 in 71 contests. His last year (1955), he got into only a few games. He played his last major league contest on May 8, 1955, in Chicago against the Tigers. After his big league career was over, he stayed active in baseball by managing for several years in the minors in addition to coaching and scouting for the Tigers and the New York Mets.

84. TOMMY HOLMES

Born: March 29, 1917, Brooklyn, New York *Bats*: Left *Throws*: Left *Height*: 5 feet, 10 inches *Weight*: 180 *Major league debut*: April 14, 1942 (Boston at Philadelphia [NL]) *Last major league game*: September 28, 1952 (Boston at Brooklyn [NL])

Major league Iron Man from: September 14, 1944, to July 14, 1946 *Consecutive games played*: 454 *Games as major league Iron Man*: 250 (consecutive games 205 through 454) *Team played for during streak*: Boston Braves (NL) *Primary position played*: Outfield *Game missed before streak*: July 29, 1943 (Boston at Cincinnati) *First game played of streak*: July 30, 1943 (first game) (Boston at Cincinnati) *Last game played of streak*: July 13, 1946 (second game) (Boston at Cincinnati) *Game missed to end streak*: July 14, 1946 (first game) (Boston at Pittsburgh)

Consecutive Game Streak's Statistical Totals

Year	G	AB	R	H	2B	3B	HR	RBI	BB	SO	AVG	SLG	SB
1943	67	277	38	74	13	3	2	19	25	12	.267	.357	4
1944	155	631	93	195	42	6	13	73	61	11	.309	.456	4
1945	154	636	125	224	47	6	28	117	70	9	.352	.577	15
1946	78	299	43	90	20	5	3	43	33	11	.301	.431	4
Total	454	1843	299	583	122	20	46	252	189	43	.316	.479	27

Tommy Holmes' name is known in baseball circles mainly as the modern day National League record holder of most consecutive games (37 contests) with a base hit from 1945 to 1978. His record (from June 6 to July 8, 1945) was broken by Cincinnati's Pete Rose in 1978 when Rose put together a 44-game streak. Holmes played his entire 11-year career in the National League, first with the Boston Braves for 10 years and then a portion of a season with the Brooklyn Dodgers. Prior to entering the big leagues, he was the property of the New York Yankees and played for their farm team in Newark. In early December 1941, the Yankees traded him to the Braves.

Holmes was the Braves' starting center fielder when Boston opened the 1942 season in Philadelphia. During his rookie season he played in 141 games and batted .278, good for second place on the club behind the league's batting champion, catcher Ernie Lombardi. Unfortunately, the Braves finished in seventh place for the fourth consecutive year. The next year Holmes missed only one game (July 29) the whole season. Starting July 30, he played the last 67 games on the 1943 schedule. He finished with a .270 batting average, led the National League in at-bats (629) and the Braves in hits (170), doubles (33) and triples (10). He also led all the league's outfielders with a .993 fielding average. The Braves were still in the second division of the standings as the team finished in sixth place. The 1944 season turned out to be Holmes' last season as the Braves' center fielder. On September 14, he became the majors' Iron Man when the Cubs' Phil Cavarretta sat out the second game of a double-header. Holmes finished the season with 222 consecutive games played, a batting average of .309, and team-leading totals in hits (195), doubles (42) and RBI (73). In addition, he was the league's hardest player to strike out as he finished with only 11 strikeouts in 631 at-bats. His offensive achievements did not seem to help the Braves much as the team finished in sixth place for the second consecutive year. The 1945 season found Holmes shifting over to play left field. At the plate, it was a career year for Holmes. In fact, with the possible exception of Cavarretta, Holmes had the best year of any player in the league that season. Playing in all 154 games (and extending his playing streak to 376 games), Holmes led the league in hits (224), doubles (47), home runs (28), slugging average (.577), total bases (367) and extra-base hits (81). He had the record hitting streak of 37 consecutive games in June and July. In addition, his batting average finished at .352, runner-up to Cavarretta's .355. He also repeated as the league's hardest player to fan with only nine strikeouts in 636 at-bats. He finished in second place to Cavarretta in voting for the league's Most Valuable Player. Even with the huge year Holmes had in 1945, this did not help the Braves. The team finished with a 67–85 record, good for only sixth place in the standings.

In the 1946, Holmes led the Braves in nearly every major offensive category although his batting average dipped to .310 and his home run total drastically dropped to a measly six clouts. For the third consecutive season, he was the hardest player to fan, finishing with 14 strikeouts in 568 at-bats. On July 14, 1946, Holmes' consecutive-games-played streak ended at 454 when he was rested by the Braves during the first game of a double-header at Pittsburgh. There was good news that year as the Braves finally had a winning season when they finished in fourth place, 15½ games behind the first-place St. Louis Cardinals. The next year (1947), Holmes led the league in hits (191) and finished with a .309 average. The Braves had another winning season and claimed third place, just eight games behind the Brooklyn Dodgers. In 1948, the Braves won the pennant by finishing six and a half games ahead of the Cardinals. Holmes participated in 139 contests, finished with a .325 average and led the Braves in several statistical categories. In the 1948 World Series, the Braves were beaten by the Cleveland Indians in six games. Holmes led all the series' batters with 26 at-bats. He managed but five singles, one RBI and hit for only a .192 average. During the 1949 season, Holmes played in only 117 games while the Braves slipped back to fourth place. His batting average fell to .266, dropping nearly 60 points. The only note of accomplishment that year for Holmes was that it was the fourth time he was the league's hardest batter to fan. He struck out only six times in 380 at-bats. During the 1950 season, his average improved to .298 but he was not playing as frequently as he took in only 88 games in the field and played a total of 105 for the season. The team started using him more for pinch hitting duties. For a while, it looked like 1950 would be Holmes' last year in the majors. He started out in 1951 as the player-manager for Hartford of the Eastern League. In mid–June, he got a call to become player-manager of the Braves, replacing his old skipper, Billy Southworth. The team played .500 ball for their new manager but they finished in fourth place again for the third consecutive year. Holmes used himself in the lineup for only a few games. During 1952, Holmes decided to concentrate on managing instead of playing. Unfortunately, the Braves got off to a slow start and Holmes was released as manager on June 1. Within a couple of weeks, the Brooklyn Dodgers acquired him with the main purpose of using him as a pinch hitter although he was still able to get into about a half dozen games in the field. The Dodgers won the pennant and Holmes was in another World Series. They went up against the powerful Yankees and lost in seven games to the Bronx Bombers. In the series, Holmes made only three token appearances and had but one at-bat. After the series, Holmes spent the rest of his baseball career in the minors, playing occasionally, but mostly managing and scouting. When Rose broke his hitting record in 1978, Holmes was happy that he was remembered for his accomplishments on the baseball diamond.

85. Eddie Lake

Born: March 18, 1916, Antioch, California *Died*: June 7, 1995, Castro Valley, California *Throws*: Right *Bats*: Right *Height*: 5 feet, 7 inches *Weight*: 160 *Major league debut*: September 26, 1939 (first game) (St. Louis at Cincinnati [NL]) *Last major league game*: September 30, 1950 (Cleveland at Detroit [AL])

Major league Iron Man from: July 14, 1946, to April 20, 1948 *Consecutive games played*: 442 *Games as major league Iron Man*: 235 (consecutive games 208 through 442) *Teams played for during streak*: Boston Red Sox (AL) (1945) and Detroit Tigers (AL) (1946–1947) *Primary position played*: Shortstop *Game missed before streak*: May 26, 1945 (St. Louis at Boston) *First game played of streak*: May 27, 1945 (first game) (Chicago at Boston) *Last game played of streak*: September 28, 1947 (Detroit at Cleveland) *Game missed to end streak*: April 20, 1948 (Detroit at Chicago)

Consecutive Game Streak's Statistical Totals

Year	G	AB	R	H	2B	3B	HR	RBI	BB	SO	AVG	SLG	SB
1945	129	471	80	132	27	1	11	51	105	37	.280	.412	9
1946	155	587	105	149	24	1	8	31	103	69	.254	.339	15
1947	158	602	96	127	19	6	12	46	120	54	.211	.322	11
Total	442	1660	281	408	70	8	31	128	328	160	.246	.354	35

Eddie Lake played in the major leagues for 11 seasons for three teams. He started out in the National League with the St. Louis Cardinals (1939–1941) but spent most of his career in the American League with the Boston Red Sox (1943–1945) and the Detroit Tigers (1946–1950). Lake was a very weak hitter and because of this was a regular player for only three of the 11 seasons he was a major leaguer.

He made his major league debut on September 26, 1939, in the first game of a doubleheader against Cincinnati. He pinch-ran for the Cards' first baseman, Johnny Mize, in the ninth inning. In that first season, Lake appeared in only one other game and went 1 for 4 with a walk. During the next two seasons with the Cards, he was sparingly used as a substitute infielder and appeared in only 77 games with a batting average of .155. In 1942, he did not play major league ball. The Red Sox picked him up as a backup shortstop for Skeeter Newsome for the 1943 season. He played in 75 games and hit a paltry .199 for the season. The Red Sox did not have a good year either, finishing in seventh place with a 68–84 season. The 1944 season was the same for Lake as he was primarily used as the backup for Newsome at shortstop where he played in only 57 games. He also appeared in six games as a relief pitcher. He finished five of the games and had a 4.19 earned run average. The Red Sox improved to a 77–77 record with a fourth-place finish, 12 games behind the pennant-winning St. Louis Browns. The 1945 season found Newsome still filling the Red Sox shortstop role and Lake sitting on the bench. In fact, Lake appeared in only four of the first 28 games to begin the season. In late May, Cronin made Lake his new shortstop and shifted Newsome over to second base. The shortstop job was Lake's for the rest of the season. He played the last 129 games on the schedule, starting with the commencement of his consecutive playing streak on May 27, 1945. He led the American League shortstops that year in assists and double plays. He had his best year at the plate with a .279 batting average. In addition, he led all American League hitters in on base percentage (.412). Unfortunately, the Red Sox finished in next-to-last place, ahead of the hapless Philadelphia Athletics, who claimed the doormat position.

On January 3, 1946, the Red Sox traded Lake to the Detroit Tigers for power-hitting first baseman Rudy York. Lake became the Tigers' shortstop, replacing Skeeter Webb, who was relegated to the backup shortstop role. In his first season with his new team, Lake played all 155 games at shortstop as the Tigers finished second to Lake's old team, the Red Sox, by a dozen games. The turnaround for the Red Sox had been the return of their key players (Williams and company) from the war effort. Lake had a very respectable year. He batted .254 and led the Tigers in runs scored with 105, walks with 103 and stolen bases with 15. On July 14 of that year, the Braves' Tommy Holmes missed a game, ending his playing streak. Lake took over the major league baseball Iron Man title with just 208 consecutive games played. The 1947 season showed that Lake again played all the Tigers' games at shortstop. Although he did walk 120 times and led the team in stolen bases again with 11 swipes, Lake's batting average really suffered. He batted only .211, which was the second-lowest batting average among all regular American League players that season. Eddie Joost of the Athletics was the lowest with a .206 average. The Tigers again finished runner-up in the standings by a dozen games, this time to the Yankees. Lake lost his shortstop job to Neil Berry during the 1948 training camp. He missed the season opener at Chicago, thus ending his consecutive game streak. After participating in 442 consecutive games the previous three seasons, Lake played in only 64 total contests the entire 1948 season, due mainly to losing his starting job and later to an injured finger. When he was in the lineup, he didn't play shortstop but was shifted between the second and third base positions. A review of Lake's statistics shows that although he was a weak hitter, his batting stats during the streak were very good except for the .211 he batted in 1947. He also had a tendency to draw walks and topped the 100 plateau each year in bases on balls when he played regularly (1945–1947). In his last two seasons (1949 and 1950), he played in only 94 and 20 games respectively. In fact, during his last season, he was used mainly as a pinch hitter or pinch runner and got into only a couple games in the field. His last appearance in his career was on September 30, 1950, as the Tigers beat Cleveland 3–1. Just like his initial major league appearance back in 1939, he was used as a pinch runner, this time for Vic Wertz in the seventh inning. His major league career came to an end with the finish of the 1950 season.

86. Mickey Vernon

Born: April 22, 1918, Marcus Hook, Pennsylvania *Bats*: Left *Throws*: Left *Height*: 6 feet, 2 inches *Weight*: 170 *Major league debut*: July 8, 1939 (first game) (Washington at Philadelphia [AL]) *Last major league game*: September 27, 1960 (Cincinnati at Pittsburgh [NL])

Major league Iron Man from: April 20, 1948, to July 6, 1948 *Consecutive games played*: 369 *Games as major league Iron Man*: 70 (consecutive games 300 through 369) *Team played for during streak*: Washington Senators (AL) *Primary position played*: First base *Game missed before streak*: April 27, 1946 (New York at Washington) *First game played of streak*: April 28, 1946 (New York at Washington) *Last game played of streak*: July 5, 1948 (second game) (Philadelphia at Washington) *Game missed to end streak*: July 6, 1948 (Philadelphia at Washington)

Consecutive Game Streak's Statistical Totals

Year	G	AB	R	H	2B	3B	HR	RBI	BB	SO	AVG	SLG	SB
1946	144	577	88	202	49	8	8	82	49	64	.350	.504	14
1947	154	600	77	159	29	12	7	85	49	42	.265	.388	12
1948	71	270	39	70	9	3	1	25	24	22	.259	.326	7
Total	369	1447	204	431	87	23	16	192	122	128	.298	.423	33

After missing the 1944 and 1945 seasons due to his service in World War II, Mickey Vernon returned to major league baseball at the startup of the 1946 season. He reclaimed his old job as the Senators' first baseman. His season started slowly when he missed seven of the first 11 games played that year. Starting with the April 28 game against the New York Yankees, Vernon initiated his new playing streak, appearing in the final 144 games on the Senators' 1946 schedule. He also had a great year statistically as he won his first American League batting crown with a .353 batting average. He also led the league with 51 doubles. The return of Vernon from the war did not benefit the Senators in the standings because after finishing in second place in 1945, they won 11 fewer games and finished in fourth place, 28 games behind the pennant-winning Boston Red Sox. The 1947 season was not a good year for either Vernon or the Senators. Vernon lost nearly 100 points in his batting when he finished at a .265 average but he did lead the team in doubles (29) and RBI (85) along with most games played (152) by a first baseman. At season's end, he was in second place behind Eddie Lake in consecutive games with 298 games. The Senators finished a dismal seventh, only five games out of the cellar.

The beginning of the 1948 season found the Senators with a new manager in Joe Kuhel (replacing Ossie Bluege) and major league baseball with a new reigning Iron Man. Eddie Lake started out on the bench for the Tigers and because his streak ended, Vernon became the major league's Iron Man for the second time in his career. It seems that this second streak took a toll on Vernon during the 1948 season. He was in a long batting slump and all his key offensive numbers were drastically down from his previous levels. His playing streak came to an end after 369 games when he took a day off on July 6, 1948, after complaining of having a fever. Vernon's stats by the end of the 1948 season showed that he had had an awful year at the plate. In 150 games played, his final batting average was .242 and he drove in 48 runners, down from 85 the previous year. The Senators also had another dismal year, finishing 40 games out of first place with a seventh-place showing in the standings. In the off-season (December 1948), the Senators traded their long-time first baseman to the Cleveland Indians. During Vernon's first year with the Tribe, his batting average rebounded to .291. He also led the Indians with 27 doubles and 83 RBI. In the first baseman fielding stats, he was the leader in games played (153), putouts (1,438) and assists (155). Vernon played only 28 games for Cleveland in 1950 when he was traded back to the Senators in mid–June. Vernon finished the 1950 season with a .281 batting average and 75 RBI. Over the next couple of years, his most noteworthy accomplishment was that he was the American League's best fielding first baseman for three straight seasons from 1950 through 1952.

In 1953, Vernon had an awesome year offensively. He won his second American League batting crown with a .337 average along with driving home 115 runs. He played all Senator games and topped the league with 43 doubles. In the fielding department, he led first sackers with 1,376 putouts and 158 double plays. The following year (1954), Vernon had another good season, repeating as the doubles king with 33 two-baggers, having a career best in home runs with 20 clouts and hitting for a .290 average. He again led first basemen in games played (148), putouts (1,365), double plays (144) and fielding average (.992). Vernon continued his best on the worst team in the league. In what turned out to be his final season in a Senators uniform, he hit .301, drove home 85 runs and had 23 doubles to pace the team again. In November 1955, the Senators traded him to the Boston Red Sox. Vernon spent the next two years with Boston as the club's first baseman. His first year with the Red Sox, he batted a solid .310 along with bringing 84 runners home. His playing time (102 games) and batting average (.241) were reduced in 1957. In January 1958, the Red Sox no longer required his services and he was picked up by one of his former teams, the Cleveland Indians. He had one more relatively decent year as he was the regular first sacker for the Indians for most of the year. He finished with 119 games and a .293 average. Unfortunately for Vernon, the Indians had acquired Vic Power to eventually take over the first baseman job in Cleveland. Vernon spent just the one year in Cleveland before he was dealt to the National League's Milwaukee Braves in the first week of the 1959 season. The Braves used him as a pitch hitter and backup first sacker to the power-hitting Joe Adcock. Vernon's career was nearing the end of the line. In his limited playing time with the Braves, he hit a paltry .220 in 74 contests. He was released by the Braves at the end of the season. He hooked up with the Pirates in his final major league season for a few games during Pittsburgh's 1960 World Championship season. Vernon was not used during the Pirates' seven-game victory over the Yankees.

After the 1960 season, Vernon retired from active play. He finished with nearly 2,500 hits in his career along with a final .286 batting average. During the off-season, Vernon's old team, the Washington Senators, had moved to Minnesota to become the Twins. A new franchise was granted to the D.C. area and Vernon was named the first manager of the new Washington Senators. He guided the Senators for just over two seasons with dreadful results until he was replaced as skipper by former Dodgers great Gil Hodges.

87. Frankie Gustine

Born: February 20, 1920, Hoopeston, Illinois *Died*: April 1, 1991, Davenport, Iowa *Bats*: Right *Throws*: Right *Height*: 6 feet *Weight*: 175 *Major league debut*: September 13, 1939 (first game) (New York at Pittsburgh [NL]) *Last major league game*: May 17, 1950 (New York at St. Louis [AL])

Major league Iron Man from: July 6, 1948, to July 20, 1948 *Consecutive games played*: 260 *Games as major league Iron Man*: 12 (consecutive games 249 through 260) *Team played for during streak*: Pittsburgh Pirates (NL) *Primary position played*: Third base *Game missed before streak*: September 10, 1946 (Pittsburgh at New York) *First game played of streak*: September 11, 1946 (first game) (Pittsburgh at New York) *Last game played of streak*: July 19, 1948 (Boston at Pittsburgh) *Game missed to end streak*: July 20, 1948 (Philadelphia at Pittsburgh)

Consecutive Game Streak's Statistical Totals:

Year	G	AB	R	H	2B	3B	HR	RBI	BB	SO	AVG	SLG	SB
1946	23	96	10	15	2	1	3	9	6	8	.156	.292	0
1947	156	616	102	183	30	6	9	67	63	65	.297	.409	5
1948	81	318	52	94	16	2	7	30	31	43	.296	.425	5
Total	260	1030	164	292	48	9	19	106	100	116	.283	.403	10

Frankie Gustine was an infielder for the Pittsburgh Pirates for 10 seasons from 1939 through 1948. With the Pirates, he was a three-time all-star game participant. He closed out his major league career with portions of seasons spent with the Chicago Cubs and St. Louis Browns. The Pirates had an eye on him early and signed him to a contract at 16 years old.

He made his major league debut in mid–September 1939 during the first game of a twin bill against the New York Giants at Pittsburgh. He was only 19 years old and was the second-youngest player in the league that season. The only player younger that season was the Braves infielder Sibby Sisti. Gustine got into 22 games at third base but was not too impressive at the plate his rookie year as he hit for only a .186 average. In his first full major league season (1940), Gustine shifted over to play second base for the Pirates' new manager, Frankie Frisch (who had replaced longtime Pirate great Pie Traynor). Gustine had a pretty good year by finishing with a .281 average in 133 games played. The Pirates finished in the middle of the pack and were just over 20 games behind the pennant-winning Cincinnati Reds. Over the next two seasons, he kept the Pirates' regular shortstop job. He batted .270 in 1941 but slumped badly the following year (1942) when his hitting dropped to a .229 average. In both years, the Pirates stayed in the middle of the standings and were not much of a threat to the powerhouse teams. In 1943, his services were curtailed by an assortment of injuries. He was in only 112 games, splitting his fielding duties between shortstop and second base. He finished with a .290 average. The Pirates finished above .500 but were still in fourth, some 25 games behind the mighty Cardinals. The next season, Pirates manager Frisch shifted Gustine over to shortstop where he finished with a .230 batting average in 127 games played. Although his average dropped 60 points, the move helped the team improve their place in the league standings and they finished in second behind the Cardinals. Getting used to playing shortstop, Gustine's batting average regained 50 points the next year as he hit for a .280 mark. As his average went north, the Pirates' place in the standings went south; the team came in fourth after finishing runner-up the previous year.

In 1946, Gustine again changed playing positions when he was put back at second base. He played in 131 contests and finished with a .259 batting average. In midseason, he was chosen to play in his first all-star game. He took over the second baseman position in the sixth inning when he replaced starting second baseman Red Schoendienst. Gustine started his game-playing streak on September 11, 1946, during a Pirates visit to New York against the Giants. He completed the season with a .259 average but the Pirates had a terrible year, dropping to seventh place with a 63–91 record. The 1947 campaign found him going back to his old playing position at third base, replacing the departed Lee Handley, who left in the off-season to play for the Philadelphia Phillies. Gustine played in all the Pirates' games in 1947 and extended his playing streak to 179 games. The season was also his best year offensively. He had career highs in many categories, including batting average (.297), hits (183), runs (102) and RBI (67). He led all National League third basemen in games played (156), put outs (193), assists (330) and double plays (35). He was the starting third baseman in the 1947 all-star game. Unfortunately, his career year did not help the Pirates much in the standings. The team finished tied for last with the Phillies. The 1948 season started out to be a good year for Gustine. He was maintaining his batting average around .300. On July 6, 1948, when the Senators' Mickey Vernon missed a game, his playing streak ended. Gustine inherited the Iron Man title with 249 consecutive games played. He would not keep this honor long. Less than two weeks later, the Pirates' manager, Billy Meyer, benched his third baseman on July 20 due to a batting slump. This decision ended Gustine's consecutive streak at 260 games. When the 1948 season concluded, the Pirates improved in the standings by coming in fourth place, only eight and a half games behind the front-running Boston Braves. It also turned out to be Gustine's last year in Pittsburgh as the Pirates traded him in December to the Chicago Cubs. After leaving Pittsburgh, he played in only 85 more games over the last two years of his major league career with the Cubs and the St. Louis Browns.

88. Vern Stephens

Born: October 23, 1920, McAlister, New Mexico *Died*: November 4, 1968, Long Beach, California *Bats*: Right *Throws*: Right *Height*: 5 feet, 10 inches *Weight*: 185 *Major league debut*: September 13, 1941 (St. Louis at Boston [AL]) *Last major league game*: June 30, 1955 (Detroit at Chicago [AL])

Major league Iron Man from: July 20, 1948, to June 10, 1950 *Consecutive games played*: 464 *Games as major league Iron Man*: 279 (consecutive games 186 through 464) *Teams played for during streak*: St. Louis Browns (AL) (1947) and Boston Red Sox (AL) (1948–1950) *Primary position played*: Shortstop *Game missed before streak*: June 15, 1947 (second game) (St. Louis at New York) *First game played of streak*: June 17, 1947 (St. Louis at Boston) *Last game played of streak*: June 9, 1950 (St. Louis at Boston) *Game missed to end streak*: June 10, 1950 (Detroit at Boston)

Consecutive Game Streak's Statistical Totals

Year	G	AB	R	H	2B	3B	HR	RBI	BB	SO	AVG	SLG	SB
1947	104	393	54	121	13	3	9	52	49	40	.308	.425	5
1948	155	635	114	171	25	8	29	137	77	56	.269	.471	1
1949	155	610	113	177	31	2	39	159	101	73	.290	.539	2
1950	50	215	52	66	14	4	13	61	28	17	.307	.591	1
Total	464	1853	333	535	83	17	90	409	255	186	.289	.498	9

Vern "Junior" Stephens was a power-hitting shortstop (ahead of his time) who played in 15 seasons during the 1940s and 1950s for several American League teams and was an eight-time all-star. He was signed by the St. Louis Browns at an early age and before he reached his 22nd birthday he was the regular shortstop for the team. He made his debut in mid–September 1941 and got into a couple of other Browns games that year. In 1942, Browns manager Luke Sewell inserted the rookie as his shortstop, replacing John Berardino, who later that year joined the military for World War II service. Berardino would eventually go on to fame after his major league career to play Dr. Steve Hardy in the television soap opera *General Hospital*. Stephens' first full season was rather successful. He wound up with a .294 average along with 14 homers. He led the Browns with 169 base hits. In 1943, Stephens proved he was the real thing by batting .289, slugging 22 homers and knocking in 91 runs. The 1944 season was a great year for Stephens and the Browns. The Browns won the American League pennant by edging the Detroit Tigers by one game. Stephens finished with a .293 average, hit 20 homers and led the American League with 109 RBI. The Browns took on their crosstown rivals, the St. Louis Cardinals, in the World Series. The Cardinals defeated the Browns in six games to claim baseball's world championship. Stephens had five hits in 22 at-bats for a .227 average in what turned out to be his only World Series appearance.

Stephens had another excellent year in 1945 as he led the league in round-trippers with 24 clouts and the Browns in just about every major offensive category. The Browns fell back to third place after having won the pennant the previous year. The next couple of seasons were not good for the Browns as they finished near or at the bottom of the standings although Stephens consistently put up the offensive numbers that were expected of him. On June 17, 1947, he started his consecutive games streak in Boston (his future home) and played in the last 104 games on the Browns' schedule. He led the American League shortstops in assists with 494. After landing in the basement in 1947, the Browns had to make some changes. One of them was trading Stephens, their star player, to the Boston Red Sox in November 1947. He was now with one of the best teams in baseball and looked forward to playing for his new team knowing full well that he would be batting in the same lineup as the great Ted Williams. The Red Sox also had a new manager, former Yankee skipper Joe McCarthy, who replaced long-time manager Joe Cronin in that position. Stephens' first season (1948) in Boston saw the Red Sox tying the Cleveland Indians for first place in the American League but the Sox lost to the Indians in a one-game playoff. He played shortstop in all the team's 155 games and led the Sox with 29 homers and 137 RBI although his batting average sunk to a then career low of .269. He also paced the league's shortstops in games played (155) and assists (540). Stephens became the active leader in consecutive games with only 186 games to his credit when the Pirates' Frankie Gustine sat out a contest on July 20, 1948. The next season, his average rebounded to .290 as he clubbed 39 homers (good for second place behind Ted Williams) and was tied for the league lead with Williams in RBI as both players drove home

159 runs. Stephens extended his playing streak to 414 games as he participated in all 155 games for the Red Sox in 1949. In the fielding categories, he led all the league's shortstops in games played (155), assists (508) and double plays (128). The Red Sox had another strong year and finished runner-up by just one game to the New York Yankees. Stephens' Iron Man streak of 464 consecutive games came to an end on June 10, 1950, when he was rested because of a pulled tendon in one of his legs. Because Stephens always put up consistent numbers, the streak did not have a negative effect on his offensive production. In fact, the streak occurred during his prime years as a ballplayer when he was at the top of the league leaders in home runs and RBI. Stephens finished 1950 with another impressive year offensively, batting .295 and clubbing 30 homers in 149 games played. He also was tied, with teammate Walt Dropo, for the league lead in the RBI category with 144. The Red Sox fell back to third place as the team played most of the second half of the season without Ted Williams, who fractured an elbow in the 1950 all-star game.

During the 1951 campaign, Stephens suffered a leg injury that limited his activity to only 109 games. He still batted .300, hit 17 homers and drove in 78 runners. Even with Stephens out for many games and Ted Williams about to go off and fight in the Korean War, the Red Sox had a decent year, coming in third place and playing 20 games above .500 ball. The next season, Stephens suffered another injury, this time to his knee, and he played in only 92 games. His production fell off because of these injuries and his career was nearing an end. His time with the Red Sox ended when during the 1952 off-season, he was traded to the Chicago White Sox. He spent the next three seasons bouncing between Chicago to St. Louis to Baltimore and back to Chicago. In those last three years, he played in only 216 more games. He spent some time with Seattle of the Pacific Coast League before leaving baseball after the 1956 season.

89. GIL HODGES

Born: April 4, 1924, Princeton, Indiana *Died*: April 2, 1972, West Palm Beach, Florida *Bats*: Right *Throws*: Right *Height*: 6 feet, 1½ inches *Weight*: 200 *Major league debut*: October 3, 1943 (Brooklyn at Cincinnati [NL]) *Last major league game*: May 5, 1963 (second game) (San Francisco at New York [NL])

Major league Iron Man from: June 10, 1950, to July 17, 1950 *Consecutive games played*: 352 *Games as major league Iron Man*: 33 (consecutive games 320 through 352) *Team played for during streak*: Brooklyn Dodgers (NL) *Primary positions played*: First base and catcher *Game missed before streak*: May 31, 1948 (second game) (New York at Brooklyn) *First game played of streak*: June 1, 1948 (New York at Brooklyn) *Last game played of streak*: July 17, 1950 (first game) (Brooklyn at St. Louis) *Game missed to end streak*: July 17, 1950 (second game) (Brooklyn at St. Louis)

Consecutive Game Streak's Statistical Totals

Year	G	AB	R	H	2B	3B	HR	RBI	BB	SO	AVG	SLG	SB
1948	119	442	46	113	17	5	10	65	40	54	.256	.385	7
1949	156	596	94	170	23	4	23	115	66	64	.285	.453	10
1950	77	282	48	85	18	1	12	53	42	32	.301	.500	2
Total	352	1320	188	368	58	10	45	233	148	150	.279	.440	19

Gil Hodges was one of the most popular players ever to wear a baseball uniform. Some people say he was the Dodgers version of Lou Gehrig. He was quiet and strong yet forever the gentle giant. He played major league ball for 18 seasons with the Brooklyn–Los Angeles Dodgers and the New York Mets. He consistently hit over 20 homers and hit over 100 RBI for many seasons. Signed as a free agent by the Dodgers in 1943, he made his debut at the tender age of 19 in the Dodgers' last game of the 1943 season. His career was put on hold for a couple of years while he served in the military during World War II. After the war, he played in the minors for Newport News during the 1946 season.

In 1947, Hodges was promoted to the Dodgers. He started his career as a catcher by serving as the occasional replacement for the Dodgers' regular backstop, Bruce Edwards. The Dodgers won the National League pennant in 1947 but lost the World Series in seven games to the New York Yankees. Hodges got into the series but struck out in his one pinch-hit appearance. He started out 1948 as the team's main catcher but in June, Dodgers manager Leo Durocher switched Hodges over to first base and made rookie Roy Campanella the Dodgers' new backstop. Hodges' consecutive game streak started on June 1, 1948, during a game in Brooklyn against the New York Giants. Hodges' rookie numbers showed he batted .249 in 134 games with 11 homers and 70 RBI while helping the Dodgers finish in third place, seven and a half games behind the first-place Boston Braves. The next season, he played in every one of the Dodgers' games and extended his playing streak to 275 consecutive contests. With the help of Hodges' 23 round-trippers and 115 runs batted in, the Dodgers edged the St. Louis Cardinals by one game to claim the National League crown in 1949. The Dodgers again met the Yankees that year in the series but were beaten again in five games. Hodges batted .235 in the series and hit a three-run homer in the seventh inning of game five off Yanks pitcher Vic Raschi. Hodges also proved his value defensively in 1949 by leading the league's first sackers in games played (156), putouts (1336), double plays (142) and fielding average (.995). In 1950, he smacked 32 homers along with knocking in 113 runs. He repeated as fielding champ for the league's first basemen with a .994 average along with a top mark of 159 double plays. On June 10 of that year, Hodges took over the Iron Man consecutive-game title from Boston's Vern Stephens. Hodges kept his streak going for another five weeks. On July 17, 1950, his 352-game streak came to an end when he badly bruised his left thigh while trying to catch a foul ball hit by the Cardinals' Stan Musial in the sixth inning of the first game of a double-header. He crashed into a big tarpaulin roller that had not been put back in its normal place near the stands. Hodges wanted to play in the nightcap and used ice pack applications and taped his leg to lessen the pain, but this did not work. The Dodgers, meanwhile, finished the season runner-up by two games to the Whiz Kids of Philadelphia.

After the 1950 season, Hodges played with the Dodgers for another 11 seasons. He was chosen for the all-star game roster six times. Besides the 1947 and 1949 pennants, he helped lead the Dodgers to win an additional five National League pennants (1952, 1953, 1955, 1956 and 1959) and appearances in the World Series. In the 1952 series, he went through one of the worst slumps in post-season play by going 0 for 21 in the seven-game series against the Yankees. In 1955, the Dodgers finally beat the Yankees in the series to take home the World Championship. Hodges played his part, batting .292 and driving in five runners. The Dodgers also won the 1959 World Championship by beating the Chicago White Sox in six games. Hodges was tied with Chicago's Ted Kluszewski for the highest series batting average with a .391 mark by going 9 for 23 with a triple, homer and a couple of RBI. His years with the Dodgers came to an end when he was selected in the expansion draft by the New York Mets in October 1961. He played in only 65 games for the Mets in two partial seasons. In late May 1963 (with his playing days behind him), he was traded to the Washington Senators with the express purpose of taking over as manager of the club, replacing Mickey Vernon. He managed the Senators for nearly five years with some respectable results for a team that normally finished near or at the bottom of the standings. After the 1967 season, the Mets were looking for a new manager and worked out a trade with the Senators to have Hodges return to New York to manage the Mets.

He got pretty quick results by leading the underdog "Miracle" Mets to a World Series championship in 1969 over the very powerful Baltimore Orioles in five games. The following couple of years resulted in third- and fourth-place finishes for the Mets in the National League's Eastern Division. As Hodges was getting the Mets ready for the 1972 season, he suffered a massive heart attack in training camp and passed away just two days shy of his 48th birthday. Like another former Senators manager (Mickey Vernon), questions remain why this great player and manager has not been selected for baseball's Hall of Fame.

90. GRANNY HAMNER

Born: April 26, 1927, Richmond, Virginia *Died*: September 12, 1993, Philadelphia, Pennsylvania *Bats*: Right *Throws*: Right *Height*: 5 feet, 10 inches *Weight*: 163 *Major league debut*: September 14, 1944 (Philadelphia at New York [NL]) *Last major league game*: August 1, 1962 (second game) (Kansas City at Detroit [AL])

Major league Iron Man from: July 17, 1950, to September 19, 1951 *Consecutive games played*: 473 *Games as major league Iron Man*: 222 (consecutive games 252 through 473) *Team played for during streak*: Philadelphia Phillies (NL) *Primary position played*: Shortstop *Game missed before streak*: September 12, 1948 (second game) (Boston at Philadelphia) *First game played of streak*: September 14, 1948 (St. Louis at Philadelphia) *Last game played of streak*: September 18, 1951 (Philadelphia at Chicago) *Game missed to end streak*: September 19, 1951 (Philadelphia at Chicago)

Consecutive Game Streak's Statistical Totals

Year	G	AB	R	H	2B	3B	HR	RBI	BB	SO	AVG	SLG	SB
1948	17	71	9	22	5	0	2	11	3	3	.310	.465	1
1949	154	662	83	174	32	5	6	53	25	47	.263	.353	6
1950	157	637	78	172	27	5	11	82	39	35	.270	.380	2
1951	145	569	56	143	22	6	9	70	26	28	.251	.359	10
Total	473	1939	226	511	86	16	28	216	93	113	.264	.368	19

Granny Hamner was the shortstop with the Philadelphia Phillies teams of the 1940s and 1950s. In 1944, at the age of 17, the Phillies signed him to a contract. During his first four seasons with the Philadelphia organization, he perfected his skills in the minors with an occasional call-up to the parent club for management to monitor his progress. In 1948, he made the club's roster permanently and was mostly at second base during the 129 games he played that year. He commenced his consecutive-game streak on September 14, 1948, in a Phillies' home game against the St. Louis Cardinals. The Phillies placed sixth in the final 1948 standings. The team was going through some growing pains and employed three managers that year. The youth of the team was really noticeable because, with the exception of shortstop Eddie Miller (who was 31), all of the starters were under 28 years of age. In 1949, Phillies manager Eddie Sawyer moved Miller over to second base and made Hamner the regular shortstop. He played all 154 games and extended his games-played streak to 171 by the end of the season. His batting average was .263 with six homers and 53 RBI. He also led the National League in at-bats (662), most assists by a shortstop (506), and most double plays by a shortstop (101). The team greatly improved, finishing in third place and winning 15 more games than during the previous year.

Between 1916 and 1979, the Phillies won only one National League pennant. That was in 1950 and it was known as the year of the Whiz Kids. With one of the youngest teams in major league baseball, Phillies manager Sawyer led the team to the league title by finishing two games ahead of the more powerful Brooklyn Dodgers. Unfortunately, when they got to the World Series, the New York Yankees were waiting for them. It was an extremely defensive series and only 16 runs were scored by both teams combined. The Yankees outscored them 11–5 in runs and swept the series in four games. The sweep was no fault of Hamner's, though, as he tied with the Yanks' Gene Woodling for highest batting total in the series, going 6 for 14 for a .429 average. During the regular season, Hamner maintained a consistent average of .270 and chipped in with 11 round-trippers and 82 RBI. In mid-July 1950, he became baseball's Iron Man when Brooklyn's Gil Hodges injured himself during a game against the Cardinals. Hamner extended his playing streak to 328 games by appearing in all 157 of the Phillies' contests. He also led the league's shortstops in games played. The following year (1951), the Phillies won close to 20 fewer games and finished in fifth place, some two dozen games behind the senior circuit champion New York Giants. Hamner hit a little below his career hitting totals with a .255 average. He was starting to close in on 500 consecutive games played when a sore arm late in the 1951 season (September 19) sidelined him for several games and brought his Iron Man reign to an end at 473 games. His batting average, if you look at his entire career, was maintained at a relatively consistent pace throughout his playing streak. His peak offensive years, though, were the first three years after his streak ended.

Hamner continued to play for the Phillies for many more years. He shifted back and forth between shortstop and second base during those years with an occasional appearance at third base. He played in three consecutive all-star games for the National League from 1952 to 1954. He started the 1952 game at shortstop and the 1954 game at second base. Starting with the 1955 season, his offensive stats started dropping and his average sometimes finished below .230. His last season as a regular player was in 1957, when he got into 133 contests. In May 1959, he was traded to the Cleveland Indians. He played only 27 games with the Tribe and was released after the 1959 season. A few years later, he hooked up with the Kansas City Athletics for a few games as a knuckleball pitcher. His career came to a close after those pitching appearances in 1962.

91. Eddie Yost

Born: October 13, 1926, Brooklyn, New York *Bats*: Right *Throws*: Right *Height*: 5 feet, 10 inches *Weight*: 170 *Major league debut*: August 16, 1944 (Chicago at Washington [AL]) *Last major league game*: July 28, 1962 (Los Angeles at Detroit [AL])

Major league Iron Man from: September 19, 1951, to May 12, 1955 *Consecutive games played*: 829 *Games as major league Iron Man*: 500 (consecutive games 330 through 829) *Team played for during streak*: Washington Senators (AL) *Primary position played*: Third base *Game missed before streak*: August 29, 1949 (Washington at St. Louis) *First game played of streak*: August 30, 1949 (Washington at Chicago) *Last game played of streak*: May 11, 1955 (Detroit at Washington) *Game missed to end streak*: May 12, 1955 (Cleveland at Washington)

Consecutive Game Streak's Statistical Totals

Year	G	AB	R	H	2B	3B	HR	RBI	BB	SO	AVG	SLG	SB
1949	31	112	15	34	4	3	0	9	22	5	.304	.393	1
1950	155	573	114	169	26	2	11	58	141	63	.295	.405	6
1951	154	568	109	161	36	4	12	65	126	55	.283	.424	6
1952	157	587	92	137	32	3	12	49	129	73	.233	.359	4
1953	152	577	107	157	30	7	9	45	123	59	.272	.395	7
1954	155	539	101	138	26	4	11	47	131	71	.256	.380	7
1955	25	83	16	15	2	2	1	8	21	12	.181	.289	2
Total	829	3039	554	811	156	25	56	281	693	338	.267	.390	33

Eddie Yost

Eddie Yost was one of the most dependable and durable third basemen to ever play major league ball. He was in the big leagues for 18 seasons with the Washington Senators, Detroit Tigers and Los Angeles Angels and never played in the minor leagues. Unfortunately, the teams he did play for always seemed to finish in the second division or near the bottom of the standings. Signed by the Senators as a free agent in 1944, he got into several games that year before leaving to serve in the military. He lost nearly two years to military service before returning to get into some contests during the 1946 season. The following year, in his first full season in the majors, he won the Senators' third baseman job. He played in 115 games and finished with a .238 average and 14 RBI. The Senators finished in seventh place in both the 1947 and 1948 seasons. In 1948, Yost's average improved to .249 as he led the Senators in doubles and walks and American League third basemen with 189 putouts. As the Senators finished in the basement of the American League standings in 1949, Yost played in 124 games with a .253 batting average and again led the team in walks. On August 30 of that season, his playing streak started in a game played in Chicago against the White Sox. He played in the last 31 games of the 1949 season and batted .304 during that stretch.

The Senators improved to fifth place in 1950 with manager Bucky Harris back for his third try as Senators skipper. Yost played nearly every inning as his batting average improved over 40 points to .295. He was one of the Senators' offensive leaders as he was the league leader in getting on base (318) and walks (141). Defensively, he led the league's third sackers in putouts (205), double plays (45) and errors (30). The end of the 1951 campaign again found the Senators finishing near the bottom of the standings in seventh place. Yost had a .283 average with a team high in homers with a dozen round-trippers. He was the league leader in doubles with 36 two-baggers. Yost again led the American League's third sackers with 203 putouts at the hot corner. He also played a few games in the outfield in 1951 with Sam Dente covering third base in those instances. In mid–September 1951, he became the Iron Man title holder, succeeding the Phils' Granny Hamner. Yost closed out the season with a 340-consecutive-game streak actively running. In 1952, he stretched his game streak to 497 games, but he suffered through one of his worst offensive years at the plate as his batting average fell 50 points (.233). In fact, in July 1952, Senators manager Harris was contemplating whether to bench Yost because he was going through one of the worst batting slumps of his career. The benching never happened as Yost

Eddie Yost: He was a steady third baseman for the Washington Senators of the 1940s and 1950s. His 829-games-played streak, which ended in May 1955, was the longest stretch since Gehrig's streak closed out in 1939.

broke out of his prolonged slump. Also, it did not stop him from leading the league in walks along with getting selected to his only all-star game. Ironically, he never made it into the game's lineup, so he did not appear in the midsummer classic. In addition, he again led all third basemen of the American League in games played (157) and putouts (212). The Senators improved by winning an additional 16 games over the previous year and jumped two places to finish in fifth place in the standings. Early in the 1953 campaign, Yost became the 18th player in major league history to play 500 consecutive games. He kept the streak going and stretched it to 649 games by season's end while at the same time improving his average to .272, up nearly 40 points from the previous season, and again leading the American League in bases on balls with 123 free passes. The Senators, in the meantime, maintained the status quo, finishing in fifth place for the second year in a row. The following year, Yost played another full slate of games (for the fifth straight year) and ended the season with 804 consecutive contests played. This was the longest streak of games played since Lou Gehrig ended his streak back in the early part of the 1939 baseball campaign. The streak nearly ended, however, late in the 1954 season when Yost was beaned by Boston pitcher Russ Kemmerer in a game on September 17. With only nine games to go until the end of the regular season, Harris had Yost make token appearances (to extend the streak) in those last nine games and replaced him each time at third base with Wayne Terwilliger once Yost was credited with a game played. The 1955 baseball season in Washington found a new manager for the Senators in Charlie Dressen. Regrettably, things only got worse as the team went 53–101 and finished in the basement of the standings. On May 12, 1955, Yost's streak finally came to an end when he was sidelined in a game against the Cleveland Indians due to a severe case of tonsillitis. The streak lasted 829 games and he had been the reigning Iron Man for over three seasons. Another streak broken that day was the major league record for most consecutive games played by a third baseman. Yost established the hot corner mark with 576 consecutive games from July 3, 1951, to May 11, 1955. By season's end, he finished with a .243 average with seven homers and 48 RBI.

Yost spent three more uneventful seasons as the Senators' third baseman before being traded to the Detroit Tigers in October 1958. His first season with the Tigers turned out to be his best year career-wise as he led the American League in runs (115), walks (135) and on base percentage (.435). He also led the league's third basemen in fielding average (.964) for the second consecutive year. The next season, his last as a starting player, he repeated as league champ in walks (125) and on base percentage (.414). He left the Tigers in December 1960 when he was selected by the Los Angeles Angels in the Expansion Draft. He finished his career after playing with the Angels for two seasons. Upon his retirement as a player, he had set many fielding records at third base (besides most consecutive games). These included most games (2,008), putouts (2,356), assists (3,659) and total chances (6,285). In addition, he established the record for most home runs leading off a game with 27 round-trippers (he had league-leading totals in this statistic during the 1950, 1956, 1959 and 1960 seasons). This record was broken by Bobby Bonds of the San Francisco Giants in 1973. After his playing career, Yost was a long-time coach for the Washington Senators, New York Mets and Boston Red Sox. He also had a chance to manage one game for the Senators in between the reigns of Mickey Vernon and Gil Hodges in Washington.

92. ROY MCMILLAN

Born: July 17, 1929, Bonham, Texas *Died*: November 2, 1997, Bonham, Texas *Bats*: Right *Throws*: Right *Height*: 5 feet, 11 inches *Weight*: 170 *Major league debut*: April 17, 1951 (Cincinnati at Chicago [NL]) *Last major league game*: August 3, 1966 (San Francisco at New York [NL])

Roy McMillan

Major league Iron Man from: May 12, 1955, to August 7, 1955 *Consecutive games played*: 584 *Games as major league Iron Man*: 85 (consecutive games 500 through 584) *Team played for during streak*: Cincinnati Reds (NL) *Primary position played*: Shortstop *Game missed before streak*: September 15, 1951 (Philadelphia at Cincinnati) *First game played of streak*: September 16, 1951 (first game) (Boston at Cincinnati) *Last game played of streak*: August 7, 1955 (first game) (New York at Cincinnati) *Game missed to end streak*: August 7, 1955 (second game) (New York at Cincinnati)

Consecutive Game Streak's Statistical Totals

Year	G	AB	R	H	2B	3B	HR	RBI	BB	SO	AVG	SLG	SB
1951	11	36	2	8	0	0	0	1	3	5	.222	.222	0
1952	154	540	60	132	32	2	7	57	45	81	.244	.350	4
1953	155	557	51	130	15	4	5	43	43	52	.233	.302	2
1954	154	588	86	147	21	2	4	42	47	54	.250	.313	4
1955	110	350	38	94	16	2	1	29	37	24	.269	.334	2
Total	584	2071	237	511	84	10	17	172	175	216	.247	.322	12

Roy McMillan was a gritty player and exemplary fielding shortstop who played in the National League for 16 seasons with the Cincinnati Reds (1951–1960), Milwaukee Braves (1961–1964) and the New York Mets (1964–1966). Signed as a free agent at 17 years old by the Reds, he spent his first four seasons in the minor leagues, mostly in his home state of Texas. The Reds brought him up to the big club for the 1951 season. He was being groomed to replace Virgil Stallcup as the Reds' shortstop, but by midseason the job was his for the taking. His consecutive-game streak started on September 16, 1951, during the first game of a double-header in Cincinnati against the Braves. He finished his rookie year with a batting average of only .211 but the Reds were more interested in his glove than in his bat.

In his second season (1952), McMillan was the youngest starting shortstop in the majors and came close to playing nearly every inning that year as he compiled a .244 batting average. He also had the top stats among the league's shortstops in games played and total assists. The Reds came in sixth place, nearly 30 games behind the pacesetting Brooklyn Dodgers. The 1953 season found McMillan playing another full slate of games as he extended his playing streak to 320 consecutive contests. He also finished with a .233 average along with five homers and 43 RBI. He again led the shortstops in games played, assists and double plays. As for the Reds, they compiled a 68–86 record, good enough for a sixth-place finish for the second straight year. This time the team was 37 games behind the repeating champion Dodgers. With a new manager in Birdie Tebbetts, the Reds showed some improvement the following year (1954) and finished in fifth position with a 74–80 record. McMillan played in another 154-game schedule and extended the playing streak to 474. This mark was good only for the second-longest streak as Eddie Yost's streak was still going. Although he hit .250 for the season and lead the senior circuit with 31 sacrifice hits, it was still McMillan's defensive skills that kept the Reds happy, as his games played, putouts and double play totals led all the shortstops of the National League.

As McMillan achieved the 500-consecutive-game milestone, he finally became the major league Iron Man on May 12, 1955, when Yost got sick and had to sit out a game. McMillan's own streak ended nearly three months later due to a sprained thumb. During a game played on August 6, 1955, McMillan was fielding a grounder off the bat of the Giants' Hank Thompson when the ball took a bad bounce and struck McMillan's right thumb. The next day, he pinch-hit in the first game of a double-header against New York to extend the streak; however, he sat out the nightcap game, ending his playing streak at 584 games. At season's end, the Reds were fifth-place finishers again. McMillan had one of his better years at the plate with a .268 average in 151 games. In reviewing his stats from his streak, McMillan compiled a .247 average and when compared to his career .243 average, it is obvious he maintained a consistent offensive performance level throughout his consecutive-games streak.

McMillan played another five years as the Reds' shortstop before being traded to the Milwaukee Braves in December 1960. During those five years, the Reds finished no better than third place (1956) but he continued to anchor the Reds' infield by leading the shortstops in the senior circuit in fielding average for three straight years (1956–1958). He also was the starting shortstop for the National League squad in the 1956 and 1957 all-star games. He spent the rest of his career with teams in Milwaukee and New York that never finished out of the second division. His playing career ended in October 1966 with his release from the Mets. From there, he spent some time in the minors, both playing and managing. In 1970, he was hired to be a coach with the Milwaukee Brewers, serving for three years and filling in for a couple of games in 1972 as their interim manager. He also later served as coach with the New York Mets from 1973–1976. When Yogi Berra was let go as the Mets' manager in the summer of 1975, McMillan took over as the skipper for the last 53 games on the schedule, compiling a 26–27 won-lost record.

93. Stan Musial

Born: November 21, 1920, Donora, Pennsylvania *Bats*: Left *Throws*: Left *Height*: 6 feet *Weight*: 175 *Major league debut*: September 17, 1941 (second game) (Boston at St. Louis [NL]) *Last major league game*: September 29, 1963 (Cincinnati at St. Louis [NL])

Major league Iron Man from: August 7, 1955, to August 23, 1957 *Consecutive games played*: 895 *Games as major league Iron Man*: 325 (consecutive games 571 through 895) *Team played for during streak*: St. Louis Cardinals (NL) *Primary positions played*: Outfield and first base *Game missed before streak*: September 30, 1951 (second game) (St. Louis at Chicago) *First game played of streak*: April 15, 1952 (Pittsburgh at St. Louis) *Last game played of streak*: August 22, 1957 (St. Louis at Philadelphia) *Game missed to end streak*: August 23, 1957 (St. Louis at Philadelphia)

Consecutive Game Streak's Statistical Totals

Year	G	AB	R	H	2B	3B	HR	RBI	BB	SO	AVG	SLG	SB
1952	154	578	105	194	42	6	21	91	96	29	.336	.538	7
1953	157	593	127	200	53	9	30	113	105	32	.337	.609	3
1954	153	591	120	195	41	9	35	126	103	39	.330	.607	1
1955	154	562	97	179	30	5	33	108	80	39	.319	.566	5
1956	156	594	87	184	33	6	27	109	75	39	.310	.522	2
1957	121	468	75	159	32	3	29	97	57	32	.340	.607	1
Total	895	3386	611	1111	231	38	175	644	516	210	.328	.574	19

Musial returned to the St. Louis Cardinals in 1946 after serving for a year in the military. He picked up where he left off by playing every game that year, leading the league in batting (with a .365 average) and several other important offensive categories. In addition, he switched over to play first base because Ray Sanders, who had played that position for four years with the Cards, was sold to the Boston Braves in April 1946. Musial's performance in 1946 earned him the National League's Most Valuable Player award for the second time in his relatively young major league playing career. The National League pennant race that year ended in a tie with the Cardinals and Dodgers. The Cardinals took the title by winning both games from the Dodgers in a best-of-three playoff series. St. Louis met the Boston Red Sox for baseball's World Championship. The World Series was a very close affair and came down to an exciting seventh game in St. Louis, which the Cards won 4–3 when Enos Slaughter sprinted from first base on a line drive double hit by Harry Walker to score the winning run in the bottom of the eighth inning. Although Musial finished the series with a .222 average by going 6 for 27, he still contributed four doubles, a triple and four RBI to the Cardinal's offensive arsenal. This was his fourth World Series appearance in his first four full years of playing big league ball. This also turned out to be his last, because the Cardinals would not play in another fall classic until 1964 (the year after Musial's retirement).

In 1947, Musial ended the year with his lowest batting average up to that time (.312), but he still led the team in hitting as the Cards finished in second place behind the Brooklyn Dodgers. He rebounded the following year in 1948 by winning his third batting crown and completely dominating the stat charts by leading the league in every major category except home runs. He was rewarded with his third Most Valuable Player award. In addition, he returned to playing in the outfield after two seasons at first base. Nippy Jones took Musial's place at first base. The Cards again finished runner-up in the standings, this time to Boston's Braves. Over the next three seasons, Musial continued to put up some very impressive numbers. Along the way, he picked up his fourth and fifth batting titles and placed runner-up each year (1949, 1950 and 1951) in the MVP voting. He sat out the final game of the 1951 season. This is noteworthy, because he would not miss another game until August 1957. On Opening Day (April 15th) of the 1952 season, Musial played the first of 895 consecutive contests. This mark became the National League record of most consecutive games played. In the 154 games he played that year, he put up numbers that were becoming the norm for the Cardinals' star player. He claimed his sixth league batting crown by hitting .336 along with 21 homers and 91 RBI. The Cardinals had a new manager that year in Eddie Stanky and he guided the team to a third-place finish, eight and a half games behind the Dodgers. In 1953, Musial again was putting the punch in the Cardinals' offense by hitting .337, clubbing 30 homers, knocking in 113 runs and leading the league in doubles (53) and in on base percentage (.437). The Cardinals, however, were at a standstill as Stanky led them to another third-place finish, tied with the Phillies, some 22 games behind the top spot in the standings. Musial had another outstanding year in 1954 with a .330 average along with topping the league in runs and doubles. By the end of the 1954 season, Musial's streak had reached 464 consecutive games. Unfortunately, the Cardinals had their worst showing since the 1938 season as the 1954 version came in sixth place with a 72–82 record. The 1955 season was another bad year for the Cards as they finished in next-to-last place, eight games ahead of the basement-winning Pittsburgh Pirates. Musial was the only Cardinal to hit above .300 as he finished with a .319 average along with leading the team in most of the offensive categories. He also started appearing in more games at first base than in the outfield. As for his consecutive streak, when the Reds' Roy McMillan ended his on August 7, 1955, due to an injury, Musial became a two-time holder of the Iron Man title. A few weeks later, in the middle of September, his streak nearly ended when he pulled a leg muscle in the fourth inning of a game against the Milwaukee Braves. Although he was pulled from that game, the injury did not sideline him and he was able to play the rest of the schedule without missing a contest and extend his playing streak to 618 games. In 1956, Musial finished the year with only a .310 batting average. This was the lowest in his career up to that time and, amazingly, it was his 15th year in the majors. Just because his average dropped did not mean he was not producing. Musial still had 27 homers and led the senior circuit with 109 RBI as he led the improved Cardinals to fourth place under new manager Fred Hutchinson.

During the opening game of the 1957 season against the Reds, Musial suffered a back muscle injury that seriously jeopardized his streak. Fortunately, his back responded to treatment and he was able to continue playing. On June 12, 1957, he broke Gus Suhr's National League game mark of 822 consecutive contests played. About a month later, playing double-headers was starting to become hard for Musial so he decided that he would sit out the final games of any future double-headers. His streak nearly ended on July 21, 1957, when he was rested during the nightcap of a double-header. Fortunately, this game was suspended until a future date. Musial's second Iron Man streak run ended when he suffered a wrenched shoulder when swinging at a high, outside curve pitch in the fourth inning of the August 22, 1957, game at Philadelphia. Four days later, manager Hutchinson had him pinch-run in the top of the ninth inning and then play first base in the bottom of the last inning of the game suspended from July 21, 1957. This action officially gave Musial 895 consecutive games played. If he had not played in that resumption of the suspended game, his consecutive game streak would have ended on July 21 with 862 consecutive games. As with his previous Iron Man streak, the 895-game streak did not affect his numbers as he had a .328 batting average and he consistently smacked at least 25 homers and drove home over 100 runs every season. When he returned from his injury, he played only 13 more games by the end of the year. He won his seventh and final batting crown with a .351 average along with 29 homers and 102 runs knocked in. The Cards finished runner-up to the Milwaukee Braves by eight games.

Musial went on to play another six years before retiring from baseball after the 1963 season. He finished his career with 3,630 base hits, good for second place all-time (at the time) behind Ty Cobb. After his retirement, he served as the Cards' general manager for one season. After his tenure as general manager came to an end, he continued to serve the Cardinals in various positions for many years. He was elected in his first year of eligibility into baseball's Hall of Fame in 1969.

94. NELLIE FOX

Born: December 25, 1927, St. Thomas, Pennsylvania *Died*: December 1, 1975, Baltimore, Maryland *Bats*: Left *Throws*: Right *Height*: 5 feet, 10 inches *Weight*: 160 *Major league debut*: June 8, 1947 (second game) (Philadelphia at Cleveland [AL]) *Last major league game*: July 25, 1965 (Cincinnati at Houston [NL])

Major league Iron Man from: August 23, 1957, to September 4, 1960 *Consecutive games played*: 798 *Games as major league Iron Man*: 475 (consecutive games 324 through 798) *Team played for during streak*: Chicago White Sox (AL) *Primary position played*: Second base *Game missed before streak*: August 6, 1955 (Chicago at Baltimore) *First game played of streak*: August 7, 1955 (Chicago at Baltimore) *Last game played of streak*: September 3, 1960 (Detroit at Chicago) *Game missed to end streak*: September 4, 1960 (first game) (Detroit at Chicago)

Consecutive Game Streak's Statistical Totals

Year	G	AB	R	H	2B	3B	HR	RBI	BB	SO	AVG	SLG	SB
1955	49	210	36	68	9	2	1	17	10	3	.324	.400	0
1956	154	649	109	192	20	10	4	52	44	14	.296	.376	8
1957	155	619	110	196	27	8	6	61	75	13	.317	.415	5
1958	155	623	82	187	21	6	0	49	47	11	.300	.353	5
1959	156	624	84	191	34	6	2	70	71	13	.306	.389	5
1960	129	525	73	145	22	10	1	55	44	12	.276	.362	2
Total	798	3250	494	979	133	42	14	304	291	66	.301	.381	25

Nellie Fox

Nellie Fox was the Chicago White Sox's second baseman during the 1950s and early 1960s. He was known for his tobacco chewing, using a bottle bat when batting and being an aggressive player on the field. He was a slap hitter who hit a lot of singles and doubles and, like two previous modern-day Iron Men (Sewell and Holmes), was extremely hard to strike out. His final stats show that he fanned only 216 times in 9,232 official at bats. He initially was signed to a contract by the Philadelphia Athletics and he put in parts of three seasons with that team. In October 1949, the White Sox made one of their all-time best trades by trading for Fox in exchange for a catcher named Joe Tipton. When Fox got to the White Sox, the team already had a quality second baseman by the name of Cass Michaels. By the end of May 1950, Michaels was gone (traded to the Washington Senators) and Fox was the new Sox second baseman.

Fox's first four years (1950 through 1953) in Chicago were somewhat uneventful as the New York Yankees were always winning the American League title and the White Sox were coming in no better than third place. His infield partner at shortstop during those early years was Chico Carrasquel and together they made an awesome double play combination. In 1954, Fox came in with a .319 average (second for the team, just behind Minnie Minoso's .320 average) along with a league-best 201 hits. He did not miss a game that year and had extended a playing streak to 169 games by the end of the 1954 campaign. The following season (1955), Fox again hit over .300 and had a better-than-average year in producing runs with 59 RBI. He missed only one game when White Sox manager Marty Marion rested him on August 6, 1955, thereby ending a streak of 274 games. If Fox had played that game, his final consecutive games streak would have reached 1,073 games. The next game on August 7, he started another streak that eventually set the all-time major league record of 798 consecutive contests played at second base. The White Sox in the meantime had a great year and finished in third place, just five games behind the first-place New York Yankees. In 1956, Fox had a new double play partner in rookie Luis Aparicio as Carrasquel was sent over to Cleveland. Aparicio played alongside Fox in the White Sox infield through the 1962 season. Although Fox had another decent year with a .296 average, the team was stagnant as they finished in third place for the fifth straight season. In 1957, Chicago had a new manager in former Cleveland Indians manager and major league catcher Al Lopez, who replaced Marion. The team finished in second place behind the ever-powerful New York Yankees. Fox was playing every game and his performance was superb as he led the junior circuit with 196 hits along with a team-high .317 average. On August 23, 1957, he was crowned the new major league Iron Man when Stan Musial injured his shoulder. The following campaign was the same story as the previous year for the White Sox as they again placed runner-up behind the Yankees. Fox hit an even .300, led the league for a second straight year with 187 base knocks and made his sixth straight all-star game appearance. On August 21, 1958, he broke the all-time record for most consecutive games played by an American League second baseman by besting Eddie Collins' 478-game streak, established back in May 1918. In mid–September 1958, Fox became the 22nd major leaguer to play 500 consecutive contests and finished the season with 513 continuous games played.

The 1959 season was White Sox's year. Nicknamed the Go-Go Sox, the team won their first league flag in 40 years (since the year of the Black Sox scandal) with a pitching staff led by Early Wynn. In the 1950s, there were only two seasons the Yankees did not win the American League; those years were 1954 and 1959 and both teams were managed by Al Lopez. Fox had one of his best years by bringing 70 runners home and hitting for a .306 average. His performance in leading the team to the pennant resulted in his being chosen the American League's 1959 Most Valuable Player by the baseball writers. The White Sox lost the World Series to the Los Angeles Dodgers in six games. Fox did his part by hitting .375 and finished in a tie with teammate Al Smith for the series lead in doubles with three. The 1960 season found the Yankees winning another title; Chicago put similar won-lost numbers together but they were good for only third place. As Fox's streak was progressing, his numbers were always very consistent. The pressures of playing every day without taking a day off did not negatively affect his performance. The streak was nearing 800 games when he came down with a virus during the first week of September. He eventually was hospitalized for observation. As a result, it took a hospital stay to keep him out of the White Sox lineup (during the first game of a twin bill on September 4, 1960), for the time since August 1955. The streak was over after 798 games.

Fox went on to play with the White Sox for three more years before leaving Chicago after 14 years by way of a trade in December 1963 to the National League team in Houston. He put in one season as Houston's second baseman and part of another as a player-coach before being released in July 1965. He retired as a ballplayer and wound up working for Ted Williams in Washington and Texas as one of his coaches before leaving after the 1972 season.

Nellie Fox: The White Sox second baseman played 798 games until an illness forced him to miss a game during the last month of the 1960 campaign.

It should be noted that during his long major league career, Fox led the American League in many statistics. These included at-bats in 1952, 1955, 1956, 1959 and 1960; hits in 1952, 1954, 1957 and 1958; singles in 1952 and 1954 through 1960; triples in 1960; and hardest batter to strike out in 1951 and 1955 through 1963 (he also was the hardest batter to strike out in the NL in 1964). Defensively, he led the league's second basemen in games played every season from 1952 through 1959; fielding average from 1952, 1954, 1956, 1959, 1962 and 1963; putouts every season from 1952 through 1958; assists in 1952, 1955 through 1957, 1959 and 1960; double plays in 1954, 1956 through 1958 and 1960; and errors in 1955. He also won four straight Gold Glove awards (1957 through 1960) as the best fielding second baseman in the American League. Fox had to wait a long time, though, to be picked for membership in baseball's Hall of Fame. On two occasions, he just missed being selected and loyal White Sox fans were wondering if he would ever be chosen for baseball immortality. Finally, he was selected by the veterans committee in 1997 for enshrinement. Unfortunately, Fox was not around for the great honor, for he had passed away many years before from cancer on December 1, 1975, a few weeks short of his 48th birthday.

95. ERNIE BANKS

Born: January 31, 1931, Dallas, Texas *Bats*: Right *Throws*: Right *Height*: 6 feet, 1 inch *Weight*: 180 *Major league debut*: September 17, 1953 (Philadelphia at Chicago [NL]) *Last major league game*: September 26, 1971 (Philadelphia at Chicago [NL])

Major league Iron Man from: September 4, 1960, to June 23, 1961 *Consecutive games played*: 717 *Games as major league Iron Man*: 90 (consecutive games 628 through 717) *Team played for during streak*: Chicago Cubs (NL) *Primary position played*: Shortstop *Game missed before streak*: August 26, 1956 (first game) (Pittsburgh at Chicago) *First game played of streak*: August 26, 1956 (second game) (Pittsburgh at Chicago) *Last game played of streak*: June 22, 1961 (Los Angeles at Chicago) *Game missed to end streak*: June 23, 1961 (Chicago at Milwaukee)

Consecutive Game Streak's Statistical Totals

Year	G	AB	R	H	2B	3B	HR	RBI	BB	SO	AVG	SLG	SB
1956	33	131	15	35	9	2	3	16	12	18	.267	.435	1
1957	156	594	113	169	34	6	43	102	70	85	.285	.579	8
1958	154	617	119	193	23	11	47	129	52	87	.313	.614	4
1959	155	589	97	179	25	6	45	143	64	72	.304	.596	2
1960	156	597	94	162	32	7	41	117	71	69	.271	.554	1
1961	63	237	34	66	6	3	12	34	26	37	.278	.481	1
Total	717	2765	472	804	129	35	191	541	295	368	.291	.570	17

Ernie Banks was one of baseball's most popular players of all time. Everyone loved him and he loved the fans and the game of baseball with a passion. He played his entire 19-year career in a Chicago Cubs uniform and because the Cubs were a second-division mainstay, Banks never appeared in a post-season contest. He was the first black player to play for the Cubs. By his attitude ("let's play two") and play on the diamond, he became known as Mr. Cub. The Cubs signed him to a free agent contract in 1953. He started out as a shortstop but in midcareer switched over to playing first base. He made his major league debut at 22 years old on September 17, 1953, in a contest at Wrigley Field against the Philadelphia Phillies. He became the team's starting shortstop, replacing Roy Smalley Jr. From his debut date through August 10, 1956, he compiled a consecutive-games-played streak that lasted through 424 games and established a National League record for most consecutive games played at the start of a major league career. Although this streak did not qualify him to be the reigning major league Iron Man (because Stan Musial's 895-game streak completely overlapped Banks' streak), the statistical numbers show that Banks thrived without having to take a day off.

In his first full year in the big leagues (1954), he hit a modest .275 along with smacking 19 homers and driving in 79 runners. The next year (1955), he fully came into his own as he clubbed 44-round trippers, drove in 117 runs and hit .295. He finished second in homers in the senior circuit behind Willie Mays' 51 blasts that season and played in his first all-star contest. He also played the most games at shortstop his first two full seasons along with being the best fielder at this position with a .972 fielding average in the 1955 season. The unfortunate thing for the Cubs was that even though they had one of the best young players in the game in their starting lineup, they were not a very good team as the club finished near the bottom of the standings in both the 1954 and 1955 campaigns. The 1956 season was no different—worst, even—as the Cubs hit rock bottom with a 60–94 record, good for last place and 33 games behind the champion Brooklyn Dodgers. On August 11, 1956, Banks' 424-game streak ended when he was hospitalized for a seriously infected left hand and, as a result, missed 18 games. His major league Iron Man streak started upon his return to the Cubs' lineup starting with the second game of a twin bill on August 26, 1956. Although Banks played all 156 of the Cubs' games in 1957, he played only 100 games at short while taking in 58 contests at third base. While the Cubs finished tied for last place with the Pirates, the playing position change did not affect Banks as he had another great year at the plate, finishing in second place behind Hank Aaron in home runs (43) and tied for third place in RBI (102) with Stan Musial. The 1958 season found Banks back at the shortstop position. He had a stellar year at the plate and led the league in at-bats, home runs, RBI, slugging average, total bases and extra-base hits. Although the Cubs finished in sixth place, some 10 games below .500 ball, the baseball writers chose Banks for the National League Most Valuable Player honor. The next season, Banks repeated as the league's best player by hitting .304, clubbing 45 homers (second to the Braves' Eddie Mathews) and leading the senior circuit with 143 RBI. Although there have been several multiple winners of the National League MVP award, Banks became the first back-to-back winner of this honor. In addition, he stretched his consecutive-game-played streak to 498 contests by the end of the 1959 season. Although the Cubs won a couple of more games than they did the year before, the team repeated as the sixth-place finisher in the final standings. The next season, a couple of Iron Man milestones occurred in 1960. On April 13, Banks became the 23rd player in major league history to play 500 consecutive games. He hit the 600-consecutive-game mark on August 6. In early September, Nellie Fox's major league leading games-played streak came to an end and Banks became the major league Iron Man on September 4, 1960, with 628 straight games. As usual, he continued to put up the numbers by hitting 41 homers and bringing home 117 runners, while playing all the Cubs' games. He also was selected for his only Gold Glove in 1960 as the league's best fielding shortstop. At the end of the season, the Cubs finished in seventh place, just one game ahead of the cellar-dwelling Philadelphia Phillies. During the 1961 season, the streak seemed to take its toll on Banks as he had only 12 homers and 34 RBI as the season was nearing the midpoint. Bothered by a sore knee, Banks voluntarily ended his streak after 717 consecutive contests by benching himself in a game in Milwaukee on June 23, 1961. He finished the year with 29 round-trippers and 80 RBI. For the first time in his career, he was being used as an outfielder and a first baseman in addition to playing his normal shortstop position. As for the Cubs, they repeated the honor as the second-worst team in the National League in 1961, again in seventh place, just above the Phillies.

Ernie Banks: Arguably the most popular player to wear a major league uniform, Mr. Cub started his big league career with a 424-game streak. This was overlapped by Stan Musial's 895-game streak. Banks had another run of 717 games (from 1956 to 1961) and succeeded Nellie Fox as baseball's Iron Man in September 1960.

In 1962, Banks made the switch from shortstop to first base. He spent 10 more seasons with the Cubs and in those years led the senior circuit's first sackers in several fielding categories including games played (1965), putouts (1969), assists (1962, 1964 and 1967), double plays (1962) and fielding average (1969). It was not until the latter part of the 1960s that the Cubs started finishing closer to the top of the standings than the bottom. In his last few years, Banks served as a player-coach under Cubs manager Leo Durocher. In December 1971, the Cubs released Banks as an active player but he continued to serve the team he loved as a coach and instructor for many years after his playing days were over. In 1977, during his first year of eligibility, Ernie "Mr. Cub" Banks was easily elected for membership into baseball's Hall of Fame.

96. Vada Pinson

Born: August 11, 1936, Memphis, Tennessee *Died*: October 21, 1995, Oakland, California *Bats*: Left *Throws*: Left *Height*: 5 feet, 11 inches *Weight*: 170 *Major league debut*: April 15, 1958 (Philadelphia at Cincinnati [NL]) *Last major league game*: September 28, 1975 (Kansas City at Texas [AL])

Major league Iron Man from: June 23, 1961, to May 31, 1962 *Consecutive games played*: 508 *Games as major league Iron Man*: 132 (consecutive games 377 through 508) *Team played for during streak*: Cincinnati Reds (NL) *Primary position played*: Outfield *Game missed before streak*: September 21, 1958 (Milwaukee at Cincinnati) *First game played of streak*: September 26, 1958 (Cincinnati at Milwaukee) *Last game played of streak*: May 30, 1962 (second game) (Cincinnati at Milwaukee) *Game missed to end streak*: May 31, 1962 (Cincinnati at Milwaukee)

Consecutive Game Streak's Statistical Totals

Year	G	AB	R	H	2B	3B	HR	RBI	BB	SO	AVG	SLG	SB
1958	3	12	2	6	1	0	0	1	1	1	.500	.583	2
1959	154	648	131	205	47	9	20	84	55	98	.316	.509	21
1960	154	652	107	187	37	12	20	61	47	96	.287	.472	32
1961	154	607	101	208	34	8	16	87	39	63	.343	.504	23
1962	43	172	35	53	11	2	13	40	15	25	.308	.622	3
Total	508	2091	376	659	130	31	69	273	157	283	.315	.506	81

Vada Pinson patrolled the outfield for four major league teams (Cincinnati Reds, St. Louis Cardinals, Cleveland Indians and Kansas City Royals) in 18 seasons. Many baseball experts agree that Pinson had all the tools to be a great ballplayer. This included having a rocket of an arm, speed on the base paths and the skill to hit for a high average with some power. He never truly lived up to all his potential, although he did finish his career with over 2,700 base hits. Signed at the age of 18 by the Reds, he played his first few years of organized ball in the minors before being called up by the parent club for the start of the 1958 season and got into 27 games, but he spent most of that season with Seattle of the Pacific Coast League.

Pinson accomplished his Iron Man streak early in his career. His streak commenced at the end of his first season when he played the last three of the Reds' games of the 1958 season, starting with the September 26, 1958, game played in Milwaukee. The 1959 season found Pinson as the team's center fielder. He had an amazing year during which he batted .316, hit 20 homers, knocked in 84 runs in 154 games, led the National League in at-bats (648), runs (131), doubles (47) and played in his first all-star game. In addition, he led the league's outfielders in games played and putouts. All these achievements surely would have guaranteed his winning the Rookie of the Year award but in 1958 he had 96 at-bats, disqualifying him as a rookie in 1959 by only six at-bats. As for the Reds, they finished tied for fifth place with the Chicago Cubs in the league standings. The next year, Pinson followed up with another decent year as he played in both all-star games in 1960 and repeated as the league leader in at-bats and doubles although his batting average dipped to the .287 mark. He also extended his consecutive playing streak to 311 games. The Reds finished in sixth place in the final standings, but that was about to change. The 1961 Reds surprised the baseball world as the team won the National League title by four games over the Los Angeles Dodgers. Power-hitting Frank Robinson led the Reds to win their first league championship since the 1940 season. Although Robinson was the main offensive force for the team, Pinson greatly contributed to the Reds' success by hitting .343 (good for second place behind the Pittsburgh Pirates' Roberto Clemente's league-leading .351 average), smacking 16 home runs and knocking in 87 runs. Additionally, Pinson became baseball's Iron Man with 377 straight games played when the Cubs' Ernie Banks sat out a game on June 23, 1961. In the World Series, the Reds faced the almighty New York Yankees. Many baseball experts agree that the 1961 Yankees were probably the best team in baseball since the 1927 Yankees. The Reds were no match for these Yankees as the Bronx Bombers beat the Reds for the world title in five games. Pinson had an awful time at the plate during the series, as he hit only .091 by going 2 for 22 in the five-game affair. The following year, he was off to a great start with a .308 average, 13 homers and 40 RBI as the end of May neared. Unfortunately, he suffered an injury when he pulled a leg muscle in the opener of the May 30, 1962, twin bill against the Milwaukee Braves. He kept his streak going by pinch hitting in the nightcap but the injury caused him to sit out the May 31 contest against the Braves, ending his streak at 508 contests. The injury also required him to miss several more games before he could return to the Reds' lineup. He still plated 100 runs by season's end but hit only 10 more homers after his return from the injury. The Reds repeated with another year of about .600 ball, but they finished in third place behind the Giants and Dodgers, who both won over 100 games in the 1962 season.

Although Pinson would play for another 13 years in the majors for several teams, he would never again appear in any more post-season or all-star games. He maintained his position as the Reds' center fielder through the 1968 season. In October 1968, the Reds traded him to the St. Louis Cardinals. After one year in St. Louis, he left the National League and wound up in the junior circuit with the Cleveland Indians. He was traded two more times before signing a contract with the Milwaukee Brewers in January 1976. He never played for Milwaukee because, once spring training ended, the Brewers released him from his playing contract in April 1976. With his playing days over, he served as a coach with the Seattle Mariners (twice), Chicago White Sox and Detroit Tigers through the 1990 season. Although he has not been selected for membership in the baseball Hall of Fame, in the future his career numbers give him a slight chance for selection by the veterans committee.

97. ROCKY COLAVITO

Born: August 10, 1933, New York, New York *Bats*: Right *Throws*: Right *Height*: 6 feet, 3 inches *Weight*: 190 *Major league debut*: September 10, 1955 (Cleveland at Boston [AL]) *Last major league game*: September 28, 1968 (New York at Boston [AL])

Major league Iron Man from: May 31, 1962, to May 22, 1963 *Consecutive games played*: 458 *Games as major league Iron Man*: 155 (consecutive games 304 through 458) *Team played for during streak*: Detroit Tigers (AL) *Primary position played*: Outfield *Game missed before streak*: June 19, 1960 (second game) (Baltimore at Detroit) *First game played of streak*: June 21, 1960 (New York at Detroit) *Last game played of streak*: May 21, 1963 (Detroit at Baltimore) *Game missed to end streak*: May 22, 1963 (Detroit at Baltimore)

Consecutive Game Streak's Statistical Totals

Year	G	AB	R	H	2B	3B	HR	RBI	BB	SO	AVG	SLG	SB
1960	98	387	46	101	13	1	25	64	29	50	.261	.494	2
1961	163	583	129	169	30	2	45	140	113	75	.290	.580	1
1962	161	601	90	164	30	2	37	112	96	68	.273	.514	2
1963	36	135	23	32	4	0	4	14	21	17	.237	.356	0
Total	458	1706	288	466	77	5	111	330	259	210	.273	.519	5

Rocky Colavito was one of the game's premier power hitters in the late 1950s and early 1960s. Signed to a contract by the Cleveland Indians in 1951, he spent four years in the Indians' farm system before being called up in September 1955. Although he played for six teams in his 14-year major league career, his most productive years were in the American League with the Indians and the Detroit Tigers. He earned a reputation as a very dangerous hitter and many pitchers were intimidated when Colavito came to the plate. He also had a rocket for an arm, so very few base runners were willing to challenge his throwing accuracy. Upon his call-up to the majors, he saw action in just five games and impressed the Indians' management by hitting .444 in those contests.

Starting with the 1956 season, Colavito spent four seasons with the Tribe and became the team's most dangerous batter. His performances in 1958 and 1959 were especially impressive as he led all American League batters in slugging average (.620) in 1958 and home runs (42, tied with Harmon Killebrew) in 1959. In addition, he led the league in extra-base hits and knocked in more than 110 runs in both years. On June 10, 1959, he tied a major league record by clubbing four consecutive homers in a game against the Baltimore Orioles. This record is held jointly by Colavito, Lou Gehrig, Mike Schmidt, Bobby Lowe, Mike Cameron and Carlos Delgado. In 1959, Cleveland finished in second place, just five games behind the junior circuit champion Chicago White Sox. Things were looking up for the Tribe in 1960 when a move was made that stunned the Indians' faithful. Cleveland general manager Frank Lane traded Colavito, the reigning home run champion, to the Detroit Tigers for reigning batting champ Harvey Kuenn. The Tigers got the better of the deal, because Colavito played with the Tigers for four seasons, while Kuenn spent only one year with Cleveland before getting shipped off to the San Francisco Giants in another transaction.

In Colavito's first year in Detroit, he led the Tigers in homers and RBI although he managed only a .249 batting average while the team finished in sixth place in the final standings. He started his consecutive playing streak with a Tigers' home game against the Yankees on June 21, 1960. Colavito had his career year in 1961 when he slammed 45 round-trippers and drove home 140 runners. In most years, these run-producing totals realistically would have led a league, but this was 1961, the same year that Mickey Mantle and Roger Maris made their historic run at Babe Ruth's 60 home run mark. Colavito appeared in all the Tigers' games that year and closed out the season with 261 consecutive games played. As for the Tigers, the team was at the top of the American League standings at the all-star break but eventually was overtaken by the vastly superior Yankees in the second half of the season. In the final standings, Detroit finished in second place, eight games behind the New Yorkers. The following season, he took over the major league Iron Man role with 304 games played when the Reds' Vada Pinson missed a game on May 31, 1962. Colavito completed the year with 422 straight contests played as he smashed 37 homers and knocked in 112 runners. The Tigers won 16 fewer games in 1962 and claimed fourth place behind the Yankees, Twins and Angels. The 1963 campaign turned out to be Colavito's last year with the Tigers. In the latter part of May, Colavito was going through a relatively prolonged hitting slump. His batting average was about 40 points below his normal numbers. On May 22, 1963, Tigers' manager Bob Scheffing benched Colavito for a game or two because of his hitting shortcomings. His Iron Man streak was over after 458 consecutive games. By the end of the season, his batting numbers had rebounded as he finished with a .271 average but he hit only 22 homers while knocking in 91 runs. The Tigers came in under the .500 winning percentage and finished in the middle of the pack in sixth place. In November 1963 (a few days before President Kennedy's assassination), Colavito was traded by the Tigers to the Kansas City Athletics.

After his trade to Kansas City, Colavito had three more productive years. He stayed with the Athletics for just one season where he hit over 30 homers and produced over 100 runs. In February 1965, he was traded back to Cleveland where in 1965 he led the league in RBI and walks. He also played that entire season without making a single miscue in the outfield. He had a decent year in 1966 with the Tribe, swatting 30 homers, but his second tour with Cleveland was brief as he was traded in midseason of the following year (1967) to the Chicago White Sox. His time with the White Sox lasted till the end of the year. He spent his last season (1968) seeing some action with the Los Angeles Dodgers and New York Yankees. At the end of the season, the Yankees released him and his days as a ballplayer were over. After doing some scouting for the Yankees, he served as a coach for the Indians for about five years.

98. BROOKS ROBINSON

Born: May 18, 1937, Little Rock, Arkansas *Bats*: Right *Throws*: Right *Height*: 6 feet, 1 inch *Weight*: 180 *Major league debut*: September 17, 1955 (Washington at Baltimore [AL]) *Last major league game*: August 13, 1977 (Oakland at Baltimore [AL])

Major league Iron Man from: May 22, 1963, to September 2, 1963 *Consecutive games played*: 483 *Games as major league Iron Man*: 100 (consecutive games 384 through 483) *Team played for during streak*: Baltimore Orioles (AL) *Primary position played*: Third base *Game missed before streak*: September 5, 1960 (second game) (Baltimore at Washington) *First game played of streak*: September 7, 1960 (Baltimore at Cleveland) *Last game played of streak*: September 2, 1963 (first game) (Baltimore at Boston) *Game missed to end streak*: September 2, 1963 (second game) (Baltimore at Boston)

Consecutive Game Streak's Statistical Totals

Year	G	AB	R	H	2B	3B	HR	RBI	BB	SO	AVG	SLG	SB
1960	20	80	11	18	4	1	2	14	2	4	.225	.375	0
1961	163	668	89	192	38	7	7	61	47	57	.287	.397	1
1962	162	634	77	192	29	9	23	86	42	70	.303	.486	3
1963	138	510	58	132	24	3	9	63	38	73	.259	.371	2
Total	483	1892	235	534	95	20	41	224	129	204	.282	.419	6

Brooks Robinson was one of the greatest fielding third basemen the game has ever witnessed. He played for the Baltimore Orioles for 23 years. Nicknamed the "human vacuum cleaner," he saved many a run from scoring against the Orioles with his fielding skills. Signed by Baltimore as a free agent in 1955, he got into several games in September of that year. During his first few years, he spent most of the time in the minors, with an occasional call-up to the parent club to fill in for an injured player. It was not until 1958 that he became the team's starting third baseman when he replaced the veteran George Kell at the hot corner. Robinson played 145 contests and batted .238 his first full season. The next year (1959), Robinson played only 88 games because the Orioles thought he still needed some more seasoning, so he put some more time in the minors with Vancouver of the Pacific League.

Starting with the 1960 season, the Orioles would not need to worry about the third base spot for the next 16 years. Robinson took over as Baltimore's permanent hot corner occupant, a position he held into the 1976 campaign. On September 7, 1960, with 20 games left in the year, Robinson commenced his playing streak in a game in Cleveland against the Indians. He finished 1960 with a .294 average along with 14 homers and 88 RBI. The Orioles had the franchise's best year since 1945 (when the team was known as the St. Louis Browns) when they secured second place by finishing eight games behind the pennant-winning New York Yankees. In 1961, Robinson played all the Orioles' 163 games at third base as the team had another decent year with a 95–67 record and a third-place finish. Robinson came in with a .287 average but was below average in the run-producing column with only seven homers and 61 RBI. Robinson again appeared in all games at third base for the Orioles in 1962 as he extended his playing streak to 345 games. He pleasantly surprised the team's management by swatting 23 homers and hitting over .300 for the first time in his major league career. The Orioles, on the other hand, dropped to seventh place, nearly 20 games out of the top spot. His 1963 batting numbers dropped off quite a bit as he hit only 11 homers, knocked in 67 runs and hit for a .251 average (a drop of 52 points from the previous year). On May 22, 1963, he became the big league's Iron Man with 384 consecutive appearances when Rocky Colavito of the Detroit Tigers sat out a contest. Robinson's streak nearly ended a few months later on August 10 in a game against the Washington Senators. He was benched by the Orioles' manager, Bill Hitchcock, for poor hitting. Eventually, Robinson did get in the game (and extended his streak) when he pinch-hit for pitcher Stu Miller in the eighth inning. He grounded out as the Senators beat the Orioles 6–5 despite the three home runs hit that day by his teammate Boog Powell. Robinson's streak did end less than a month later when he sat out the nightcap of a double-header at Boston on September 2, 1963. His 483-consecutive-games streak was Baltimore's all-time team record until another Oriole by the name of Cal Ripken put a pretty long consecutive streak together.

Robinson kept playing until the latter part of the 1977 season. During his remarkable career in an Orioles uniform, he set many major league records for third basemen and also led the American League in numerous hitting and fielding categories. These included at-bats in 1961; RBI 1964; and sacrifice flies in 1962, 1964, 1967 and 1968. As the third baseman, he led the league in games played from 1960 through 1964, 1966, 1968 and 1970; fielding average from 1960 through 1964, 1966 through 1969, 1972 and 1975; putouts in 1958, 1960 and 1964; assists from 1960, 1963, 1964, 1966 through 1969 and 1974; and double plays in 1963, 1964 and 1974. In addition, he won an amazing 16 straight Gold Glove awards (1960 through 1975) as the best fielding second baseman in the American League. He played in 18 all-star games and four World Series and was on the winning team twice (1966 and 1970). He also was the American League MVP during the 1964 season, all-star game MVP in 1966, and World Series MVP in 1970 when he almost won the series all by himself with an amazing fielding display that is still talked about over 30 years later. In 1983, he was selected for Hall of Fame enshrinement in his first year of eligibility. After his retirement, he has kept active in baseball circles as a broadcaster of the Orioles' games and also as president of the Major League Players' Alumni Association.

99. RON SANTO

Born: February 25, 1940, Seattle, Washington *Bats*: Right *Throws*: Right *Height*: 6 feet *Weight*: 190 *Major league debut*: June 26, 1960 (first game) (Chicago at Pittsburgh [NL]) *Last major league game*: September 29, 1974 (Chicago at Oakland [AL])

Major league Iron Man from: September 2, 1963, to April 18, 1964 *Consecutive games played*: 371 *Games as major league Iron Man*: 29 (consecutive games 343 through 371) *Team played for during streak*: Chicago Cubs (NL) *Primary position played*: Third base *Game missed before streak*: August 14, 1961 (Philadelphia at Chicago) *First game played of streak*: August 15, 1961 (Philadelphia at Chicago) *Last game played of streak*: April 17, 1964 (Philadelphia at Chicago) *Game missed to end streak*: April 18, 1964 (Philadelphia at Chicago)

Consecutive Game Streak's Statistical Totals

Year	G	AB	R	H	2B	3B	HR	RBI	BB	SO	AVG	SLG	SB
1961	44	156	20	41	7	1	11	25	22	12	.263	.532	0
1962	162	604	44	137	20	4	17	83	65	94	.227	.358	4
1963	162	630	79	187	29	6	25	99	42	92	.297	.481	6
1964	3	9	4	5	2	1	1	3	3	1	.556	1.333	0
Total	371	1399	147	370	58	12	54	210	132	199	.264	.439	10

Ron Santo was the Cubs' star third baseman in the 1960s and early 1970s. Although he consistently put together decent batting and fielding stats throughout his career, he unfortunately played for Cubs' teams that did not fare too well in the standings. Signed to a contract by the Cubs in 1959, he made his major league debut in the first game of a double-header on June 26, 1960, in Pittsburgh. He made an immediate impression by playing both games of the twin bill and getting three hits in seven at-bats with five runs knocked in as the Cubs swept the Pittsburgh Pirates. He finished his rookie year with respectable numbers, hitting .251 in 95 games played at the hot corner.

In his second year (1961), the 21-year-old third baseman clubbed 23 homers and improved his batting average to .284 while the Cubs were finishing in seventh place for the second straight year. With 44 games left in the 1961 schedule, Santo started his consecutive-games-played streak on August 15, 1961, in a contest at Wrigley Field against the Phillies. Although Santo swatted 17 homers and pushed across 83 runners while playing in all the Cubs' games in 1962, it was hard to imagine why he did not take a day or two off that year because his hitting (.227) fell nearly 60 points — the lowest batting numbers for a regular player in the National League during that season. The Cubs came in with a dismal 59–103 record for ninth place in the final standings. Santo rebounded the next year (1963) by hitting .297 (a jump of 70 points) and contributing to the club's offense with 25 round-trippers and 99 RBI. On September 2, 1963, Santo succeeded the Baltimore Orioles' Brooks Robinson as the majors' Iron Man with a 343-consecutive-game streak actively running. Santo finished the year with 368 straight games played and the Cubs dramatically improved by winning 23 more games than during the previous season, but they still ended up in seventh place, 17 games behind the National League champion Los Angeles Dodgers.

Santo started the 1964 season on fire by hitting .556 along with an amazing slugging average of 1.333 after three games. However, during the Cubs' 1964 home opener at Wrigley Field, Santo suffered a freak accident when Danny Cater of the Phillies accidentally hit Santo in the back of the head with his elbow while running to third base. Santo was trying to catch an inning-ending windblown pop-up. The injury caused Santo to miss the April 18, 1964, contest against the Phillies, thus ending his consecutive games Iron Man streak at 371 games.

This game turned out to be the only game he missed the entire 1964 season. Upon returning to action, Santo put together another long playing streak (390 games). This second streak did not qualify him for Iron Man status because his Cubs teammate Billy Williams was in the middle of establishing a National League record with his 1,117-game streak that occurred from 1963 through 1970. As part of his later streak, Santo did establish a league record by appearing in 364 consecutive games at third base from April 19, 1964, to May 31, 1966. Although his Iron Man streak had ended in the early portion of the season, Santo had an extremely productive year by batting for a .313 average, hitting 33 doubles, 13 triples (the league high that year), 30 home runs and a slugging average of .564.

After the 1964 campaign, Santo continued to hold down the Cubs' third base job through the 1973 season. Although he never made an appearance in the postseason, Santo did appear in eight all-star games and led the senior circuit in a variety of offensive categories (bases on balls, on base percentage, total times on base, and sacrifice flies) and defensive (by a third baseman) categories (games played, putouts, assists, errors, double plays and fielding average). In December 1973, the Cubs traded their long-time third baseman to the crosstown rival Chicago White Sox. Santo spent one unimpressive season with the White Sox before retiring at the end of the 1974 season. Although he has not made it into baseball's Hall of Fame, a strong argument could be presented to include Santo in that institution's membership. Another thing that seems to be amazing about Santo's streaks, and his major league career in general, is that he played this entire time as a diabetic. It is difficult to play every day, but the added burden of this physical condition makes it all the more incredible. Today, Santo does baseball broadcasting in Chicago but problems with his diabetes has resulted in removal of one of his legs and other medical complications.

100. BILL WHITE

Born: January 28, 1934, Lakewood, Florida *Bats*: Left *Throws*: Left *Height*: 6 feet *Weight*: 185 *Major league debut*: May 7, 1956 (New York at St. Louis [NL]) *Last major league game*: September 24, 1969 (St. Louis at New York [NL])

Major league Iron Man from: April 18, 1964, to May 15, 1964 *Consecutive games played*: 284 *Games as major league Iron Man*: 24 (consecutive games 261 through 284) *Team played for during streak*: St. Louis Cardinals (NL) *Primary position played*: First base *Game missed before streak*: June 24, 1962 (first game) (St. Louis at Philadelphia) *First game played of streak*: June 24, 1962 (second game) (St. Louis at Philadelphia) *Last game played of streak*: May 14, 1964 (St. Louis at Philadelphia) *Game missed to end streak*: May 15, 1964 (Milwaukee at St. Louis)

Consecutive Game Streak's Statistical Totals

Year	G	AB	R	H	2B	3B	HR	RBI	BB	SO	AVG	SLG	SB
1962	94	363	53	133	20	1	9	53	32	27	.366	.501	4
1963	162	658	106	200	26	8	27	109	59	100	.304	.491	10
1964	28	111	15	28	6	0	3	9	11	22	.252	.387	0
Total	284	1132	174	361	52	9	39	171	102	149	.319	.484	14

Bill White was a slick fielding first baseman who played for 13 seasons in the major leagues. His career started with the New York Giants but he spent the great majority of his time with the St. Louis Cardinals and Philadelphia Phillies. When he made his major league debut on May 7, 1956, he took over the job as the Giants' first baseman and did not miss one contest the rest of the season. In his debut game, he belted a homer in his first big league at-bat. In his rookie year, he led the National League first basemen in games played, putouts and assists. He did not play at all in 1957 due to military service and made only a couple of dozen appearances the following year when he made it back to the majors in July 1958. With White in the military, the Giants found a new first baseman in Orlando Cepeda. Since the Giants had two capable first sackers, a decision was made to trade White to the St. Louis Cardinals on March 25, 1959. In his first year with the Cards, the team rotated him between first base and the outfield because the Cards still had Stan Musial in their lineup. Due to his age, Musial was primarily used at first base. That year (1959), the Cards finished in seventh place, just ahead of the cellar-dwelling Phillies. White got into 138 games his first season back from military service and finished with a .302 batting average, a dozen homers and 72 RBI.

In 1960, White took over the Cards' first base position permanently as he helped them win 15 more games than they did in 1959. The team finished in third place, just nine games behind the league titleholders, the Pittsburgh Pirates. He played in both all-star games that year, led the National League's first sackers in double plays and won his first of seven straight league Gold Gloves at first base. The following year (1961), he clubbed 20 homers and drove in 90 runs in 153 games and led the first basemen in games played as the Cards finished fifth. In 1962, White appeared in 159 games and started a consecutive playing streak on June 24 when he played in the second game of a double-header in Philadelphia against the Phillies. He played the last 94 games on the 1962 schedule and batted .366 during that stretch as the Cards finished in sixth place in the final standings. He won his third Gold Glove and finished among the fielding leaders at first base with a .993 average. The 1963 season found White playing every Cardinals game at first base as he helped them to a second-place finish, just six games behind the Los Angeles Dodgers. He had one of his best years offensively as he led the Cards in homers with 27 clouts and drove home 109 runners as he finished with a .304 batting average. He started out the 1964 season with a 256-consecutive-game streak and replaced the Cubs' Ron Santo as the major league Iron Man a few days after the start of the season. White held onto the Iron Man title for only 24 games. On May 15, 1964, his playing streak ended at 284 games as he was rested during a home game against the Milwaukee Braves. He was rested because he was hitting only .252, a figure that was well below his normal batting levels. White went on to finish with a .303 average along with 21 homers and 102 RBI. His performance helped the Cards win the 1964 National League championship as they edged the Cincinnati Reds and Philadelphia Phillies by one game, thanks to a major collapse by the Phillies in the final two weeks of the season. In the 1964 World Series, the Cards defeated the New York Yankees in seven games to claim baseball's world championship. Despite the Cards' win, White had a simply awful time at the plate as he produced only three hits and batted a paltry .111 average.

White played one more year with the Cards before being traded to Philadelphia in late October 1965. His first year (1966) with the Phillies was to be his last productive year as he hit 22 homers and knocked in 103 runs. He would stay in Philadelphia for three years before being traded back to the Cardinals in early April 1969 (his final playing season). In his last year, he played in only 49 games and hit .211, some 75 points below his career batting average. He retired from active playing after the 1969 season but a couple of years later was hired to work alongside New York Yankees broadcaster and former Bronx Bomber shortstop Phil Rizzuto, and provide color commentary on radio and television for Yankees games. He stayed with the Yankees until 1989 when he was hired to replace Bart Giamatti as National League president. White would serve as the senior circuit's president until 1994.

101. KEN BOYER

Born: May 20, 1931, Liberty, Missouri *Died*: September 7, 1982, St. Louis, Missouri *Bats*: Right *Throws*: Right *Height*: 6 feet, 1½ inches *Weight*: 190 *Major league debut*: April 12, 1955 (St. Louis at Chicago [NL]) *Last major league game*: August 9, 1969 (Chicago at Los Angeles [NL])

Major league Iron Man from: May 15, 1964, to April 23, 1965 *Consecutive games played*: 306 *Games as major league Iron Man*: 142 (consecutive games 165 through 306) *Team played for during streak*: St. Louis Cardinals (NL) *Primary position played*: Third base *Game missed before streak*: May 5, 1963 (second game) (St. Louis at Cincinnati) *First game played of streak*: May 7, 1963 (Los Angeles at St. Louis) *Last game played of streak*: April 21, 1965 (Milwaukee at St. Louis) *Game missed to end streak*: April 23, 1965 (St. Louis at Cincinnati)

Consecutive Game Streak's Statistical Totals

Year	G	AB	R	H	2B	3B	HR	RBI	BB	SO	AVG	SLG	SB
1963	136	527	73	151	25	2	21	89	58	76	.287	.461	1
1964	162	628	100	185	30	10	24	119	70	85	.295	.489	3
1965	8	33	3	11	2	0	0	6	2	6	.333	.394	0
Total	306	1188	176	347	57	12	45	214	130	167	.292	.474	4

Ken Boyer was one of three brothers who played in the majors. The oldest, Cloyd, was a pitcher in the early 1950s and the youngest sibling, Clete, was the spectacular fielding third baseman for the New York Yankees during the late 1950s and early 1960s Bronx Bomber dynasty. Ken was also a third baseman and is considered by many baseball sources to be the best third baseman in St. Louis Cardinals history. Signed to a contract at the age of 18 in 1949 by the Cards, he initially fine-tuned his skills for several years in the minors along with serving a two-year stint in the military.

After the 1954 season, the Cards sent their third baseman, Ray Jablonski, to the Cincinnati Reds. With this transaction, Boyer took over the hot corner for the Cards. He put a solid year together his rookie season with 18 clouts and 62 runs. He followed up the next year (1955) with 26 homers, 98 RBI and a .306 batting average. Although he had very good years his first two seasons in the big leagues, he was replaced at third base by Eddie Kasko and switched over to center field for most of the 1957 campaign. Boyer's stats suffered some when his batting average dropped to .265 (down by over 40 points). In 1958, Kasko went to shortstop and Boyer returned to third base with the arrival of the 20-year-old Curt Flood, who took over in center field. Boyer's numbers rebounded to previous levels as he led the team in homers (23) and RBI (90) during the 1958 campaign. He repeated as the Cardinals' leader in homers and RBI in 1959. It was obvious by 1960 that along with the aging Stan Musial, Boyer was the Cards' best player. He led the team in several offensive stats as the Cards put together a solid effort for manager Solly Hemus and finished in third place, just nine games behind the league champion Pittsburgh Pirates. During 1961 and 1962, Boyer continued to maintain his level of performance by leading the Cards in many offensive categories.

The 1963 season found Boyer starting his consecutive-games-played streak on May 7 in St. Louis against the Dodgers. He played the final 136 games on the schedule and maintained stable statistical numbers throughout as he again led St. Louis with 111 RBI. The team finished second behind the Dodgers by six games. The 1964 season was a very pleasant time for Boyer and his Cardinals. He led the team to the National League pennant by leading the league with 119 RBI and winning the league's Most Valuable Player award. He appeared in all 162 games that season and became the Iron Man of baseball on May 15, 1964 (with only 165 straight games played to his credit), when teammate Bill White's streak ended. By season's end, Boyer's playing streak reached 298 consecutive games. As for the team, thanks to a late-season collapse by the Philadelphia Phillies, the Cards won the league title by one game over both the Phillies and the Cincinnati Reds. The Cards went on to beat the New York Yankees in the 1964 World Series in a very exciting seven-game confrontation. Boyer's clutch hitting during the series lifted the team to the championship. He hit a grand slam in the fourth game to account for all the Cards' runs in a 4–3 win and then smashed a critical seventh-inning homer in game seven to lift the Cards to a 7–5 victory. In the off-season, manager Johnny Keane left the Cards and signed on to manage the Yankees, who were fresh from firing Yogi Berra. Long-time Cardinal Red Schoendienst took over the Cards' helm as manager. The bottom completely dropped out of the club's performance as they finished just below .500 ball with an 80–81 record and a seventh-place finish in the standings. Boyer's performance suffered the same fate as the team's when he came in with only 13 homers, 75 RBI and a .260 batting average. As for his playing streak, just eight games into the 1965 season, Boyer scratched himself from the lineup because of an inflamed muscle in the lower left side of his back. His streak, along with his Iron Man reign, was over after 306 straight games. Right after the season, Boyer's tenure as the Cardinals' third baseman ended when he was shipped off in a trade to the New York Mets in October 1965.

Boyer played only four more rather uneventful years in the majors (with the Mets, Chicago White Sox and Los Angeles Dodgers). His final appearance came on August 9, 1969, when he made a pinch-hit appearance in the ninth inning of a Dodgers' 4–0 loss to the Chicago Cubs. The Dodgers released him after the season. He spent a couple of years in the early 1970s coaching for the Cardinals. In early 1978, he was named the Cards' manager, replacing Vern Rapp. He put in a couple of years as their skipper with average results before he was replaced by Whitey Herzog about 50 games into the 1980 season. Soon after his release as manager, it was discovered that Boyer had lung cancer and he passed away from the dreaded disease a couple of years later at the age of 51.

102. JOHNNY CALLISON

Born: March 12, 1939, Qualls, Oklahoma *Bats*: Left *Throws*: Right *Height*: 5 feet, 10 inches *Weight*: 175 *Major league debut*: September 9, 1958 (Boston at Chicago [AL]) *Last major league game*: August 17, 1973 (New York at Texas [AL])

Major league Iron Man from: April 23, 1965, to June 10, 1965 *Consecutive games played*: 323 *Games as major league Iron Man*: 45 (consecutive games 279 through 323) *Team played for during streak*: Philadelphia Phillies (NL) *Primary position played*: Outfield *Game missed before streak*: June 8, 1963 (Cincinnati at Philadelphia) *First game played of streak*: June 9, 1963 (first game) (Cincinnati at Philadelphia) *Last game played of streak*: June 9, 1965 (Los Angeles at Philadelphia) *Game missed to end streak*: June 10, 1965 (Los Angeles at Philadelphia)

Consecutive Game Streak's Statistical Totals

Year	G	AB	R	H	2B	3B	HR	RBI	BB	SO	AVG	SLG	SB
1963	109	450	75	138	26	10	22	62	30	72	.307	.556	6
1964	162	654	101	179	30	10	31	104	36	95	.274	.492	6
1965	52	203	28	56	13	6	12	34	15	38	.276	.576	0
Total	323	1307	204	373	69	26	65	200	81	205	.285	.527	12

Johnny Callison played in the majors for 16 seasons with four teams but was most notably known as a star right fielder with the Philadelphia Phillies in the 1960s. Signed to a contract at the age of 18 by the Chicago White Sox in 1957, he spent a short tenure in the minors before being called up in early September 1958. He made his debut with the White Sox in a home game against Boston on September 9. He got into 18 games that season, playing primarily in left field, and made a favorable impressive at the plate by finishing with a .297 batting average. The following year (1959) found him back in the minors with Indianapolis of the American Association for further seasoning. He did eventually get a call-up to the White Sox but hit only .173 in the 49 games he appeared in that season.

In December 1959, Callison was traded by the White Sox to the Phillies for third baseman Gene Freese. Callison immediately became one of the Phillies' starting outfielders, rotating between the three outfield positions. The 21-year-old got into nearly 100 games, but he missed some games due to a knee injury. He finished his first full major season with a .260 average. During the 1961 season, he hit at a .266 clip and led the last-place Phillies with 121 hits and 20 doubles. Callison had one of his better seasons in 1962 when he clubbed 23 homers, knocked in 83 runs, hit a career-best .300 and tied Willie Davis, Bill Virdon, and Maury Wills for the National League lead in triples with 10 three-baggers. It was also the year that Callison made the permanent switch to right field. His 24 assists topped all league outfielders in that category. A couple of months into the 1963 campaign, Callison's consecutive games streak started on June 9 during the first game of a twin bill in Philadelphia against the Cincinnati Reds. He appeared in the last 109 games on the schedule and kept his statistical numbers above the norm. He clubbed 22 of his 26 homers that season during that stretch. He was gaining a reputation for having an accurate throwing arm as he again led the National League's outfielders with 26 assists. When the season came to a close, he had helped the Phillies to a fourth-place finish, as the club was just a dozen games out of first place. The 1964 season was a year to remember. Callison probably had his best year as he played all 162 games (extending his streak to 271 games), smacked 31 round-trippers, drove in 104 runs, led the outfielders in assists (19) for the third consecutive year and hit a dramatic two-on and two-out ninth-inning homer that gave the National Leaguers a 7–4 victory in the all-star game. His performance resulted in his selection as that game's MVP. Additionally, he finished in second place in the league's MVP voting (243 to 187) behind the Cards' Ken Boyer. The Phillies finished just one game out of first place when the season ended but the team's collapse is all that was remembered by many Phillies fans. All of Callison's accomplishments could not prevent the team from losing 10 games in a row late in the year and seeing a six and a half-game lead disappear in the last two weeks of the season. In the early portions of the following year, Callison took over the Iron Man title from Boyer on April 23, 1965. Callison held onto the title for 45 games. The Phillies' manager, Gene Mauch, rested Callison on June 10, 1965, against the Dodgers, thereby ending his playing streak at 323 games. He finished the year with a .262 batting average, homered 32 times, knocked in 101 runners and led the league with 16 triples. For the fourth year running, he paced all outfielders of the National League with 21 assists. As for the Phillies, they finished in the middle of the pack (sixth place), nearly a dozen games behind the front-running Los Angeles Dodgers.

Even though Callison would lead the league in doubles with 40 two-baggers in 1966, his best years of production were behind him. He played four more years in right field for the Phillies, with relatively below-average numbers, before being traded in November 1969 to the Chicago Cubs. He stayed for two years with the Cubs' organization and then was sent over to the New York Yankees in January 1972. He played in 137 contests for the Yankees over the next two seasons. On August 17, 1973, he made his final appearance in a major league game when in the eighth inning of a game at Texas, he took Ron Blomberg's place in right field. The next day, the Yankees released Callison because he was hitting only .176 in 45 contests. His baseball career came to an end with his release from the Yankees.

103. CURT FLOOD

Born: January 18, 1938, Houston, Texas *Died*: January 20, 1997, Los Angeles, California *Bats*: Right *Throws*: Right *Height*: 5 feet, 9 inches *Weight*: 165 *Major league debut*: September 9, 1956 (Cincinnati at St. Louis [NL]) *Last major league game*: April 25, 1971 (Milwaukee at Washington [AL])

Major league Iron Man from: June 10, 1965, to June 14, 1965 *Consecutive games played*: 294 *Games as major league Iron Man*: 5 (consecutive games 290 through 294) *Team played for during streak*: St. Louis Cardinals (NL) *Primary position played*: Outfield *Game missed before streak*: July 13, 1963 (Milwaukee at St. Louis) *First game played of streak*: July 14, 1963 (first game) (Chicago at St. Louis) *Last game played of streak*: June 13, 1965 (second game) (Milwaukee at St. Louis) *Game missed to end streak*: June 14, 1965 (Pittsburgh at St. Louis)

Consecutive Game Streak's Statistical Totals

Year	G	AB	R	H	2B	3B	HR	RBI	BB	SO	AVG	SLG	SB
1963	74	299	52	104	18	4	3	31	18	25	.348	.465	6
1964	162	679	97	211	25	3	5	46	43	53	.311	.378	8
1965	58	239	35	71	12	1	7	29	17	18	.297	.444	4
Total	294	1217	184	386	55	8	15	106	78	96	.317	.412	18

Curt Flood was an impeccable fielding center fielder for the St. Louis Cardinals and a couple of other teams in the 1950s and 1960s. Although he was a fine player, most of his fame came from challenging the reserve clause in baseball that tied a player to a team without giving him the chance to file for free agency. The astronomical salaries that modern day baseball players make today are directly attributed to the actions Flood took in early 1970. Unfortunately, Flood never benefited from this change in baseball's salary structure.

Flood was signed to a Cincinnati Reds contract in 1956, but in two seasons with the Reds, he got into only eight games at the major league level because most of the time was spent in the Reds' minor league system. In December 1957, the Reds traded him to St. Louis. During the 1958 campaign, Flood took over the Cards' center field position and (except for the 1959 season, when several players rotated positions in the outfield) held down the spot for 12 seasons. His performance the first three years in a Cardinal uniform was relatively mediocre as he hit around .250 with little run production, although he did lead National League outfielders in fielding in 1960 with a .993 percentage. The next season (1961), he had one of his better years with the bat as he hit .322, but his run making was still very low. He only hit two homers and drove home 21 runners. In 1962, his batting slipped some (.296) but he made up for it by hitting a dozen homers and driving in 70 runs. The 1963 season found Flood finishing with a .302 average in 158 games played while leading the senior circuit in at-bats and outfield putouts and capturing his first of seven straight Gold Gloves. He also helped the Cards finish six games behind the Dodgers, good for second place. On July 14, 1963, he played the first game of his consecutive games streak in St. Louis against the Chicago Cubs. He finished the year participating in the team's last 74 scheduled games. The following year (1964), Flood made it into the lineup of every Cardinals game (extending his games-played streak to 236 games) as he again paced the National League in at-bats, won another Gold Glove and played in his first all-star contest. He was one of the key team members in leading the Cardinals to the 1964 National League championship. The Cards also won the World Series by besting the New York Yankees in seven games as Flood contributed six hits and knocked in three runs. The next year on June 10, 1965, Flood became the majors' Iron Man title holder when the Phils' Johnny Callison sat out a game. Only days later, Flood's own streak ended at 294 games when he missed the June 14 home game against the Pittsburgh Pirates because of a painfully huge knot on his right thigh. Despite this, he had a good year by leading the Cardinals in batting, hits and RBI. Unfortunately, the Cardinals did a complete turnaround in the standings from being the world champs in 1964 to finishing a disappointing seventh in the 1965 final standings under the guidance of their new manager, Red Schoendienst.

After the 1965 season, Flood played four more productive seasons in center field for the Cardinals and helped them win the National League pennants in 1967 and 1968. The team won the 1967 World Series by defeating the Boston Red Sox in seven games although Flood hit a disappointing .179 in the affair. The next year (1968), the Cards found themselves in another seven-game series; this time against the Detroit Tigers and their 31-game-winning pitcher, Denny McLain. One of the surprises of the series was that McLain won only one contest and the Tigers' other pitcher, Mickey Lolich, won the other three as Detroit edged out the Cards in seven games. Although Flood had a much better series this time around (with a .286 average), most fans will remember the line shot that the Tigers' Jim Northrup hit to center field that Flood misjudged into a triple during a crucial part of the deciding seventh game which led to a Tigers' 4–1 victory. After another season with the Cardinals in 1969, Flood found himself being traded to the Philadelphia Phillies right after the season ended. Not wanting to play in Philadelphia, Flood refused to report to his new club and filed a legal suit in January 1970 against baseball's reserve clause. While the case was pending, he sat out the entire 1970 season. In the interim, he was traded by the Phillies to the Washington Senators in early November 1970. With assurances that his case against the reserve clause would not be jeopardized, he decided to report to the hapless Senators. His career in Washington lasted just 13 games and he was released. With his release from the Senators, his playing career was over. Eventually, his case went before the U.S. Supreme Court, but he lost his suit in a 5–3 decision; however, due to the close decision, the owners agreed to an arbitration solution, which brought the reserve clause to an end.

104. Leo Cardenas

Born: December 17, 1938, Matanzas, Cuba *Bats*: Right *Throws*: Right *Height*: 5 feet, 11 inches *Weight*: 150 *Major league debut*: July 25, 1960 (Cincinnati at Chicago [NL]) *Last major league game*: September 26, 1975 (Kansas City at Texas [AL]).

Major league Iron Man from: June 14, 1965, to September 1, 1965 *Consecutive games played*: 344 *Games as major league Iron Man*: 75 (consecutive games 270 through 344) *Team played for during streak*: Cincinnati Reds (NL) *Primary position played*: Shortstop *Game missed before streak*: August 4, 1963 (first game) (Pittsburgh at Cincinnati) *First game played of streak*: August 4, 1963 (second game) (Pittsburgh at Cincinnati) *Last game played of streak*: September 1, 1965 (first game) (Milwaukee at Cincinnati) *Game missed to end streak*: September 1, 1965 (second game) (Milwaukee at Cincinnati)

Consecutive Game Streak's Statistical Totals

Year	G	AB	R	H	2B	3B	HR	RBI	BB	SO	AVG	SLG	SB
1963	50	175	17	49	9	0	3	15	8	19	.280	.383	1
1964	163	597	61	150	32	2	9	69	41	110	.251	.357	4
1965	131	472	55	136	23	8	9	48	52	90	.288	.428	1
Total	344	1244	133	335	64	10	21	132	101	219	.269	.387	6

Leo Cardenas was a shortstop with extremely reliable fielding who toiled for 16 seasons in the big leagues with five major league teams. His fielding was so consistent that he eventually acquired the nickname of "Mr. Automatic" to show how reliable he was at the position. The first half of his career was spent with the Cincinnati Reds. Making his debut at 21 years of age, he spent his first two major league seasons being groomed as the Reds' shortstop of the future. He got into 48 and 74 games during those years. He learned to play the shortstop position better by observing Roy McMillan and Eddie Kasko on a daily basis. The 1961 season was very successful for the Reds as they won the National League title. They lost that year's World Series to the ultrapowerful New York Yankees in five games. Cardenas made his only World Series appearances as a ballplayer in that series and had a double in three pinch-hitting appearances.

With the beginning of the 1962 campaign, Reds' manager Fred Hutchinson decided the time was right to install Cardenas as the team's regular shortstop as Kasko was moved over to third base. Cardenas got into 153 contests and compiled a .294 batting average with 10 homers and 60 RBI. Although the Reds did not repeat as league champs, they did finish a respectable third, only three and a half games behind the pace-setting San Francisco Giants. In 1963, Cardenas batted only .235 and drove in 48 runs. Although he led the team in strikeouts, he was steady in the field as he led all National League shortstops in fielding with a .972 percentage. His Iron Man streak started when he appeared in the lineup of the nightcap of a twin bill on August 4, 1963. He played the last 50 games on the schedule and hit .280 during this stretch (some 45 points higher than his overall average). The following year, Cardenas played in all 163 games and extended his playing streak to 213 games by the end of the year. He played in his first all-star game and led the league's shortstops in games played (163) and putouts (336). His average was up a little (.251) from the previous year but he had the undistinguished honor of leading the Reds in strikeouts (110) for the third straight season. The Reds just missed winning the league championship as they finished in second place with the Philadelphia Phillies, just a game behind the first-place St. Louis Cardinals.

During the 1965 season, Cardenas played 156 games, batted .287, belted out 11 homers and drove home 57 runs. He led the National League in intentional walks (25), games played by a shortstop (155), putouts (292) and double plays (92). On June 14, 1965, he became the majors' Iron Man when the Cards' Curt Flood missed a game. Cardenas' reign as Iron Man lasted just a few months and ended when he missed the nightcap of a double-header in Cincinnati against the Milwaukee Braves on September 1, 1965, due to an inflamed right eye. His streak ended at 344 games and his statistics showed he maintained a consistent productive pace. At the end of the 1965 campaign, he won his first and only Gold Glove at shortstop. The Reds finished in fourth place, some eight games out of first place. The next season (1966), Cardenas had his best career totals in home runs (20) and RBI (81) but hit only .255 (a drop-off of 32 points from the 1965 season). He played two more seasons with the Reds before being traded to the Minnesota Twins of the American League in November 1968. After three years in a Twins uniform, where he put good numbers together each season and led the shortstops of the junior circuit in fielding in 1971, he was sent out to the West Coast in November 1971 via a trade to the California Angels. After one year with the Angels, he was back in Ohio, this time with the Cleveland Indians. He got into only 72 games with the Tribe in 1973 when he was again sent packing; on this occasion it was to the Texas Rangers where he served as a utility infielder for two seasons. His major league career came to an end when Texas released him during the 1976 training camp.

105. Billy Williams

Born: June 15, 1938, Whistler, Alabama *Bats*: Left *Throws*: Right *Height*: 6 feet, 1 inch *Weight*: 175 *Major league debut*: August 6, 1959 (Philadelphia at Chicago [NL]) *Last major league game*: October 2, 1976 (California at Oakland [AL])

Billy Williams

Major league Iron Man from: September 1, 1965, to September 3, 1970 *Consecutive games played*: 1117 *Games as major league Iron Man*: 812 (consecutive games 306 through 1,117) *Team played for during streak*: Chicago Cubs (NL) *Primary position played*: Outfield *Game missed before streak*: September 21, 1963 (Milwaukee at Chicago) *First game played of streak*: September 22, 1963 (Milwaukee at Chicago) *Last game played of streak*: September 2, 1970 (Philadelphia at Chicago) *Game missed to end streak*: September 3, 1970 (Philadelphia at Chicago)

Consecutive Game Streak's Statistical Totals

Year	G	AB	R	H	2B	3B	HR	RBI	BB	SO	AVG	SLG	SB
1963	6	22	3	6	1	0	2	5	3	3	.273	.591	2
1964	162	645	100	201	39	2	33	98	59	84	.312	.532	10
1965	164	645	115	203	39	6	34	108	65	76	.315	.552	10
1966	162	648	100	179	23	5	29	91	69	61	.276	.461	6
1967	162	634	92	176	21	12	28	84	68	67	.278	.481	6
1968	163	642	91	185	30	8	30	98	48	53	.288	.500	4
1969	163	642	103	188	33	10	21	95	59	70	.293	.474	3
1970	135	536	117	170	27	4	36	112	58	53	.317	.584	6
Total	1117	4414	721	1308	213	47	213	691	429	467	.296	.511	47

Billy Williams was a quiet player who let his bat do most of the talking. He put in 18 seasons in the major leagues, most of which were spent with the lowly Chicago Cubs (from 1959 through 1974). A trade late in his career sent him to the American League's Oakland Athletics where he was that team's designated hitter for two seasons. Signed to a contract by the Cubs in 1956 at the age of 18, he was assigned to various minor league teams in the Cubs' farm system to give him the seasoning needed to eventually become a member of the parent club. In 1959 and 1960, he was called up to the Cubs for brief trial periods to get him used to the big leagues.

The 1961 season found Williams with the Cubs as their left fielder, a position he filled through the 1973 campaign (except for 1965 and 1966 when he shifted over to right field). Although he had 30 major league contests under his belt before the start of the 1961 season, Williams still met the qualifications to be a rookie. That season, he impressed many by clubbing 25 homers, knocking in 86 runners and producing a .278 batting average that resulted in his being chosen the National League's Rookie of the Year for the 1961 season. His sophomore year, he played in 159 games and led the Cubs with 184 hits, 22 home runs and 91 RBI. In addition, he played in his first of six career all-star games for the National League squad.

Billy Williams: The Chicago Cubs outfielder broke Stan Musial's National League consecutive games record and stretched it to 1,117 games until he voluntarily sat out a contest in early September 1970.

Williams was gaining the reputation of being a very consistent player as he compiled similar statistics during the 1963 season. He led the Cubs in doubles (36), tied for the team lead in homers (25 with Ron Santo), had 95 RBI and hit for a .286 batting average. He also played in every one of the team's games except for the Cubs' home game on September 21, 1963, against the Milwaukee Braves. After sitting out that contest, he started his long consecutive-games-played streak the next day at Wrigley Field against those same Braves. The 1964 season found Williams putting in another solid performance as he led the Cubs in several important statistical categories. He had his best year up to that time as he played all 162 games and finished with a .312 batting average, 33 homers and 98 runs driven home. The Cubs finished in eighth place, only 17 games out of the top spot, as several teams were in close contention for the National League crown right down to the final week of the season.

Williams followed up his 1964 performance with even better numbers in 1965. He was the team leader in every major statistical category, had over 200 hits, drilled 34 homers and batted in 108 runners along with leading the league with 79 extra-base hits. On September 1, 1965, he replaced the Reds' Leo Cardenas as the major league Iron Man with an active streak of 306 consecutive games. Playing every day did not affect Williams' performance but it did not help the Cubs much as the team again finished in eighth place. The next season (1966), his production numbers dropped off some but not enough to have him taken out of the lineup as his streak continued to grow. The Cubs, with new manager Leo Durocher at the helm, were found residing 36 games out of first place, in last place, with a 59–103 record. In 1967, the Cubs and their faithful fans had something to cheer about as the team finished in third place with an 87–74 record, their best finish since the 1946 campaign. Williams had another consistent year with 28 homers along with 84 RBI and a .278 average. His consecutive streak stood at 656 games by the end of the 1967 season. In 1968, he achieved a couple of unique hitting accomplishments. First, he hit for the cycle in early July and then later slugged three homers in a game in September. He finished the year with 30 homers, 98 RBI and paced all National League batters in total bases (321) and extra-base hits (68). The Cubs had another winning season and repeated their third-place finish in the standings. He was fast approaching the senior circuit record that Stan Musial held for most consecutive games played. This almost did not happen because in mid–June 1969, Williams suffered a minor foot injury during a game in Cincinnati. During the next three contests he was used as a pinch hitter to keep the streak active. Within a couple of days, his foot was better and he returned to the starting lineup. On June 29, 1969, he officially passed the 895-game streak that Musial had established back in the 1957 season. Williams' streak nearly came to an end again late in the year but another pinch hitting appearance in the September 27 game in Pittsburgh kept it alive. When the 1969 season ended, his consecutive streak stood at 982 games and counting. He also finished with another decent year as he hit 21 homers, knocked in 95 runners and led the Cubs in hits (188), triples (10) and batting average (.293). Additionally, his efforts contributed to the Cubs finishing second, just eight games behind the miracle New York Mets. Williams' 1970 season was his most productive of his career as he had league highs in runs scored (137), hits (205), total bases (373) and led the Cubs in all major statistical categories as he finished with 42 homers, 129 RBI and a .322 batting average. On April 30, 1970, he became the first National Leaguer to play in 1,000 consecutive contests. He now had the fourth-longest playing streak in the game's history behind Lou Gehrig, Everett Scott and Joe Sewell. His streak came close to ending again on June 29 and August 7, 1970, but he was able to get into the lineup in both those games by either pinch hitting or being used as a defense replacement. Finally, on September 3, 1970, Williams asked Durocher to let him sit out the game. After serving as the Iron Man of the major leagues for just over five years, his streak was over after

1,117 games. This mark stood as the National League record until the Padres' Steve Garvey passed it in mid-April 1983. Williams' great year again helped the Cubs to another second-place finish in the senior circuit's Eastern Division behind the Pittsburgh Pirates.

After his streak ended, Williams put in four more productive years with the Cubs. In fact, the 1972 season was special as he led the National League in slugging (.606), total bases (348) and extra-base hits (77) and as well as winning his only league batting title with a .333 average. After the 1974 season, the Cubs traded Williams to the Athletics where they used him primarily as their designated hitter. He put in two seasons with Oakland before being released from the team in November 1976. A year later, he was back with the Cubs as the team's hitting instructor. Eventually, he became one of their regular coaches in 1980. A couple of years later, he left the Cubs and moved back to the Athletics as a coach for three years before returning to the Cubs' coaching staff for a couple of more seasons. He almost was elected to baseball's Hall of Fame in 1986 but missed being selected by a mere four votes. The next year was a slam dunk in the writers' voting as Williams led all vote-getters and easily was selected for Hall of Fame membership along with former pitcher Catfish Hunter.

106. SANDY ALOMAR

Born: October 19, 1943, Salinas, Puerto Rico *Bats*: Switch Hitter *Throws*: Right *Height*: 5 feet, 9 inches *Weight*: 140 *Major league debut*: September 15, 1964 (first game) (St. Louis at Milwaukee [NL]) *Last major league game*: September 30, 1978 (Texas at Seattle [AL])

Major league Iron Man from: September 3, 1970, to May 22, 1973 *Consecutive games played*: 648 *Games as major league Iron Man*: 380 (consecutive games 269 through 648) *Team played for during streak*: California Angels (AL) *Primary position played*: Second base *Game missed before streak*: May 14, 1969 (Washington at California) *First game played of streak*: May 16, 1969 (California at New York) *Last game played of streak*: May 20, 1973 (Texas at California) *Game missed to end streak*: May 22, 1973 (California at Chicago)

Consecutive Game Streak's Statistical Totals

Year	G	AB	R	H	2B	3B	HR	RBI	BB	SO	AVG	SLG	SB
1969	134	559	60	140	10	2	1	30	36	48	.250	.281	18
1970	162	672	82	169	18	2	2	36	49	65	.251	.293	35
1971	162	689	77	179	24	3	4	42	41	60	.260	.321	39
1972	155	610	65	146	20	3	1	25	47	55	.239	.287	20
1973	35	112	9	21	0	0	0	6	3	7	.188	.188	9
Total	648	2642	293	655	72	10	8	139	176	235	.248	.292	121

Sandy Alomar played portions of 15 seasons in the major leagues with six ball clubs. He played every position except catcher and pitcher although a great majority of the games played were spent at second base. Signed to a professional contract by the Milwaukee Braves in 1960, he did not make it to the big leagues with the Braves until the middle of September 1964. In his time with the Braves, he was in only 117 games over a three-year period with very little production to show for it. During 1967 spring training, the Braves traded him to the New York Mets. His tour with the Mets was short lived (15 games) as he found himself traded again, this time to the Chicago White Sox in August 1967 where he played in a dozen games for the Sox by season's end. The following season (1968) found him in competition with Tim Cullen for the Sox's second baseman job. Soon after, Cullen was traded to the Washington Senators and the second baseman job was Alomar's to fill on a regular basis.

His 1968 stats indicate that he played in 133 games with a .253 average and only 12 RBI along with making more errors than any other second baseman in the American League with 18 miscues.

He started 1969 with the White Sox but was traded to the California Angels on May 14, 1969, when the teams swapped second basemen (Alomar for Bobby Knoop). Alomar immediately took over the role as the Angels' second sacker and played in the last 134 games on the Angels' schedule. In addition, he hit his first major league career homer that season as he finished with a .250 average along with 30 RBI. He also led all the league's second basemen with 156 games played and 23 errors. The Angels finished with a 71–91 record and came in third place in the American League's Western division. The next season, Alomar took over the Iron Man title from the Cubs' Billy Williams in early September 1970. Alomar played in all 162 of California's games that year and extended his playing streak to 296 contests. Although it did not jeopardize his streak, he made a token appearance in the last game of the season on October 1 where he played just one inning at second and then was removed from the game in the top of the second inning. He played in his only all-star game that year, finished the season with a .251 average at the plate along with driving home 36 runners. He paced the league's second basemen with 119 double plays. Although the Angels again placed third in their division during 1970, the team's 86–76 record improved by 15 games from the previous season. Alomar extended his consecutive games streak to 458 by again playing a full slate of games through the 1971 season. He led all junior circuit batters with 689 at-bats. He batted .260, finished with 179 hits (second behind the Twins' Cesar Tovar for most hits in the American League) and was one of the best fielding league second basemen with a .989 fielding accuracy. The Angels regressed to a losing record (76–86) in 1971 along with a fourth-place finish in the standings. In the 1972 season, Alomar extended his streak to 613 games but it was obvious that he was in the lineup for his glove rather than his bat as he produced a .239 average with a homer and only 25 RBI. Two games that year nearly ended his streak. During games on July 28 and July 30, he did not start either contest and was inserted into the lineup in the seventh inning of both games as a defensive replacement. The team continued its losing ways by finishing in fifth place, 18 games behind the division-leading Oakland Athletics. In the early portion of the next season (1973), Alomar was having serious problems at the plate. Angels' skipper Billy Winkles did not start Alomar on May 9 but he did make a defensive replacement appearance in the bottom of the seventh. In three straight games from May 18 through May 20, Winkles used Billy Grabarkewitz at second base but Alomar still got into those contests late in the game to replace Grabarkewitz. Finally a decision had to be made and although Winkles regretted having to terminate Alomar's streak, for the good of the team he was benched due to his slow start. His streak was over after 648 games which spanned just over four years. Soon his tour with the Angels was over and he was shipped off to the New York Yankees in July 1974.

With the Yankees in search of a second baseman since Horace Clarke lost the job, Alomar immediately took over that position. He finished that year and two more seasons with the Bronx Bombers when he was traded a final time in mid-February 1977 to the Texas Rangers. Texas used him when needed as a utility fielder in their lineup over the next two seasons. After the completion of the 1978 campaign, his career came to an end with his release from the Rangers in October 1978. Afterward, he did some managing in Puerto Rico and later coached the San Diego Padres. Today, he is better known as the father of two modern-day major leaguers, second baseman Roberto Alomar and catcher Sandy Alomar Jr.

107. ROY WHITE

Born: December 27, 1943, Los Angeles, California *Bats*: Switch Hitter *Throws*: Right *Height*: 5 feet, 10 inches *Weight*: 160 *Major league debut*: September 7, 1965 (first game) (Baltimore at New York [AL]) *Last major league game*: September 27, 1979 (Cleveland at New York [AL])

Major league Iron Man from: May 22, 1973, to May 22, 1974 *Consecutive games played*: 388 *Games as major league Iron Man*: 166 (consecutive games 223 through 388) *Team played for during streak*: New York Yankees (AL) *Primary position played*: Outfield *Game missed before streak*: August 29, 1971 (New York at Kansas City) *First game played of streak*: August 31, 1971 (Washington at New York) *Last game played of streak*: May 21, 1974 (New York at Boston) *Game missed to end streak*: May 22, 1974 (New York at Boston)

Consecutive Game Streak's Statistical Totals

Year	G	AB	R	H	2B	3B	HR	RBI	BB	SO	AVG	SLG	SB
1971	29	102	19	34	2	1	4	16	21	11	.333	.490	3
1972	155	556	76	150	29	0	10	54	99	59	.270	.376	23
1973	162	639	88	157	22	3	18	60	78	81	.246	.374	16
1974	42	156	19	39	6	4	2	12	23	13	.250	.378	3
Total	388	1453	202	380	59	8	34	142	221	164	.262	.383	45

Roy White was one of the New York Yankees' most consistent performers during the late 1960s and early 1970s. In July 1961, the Yankees signed the switch-hitting 17-year-old to a contract and he wound up playing his entire 15-year major league career in pinstripes. He started playing in the Yankees' minor league system commencing in 1962 and spent that time in Greensboro, Fort Lauderdale and Columbus fine-tuning his ballplaying skills until his call-up to the parent club during the last month of the 1965 season. He made his debut on September 7, 1965, during a Yankees' home game against the Baltimore Orioles. He got into 14 games by the end of the year and hit for a .333 average. The following season (1966), he was a permanent part of the Yankees' team, but was mainly used as their extra outfielder. He got into 115 contests, hit .225 with seven homers and 20 RBI. The 1967 season found him back in the minors for more seasoning but because he tore up the Pacific Coast League pitching with close to a .350 average, the Yankees could not help but return him to the big club's roster. After his recall, he hit only .224 in 70 games and showed little run production while in the lineup, but management decided to stick with him and made him the team's regular left fielder in 1968. He filled that playing position on the Yankees' roster for the next 10 years.

In 1968, White showed much improvement as he upped his average to .267 and led the Yankees with 89 runs scored, 154 hits, 20 doubles and 62 RBI. He also tied for the team lead in both triples (with Bill Robinson) and stolen bases (with Horace Clarke). He further improved on his stats in 1969 as he again paced all Yankees with 30 doubles while hitting .290 and driving home 74 runners in 130 games. In addition, he led the American League with 11 sacrifice flies and was selected to appear in his only all-star game. During the 1970 campaign, White missed one game and was tied with Sandy Alomar for the American League lead for most games played (162). He had his most productive season as a major leaguer. He hit at a .296 clip while clubbing 22 homers, knocking in 94 runs and again leading the Yankees with 30 doubles for the third straight season. He put in another solid performance in 1971 with the bat as he hit for a .292 average, clubbed 19 homers, drove in 84 runners and again was the league leader with 17 sacrifice flies. Additionally, he was perfect in left field and led the outfielders of the American League with a 1.000 fielding average as he handled 314 fielding chances without a single miscue. On the last day of August 1971, he started his consecutive playing streak at Yankee Stadium against the Washington Senators. During the early part of his playing career, the Yankees usually were in the middle of the pack in the standings. The 1971 season was no different as the team placed fourth in the Eastern Division, a solid 21 games behind the division-leading Baltimore Orioles. The following year (1972), White was in the Yankee lineup every game and extended his playing streak to 184 contests. Additionally, he led the league outfielders with 155 games played, topped the league with 99 walks and finished with 10 homers, 54 RBI and a .270 batting average. The Yankees again finished in fourth place (only six and a half games out of the lead) in the East, only on this occasion it was the Detroit Tigers who won the division crown. White completed another full schedule of games in 1973 as he batted .246, smacked 18 homers and drove home 60 runners. On May 22, his playing streak had reached 223 straight contests when he took over the majors' Iron Man title from Sandy Alomar of the California Angels. As the year closed out, he was still the Iron Man as he stretched his playing streak to 346 contests. The final Eastern Division standings in 1973 found the Orioles back on top with the Yanks a distant 17 games back in the fourth position. In the off-season, Ralph Houk stepped down as the Yankees' skipper and was replaced by former Pittsburgh Pirate Bill Virdon. When the 1974 season started, Virdon decided to rotate White between left field and the designated hitter position. During the 42nd game of the year, White strained his left leg hamstring in the eighth inning of a 14–6 loss at Boston. He was attempting to go from first to third on a Ron Blomberg single but pulled up lame and was easily tagged out on the play. The next day (May 22, 1974), he was out of the Yankees' lineup for the first time in 388 games. By season's end he would miss 26 games as he came in with a .275 average but with just seven homers and 43 RBI to show for his efforts. The team flourished under Virdon as he led them to a second-place finish, just two games behind the repeat division champion Orioles.

White played for five more seasons in Yankees pinstripes. His most noted accomplishment during these years was that he led the American League with 104 runs scored in 1976. During this period, the Yankees returned to their past glory as the team made it to the World Series three consecutive years from 1976 through 1978. White had a horrible fall classic in 1976 as he hit only .133 (2-for-15) as the Cincinnati Reds (the big Red Machine) rolled over them and swept the series in four games. The following year (1977) against the Los Angeles Dodgers, he made only two pinch-hitting appearances as the Yankees won in six games and achieved their first world championship since 1962. In a repeat appearance with the Dodgers in 1978, White was one of the top performers as he batted .333 (8-for-24), had a homer, drove in four runners and led all series players with nine runs scored as the Yankees repeated as world champions. After sharing the left field duties with Lou Piniella in 1978, White was primarily used as a reserve outfielder in 1979 and played in only 81 contests in what turned out to be his last season as a major leaguer. After the 1979 season, he filed for free agency but then decided to play in Japan. He played for a few seasons with the Yomiuri Giants and put up some decent offensive numbers among which was the 29 homers he hit in 1980. When he returned from Japan in 1983, he was back in pinstripes as one of Bombers' coaches. He served for a few seasons and then later returned to the Yankees as their first base coach.

108. Eddie Brinkman

Born: December 8, 1941, Cincinnati, Ohio *Bats*: Right *Throws*: Right *Height*: 6 feet *Weight*: 170 *Major league debut*: September 6, 1961 (Washington at New York [AL]) *Last major league game*: September 28, 1975 (Baltimore at New York [AL])

Eddie Brinkman

Major league Iron Man from: May 22, 1974, to August 10, 1974 *Consecutive games played*: 434 *Games as major league Iron Man*: 76 (consecutive games 359 through 434) *Team played for during streak*: Detroit Tigers (AL) *Primary position played*: Shortstop *Game missed before streak*: September 25, 1971 (New York at Detroit) *First game played of streak*: September 26, 1971 (New York at Detroit) *Last game played of streak*: August 9, 1974 (Detroit at Texas) *Game missed to end streak*: August 10, 1974 (Detroit at Texas)

Consecutive Game Streak's Statistical Totals

Year	G	AB	R	H	2B	3B	HR	RBI	BB	SO	AVG	SLG	SB
1971	3	7	0	2	0	0	0	0	1	1	.286	.286	0
1972	156	516	42	105	19	1	6	49	38	51	.203	.279	0
1973	162	515	55	122	16	4	7	40	34	79	.237	.324	0
1974	113	379	40	84	9	3	10	42	22	49	.222	.340	1
Total	434	1417	137	313	44	8	23	131	95	180	.221	.312	1

Eddie Brinkman was your typical no-hit, all-glove shortstop of the 1960s and 1970s. Growing up in Cincinnati, he played with Pete Rose (baseball's all-time hits leader and two-time major league Iron Man) on their high school team. Signed by Washington in 1961, the Senators groomed him to be their future shortstop. He made his big league debut in September 1961 but got into only a few games that year. He put in one more part-time year (1962) before taking over the starting shortstop role for the Senators in 1963. His first full year he put up some decent numbers for a player who was in the lineup for his glove. Although he hit only .228, he hit seven homers and drove in 45 runners. Ironically, one of the areas he led the American League in that season was errors by a shortstop with 37 miscues. He also had more double plays (97) than any other league shortstop. As for the Senators, they were the perennial cellar dwellers in those years and 1963 was no different as they finished in last place with a 56–106 record.

Over the next three seasons, Brinkman held down the Senators' shortstop position until the 1967 season. That year, Senators manager Gil Hodges decided to alternate Brinkman and rookie Tim Cullen at shortstop because Brinkman was not producing much offensively to justify his being in the lineup on a daily basis. His final 1967 stats bore this reasoning out when he came in with just a .188 batting average, a homer and 18 RBI in 109 games. Before the following year (1968) started, Cullen was shipped off to the Chicago White Sox. One of the players obtained in that trade was Ron Hansen. When the 1968 campaign began, Hansen was the main shortstop with Brinkman as his primary backup. In August of that year, Hansen was traded back to the White Sox in exchange for Cullen. With Cullen back with the Senators, the shortstop job was back on a rotating basis between Cullen and Brinkman. Brinkman's numbers were getting even worse as he took part in 77 games and showed only a .187 average with no homers and just six RBI. Since the Senators again finished dead last in the standings, a change was needed and baseball great Ted Williams was hired to take over the team for the 1969 season. This was a turning point in Brinkman's career. Working with Williams, a decision was made to change Brinkman's batting style. Brinkman's batting and the team's performance improved immediately. By year's end, he came in with a .266 average (an improvement of 79 points), a couple of homers and 43 RBI in 151 games. The team improved by 21 games and had an 86–76 record, good for a solid fourth-place finish in the American League standings. The next year (1970), he repeated his performance by hitting .262 with a homer and 40 RBI. In the field, he paced the league's shortstops in putouts (301), assists (569) and double plays (103) in 158 contests. The Senators unfortunately returned to their losing ways as they went 70–92 and came in last place in the Eastern Division.

After having played with Washington for 10 years, Brinkman was traded to the Detroit-

Tigers in October 1970. He immediately took over as Detroit's new shortstop, replacing Cesar Gutierrez. Brinkman was finally with a consistently winning team after having endured the losing atmosphere in the Senators' clubhouse for so many years. That first season in Detroit (1971), he manned the shortstop position for 159 games and came in with a .228 average, a homer and 37 RBI. Without the Splendid Splinter there to guide him, Brinkman's batting average reverted to his pre-Williams' days. In fielding, he led the league's shortstops with 159 games played and 513 assists. Near the end of the season, he started his consecutive playing streak when he played in the Tigers' final three contests of the 1971 season. Detroit finished in second place, a dozen games behind the Baltimore Orioles. Brinkman played in all 156 of the Tigers' games in 1972 and hit .203 along with six homers and 49 RBI. He had a fantastic year in the field as he made just seven errors and led the shortstops with a .990 fielding average. He also set a couple of records for shortstops by playing 72 straight errorless contests and handling 331 consecutive chances without an error. On August 5, in a game against Cleveland, he committed a miscue that ended both of these streaks. For his superb year in the field, he was selected as the American League Gold Glove shortstop winner for the 1972 season. Additionally, he contributed to the Tigers winning the Eastern Division championship and a berth in the league championship series against the Oakland Athletics. Tigers skipper Billy Martin decided not to use Brinkman during the series so Martin switched second baseman Dick McAuliffe to shortstop and inserted Tony Taylor at second base. That left Brinkman on the bench for his first post-season opportunity. He did get in one game at shortstop and made the best of it by going 2-for-4 with a couple of doubles. Unfortunately, the Tigers lost an exciting series 3–2 to the Athletics and Oakland eventually went on to win the 1972 World Series. Brinkman extended his playing streak to 321 games when he competed in all of the Tigers games in 1973. The streak came close to ending when he was not in the starting lineup for the last two games of the year. In both contests, he replaced the game's starting shortstop, Tom Veryzer, in the late innings to keep the streak alive. Brinkman's average jumped over 30 points to .237 as he contributed seven homers and 40 RBI along the way. The Tigers came in third place, behind the Orioles by 12 games. The 1974 season found Brinkman becoming the Iron Man of baseball on May 22 when the Yankees' Roy White suffered an injury. Brinkman ran his streak to 434 games before manager Ralph Houk rested him on August 10, 1974. During his Iron Man run, Brinkman had a low offensive production but that was quite normal for him. It must be remembered that he was in the lineup for his glove, not his bat. By season's end, the Tigers came in last in the standings and changes would soon occur.

Brinkman's streak occurred in the latter stages of his playing career. When his streak ended, he had only one more year in the majors and his suitcase suddenly became very busy. In December 1974, the Tigers traded him to the National League's St. Louis Cardinals. He spent half the year there and then was shipped off to Texas in June. Nine days later, another trade took him to the New York Yankees. He stayed with the Bronx Bombers till his release as a major leaguer during the 1976 spring training camp. Between 1979 and 1988, he stayed active in baseball circles by serving on the coaching staffs in Detroit, San Diego, and Chicago (White Sox).

109. MIKE SCHMIDT

Born: September 27, 1949, Dayton, Ohio *Bats*: Right *Throws*: Right *Height*: 6 feet, 2 inches *Weight*: 195 *Major league debut*: September 12, 1972 (New York at Philadelphia [NL]) *Last major league game*: May 28, 1989 (Philadelphia at San Francisco [NL])

Major league Iron Man from: August 10, 1974, to May 27, 1975 *Consecutive games played*: 231 *Games as major league Iron Man*: 90 (consecutive games 142 through 231) *Team played for during streak*: Philadelphia Phillies (NL) *Primary position played*: Third base *Game missed before streak*: August 31, 1973 (Montreal at Philadelphia) *First game played of streak*: September 1, 1973 (Montreal at Philadelphia) *Last game played of streak*: May 26, 1975 (San Francisco at Philadelphia) *Game missed to end streak*: May 27, 1975 (San Francisco at Philadelphia)

Consecutive Game Streak's Statistical Totals

Year	G	AB	R	H	2B	3B	HR	RBI	BB	SO	AVG	SLG	SB
1973	28	78	6	12	1	0	3	11	16	39	.154	.282	5
1974	162	568	108	160	28	7	36	116	106	138	.282	.546	23
1975	41	153	16	29	9	0	6	18	18	56	.190	.366	3
Total	231	799	130	201	38	7	45	145	140	233	.252	.486	31

Mike Schmidt is considered one of the best third basemen the game has ever seen along with being the best Philadelphia Phillies' player of all time. He was a dangerous power hitter at the plate and a Gold Glover when fielding his position at the hot corner. He played his entire 18-year major league career with the Phillies. Selected by the Phillies in the second round of the 1971 free agent draft, he was brought up to the majors in late 1972 and made his debut on September 12 in Philadelphia against the New York Mets.

At the start of the 1973 season, he took over the third base job from the departed Don Money. Schmidt's first full year was not that impressive as he hit only .196 but he did have 18 homers and 52 RBI. The Phillies finished in last place with a 71–91 record. Schmidt's Iron Man streak occurred early in his career beginning September 1 in a game in Philadelphia against the Montreal Expos; he went on to play the last 28 contests on the 1973 schedule. In 1974, he produced the type of offensive numbers that the Phillies were expecting from their prospect. He led the National League with 36 homers, 138 strikeouts and a .546 slugging average while helping the Phillies to an 80–82 record and a third-place finish (just eight games behind the division-champion Pittsburgh Pirates). In addition, he paced the league's third basemen in games played (162) and assists (404). On August 10, he took over the Iron Man title from Detroit's Ed Brinkman with just 142 consecutive games played to date (this turns out to be one of the lowest totals in modern times to ever become baseball's Iron Man). By the completion of the 1974 season, his consecutive streak was extended to 190 games played. Schmidt was having hitting problems at the beginning of the 1975 season. The Phillies' manager, Danny Ozark, determined that Schmidt needed a rest and benched him on May 27, 1975. His streak was over after 231 consecutive games played. After returning from the bench, he recovered his hitting stroke and finished the 1975 campaign with a senior circuit high in homers with 38 clouts along with driving in 95 runners as the Phillies claimed second place behind the Pittsburgh Pirates for the division championship.

During the rest of his superstar career with the Phillies from 1976 through 1989, Schmidt was the dominant force in the team's offensive arsenal as he led the National League in homers in 1976, 1980, 1981, 1983, 1984 and 1986; runs scored in 1981; RBI during 1980, 1981, 1984 and 1986; walks in 1979, 1981 through 1983; on base percentage from 1981 through 1983; and slugging percentage from 1980 through 1982 and 1986. Defensively, he led the third basemen of the National League in games played in 1976; assists in 1976, 1977 and 1980 through 1983; double plays from 1978 through 1980, 1982, 1983 and 1987; and fielding percentage in 1986. He also was honored with 10 Gold Gloves for third basemen (1976 through 1984 and 1986). He was picked to play in 10 all-star games for the National League squad. He also was chosen the league's Most Valuable Player in 1980, 1981 and 1986 and was one of the key players who led the Phillies to the World Series in 1980 and 1983. In the 1980 series (the Phillies' first World Series appearance since 1950) against the Kansas City Royals, he batted .381 (8-for-21) and led all series participants with six runs scored. The Phillies claimed the world championship by beating the Royals in six games. His performance resulted in his being selected the series' Most Valuable Player. The Phillies made it back to the fall classic a few years later in 1983 but lost to the Baltimore Orioles in five games. On this occasion, Schmidt had a horrible time against the Orioles as he had only a single hit in 20 at-bats for a .050 average. In his last two years (1988–1989), he started having problems with the injury bug. It was, in fact, a shoulder ailment that finally made him decide to hang up his cleats and glove in late May 1989. Concluding his career with offensive numbers that could not be ignored, Schmidt was voted into baseball's Hall of Fame in 1995.

110. Dave Cash

Born: June 11, 1948, Utica, New York *Bats*: Right *Throws*: Right *Height*: 5 feet, 11 inches *Weight*: 170 *Major league debut*: September 13, 1969 (New York at Pittsburgh [NL]) *Last major league game*: October 5, 1980 (San Diego at San Francisco [NL])

Major league Iron Man from: May 27, 1975, to September 26, 1976 *Consecutive games played*: 494 *Games as major league Iron Man*: 276 (consecutive games 219 through 494) *Teams played for during streak*: Pittsburgh Pirates (NL) (1973) and Philadelphia Phillies (NL) (1974–1976) *Primary position played*: Second base *Game missed before streak*: September 17, 1973 (New York at Pittsburgh) *First game played of streak*: September 18, 1973 (New York at Pittsburgh) *Last game played of streak*: September 26, 1976 (first game) (Philadelphia at Montreal) *Game missed to end streak*: September 26, 1976 (second game) (Philadelphia at Montreal)

Consecutive Game Streak's Statistical Totals

Year	G	AB	R	H	2B	3B	HR	RBI	BB	SO	AVG	SLG	SB
1973	15	68	8	23	3	1	0	6	3	6	.338	.412	0
1974	162	687	89	206	26	11	2	58	46	33	.300	.378	20
1975	162	699	111	213	40	3	4	57	56	34	.305	.388	13
1976	155	650	88	181	14	11	1	54	51	12	.278	.338	10
Total	494	2104	296	623	83	26	7	175	156	85	.296	.370	43

Dave Cash was an infielder who played in the majors for 12 seasons with four National League teams: the Pittsburgh Pirates, Philadelphia Phillies, Montreal Expos and San Diego Padres. In June 1966, he was selected in the fifth round of the free agent draft by the Pirates. Pittsburgh had Cash in mind as the eventual replacement at second base upon Bill Mazeroski's retirement. Cash's first few years were spent in the minors before being called up to the parent club in late 1969. He made his major league debut on September 13 in the Pirates' 5–2 loss at Forbes Field against the New York Mets. He got into 18 games by season's end and finished with a .279 batting average.

Cash served primarily as Mazeroski's backup at second base in 1970 as he appeared 64 times in the lineup. He contributed offensively by hitting .314 as the Pirates secured the league's Eastern Division title by five games over the Chicago Cubs. The Pirates went out quickly in the championship series as they were swept in three games by the Cincinnati Reds. Cash had only one hit in eight at-bats during that series for a .125 batting average. He played more games at second base during the 1971 season than any other Pirate, including Mazeroski, who was still considered the top man at the position. Cash hit .289 for the year along with a couple of homers and brought home 34 runners as the Pirates took the senior circuit's Eastern Division crown by seven games over the St. Louis Cardinals. After disposing of the San Francisco Giants in the league championship in four games (where Cash hit .421 with eight hits in 19 at-bats), the Pirates went from losing the first two games to defeating the Baltimore Orioles in the fall classic in an exciting seventh game to claim baseball's championship. Cash played all seven games at second base but went only 4 for 30 (.133) in the series. In 1972, Cash permanently took over as the Pirates' second baseman and contributed to another divisional crown. The team ran into the ever-powerful Reds and lost the league title in five games. The following year (1973), manager Bill Virdon decided to rotate Cash and Rennie Stennett at second. Sometimes Cash would also play the hot corner to give the regular third baseman, Richie Hebner, a rest. Cash started his playing streak on September 18 in Pittsburgh against the New York Mets as he appeared in the final 15 Pirates games of the season. At the end of the year, the Pirates decided to give Stennent the second base job permanently and made the decision to trade Cash to the Phillies in October 1973.

The 1974 season found Cash as the Phillies' man at second, replacing Denny Doyle who went off to play in the American League for the California Angels. Batting lead-off in the lineup, Cash finally got a real chance to be a full-time player. Playing all 162 games along with teammates Mike Schmidt and Larry Bowa, he batted an even .300 and drove in a career-high 58 runners as he contributed to the Phillies' improvement and a third-place finish. In addition, he had more at-bats (687) than any other league player and topped all National League second basemen in assists and double plays. He also appeared in his first of three straight all-star game appearances. He was close behind teammate Mike Schmidt for most consecutive games by a major leaguer with 177 contests to his credit. On May 26, Cash had the third-longest playing streak with the Phillies (and in major league baseball) behind teammates Schmidt and Bowa. In that game, Bowa (whose streak was eight games behind Schmidt's and five contests ahead of Cash's) suffered a broken left thumb on a pick-off play. The next Phillies game on May 27, both Schmidt (benched) and Bowa (injured) were out of the team's lineup and Cash took over baseball's Iron Man role. Cash again took in all 162 of the Phillies' game in 1975 at second base and extended his playing streak to 339 games by season's end. In addition to leading the National League for the second straight season in total at-bats, he topped all hitters with 213 base hits. During the 1976 season, Cash's average dropped about 20 points but he still hit a respectable .284 along with driving in 56 runners. For the third consecutive year, he led the National League in at-bats (666) in addition to a top total of 12 triples. He also paced the league's second basemen in double plays and fielding average. There were several occasions during the 1976 season that his streak nearly ended. On June 11, he pinch-hit in the eighth inning and then took over at second base. His National League record for most consecutive games (443) at second base came to an end on August 6 where his only appearance in the game was as a pinch hitter for pitcher Jim Lonborg in the top of the seventh. He also pinch-hit for pitcher Jim Kaat in the top of the eighth on September 1, 1976. Cash's streak finally did end when he sat out the second game of a double-header against the Montreal Expos on September 26, 1976. Although the Phillies beat the Expos in the game 2–1, the game was called after seven innings, so you have to wonder if Phillies' skipper Danny Ozark would have used Cash if the game had gone the distance. As a result, his streak ended at 494 games, just six games short of reaching 500 consecutive games. The Phillies won the Eastern Division in 1976 by nine games over the Pirates but were swept by the Reds in three games in the league championship series.

Cash left the Phillies after the 1976 season via free agency to the Montreal Expos. He spent three years at third base for the Expos before being traded to the San Diego Padres. In

1980, he hit a relatively paltry .227 in 130 games for the Padres. The Padres released him from their roster just before the start of the 1981 season. With his big league career over, Cash would eventually coach for a while in the Phillies' minor league system.

111. PETE ROSE

Born: April 14, 1941, Cincinnati, Ohio *Bats*: Switch Hitter *Throws*: Right *Height*: 5 feet, 11 inches *Weight*: 192 *Major league debut*: April 8, 1963 (Pittsburgh at Cincinnati [NL]) *Last major league game*: August 17, 1986 (San Diego at Cincinnati [NL])

Major league Iron Man from: September 26, 1976, to May 7, 1978 *Consecutive games played*: 678 *Games as major league Iron Man*: 195 (consecutive games 484 through 678) *Team played for during streak*: Cincinnati Reds (NL) *Primary positions played*: Outfield and third base *Game missed before streak*: September 26, 1973 (San Diego at Cincinnati) *First game played of streak*: September 28, 1973 (San Francisco at Cincinnati) *Last game played of streak*: May 7, 1978 (first game) (Montreal at Cincinnati) *Game missed to end streak*: May 7, 1978 (second game) (Montreal at Cincinnati)

Consecutive Game Streak's Statistical Totals

Year	G	AB	R	H	2B	3B	HR	RBI	BB	SO	AVG	SLG	SB
1973	3	14	2	1	1	0	0	0	1	1	.071	.143	0
1974	163	652	110	185	45	7	3	51	106	54	.284	.388	2
1975	162	662	112	210	47	4	7	74	89	50	.317	.432	0
1976	162	665	130	215	42	6	10	63	86	54	.323	.450	9
1977	162	655	95	204	38	7	9	64	66	42	.311	.432	16
1978	26	115	20	37	8	1	3	16	8	4	.322	.487	2
Total	678	2763	469	852	181	25	32	268	356	205	.308	.427	29

Pete Rose, baseball's all-time hits leader, was a two-time holder of the Iron Man title — the first since the Cardinals' Stan Musial. He put in 24 seasons in the majors playing every position on a relatively regular basis (except pitcher, catcher and shortstop) at one time or another. He played for the Cincinnati Reds (1963–1978 and 1984–1986), Philadelphia Phillies (1979–1983) and Montreal Expos (1984). Nicknamed "Charlie Hustle," he always gave that extra effort on the diamond. Signed to a free agent contract in July 1960, he won the Reds' second base job from Don Blasingame in the 1963 training camp and made his big league debut on Opening Day of 1963. In his rookie year, he appeared in 157 contests and finished with a .273 average, six homers and 41 RBI. This performance earned him the National League's 1963 Rookie of the Year honors.

Rose played nearly 10 years of major league ball before he started his first Iron Man run. During that first decade with the Reds, he was one of the team's most reliable players and consistently hit above .300 every year. The Reds during the early years were just a mediocre team and their "Big Red Machine" era was on the horizon. After being the Reds' second baseman for his first four years in the majors, Rose switched to the outfield starting with the 1967 season. The following two years, he won consecutive league batting titles with averages of .335 (1968) and .348 (1969). He won his only Gold Gloves in 1969 and 1970 while playing in right field for the Reds. In the 1970 all-star game, he scored the game's winning run for the National League in his famous home plate collision with the American League's catcher, Ray Fosse of the Cleveland Indians. Rose played on his first pennant-winning team that year when the Reds swept the Pittsburgh Pirates in three games to win the league championship series. In the 1970 World Series, Rose hit only .250 as the Reds were beaten in five games by the Baltimore Orioles. Two years later, the Reds again beat the Pirates in the league championship series. This time the Reds faced the Oakland Athletics in the series. The series went the fully contested seven games but the Reds again lost. Rose had another relatively lousy series as he batted only .214, although he did lead all series players with 28 at-bats.

In 1973, Rose took in his third National League batting title with a .338 average along with winning the league's Most Valuable Player award as he helped the Reds win the Western Division crown. Although the New York Mets defeated the Reds to claim the league championship in 1973, Rose finally had a decent postseason by hitting .381 average in the five-game affair. With three games left on the schedule in 1973, he started his consecutive streak in a game at Cincinnati against the San Francisco Giants. Playing the full slate of games in 1974, Rose's batting average plummeted over 50 points as he hit below .300 for the first time since the 1964 season. The Reds finished runner-up to the Los Angeles Dodgers in the Western Division standings. Rose made another position switch in 1975 as he took over at third base from Dan Driessen. Rose's average rebounded to .317 and he extended his playing streak to 328 games as the season came to a close. The Reds won the division title by 20 games over the Dodgers, swept the Pirates in the league championship series and won their first World Series since 1940 when they beat the Boston Red Sox 4–3 in the seventh game on a ninth-inning bloop single by Reds second baseman Joe Morgan. Rose led all World Series hitters with a .370 average and was chosen the series' Most Valuable Player. During the 1976 season, he hit .323, led the league with 215 hits and extended his playing streak to 490 straight contests. Near the end of the season, he took over the Iron Man title from the Phillies' Dave Cash on September 26, 1976. The 1976 postseason was a repeat performance as the Reds ran through all their opponents and demolished the New York Yankees in the World Series in four games. Although the Reds had won the series, Rose hit for only a paltry .188 average against the Yankees. Playing all the Reds' game in 1977 for a fourth consecutive year, Rose crossed over the 500-game plateau early in the year and extended his streak to 652 games. He again hit over the .300 mark with a .311 average and drove home 64 Reds. The Reds' chances for a third consecutive major league title ended when they finished 10 games behind in the standings to the division-winning Dodgers. The following year (1978), Rose was off to a decent start with a .322 batting average, three homers and 16 RBI after 26 games when his consecutive game streak came to an abrupt end after 678 contests. On May 7, 1978, he sat out the second game of a double-header against the Montreal Expos in Cincinnati because of severe stomach cramps. He would miss only one other game that year, on August 31 against the St. Louis Cardinals, when he would start another long playing streak. In addition, he compiled a 44-consecutive-game hitting streak during the 1978 season that tied the all-time National League mark which he shares with Hall of Famer Willie Keeler. Details about Rose's second Iron Man streak and other aspects of his long major league career are included in a later narrative.

Pete Rose: Major league baseball's all-time hits leader achieved streaks of 678 and 745 games between 1973 and 1983 which made him the Iron Man on two occasions.

112. STEVE GARVEY

Born: December 22, 1948, Tampa, Florida *Bats*: Right *Throws*: Right *Height*: 5 feet, 10 inches *Weight*: 192 *Major league debut*: September 1, 1969 (New York at Los Angeles [NL]) *Last major league game*: May 23, 1987 (Montreal at San Diego [NL])

Major league Iron Man from: May 7, 1978, to July 29, 1983 *Consecutive games played*: 1,207 *Games as major league Iron Man*: 833 (consecutive games 375 through 1207) *Teams played for during streak*: Los Angeles Dodgers (NL) (1975–1982) and San Diego Padres (NL) (1983) *Primary position played*: First base *Game missed before streak*: September 2, 1975 (Los Angeles at San Francisco) *First game played of streak*: September 3, 1975 (Los Angeles at Cincinnati) *Last game played of streak*: July 29, 1983 (first game) (Atlanta at San Diego) *Game missed to end streak*: July 29, 1983 (second game) (Atlanta at San Diego)

Consecutive Game Streak's Statistical Totals

Year	G	AB	R	H	2B	3B	HR	RBI	BB	SO	AVG	SLG	SB
1975	24	97	16	34	7	1	4	20	6	11	.351	.567	0
1976	162	631	85	200	37	4	13	80	50	69	.317	.450	19
1977	162	646	91	192	25	3	33	115	38	90	.297	.498	9
1978	162	639	89	202	36	9	21	113	40	70	.316	.499	10
1979	162	648	92	204	32	1	28	110	37	59	.315	.497	3
1980	163	658	78	200	27	1	26	106	36	67	.304	.467	6
1981	110	431	63	122	23	1	10	64	25	49	.283	.411	3
1982	162	625	66	176	35	1	16	86	20	86	.282	.418	5
1983	100	388	76	114	22	0	14	59	29	39	.294	.459	4
Total	1207	4763	656	1444	244	21	165	753	281	540	.303	.467	59

Steve Garvey played in the major leagues for 19 seasons with the Los Angeles Dodgers and the San Diego Padres. By the time he retired from baseball in 1988, he was considered one of the best fielding first basemen the game has known and the most durable player of the 1970s and early 1980s. Originally selected by the Minnesota Twins in the third round of the 1966 free agent draft, Garvey could not come to an agreement with the Twins and two years later was picked in the first round (and 13th overall) in the 1968 draft by the Dodgers.

Called up to the Dodgers in the last month of the 1969 season, Garvey made only three pinch-hitting appearances that year. The following season (1970), he played close to three dozen games at third base and batted .269. In 1971, he took in 81 games and hit for only a .227 average along with seven homers and 26 RBI. He missed a portion of that year with a hand injury. In 1972, he was the team's regular starting third baseman; his average jumped 42 points as he finished with a .269 average in 96 games, but his power and run production totals were disappointing as he had only nine homers and 30 RBI. Since Garvey led all National League third basemen with 28 errors in 1972, Dodgers skipper Walt Alston decided to platoon him with Bill Buckner at first base in 1973 and bring in rookie Ron Cey to take over the hot corner. This would be the first year that Garvey and Cey along with second baseman Davey Lopes and shortstop Bill Russell formed the longest running infield partnership, lasting into the 1981 campaign. Playing 114 contests in 1973, Garvey hit over .300 for the first time in his career with a .304 average along with eight homers and knocking in 50 runners. In 1974, he took over the full-time duties at first base and Buckner was moved permanently to the outfield. Garvey thrived on the additional work as he played 156 games and hit a solid .312, clubbed 21 round-trippers and knocked in 111 runners. As a result of this performance, he was selected the 1974 National League's Most Valuable Player. Additionally, he was elected by the fans to his first all-star game by write-in votes as his name was not on the all-star ballots. In the game, he had a couple of hits and made an impressive defensive play that kept a couple of runs from scoring in the senior circuit's 7–2 victory. He also was chosen the game's Most Valuable Player. The Dodgers won the Western Division title by four games over the second-place Cincinnati Reds in 1974. In the league championship series, Los Angeles disposed of the Pittsburgh Pirates in four games as Garvey hit .389 along with a series-leading five RBI. They faced the Oakland Athletics in the 1974 World Series but lost to the more talented Athletics in five contests. Garvey was one of the bright spots on the Dodgers roster as he paced all series players with 21 at-bats, eight hits and a .381 batting average.

Garvey followed up the previous season's performance with another splendid year in 1975 as he led the Dodgers with 659 at-bats, 210 hits, 38 doubles, .319 batting average and .476 slugging percentage. He also started his National League record of 1,207 consecutive games by appearing in the final 24 games on the 1975 schedule, commencing with the September 3 game in Cincinnati. Although Garvey had another great year, the Dodgers finished a distant second by 20 games in their division behind the powerful Cincinnati Reds. Playing all the Dodgers' games at first base in 1976, he again paced the team in hits, doubles and a .317 batting average as the team finished runner-up again to the Reds in the divisional standings. Garvey had another super year at the plate in 1977 by hitting .297 and leading the Dodgers with 192 hits, 33 homers and 115 RBI. He played all the team's contests for the second straight year and extended his playing streak to 348 games. All his games in the field in 1977 were at first base except for two-pinch hitting appearances on May 28 and August 15. The Dodgers won the Western Division by 10 games over the Reds, disposed of the Philadelphia Phillies in four games in the league championship and faced the New York Yankees in the World Series for the first time since 1963. Although the Dodgers lost to the Yankees in six games, Garvey had a fine series; he hit .375 and tied the Yanks' Reggie Jackson for the most hits in the series with nine base knocks. Early the next season, on May 7, 1978, Garvey took over the major league Iron Man title from Cincinnati's Pete Rose. The season was another productive year for the Dodgers' first baseman as he hit a solid .316 along with hitting 21 homers and producing 113 runs. He also came away with his second all-star game Most Valuable Player award. The Dodgers again earned a World Series berth by getting past the Phillies in four games. Facing the Yankees for a second straight year in the World Series, the Dodgers lost again in six games. Garvey had an awful series, going 5 for 24 for a .208 average. In 1979, he again proved

Steve Garvey: He was a first baseman for the Los Angeles Dodgers and San Diego Padres. He set the all-time National League mark with 1,207 consecutive games. His streak ended in late July 1983 when he suffered a hand injury during a play at the plate.

his playing streak had no negative ramifications as he played all 162 games at first and led the Dodgers in the majority of the offensive categories, which included a .315 batting average. The Dodgers had their worst season on the field since 1968 when they finished with a 79–83 record and finished third behind the Reds. Garvey hit over .300 for the final time in his career (and seventh time in the last eight seasons) in 1980 when he led the league in hits for a second time. He played in all but one game at first base and extended his playing streak to 835 contests as the 1980 season came to a close. The only game he did not appear on defense in 1980 was the second game of a double-header on May 26 in Cincinnati. Garvey pinch-hit for pitcher Charlie Hough in the top of the ninth to keep his streak alive. The Dodgers reverted to their winning ways by finishing in second place behind the Houston Astros by one game. In fact, they and the Astros were tied at the end of the year and the teams played a one-game playoff that saw Houston come out on top. In the strike-shortened 1981 season, Garvey continued his streak by taking in all 110 Dodgers' contests but finished with his lowest average (.283) since 1972. When the strike occurred, the Dodgers were sitting in first place. They came in fourth for the second half of the year and took on Houston for the league championship. The Dodgers came back from a two-game deficit to beat the Astros in five games and earn a place in the 1981 World Series against their old nemesis, the Yankees. In the series, the Dodgers fell behind 2–0 but came back to defeat the Yankees (for only the third time in a World Series) in six games. Garvey hit a team-high .417 and led all series players with 10 hits. The 1982 season turned out to be Garvey's last in a Dodgers uniform. In a 13–1 loss to the Montreal Expos on May 2, he did not start but pinch-hit for the pitcher in the fifth inning. On June 7, 1982, he became just the fifth player in major league history to appear in 1,000 consecutive contests. In early July, he was hampered by a pulled right hamstring but continued to play for a few innings in each game and then rest. The injury seemed to get worse and it looked like the streak might end but Garvey was determined to keep it going because he was within 90 games of breaking the National League record of 1,117 games held by the Cubs' Billy Williams. There were several games in the middle of July that he was used only as a pinch hitter. Eventually, his injury healed and he continued with the streak. He ended the year with a .282 batting mark along with 16 homers, 86 RBI and a team-high 35 doubles. The Dodgers finished one game behind the Western Division-winning Braves in the final standings. His streak stood at 1,107 games when the 1982 season came to a close, just 11 games shy of establishing a new league mark. He left the Dodgers after this season and signed a free agent contract with the San Diego Padres. On April 16, 1983, Garvey broke the all-time National League mark for consecutive games played in the Padres' 8–5 loss to the Dodgers. His streak (and his 1983 season) came to an end at 1,207 games when he dislocated a finger in a home plate collision with the Braves' pitcher, Pascual Perez, during the first game of a double-header on July 29, 1983, in San Diego. His streak stats indicate that Garvey was very dependable in putting up consistent offensive numbers along with leading the National League first basemen in fielding for several seasons.

After his playing streak ended, Garvey played for four more seasons with the Padres before retiring in January 1988 due to an arm injury. From September 23, 1984, to September 6, 1986, he played 305 straight games with the Padres to establish the team record for most consecutive games. He is the only player that presently holds two teams' record for most consecutive games (1,107 games with the Dodgers and 305 games with the Padres). His final stats might result in his someday getting chosen to baseball's Hall of Fame, although he has suffered some personal problems since retiring that might have an effect on this ultimate achievement.

113. PETE ROSE

Born: April 14, 1941, Cincinnati, Ohio *Bats*: Switch Hitter *Throws*: Right *Height*: 5 feet, 11 inches *Weight*: 192 *Major league debut*: April 8, 1963 (Pittsburgh at Cincinnati [NL]) *Last major league game*: August 17, 1986 (San Diego at Cincinnati [NL])

Major league Iron Man from: July 29, 1983, to August 24, 1983 *Consecutive games played*: 745 *Games as major league Iron Man*: 26 (consecutive games 720 through 745) *Teams played for during streak*: Cincinnati Reds (NL) (1978) and Philadelphia Phillies (NL) (1979–1983) *Primary positions played*: Third base and first base *Game missed before streak*: August 31, 1978 (Cincinnati at St. Louis) *First game played of streak*: September 1, 1978 (Cincinnati at St. Louis) *Last game played of streak*: August 23, 1983 (Philadelphia at San Francisco) *Game missed to end streak*: August 24, 1983 (Philadelphia at San Francisco)

Consecutive Game Streak's Statistical Totals

Year	G	AB	R	H	2B	3B	HR	RBI	BB	SO	AVG	SLG	SB
1978	28	108	19	34	8	0	2	16	14	2	.315	.444	3
1979	163	628	90	208	40	5	4	59	95	32	.331	.430	20
1980	162	655	95	185	42	1	1	64	66	33	.282	.354	12
1981	107	431	73	140	18	5	0	33	46	26	.325	.390	4
1982	162	634	80	172	25	4	3	54	66	32	.271	.338	8
1983	123	421	44	108	13	3	0	38	46	24	.257	.302	7
Total	745	2877	401	847	146	18	10	264	333	149	.294	.368	54

Rose started his second Iron Man streak on September 1, 1978, in a game against the Cardinals in St. Louis and appeared in the last 28 games on the 1978 Reds' schedule. He finished the year with a .302 average as the Reds finished in second place behind the Los Angeles Dodgers in the National League's Western Division. After the season, he became a free agent in November 1978 and left his hometown team, the Reds, to sign a contract to play for the Philadelphia Phillies. When he reported to the Phillies, the team was already set with Mike Schmidt at third and a solid outfield lineup of Bake McBride, Garry Maddox and Greg Luzinski. Phillies manager Danny Ozark needed to have Rose in Philadelphia's daily starting lineup so he put him at first base, replacing Richie Hebner, who had left the team for the New York Mets.

The position shift did not bother Rose as he led the 1979 Phillies in several offensive categories, which included 208 hits and a .331 batting average. Although the Phillies had a decent win-loss record, they finished in fourth place behind the Pittsburgh Pirates. While his batting average dropped by nearly 50 points in 1980, Rose helped the Phillies win the league's Eastern Division title by one game over the Montreal Expos. After eliminating the Houston Astros in five games during the league series, the Phillies faced the Kansas City Royals in the team's first World Series berth since 1950. They defeated the Royals in six games as Rose went 6 for 23 for a .261 average along with producing a double and an RBI. The 1981 season was strike shortened and this resulted in the Phillies playing just 107 games. They made the playoffs but lost to Montreal in a five-game series. While the team did not repeat as world champs, Rose had a great year as his average rebounded to .325. He led the senior circuit with 140 hits and extended his playing streak to 460 games. In addition, he broke Stan Musial's National League record of 3,630 hits when major league baseball resumed play after settling the labor unrest. During the 1982 campaign, Rose's average again plummeted over 50 points as he hit for only a .271 average (his lowest since his second season, 1964, in the big leagues). He played every game at first base for the third straight season and stretched his overall consecutive playing run to 622 contests. This streak was good for only second place on the active list behind

Steve Garvey, who was producing his National League record of 1,207 games of perfect attendance. The season's final standings saw the Phillies finishing in second place behind the St. Louis Cardinals by a few games. In 1983, time was catching up to Rose. During the season, Rose was used in a pinch-hitting role in about 15 games just to keep his playing streak from ending. When Garvey suffered a hand injury in late July, ending his record run of consecutive games, Rose became the major league Iron Man for a second time and, in addition, the oldest player to attain this title. His second time as the Iron Man was brief, lasting just 26 games. On August 24, 1983, Rose's streak ended when he did not play in the Phillies' 5–3 loss to the San Francisco Giants, thus ending his games-played streak at 745 contests. The Phillies' manager, Paul Owens, had planned to use Rose as a pinch hitter in the top of the 10th inning but the Giants' Joel Youngblood hit a two-run homer off the Phillies' Steve Carlton in the bottom of the ninth to win the game for the Giants. By the end of the year, Rose had finished with a career-low .245 average. It looked quite obvious that having missed only two games in nearly 10 years, Rose's batting average was starting to suffer. Due to this, Rose was being used more often in a pinch hitter role and Owens was trying to extend Rose's streak as long as possible without having him in the daily lineup more regularly.

After his streak ended, he finished the year out and played in his final World Series against the Baltimore Orioles. Tied with five other players for most hits in the series with five base knocks, he hit .313 (second highest on the team) but the Phillies were beaten in five games. A few days after the series ended, the Phillies released Rose. In January 1984, he signed to play for the Montreal Expos. His time with Montreal was short lived as he was dealt in mid-August 1984 to his old team, the Reds. He immediately was named player-manager of the Reds, replacing Vern Rapp. Rose continued as an active player with the Reds through 1986 and made his final appearance as a player while pinch-hitting on August 17 in a game against the Padres. During his last three playing years in the majors, he was the National League's oldest active player. He was given his release as a player in November 1986 but continued to serve as the Reds' skipper into the 1989 season when he was dismissed. The reason for his discharge was that Rose had gotten into some serious problems with betting on sporting events, including baseball. When all was said and done, baseball commissioner Bart Giamatti banned Rose from the game for life.

It must be noted that during his long career in major league baseball, Pete Rose led the National League in many statistics categories. These include at-bats (1965, 1972, 1973 and 1977), runs scored (1969 and 1974 through 1976), hits (1965, 1968, 1970, 1972, 1973, 1976 and 1981), doubles (1974 through 1976, 1978 and 1980), batting average (1968, 1969 and 1973), on base percentage (1968 and 1979), and times on base (1965, 1968, 1969, 1973 through 1976, 1979 and 1981). In addition, he led in several categories in fielding at all the different positions he played and the categories included putouts, assists and fielding average. He also established all-time major league records for most times on base (5,929), at-bats (14,053), games played (3,562) and hits (4,256). He holds the National League mark for most career doubles (746, good for second place all-time). Only Hall of Fame member Tris Speaker has more doubles with 792 two-baggers. Also, he played in 16 all-star games and six World Series. It is acknowledged that the numbers he produced on the baseball diamond easily qualify him for induction into baseball's Hall of Fame, but because of his betting problems and the lifetime ban that was issued in 1989, there is an extremely good chance he will never receive the honor. This could change if the present or future baseball commissioner decides to reinstate Rose and make him eligible for Hall of Fame membership.

114. ALFREDO GRIFFIN

Born: October 6, 1957, Santo Domingo, Dominican Republic *Bats*: Switch Hitter *Throws*: Right *Height*: 5 feet, 11 inches *Weight*: 160 *Major league debut*: September 4, 1976 (first game) (Boston at Cleveland [AL]) *Last major league game*: October 3, 1993 (Toronto at Baltimore [AL])

Major league Iron Man from: August 24, 1983, to May 27, 1984 *Consecutive games played*: 392 *Games as major league Iron Man*: 82 (consecutive games 311 through 392) *Team played for during streak*: Toronto Blue Jays (AL) *Primary position played*: Shortstop *Game missed before streak*: September 6, 1981 (Toronto at Chicago) *First game played of streak*: September 7, 1981 (Toronto at Minnesota) *Last game played of streak*: May 27, 1984 (first game) (Cleveland at Toronto) *Game missed to end streak*: May 27, 1984 (second game) (Cleveland at Toronto)

Consecutive Game Streak's Statistical Totals

Year	G	AB	R	H	2B	3B	HR	RBI	BB	SO	AVG	SLG	SB
1981	23	73	1	14	3	1	0	1	4	6	.192	.260	1
1982	162	539	57	130	20	8	1	48	22	48	.241	.314	10
1983	162	528	62	132	22	9	4	47	27	44	.250	.348	8
1984	45	151	16	34	3	1	2	14	2	12	.232	.305	2
Total	392	1291	136	310	48	19	7	110	55	110	.240	.323	21

One of the more reliable shortstops of the 1980s, Alfredo Griffin was a member of four major teams in an 18-year career. Signed by the Cleveland Indians in August 1973, he made his major league debut in early September 1976 in a game at Cleveland against the Boston Red Sox. He put in three seasons with Cleveland, where he played just 31 games and hit .184 (9 for 49) during his time with the Indians. The Tribe traded Griffin to the Toronto Blue Jays in December 1978.

Griffin won the Blue Jays' starting shortstop job from Luis Gomez. In his first full-time season in the big leagues, he played 153 games, hit .287 and led the Blue Jays in at-bats (624), runs (81), hits (179), triples (10) and stolen bases (21). On a negative note, he also led American League shortstops with 36 miscues. After the season, he was voted the league's Rookie of the Year (tied with Minnesota Twins third baseman John Castino). Although the Blue Jays had found a reliable shortstop, it did not prevent them from finishing dead last for the third consecutive season under manager Roy Hartsfield (who would lose his job after the season). The following year (1980), Griffin's batting average dropped over 30 points as he finished with a .254 average, although he again led the team in several statistical categories. He also topped the junior circuit in triples with 15 three-baggers while leading all shortstops in games played (155) and errors (37). As for the Blue Jays, they came in last again for the fourth straight year with a 67–95 record under first-year skipper Bobby Mattick. In his third year with the Jays, Griffin got into 101 contests in a strike-shortened season. He had an awful year offensively, hitting an anemic .209 with just 21 RBI as the Jays kept their tradition alive by being the Eastern Division doormat for a fifth straight year. Griffin's consecutive game streak started on September 7, 1981, in a game at Minnesota when he pinch-hit in the eighth inning. He rebounded in 1982 by lifting his batting average to .241 (an improvement of 32 points) as he appeared in all Blue Jays games at shortstop. Although Bobby Cox took over as the manager, it did not help much as it was just another year for the Blue Jays to finish at the bottom of the standings. For the second straight season, Griffin was in the team's lineup every day in 1983 as he hit .250 and drove home 47 runs. He took over the major league Iron Man honor from Pete Rose on August 24, 1983, when Rose was not used in a Phillies' game. By season's end, Griffin had extended his playing streak to 347 games. The only game he nearly missed that year was the September 11, 1983, contest against the Oakland Athletics in Toronto. He was used as a pinch runner in the bottom of the eighth inning and took over the designated hitter place in the lineup. As for the Blue Jays, they finally escaped the cellar when the team came in fourth place, just nine games behind the division-champion Baltimore Orioles. About two months into the next season, Griffin's time as major league Iron Man ended (after 392 games) during the second game of a double-header against the Indians in Toronto on May 27, 1984. Although he did get into the game when Toronto manager Bobby Cox used him as a pinch runner in the ninth inning (and he eventually scored the game's winning run on a sacrifice fly), a change to major league baseball rules in 1974 (rule 10.24(C)) states that a pinch running appearance alone by a player in a game shall not extend a consecutive playing streak. Due to this rule, his streak was considered officially ended. He did go on to play 22 more consecutive games before actually sitting out an entire contest on June 22, which would have given him 414 consecutive games had that rule not been in effect. Eventually, he would lose his job as the Jays' shortstop to Tony Fernandez and be sent in a trade to the Athletics in December 1984.

The 1985 season found Griffin as Oakland's new shortstop, replacing Tony Phillips. Griffin embarked on another playing streak as he played the entire slate of games for the Athletics in 1985 and 1986 and 23 games into the 1987 season for a stretch of 347 games. This was a team record for the Oakland franchise until it was broken by another Athletic shortstop, Miguel Tejada, in 2002. Griffin stayed in Oakland until he was traded to the Los Angeles Dodgers in December 1987. He put in four years with the Dodgers, including playing shortstop for the 1988 world champions, before returning to the Toronto Blue Jays via free agency in March 1992. He served primarily as a utility infielder in his last two major league seasons. He made token appearances in the 1992 and 1993 World Series while helping the Blue Jays win two consecutive world championship titles. His career came to an end with the conclusion of the 1993 World Series.

115. Dale Murphy

Born: March 12, 1956, Portland, Oregon *Bats*: Right *Throws*: Right *Height*: 6 feet, 4 inches *Weight*: 210 *Major league debut*: September 13, 1976 (second game) (Atlanta at Los Angeles [NL]) *Last major league game*: May 21, 1993 (Colorado at Los Angeles [NL])

Major league Iron Man from: May 27, 1984, to July 9, 1986 *Consecutive games played*: 740 *Games as major league Iron Man*: 362 (consecutive games 379 through 740) *Team played for during streak*: Atlanta Braves (NL) *Primary position played*: Outfield *Game missed before streak*: September 25, 1981 (Cincinnati at Atlanta) *First game played of streak*: September 26, 1981 (Cincinnati at Atlanta) *Last game played of streak*: July 8, 1986 (Atlanta at Philadelphia) *Game missed to end streak*: July 9, 1986 (Atlanta at Philadelphia)

Consecutive Game Streak's Statistical Totals

Year	G	AB	R	H	2B	3B	HR	RBI	BB	SO	AVG	SLG	SB
1981	9	27	4	5	0	0	2	4	5	7	.185	.407	2
1982	162	598	113	168	23	2	36	109	93	134	.281	.507	23
1983	162	589	131	178	24	4	36	121	90	110	.302	.540	30
1984	162	607	94	176	32	8	36	100	79	134	.290	.547	19
1985	162	616	118	185	32	2	37	111	90	141	.300	.539	10
1986	83	311	56	85	15	2	14	36	47	77	.273	.469	4
Total	740	2748	516	797	126	18	161	481	404	603	.290	.525	88

Dale Murphy

One of the most popular players to wear an Atlanta Braves uniform was Dale Murphy. Murphy was a very talented player with a quiet demeanor (he was also a devout Mormon) who played major league ball with the Braves, Philadelphia Phillies and Colorado Rockies in 18 seasons. Drafted by the Braves in the first round (and fifth overall) in the free agent baseball draft in June 1974, he made his major league debut (as a catcher) for the Braves on September 13, 1976, at Los Angeles in a 4–3 Dodgers victory. He had spot duty his first two years in Atlanta as he took in 37 contests behind the plate, hit a respectable .291, belted a couple of homers and drove in 23 runs when given the chance to play.

With the trade of first baseman Willie Montanez to the New York Mets on December 8, 1977, Atlanta had an opening in their infield and Murphy was chosen to take over the first base position. In his first full year in the majors, Murphy impressed the Braves organization by clubbing 23 homers (tied for the team lead with Bob Horner and Jeff Burroughs) and knocking in 79 runners. There was much room for improvement, though, as his batting average was only .226, plus he led the National League's batters with 145 strikeouts. In 1979, a knee injury curtailed his playing time to 104 games but his average did improve 50 points. Braves manager Bobby Cox shifted Murphy to centerfield for the 1980 season. It was this year that Murphy started coming into his own. Although he did lead the league again in strikeouts with 133 whiffs, he finished with 33 homers, 89 RBI and a solid .281 batting average in 156 games. He also made his first of seven appearances in the major leagues' all-star game. In 1981, the Braves lost 55 scheduled games due to a work stoppage. Murphy played in 104 contests, had 13 homers, 50 RBI and a .247 batting average. His consecutive playing streak started when he played the last nine games on the 1981 schedule beginning with the September 26 game, when he pinch-hit for pitcher Gene Garber in the ninth inning against the Cincinnati Reds. The following season (1982), Murphy put together a season that resulted in his being selected the Most Valuable Player in the National League. Besides smacking 36 homers and batting .281, he paced the league hitters with 109 RBI and won his first of five straight Gold Gloves. Although he played the majority of the games in center (115), he also took in 66 games in left and 10 games in right. The only game that year where his streak nearly ended was the Braves' home game on August 19 against the Montreal Expos, when he was used as a pinch hitter in the eighth inning. In addition to Murphy, Atlanta also had a great year as they won the Western Division crown by one game over the Los Angeles Dodgers. Unfortunately, the Braves were swept in the league's championship series by the St. Louis Cardinals in three straight games. Murphy followed up his previous season's performance by repeating as the league MVP in 1983. This selection was justified by his hitting 36 pitches out of the park, batting .302, plus winning the league RBI title (by knocking in 121 runners) for the second straight year and the slugging percentage title (.540). By playing a second consecutive season without missing a game, he stretched his games-played streak to 333 by the end of the 1983 season. His streak nearly ended on July 20 but he was inserted into the lineup defensively in the ninth inning. He also did not start the last game of the season on October 2 but pinch-hit for Brett Butler in the eighth inning of a 4–3 Atlanta victory in San Diego. The Braves came up three games short of repeating as the Western Division champs as they finished in second place behind the Dodgers. Although there was no three-peat for Murphy as the league's MVP in 1984, he did tie the Phillies' Mike Schmidt for the National League's home run title with 36 round-trippers. Additionally, he led the league in extra-base hits (76), total bases (332), repeated as the slugging percentage champion (with .547), and paced the Braves in every major offensive category except stolen bases. He took over the Iron Man title from Toronto's Alfredo Griffin on May 27, 1984, when Griffin was used only as a pinch runner in the second game of a double-header. According to major league rules, this scenario officially ended Griffin's streak because a playing streak cannot be extended by just being used as a pinch runner. By the close of the 1984 season, Murphy's streak stood at 495 straight contests. The Braves again finished runner-up in the West, this time to the San Diego Padres. The 1985 season found the team with a new manager (Eddie Haas) as the previous skipper (Joe Torre) was let go after the end of the 1984 season. Murphy had another superb year by pacing the league in several categories which included most runs (118), times on base (276), walks (90), strikeouts (141) and home runs (37) along with furthering his playing streak to 657 games. The only game he did not play in the outfield was the May 22 game at St. Louis when he pinch-hit for pitcher Bruce Mahler in the eighth inning of a 5–3 loss to the Cardinals. Atlanta dropped to fifth place in the standings as they finished 66–96 under Haas (and later Bobby Wine). The following year, in the top of the third inning of the April 29, 1986, game in Atlanta against the New York Mets, Murphy injured his right palm when his hand got stuck in the seam of the outfield fence. He was taken out of the game and needed nine stitches to close the wound. The next day, he was not in the lineup against the Mets and the streak looked broken. Braves' manager Chuck Tanner decided to use Murphy as a pinch hitter in the fifth inning and he responded by clubbing a home run as the Braves went on to an 8–1 victory over the Mets. The next game, he was back at his normal place in the Braves' lineup. On July 9, 1986, after 740 consecutive appearances, Murphy's streak ended when he was left out of the team lineup for a much-deserved rest. If he had not sat out that game, his streak would have extended to 915 games because he compiled another playing streak of 174 games until he sat out the Braves' in Philadelphia game on July 26, 1987, against the Phillies. He was replaced as Iron Man by the Orioles' Cal Ripken Jr. With this transition to Ripken, the majors would not see another player become an Iron Man until 1998. The offensive numbers Murphy compiled during his game streak were much better when compared to his overall career stats. His performance was at a higher level when he played every day.

After his consecutive game streak ended, Murphy put in nearly five more seasons with the Braves before being traded to the Phillies on August 3, 1990. He spent part of three years with the Phillies before being released after training camp in April 1993. He was quickly picked up by the Rockies that same day. His time in Colorado, however, was brief because after playing 26 games and hitting a measly .143 average, he retired.

116. CAL RIPKEN JR.

Born: August 24, 1960, Havre de Grace, Maryland *Bats*: Right *Throws*: Right *Height*: 6 feet, 4 inches *Weight*: 200 *Major league debut*: August 10, 1981 (Kansas City at Baltimore [AL]) *Last major league game*: October 6, 2001 (Boston at Baltimore [AL])

Major league Iron Man from: July 9, 1986, to September 20, 1998 *Consecutive games played*: 2,632 *Games as major league Iron Man*: 1,947 (consecutive games 686 through 2632) *Team played for during streak*: Baltimore Orioles (AL) *Primary positions played*: Shortstop and third base *Game missed before streak*: May 29, 1982 (second game) (Toronto at Baltimore) *First game played of streak*: May 30, 1982 (Toronto at Baltimore) *Last game played of streak*: September 19, 1998 (New York at Baltimore) *Game missed to end streak*: September 20, 1998 (New York at Baltimore)

Consecutive Game Streak's Statistical Totals

Year	G	AB	R	H	2B	3B	HR	RBI	BB	SO	AVG	SLG	SB
1982	118	447	76	122	23	3	25	73	42	77	.273	.506	3
1983	162	663	121	211	47	2	27	102	58	97	.318	.517	0
1984	162	641	103	195	37	7	27	86	71	89	.304	.510	2
1985	161	642	116	181	32	5	26	110	67	68	.282	.469	2
1986	162	627	98	177	35	1	25	81	70	60	.282	.461	4
1987	162	624	97	157	28	3	27	98	81	77	.252	.436	3
1988	161	575	87	152	25	1	23	81	102	69	.264	.431	2
1989	162	646	80	166	30	0	21	93	57	72	.257	.401	3
1990	161	600	78	150	28	4	21	84	82	66	.250	.415	3
1991	162	650	99	210	46	5	34	114	53	46	.323	.566	6
1992	162	637	73	160	29	1	14	72	64	50	.251	.366	4
1993	162	641	87	165	26	3	24	90	65	58	.257	.420	1
1994	112	444	71	140	19	3	13	75	32	41	.315	.459	1
1995	144	550	71	144	33	2	17	88	52	59	.262	.422	0
1996	163	640	94	178	40	1	26	102	59	78	.278	.466	1
1997	162	615	79	166	30	0	17	84	56	73	.270	.402	1
1998	154	579	63	158	26	1	14	61	50	65	.273	.394	0
Total	2632	10221	1493	2832	534	42	381	1494	1061	1145	.277	.449	36

Cal Ripken Jr. is one of the all-time greatest shortstops that the game has witnessed. He achieved many offensive and defensive milestones for shortstops but he will be most noted for his record-setting 2,632-consecutive-game streak that was achieved over a 16-year period. Born and raised near Baltimore, he was selected by his hometown team in the second round of the free agent draft in June 1978. He stayed with the Orioles for his entire big league career, which lasted 21 seasons. He made his major league debut on August 10, 1981, by pinch running for teammate Ken Singleton in the ninth inning of a 3-2 Baltimore victory over the Kansas City Royals. His initial work in the majors was not much to talk about as he took part in only 23 contests in 1981 and all he showed for it was a minuscule .128 batting average. This performance was no indication of what was to come.

Upon the start of the 1982 season, Ripken took over the third base job from Doug DeCinces (successor to the great Brooks Robinson). The historic streak soon began on May 30, 1982, with an Orioles' home game against the Toronto Blue Jays. Ripken played the first 27 games of the streak at third base. A few days later, in a game at Minnesota, his record of 8,243 consecutive innings played commenced. He would not miss another inning until five years later when he was pulled from the lineup in a lopsided loss to the Blue Jays. Another milestone occurred on July 1, when Orioles skipper Earl Weaver shifted Ripken over to the shortstop position. It would be another 2,243 consecutive games before the Orioles would see a different shortstop on a regular basis. His 28 homers, 93 RBI and a .264 batting average in 160 games earned him the American League's 1982 Rookie of the Year honors. The Orioles finished second in the league's Eastern Division, just one game behind the Milwaukee Brewers. In 1983, the sophomore jinx was not in Ripken's vernacular as he hit .318, clubbed 27 homers, brought in 102 runners and led the junior circuit with 663 at-bats, 211 hits, 47 doubles, 121 runs scored and 76 extra-base hits. He also paced the league's shortstops with 162 games played, 534 assists and 113 double plays. These achievements, along with helping the Orioles capture the Eastern Division, won him the American League's Most Valuable Player award. After escorting the Chicago White Sox out of World Series contention by beating them in four games during the league championship series, the Orioles won the 1983 world championship by defeating the Philadelphia Phillies in five games. Although Ripken was a steady force at short and recorded the final putout in the series, he went only 3 for 18 for a

.167 batting average. The Orioles were baseball's world champions for the first time since the 1970 season. He followed up his MVP season with another solid performance in 1984 as he hit .304, knocked 27 pitches out of the park and drove home 86 runners. In May, he hit for the cycle in a 6–1 Orioles win over Texas. In addition, he set a league record for assists by a shortstop (583) and again led the position holders in games placed (162), putouts (297) and double plays (122). That season, the Orioles fell to fifth place in the division, 19 games out of first place. During the second game of the 1985 season against the Texas Rangers, Ripken injured his left ankle during a third-inning pick-off attempt. He stayed in the game but had x-rays taken after the game to determine the severity of the injury. Fortunately, nothing was broken. He finished with a .282 average, 26 homers and 110 RBI during the 1985 campaign. He again led the league's shortstops in putouts (286) and double plays (123) while stretching his consecutive playing streak to 603 contests. The Orioles finished with an 83–78 record, good for a fourth-place finish in the Eastern Division.

Cal Ripken Jr.: Baseball's all-time Iron Man played for more than 16 years (and 2,632 games) without missing a single contest. He broke Gehrig's record in September 1995 and voluntarily ended the streak three years later on September 20, 1998.

On July 9, 1986, Ripken took over the major league Iron Man title from the Braves' Dale Murphy. It was game 686 of his streak and he would retain the Iron Man title for well over a decade. While he concluded the 1986 season with the streak count at 765 games, he smacked a team-high 25 round-trippers, brought in 81 runners and hit a .282 average for the second straight year. The Orioles, meanwhile, sank to the bottom of the divisional standings by finishing nearly two dozen games behind the Eastern champion Boston Red Sox. After these results, long-time manager Earl Weaver left the team and was replaced as skipper by long-time third base coach Cal Ripken Sr. (Cal's dad) for the 1987 season. On September 14, 1987, Ripken's streak of 8,243 consecutive innings played came to an end when he was pulled in the eighth inning of an 18–3 loss to the Blue Jays. In this game, Toronto set a major league record by belting 10 home runs. Ripken's final stats for 1987 season saw his hitting drop 30 points (down to a .252 average) but he still clubbed 27 homers and knocked in a team-high 98 runs. With the significant drop in his batting average and the Orioles' sixth-place finish (with a 67-95 won-loss record), some critics of the streak were calling for Cal to take an occasional rest. In the fielding department, he led the shortstops with 162 games played and 480 assists.

The following year (1988), the Orioles got off to a horrible start. Six games into the season, Cal Sr. was fired as manager and replaced by Hall of Famer Frank Robinson. The move made to replace Cal Sr. as manager did not sit well with Cal Jr. The change also had no effect on the team as they lost an amazing 21 straight games before achieving their first victory of the season. The June 25, 1988, game against the Red Sox saw him play his 1,000th consecutive contest, just the sixth player in major league history to reach that figure. Obviously, the horrendous start at the beginning of the season resulted in another cellar-dwelling finish for the Orioles. Ripken upped his average a little by hitting .264 along with having 23 homers and driving in 81 runners. During the course of the 1989 season, he appeared in his 1,208th straight contest in the middle of August and took over third place on the all-time list of consecutive games by passing the National League record holder, Steve Garvey. Ripken finished with a .257 average, 21 homers and a team-high 93 RBI as the Orioles made immense improvements under Robinson's guidance. The club made a 33-game turnaround and just missed winning the junior circuit's Eastern Division pennant by finishing two games behind the Blue Jays. Ripken further moved up the all-time list of consecutive game holders when he passed Everett Scott for second place (behind Lou Gehrig) on June 12, 1990. Although Ripken hit a then career-low .250 average, he did lead the offensive charge by pacing the Orioles in homers (21), runs (78) and RBI (84). Defensively, he was absolutely superb as he topped the American League's shortstops with 161 games played and a .996 fielding average; he committed his first error on April 13 and made just three miscues all year. Additionally, he put together fielding streaks of 95 errorless games and 431 errorless chances that set records for shortstops. When the 1990 season concluded, the Orioles had reverted to their losing ways as they finished in fifth place with a 76–85 record and a dozen games behind the first-place Red Sox. His streak stood at 1,411 games when the season closed. He had below-average numbers in offensive productivity and critics were again raising the possibility that Ripken needed to sit down for the betterment of the team and to enhance his performance on the diamond. He responded in 1991 by hitting a three-run homer in the all-star game to lead the American Leaguers to a 4–2 victory that resulted in his being selected the game's MVP. He proved he could still do the job by raising his batting average to .323, crushing 34 home runs and bringing home 114 runners. He also led the league in total bases (368) and extra-base hits (85) along with leading the Orioles in just about every major offensive category. His performance that year won him his second league MVP honor. Additionally, he picked up his first Gold Glove as he paced the shortstops again in games played, putouts, assists, double plays and fielding average. Despite Ripken's excellent year, the Orioles went through a managerial change with Robinson being replaced in May by Johnny Oates. The change did not help because Baltimore finished in next-to-last place with a 67–95 record. After having set career highs in several categories the previous season, his batting average and production numbers sunk close to career lows in 1992 as he compiled a .251 average, 14 homers and 72 RBI. He was again starting to hear cries to sit down and get the streak behind him but the only situation that threatened the streak in 1992 was when he twisted his ankle while running out a double in the September 11 game against the Milwaukee Brewers. He did not miss any action but the Orioles took the precautionary step of recalling Manny Alexander from the minors in case the situation worsened. Ripken picked up his second straight Gold Glove as he again compiled top totals among American League shortstops in games played, putouts and double plays. A bright spot was that even though he had a bad year hitting, the team responded to Oates' guidance by putting an 89–73 record together, good for a third-place finish and only seven games off the divisional lead. During the 1,790 game of the streak, a situation occurred that came the closest to ending Ripken's streak. In a game with the Seattle Mariners on June 6, 1993, he twisted his right knee during a brawl when his spikes got caught in the grass. The next day his knee was swollen but Ripken fought through the pain and played that night against Oakland. In mid-July, he clubbed his 278th career homer, setting a new major league record (a mark since broken) for shortstops. He led the American League's shortstops in games played for the ninth occasion and in assists for the seventh time. His offensive numbers improved slightly in 1993 as he hit .257, smacked 24 round-trippers and topped the team with 90 RBI. The Orioles showed no progress toward challenging for the divisional title as they came in with another third-place finish. The 1994 season was basically a washout as the players went out on strike in mid-August. About a month later, the team owners decided to cancel the rest of the season along with the World Series. In a game at Minnesota on August 1, he became just the second player to hit the 2,000-consecutive-game mark. Ripken was having a decent year with a .315 average and 75 RBI in 112 games when the strike stopped all play. Additionally, he again was the leader in games played, double plays and fielding average for all American League shortstops. When the work stoppage occurred, he had extended his streak to 2,009 games (just 121 games short of the all-time mark held by the great Lou Gehrig).

As the 1995 season approached, the strike continued. There was talk that the owners would employ replacement players to get the season started. This situation put Ripken's streak into jeopardy if replacement players were used. Orioles' owner Peter Angelos put a stop to that scenario by stating that Baltimore would not use replacement players and would forfeit any games until the striking players returned. Angelos took great pride that an Oriole was on the verge of breaking Lou Gehrig's all-time consecutive game streak and made this decision to protect Ripken's streak. The strike soon ended, the players returned in late April to start play and worries that the streak might be over were ended. Close to 20 regular season games were lost due to the strike. On September 5, 1995, before a packed house at Camden Yards in Baltimore, Ripken tied Gehrig at the 2,130-consecutive-game mark as the Orioles defeated the California Angels 8–0. He provided some of the offense by hitting a homer in the sixth inning. The next night, as a nationwide audience took in the game, a new major league record of most consecutive games played was established when the top of the fifth inning ended and the game became official. The game was stopped for over 20 minutes as Ripken took a victory lap around the field. Once the game resumed, Ripken was one of the game's heroes as he homered in the fourth inning and the Orioles went on to defeat the Angels 4–2. Withstanding the cries of critics to take the bench for so long, Ripken finally prevailed to set the new mark. He completed the year with 2,153 straight games (and counting) along with hitting .262, clubbing 17 homers and bringing home 88 runners as Baltimore came in third place, 15 games behind the Red Sox for the Eastern Division title. He again led the junior circuit shortstops in fielding (.989) for the fourth time in his career along with having league highs in games played (144) and double plays (100). In late May 1996, he passed the 2,200-game mark. A couple of nights later, he had a career game in Seattle by hitting three homers and driving in eight runs as the Orioles defeated the Mariners 12–8. A few weeks later, on June 14, he broke the world record for most consecutive games by participating in his 2,216th straight contest. The previous record holder was Japan's Sachio Kinugasa, who played for the Hiroshima Carp and compiled a 2,215-game streak from late in the 1970 season till his retirement after the 1987 campaign. A few weeks later, there was a situation that nearly put Ripken out of the lineup. During a team photo shoot for the 1996 American League all-star squad, Ripken suffered a broken nose when he was accidentally hit by a forearm of an all-star teammate. Chicago pitcher Roberto Hernandez had lost his footing, fell and hit Ripken in the face on the way down. A true Iron Man, Ripken did not miss any action and made his scheduled start in the all-star game. Ripken's streak of consecutive games at shortstop came to an end on July 15 when he was replaced after 2,216 games by Manny Alexander. Alexander lasted just six games at the shortstop spot before Ripken returned to the position. Ripken, in the interim, had made the shift back to his original position at third base. His final stats for the 1996 season were a .278 average, 26 homers and 102 RBI. The Orioles made the playoffs as the wild card by finishing in second place behind the Yankees by four games. Baltimore defeated the Cleveland Indians in four games in a best-of-five series as Ripken hit a sparkling .444 along with eight hits and three doubles. Facing the Yankees for the league championship, the Orioles were beaten in five games as Ripken went 5 for 20 for a .250 average. With the acquisition of Mike Bordick (from Oakland) during the 1996 off-season, Ripken made the permanent switch back to third base. Playing the full slate of scheduled games in 1997 for the final time in his career, he proved he could still produce the numbers by batting .270, hitting 17 homers and driving in 84 runners while helping the Orioles take first place over the Yankees by two games. In the division series against the Mariners, Ripken hit .438 as he went 7 for 16 and led the Orioles to victory in four games. He followed up that performance with a .348 average against the Indians in the league championship series but the Orioles were defeated in six games by the Tribe. In the first month of the 1998 season, Ripken hit the 2,500-consecutive-game milestone in an Orioles' home game against the Athletics. With only about a week left in the 1998 season, Ripken informed Orioles manager Ray Miller that he wanted to sit out the September 20 game against the Yankees. The game was the season's final home game for Baltimore and he desired to have the streak end where it started — in front of the family, friends and fans that he truly cherished. During the game, several of his teammates urged him to take the field, but his decision was final and baseball's greatest consecutive games streak of all time had finally come to an end. He destroyed Gehrig's previous "unbeatable" record by 502 games but it is safe to say that this is a record that probably never will be broken because it would take over 16 straight seasons (without missing a game) for a player to come close to challenging it. He was major league baseball's Iron Man from July 1986 through September 1998 — a span of over 12 seasons!

After his streak ended, Ripken played three more seasons in Baltimore before retiring after the 2001 season. During those last three years, he spent several tours on the disabled list. After nearly two decades without missing a game, the fragility of getting older finally caught up to Ripken. He still produced some good numbers offensively and in fact was selected the MVP in the 2001 all-star game. This selection was justified as he hit a homer and contributed to the American League's 4–1 victory. As for his future in baseball, though, one thing is guaranteed — he will be elected to baseball's Hall of Fame in his first year of eligibility.

117. Albert Belle

Born: August 25, 1966, Shreveport, Louisiana *Bats*: Right *Throws*: Right *Height*: 6 feet, 1 inch *Weight*: 190 *Major league debut*: July 15, 1989 (Texas at Cleveland [AL]) *Last major league game*: October 1, 2000 (New York at Baltimore [AL])

Major league Iron Man from: September 20, 1998, to June 11, 1999 *Consecutive games played*: 392 *Games as major league Iron Man*: 66 (consecutive games 327 through 392) *Teams played for during streak*: Cleveland Indians (AL) (1996), Chicago White Sox (AL) (1997–1998), and Baltimore Orioles (AL) (1999) *Primary position played*: Outfield *Game missed before streak*: September 18, 1996 (Cleveland at Chicago) *First game played of streak*: September 19, 1996 (Kansas City at Cleveland) *Last game played of streak*: June 9, 1999 (Baltimore (AL) at Florida [NL]) *Game missed to end streak*: June 11, 1999 (Baltimore (AL) at Atlanta [NL])

Consecutive Game Streak's Statistical Totals

Year	G	AB	R	H	2B	3B	HR	RBI	BB	SO	AVG	SLG	SB
1996	10	37	8	14	4	0	2	7	4	3	.378	.649	1
1997	161	634	90	174	45	1	30	116	53	105	.274	.491	4
1998	163	609	113	200	48	2	49	152	81	84	.328	.655	6
1999	58	213	33	52	3	1	10	35	47	30	.244	.408	7
Total	392	1493	244	440	100	4	91	310	185	222	.295	.550	18

Albert Belle was one of the major league's most feared power hitters during the 1990s. When he started his career he was known as Joey Belle, but he changed his name shortly thereafter to the more formal Albert Belle. During his career, he played for the Cleveland Indians from 1989 to 1996, the Chicago White Sox in 1997 and 1998 and the Baltimore Orioles in 1999 and 2000. Originally selected by the Indians in the second round of the free agent draft in June 1987, he spent time in the minors before he was called up to the parent club in July 1989. He made his big league debut on July 15 by going 1 for 4 in a 7–1 Indians victory. He finished the year playing in 62 games and hitting an unimpressive .225 along with seven homers and knocking in 37 runners. After playing a handful of games in 1990, he finally made his present position permanent in 1991 by taking over the left field spot on the Indians' roster. That first full season in the majors, Belle impressed Cleveland's management by hitting 28 of the team's 79 round-trippers, bringing home 95 runs (both of which were team highs) and hit for a .282 batting average.

In 1992, Cleveland manager Mike Hargrove decided to use Belle more as a designated hitter. Although his hitting fell over 20 points to a .260 average, he still paced all Indians hitters with 34 homers and 112 RBI. Returning to left field slot in 1993, he continued producing the ever-improving big numbers by leading the American League in RBI (129) and sacrifice flies (14) along with his blasting 38 homers and hitting for a .290 average. In the strike-shortened season of 1994, Belle came close to achieving the Triple Crown even though he did not lead the league in any of the three key categories. Belle finished just behind the Yankees' Paul O'Neill (.359) in batting as he improved his hitting to .357. He also had 36 homers and knocked in 101 runners. Belle did lead the league with 294 total bases and 73 extra-base hits. His career year came in 1995 when he led the junior circuit's batters in home runs (50) and RBI (126) but missed out on the Triple Crown by finishing nearly 40 points (.317) behind Seattle Mariners' Edgar Martinez' league-leading .356 average. Belle also topped the league with a .690 slugging percentage, 121 runs scored, 52 doubles, 377 total bases and 103 extra-base hits. His performance that season was the driving force in helping the Indians win the American League's Central Division crown. In the playoffs, the Indians swept the Boston Red Sox in three games and then beat the Mariners in six games to claim the league title. In their first World Series appearance since 1954, the Indians took on the Atlanta Braves. The series was close but Atlanta defeated Cleveland in six games. Belle went 4 for 17 for a .235 and had two of the five Cleveland homers that were hit in the series. He followed up that year's performance with another big year in 1996. Hitting .311, clubbing 48 homers and driving in a league-high 148 runners, he was the offensive leader who drove the Indians to another Central Division championship. With 10 games left on the 1996 schedule, he started his consecutive-games-played streak on September 19 during an Indians home contest against the Kansas City Royals. In the playoffs, Cleveland was eliminated by the Baltimore Orioles in four games as Belle only hit .200 but he did smack two homers and led the series with six RBI. After the season, he became a free agent and left Cleveland when he signed a contract with the Chicago White Sox that made him the highest-paid player in the game over the next four seasons.

In his first season with the White Sox, Belle had a relatively off year. His batting average dipped to .274 and he hit only 30 homers. He did prove to be a clutch hitter by driving in 116 runners. The club came in second place behind his old team, Cleveland, for the division title. He rebounded in 1998 by coming in with 49 homers, 200 hits, a .328 batting average and a career high in RBI by driving home 152 runners. This was good for second place in the American League behind the Texas Rangers' Juan Gonzalez, who finished with 157 RBI. When Ripken's all-time 2,632 games played streak ended, Belle became the reigning Iron Man on September 20, 1998 with 327 consecutive games played. Belle paced the White Sox in many offensive categories and helped the team finish in second place in the league's Central Division even though the club finished with an 80–82 record. After the 1998 season, he filed for free agency again and signed a contract to play for the Orioles. With the Orioles already having B. J. Surhoff in left and Brady Anderson in center, Belle wound up playing right field for Baltimore. It must be noted that it was rather amazing that Belle put together a long-enough games-played streak to be baseball's Iron Man. The surly manner that he displayed at times to reporters, fans or other players often resulted in his getting into trouble with his manager or the league and getting suspended or reprimanded. This type of situation is what brought his Iron Man streak to a conclusion. During the ninth inning of the June 9, 1999, game against the Florida Marlins, he got into a shouting match with his manager, Ray Miller, for failing to run out a grounder. The next Orioles' game, June 11 against the Braves, Miller benched Belle for insubordination, ending his 392-games-played streak. Ironically, Belle did not miss another game until the August 27, 2000, game in Baltimore against the Tampa Bay Devil Rays. This would have extended his streak to 625 contests if Miller had not taken disciplinary action against Belle. Belle's first year in Baltimore saw him hit .297 while leading the Orioles in home runs (37) and runs batted in (117). The club finished fourth, 20 games behind the American League Eastern Division champion New York Yankees.

Belle played only one more season in the majors. He hit just 23 homers (his lowest total since he became a regular player in the early 1990s) but still drove in 103 runners and attained a .281 batting average. His baseball career came to an abrupt end after the 2000 season when a severe medical condition involving his hip joints made it impossible for him to play baseball effectively and doctors advised him to hang up his spikes.

118. Vinny Castilla

Born: July 4, 1967, Oaxaca, Mexico *Bats*: Right *Throws*: Right *Height*: 6 feet, 1 inch *Weight*: 175 *Major league debut*: September 1, 1991 (Atlanta at Philadelphia [NL]) *Last major league game*: (still active)
Major league Iron Man from: June 11, 1999, to June 15, 1999 *Consecutive games played*: 307 *Games as major league Iron Man*: 4 (consecutive games 304 through 307) *Team played for during streak*: Colorado Rockies (NL) *Primary position played*: Third base *Game missed before streak*: June 25, 1997 (Colorado at Los Angeles) *First game played of streak*: June 26, 1997 (San Francisco at Colorado) *Last game played of streak*: June 14, 1999 (San Francisco at Colorado) *Game missed to end streak*: June 15, 1999 (San Francisco at Colorado)

Consecutive Game Streak's Statistical Totals

Year	G	AB	R	H	2B	3B	HR	RBI	BB	SO	AVG	SLG	SB
1997	85	329	48	103	15	0	21	55	20	64	.313	.550	0
1998	162	645	108	206	28	4	46	144	40	89	.319	.589	5
1999	60	228	31	62	11	0	12	36	25	25	.272	.478	1
Total	307	1202	187	371	54	4	79	235	85	178	.309	.557	6

One of the more reliable third basemen of recent times who also could hit for power, Vinny Castilla has played in the majors since the 1991 season with five teams. He started his professional baseball career by playing in the Mexican League for three years. In March 1990, he was sold to the Atlanta Braves. Working his way up through the Braves' farm system, he got called up for a look during the last month of the 1991 season. He made his big league appearance as a ninth-inning defensive replacement at shortstop in a game against the Philadelphia Phillies on September 1, 1991. By the end of the year, he saw only limited duty in a dozen games, mainly making token appearances. He spent the following year (1992) in the International League with Richmond except for another brief call-up to the Braves.

With the National League expanding for the 1993 season, Castilla was chosen in the second round of the expansion draft by the new senior circuit team, the Colorado Rockies. He finally found a permanent home with a major league club as the Rockies used him at shortstop. He appeared in 105 games and although he was on the disabled list for a while, he proved (when given the chance) that he could handle major league pitching by hitting .255 along with contributing nine homers and 30 RBI. During the 1994 season he was shuttled between Colorado and the farm team in Colorado Springs. Playing in just 52 games at various infield positions, he finished the year going 43 for 130 for a rather impressive .331 average. With Charlie Hayes going off to the Phillies, Castilla took over the third base job in 1995 on a permanent basis. This turned out to be his breakout year as he clobbered 32 homers, drove in 90 runners and finished with a .309 batting average. He helped lead the Rockies to their first post-season appearance as the club finished second to the Los Angeles Dodgers in the West and their record qualified them for the wild card spot. In spite of the Rockies being eliminated by the Braves in four games, Castilla had an awesome series, going 7 for 15 and tying all series players with three home runs and six RBI. He and Dante Bichette were the Rockies' MVPs in the series. Missing just two contests the following season (1996), Castilla hit .304 and improved his offensive production by slamming 40 round-trippers and driving home 113 runs as the Rockies finished in third place, just eight games out of the divisional top spot. In 1997, to show how consistent he had become at the plate, he produced exactly the same statistical numbers in batting average, homers and RBI as he did during the previous year. He started his consecutive game streak during a Rockies' home game on June 26, 1997, against the San Francisco Giants. The only game he did not start the rest of the season was the last game on the schedule when he made a pinch-hitting appearance. The Rockies finished in third place for the second straight year with the same won-lost record as the previous year and were seven games behind the division-pacesetting San Francisco Giants. Castilla had a career year in 1998 by playing all 162 games, hitting .319 plus leading the Rockies with 46 home runs and 144 RBI. He came in third in RBI behind the Cubs' Sammy Sosa (158) and Cards' Mark McGwire (147) during the year of their famous successful home run pursuit of Roger Maris' all-time home run mark. Unfortunately, all the runs Castilla produced for the Rockies did not help them too much in the standings as they finished 77–85, good for fourth place in their division. Starting the 1999 season with a 247 game-playing-streak, he became the major league Iron Man on June 11, 1999, when Baltimore's Albert Belle was benched by the Orioles' manager. Castilla's reign as Iron Man lasted only four games as Rockies' skipper Jim Leyland rested his third baseman on June 15, ending Castilla's consecutive playing streak at 307 contests. He completed the year with a .275 average, 33 homers and produced 102 runs as the Rockies finished dead last in the Western Division with a 72–90 record.

After the 1999 season, Castilla was traded by the Rockies to the Tampa Bay Devil Rays. He played in Tampa Bay for parts of two seasons. Early in the second season, the Devil Rays were not impressed with his play and released him on May 10, 2001. A few days later, he was picked up by the Houston Astros. He finished the year in Houston with some semblance of his previous production by knocking 23 pitches out of the park and driving in 82 runners. After the 2001 season, he became a free agent and signed on with his original team, the Atlanta Braves. He put in a couple of seasons with the Braves before going the free agent route again and hooking up with the Rockies for another tour. It is obvious that playing in Colorado agreed with Castilla, because his performance returned to that of his previous days in Colorado as he smacked 35 homers (most since the 1998 season) and drove in 131 runs (second best careerwise). Because his 2004 season was so productive, Castilla might have a few more good years left in him, despite turning 37 years old. During the 2004 off-season, he signed a free agent contract to play with the Washington Nationals (formerly the Montreal Expos) for the 2005 season. Castilla's 2005 performance was a bit disappointing for the Nationals as his home run and RBI totals fell off terribly as was evidenced by his clubbing just a dozen pitches out of the park and driving home only 66 runners.

119. B.J. Surhoff

Born: August 4, 1964, Bronx, New York *Bats*: Left *Throws*: Right *Height*: 6 feet, 1 inch *Weight*: 185 *Major league debut*: April 8, 1987 (Boston at Milwaukee [AL]) *Last major league game*: (still active)

Major league Iron Man from: June 15, 1999, to July 3, 1999; July 3, 1999, to July 5, 1999 (tied with Johnny Damon); July 5, 1999, to August 20, 1999; August 20, 1999, to August 21, 1999 (tied with Johnny Damon); August 21, 1999, to August 30, 1999; August 30, 1999, to September 6, 1999 (tied with Johnny Damon); September 6, 1999, to August 21, 2000 *Consecutive games played*: 445 *Games as major league Iron Man*: 221 (consecutive games 225 through 240, consecutive games and 241 and 242 [tied with Damon], consecutive games 243 through 281, consecutive games 282 and 283 [tied with Damon], consecutive games 284 through 291, consecutive games 292 through 298 [tied with Damon], consecutive games 299 through 445) *Teams played for during streak*: Baltimore Orioles (AL) (1998–2000) and Atlanta Braves (NL) (2000) *Primary position played*: Outfield *Game missed before streak*: September 28, 1997 (Baltimore at Milwaukee) *First game played of streak*: March 31, 1998 (Kansas City at Baltimore) *Last game played of streak*: August 20, 2000 (Atlanta at San Francisco) *Game missed to end streak*: August 21, 2000 (Atlanta at Colorado)

Consecutive Game Streak's Statistical Totals

Year	G	AB	R	H	2B	3B	HR	RBI	BB	SO	AVG	SLG	SB
1998	162	573	79	160	34	1	22	92	49	81	.279	.457	9
1999	162	673	104	207	38	1	28	107	43	78	.308	.492	5
2000	121	476	61	137	31	1	14	61	35	51	.288	.445	7
Total	445	1722	244	504	103	3	64	260	127	210	.293	.467	21

B.J. Surhoff is a second-generation professional athlete. His father played in the National Basketball Association back in the 1950s and his brother, Rich, pitched in a handful of games for the Philadelphia Phillies and Texas Rangers during the 1985 season. Surhoff has played in the majors for 19 seasons with just three teams. He originally was drafted by the New York Yankees during the 1982 free agent draft but never signed a contract with the Bronx Bombers. Instead, he opted to play ball for the United States in the 1984 Olympics. He was chosen again in the draft (this time the first overall pick) in 1985 by the Milwaukee Brewers. Surhoff played a season each in the Midwest and Pacific Coast leagues before making the Brewers' roster for the 1987 season. He debuted in the big leagues in a Milwaukee home game on April

8, 1987, against the Boston Red Sox. Primarily sharing the catching duties with teammate Bill Schroeder, Surhoff played 115 contests during his rookie season and hit for a .299 average along with blasting seven homers and driving in 58 runs.

Surhoff spent nine years in a Brewers uniform, playing a variety of positions, before being granted free agency in November 1995. Six weeks later, he signed a contract to play for the Baltimore Orioles. Having used several players at third base in 1995, the Orioles needed a stabilizing presence at the hot corner. With the acquisition of Surhoff, the team found a player who could play just about anywhere. The decision was made to use him at the third base spot. He filled in capably by posting what were then his career highs in home runs (21) and RBI (82) as he helped the Orioles qualify for the playoffs by finishing in second place behind the Yankees in the Eastern Division. The following year (1997), he made another adjustment. With the departure of outfielder Bobby Bonilla and the acquisition of shortstop Mike Bordick, the Orioles shifted Cal Ripken to third base and sent Surhoff to the outfield as the team's regular left fielder. He responded with another solid year by hitting .284, parking 18 pitches and bringing home 88 runners. The Orioles won the 1997 Eastern Divisional championship but lost the league championship series to the Cleveland Indians in six games.

Because he sat out of the final 1997 Orioles' regular season game, Surhoff's consecutive playing streak started with the 1998 season opener in Baltimore against the Kansas City Royals on March 31, 1998. He appeared in all 162 games in 1998 and was in the team's starting lineup except for about 15 contests. In those instances, rookie manager Ray Miller got Surhoff into the game as a pinch hitter. Playing every day did not affect his on-field performance as he contributed 22 home runs, 92 RBI and a .279 average to the Orioles' offense. The Orioles came in a dismal fourth with a 79–83 record and were 35 games behind the division-leading Yankees. On June 15, 1999, Surhoff became the sport's new active leader in most consecutive games with a streak of only 225 games played. Although he had the longest active playing streak, Surhoff was in close competition for the title with Kansas City Royals' Johnny Damon. In fact, between July 3 and September 6, there were three occasions (and a total of 11 games) that both players were tied for the lead in consecutive games played. When Damon's streak ended because of an injury during the second week of September, Surhoff no longer had a close competitor for the major league Iron Man honor. He had an awesome year offensively by hitting .308 and amassing career highs in hits (207), doubles (38), homers (28) and RBI (107). Additionally, he led the American League in at-bats (673) and posted a 1.000 fielding average as he played an error-free left field during the 1999 season. His Iron Man streak was still intact when he was traded to the Atlanta Braves on July 31, 2000. The streak came to an end three weeks later when after 445 games, Braves manager Bobby Cox sat him out on August 21, 2000, because of the bruised ribs Surhoff suffered from a pitched ball a few games earlier.

After his streak ended, Surhoff played in Atlanta for a couple of years. After the 2002 season, he again chose the free agent route and returned to the Orioles. Playing the last three years in Baltimore, he has continued to perform at a consistent level by hitting around .300 each season, although in 2005 he was used primarily as an extra outfielder or to fill in occasionally at first base.

120. JOHNNY DAMON

Born: November 5, 1973, Fort Riley, Kansas *Bats*: Left *Throws*: Left *Height*: 6 feet *Weight*: 175
Major league debut: August 12, 1995 (Seattle at Kansas City [AL]) *Last major league game*: (still active)

Johnny Damon

Major league Iron Man from: July 3, 1999, to July 5, 1999 (tied with B.J. Surhoff); August 20, 1999, to August 21, 1999 (tied with B.J. Surhoff); August 30, 1999, to September 6, 1999 (tied with B.J. Surhoff) *Consecutive games played*: 305 *Games as major league Iron Man*: 11 (consecutive games 241 and 242 [tied with Surhoff], consecutive games 282 and 283 [tied with Surhoff], consecutive games 292 through 298 [tied with Surhoff] *Team played for during streak*: Kansas City Royals (AL) *Primary position played*: Outfield *Game missed before streak*: September 28, 1997 (Kansas City at Chicago) *First game played of streak*: March 31, 1998 (Kansas City at Baltimore) *Last game played of streak*: September 14, 1999 (first game) (Anaheim at Kansas City) *Game missed to end streak*: September 14, 1999 (second game) (Anaheim at Kansas City)

Consecutive Game Streak's Statistical Totals

Year	G	AB	R	H	2B	3B	HR	RBI	BB	SO	AVG	SLG	SB
1998	161	642	104	178	30	10	18	66	58	84	.277	.439	26
1999	144	583	100	179	39	9	14	77	67	50	.307	.477	36
Total	305	1225	204	357	69	19	32	143	125	134	.291	.457	62

Johnny Damon is an outfielder with a relatively weak throwing arm who has made up for this deficiency with his blazing speed. He has played in the majors for the last 11 seasons with the Kansas City Royals, Oakland Athletics and Boston Red Sox. Chosen by Kansas City in the June 1992 supplemental player draft, he spent a couple of years in the minors preparing himself for the day he would make the Royals' roster. This occurred in the summer of 1995 when he was called up from Wichita of the Texas League and made his debut on August 12 in Kansas City against the Seattle Mariners. At that point, he took over the job of patrolling center field for the Royals for the rest of the season. He took in 47 games during his rookie campaign and went 53 for 188 for a .282 average.

Over the next two years, he proved he could handle major league pitching by hitting over .270 each season along with providing a quality presence in the Royals' outfield. Designated the team's center fielder for the 1998 season, he started his consecutive-games-played streak on March 31. Playing in all 161 contests on the team's schedule (in ten games he was not in the starting lineup but was inserted in the late innings as a pinch hitter or defensive replacement), he led the Royals in at-bats, runs scored and doubles along with hitting .277 and smacking an impressive 18 homers as the Royals finished in third place in the American League's Central Division, nearly 20 games behind the first-place Cleveland Indians. The following season (1999), Royals manager Tony Muser decided to go with rookie Carlos Beltran in center field and shifted Damon over to left field. When the Orioles' B.J. Surhoff became baseball's reigning Iron Man in mid-June 1999, Damon was just a couple of games behind him in consecutive games. On July 3, Damon caught up to Surhoff and they stayed tied through July 5. Damon tied him on two other occasions (August 20 and 21 and August 30 through September 6). Even though he was not the Iron Man anymore, his games-played streak continued through to September 14 when it ended after 305 straight contests. He suffered an injury during the first game of a double-header against the Anaheim Angels that ended his streak. He was out of the Royals' lineup the rest of the season except for his pinch runner appearance in the team's final game that year. He finished with a .307 batting average. He also clubbed 14 homers and drove home 77 runners in 145 games. His playing every day did not affect Damon's statistics, but the club did not benefit from it as they won 64 and lost 97 while finishing just ahead of the Minnesota Twins, who had placed dead last in the Central Division.

The next year (2000), he had his best year with the Royals by leading the American League in runs scored (136) and stolen bases (46). He had a career-best .327 average and his 214 hits were good for second place in the league behind California's Darin Erstad, who led the league with 240 base knocks. He also parked 16 homers and drove in an amazing 88 runners (quite a high total for a leadoff hitter). Although he produced very impressive offensive statistics, this did not prevent the Royals from trading him to the Athletics in January 2001. Rotating again between left and center field for the Athletics in 2001, Damon's numbers dropped off dramatically as his batting average fell to .256 and his RBI total dropped to 49 runs. After the season, he filed for free agency and signed a contract with the Red Sox in December 2001. Since his signing with Boston, he has put together four solid seasons as the team's center fielder. He also helped the Red Sox finish in second place each year in the American League Eastern Division behind the New York Yankees. During the 2004 season, he hit .304 and achieved career highs in homers (20) and RBI (94). In the league championship series against the Yankees, he hit two homers (one a grand slam) in the Red Sox's 10–3 victory in the seventh and deciding game of the championship series. Facing the St. Louis Cardinals in the World Series, he was one of the key players to help the Boston Red Sox win their first world baseball championship in 86 years as the club swept the Cardinals in four games and ended the Curse of the Bambino.

Although Damon's run-producing numbers dropped off in 2005, his batting average improved a dozen points (.316) as he again helped the Red Sox make it to the postseason. Unfortunately, Boston failed to repeat as world champions as they were swept in three games by the Chicago White Sox in the first round of the playoffs.

121. Sammy Sosa

Born: November 12, 1968, San Pedro de Macoris, Dominican Republic *Bats*: Right *Throws*: Right *Height*: 6 feet *Weight*: 165 *Major league debut*: June 16, 1989 (Texas at New York [AL]) *Last major league game*: (still active)

Major league Iron Man from: August 21, 2000, to September 19, 2000 *Consecutive games played*: 388 *Games as major league Iron Man*: 28 (consecutive games 361 through 388) *Team played for during streak*: Chicago Cubs (NL) *Primary position played*: Outfield *Game missed before streak*: July 5, 1998 (Pittsburgh at Chicago) *First game played of streak*: July 9, 1998 (Chicago at Milwaukee) *Last game played of streak*: September 18, 2000 (Chicago at Milwaukee) *Game missed to end streak*: September 19, 2000 (Chicago at Milwaukee)

Consecutive Game Streak's Statistical Totals

Year	G	AB	R	H	2B	3B	HR	RBI	BB	SO	AVG	SLG	SB
1998	76	310	67	90	5	0	33	77	38	91	.290	.626	8
1999	162	625	114	180	24	2	63	141	78	171	.288	.635	7
2000	150	579	103	185	36	1	50	136	88	160	.320	.644	7
Total	388	1514	284	455	65	3	146	354	204	422	.301	.637	22

One of the great power hitters of modern times, Sammy Sosa originally was thought to be a mediocre player with plenty of speed and the tendency to hit for power on occasion. He originally was signed as a nondrafted free agent by the Texas Rangers in the summer of 1985. Working his way up through the Rangers' minor league system, he made his major league debut in his fourth year of professional ball on June 16, 1989, at Yankee Stadium in an 8–3 New York victory over the Rangers. Ironically, in this debut, he batted leadoff. This fact alone would indicate that hitting home runs was not what his team expected of him. Later that month, he hit his first career homer against future Hall of Fame pitcher Roger Clemens. About six weeks after his debut game, the Rangers traded Sosa to the Chicago White Sox. He spent parts of three rather unimpressive seasons in a White Sox uniform before being shipped off to the crosstown rival Chicago Cubs just before the start of the 1992 season.

Before coming to play at Wrigley Field, the most circuit clouts Sosa ever hit in a professional season was 15 homers (with the White Sox in 1990). The first season (1992) he spent with the Cubs was so injury plagued that he got into the lineup for only 67 contests. In 1993, he nearly matched his home run total for all previous major league seasons (37) when he knocked 33 pitches out of the park as he finished with a .261 average and 93 RBI. During the strike-shortened 1994 season, he took over the Cubs' right field position on a regular basis. He finished that year with 25 home runs, along with hitting at or above the .300 level for the first time. Over the next three seasons, he continued his consistent power display by hitting 112 homers. He also proved quite durable by not missing a single contest during the 1995 and 1997 campaigns. Any consecutive-game stretch he put together during those years did not matter as far as becoming the Iron Man because Cal Ripken Jr. was still in the midst of playing his 2,632-game record-shattering streak.

His performance during the 1998 made Sosa a household name in the United States. He and the St. Louis Cardinals' Mark McGwire were making serious runs at baseball's all-time single-season mark of 61 home runs held by the Yankees' Roger Maris. Sosa had one of the greatest months a batter ever had in June 1998 when he set the major league mark for most home runs in a single month with 20 clouts. Just before that year's all-star game, he missed a game when he suffered a minor injury. This injury caused him to skip the midseason classic. He did not miss another regular season game that year as his Iron Man consecutive-game streak commenced in a Cubs' game during a visit to Milwaukee on July 9, 1998. As the season progressed, the nation watched as both men got ever closer to the magic 61-homer mark. Although McGwire beat him to the record in September by smacking an amazing 70 home runs, the baseball writers chose Sosa as the National League's Most Valuable Player. Besides his personality that seemed to charm the scribes, Sosa finished with 66 homers and had league highs in runs scored (134), RBI (158), and total bases (416). The Cubs also finished ahead of the Cardinals in the league's Central Division standings (and qualified for the playoffs as the wild card) to further justify his selection as the league's MVP. He followed up his record performance the following year (1999) by hitting 63 round-trippers, driving in 141 runners, hitting .288, and pacing the league's hitters in total bases (397) and extra-base hits (89). He played the full 162-game schedule in 1999 and extended his playing streak to 238 games by the end of the season. Unfortunately for the Cubs, the team returned to their traditional losing ways by coming in dead last in the divisional standings, finishing 30 games behind the first-place Houston Astros. The next year on August 21, 2000, Sosa inherited baseball's Iron Man title from the Atlanta Braves' B.J. Surhoff, who had missed his team's game that day because of sore ribs. Sosa's reign lasted only about a month because during the Cubs' September 18, 2000, game against the Milwaukee Brewers, he experienced lower back stiffness and had to be taken out of the game. The back problem did not subside the next day and he was scratched from the Cubs' lineup; as a result, his consecutive streak of games played came to an end on September 19 after 388. He finished the season by leading the National League with 50 homers and came in second place (behind the Colorado Rockies' Todd Helton) with 89 extra-base hits. Although he had another excellent year with the bat, all of Sosa's offensive production did not prevent the Cubs from finishing in the Central Division's basement for the second straight year as the club went 65–97 under new manager Don Baylor.

In recent years, Sosa has steadily climbed the list of all-time home run leaders. In the first week of the 2003 season, he joined the 500 home run club by reaching that milestone in his 15th major league season. With the conclusion of the 2004 season, he was seventh on the all-time home run list with 574 round-trippers. After a dozen seasons with the Cubs, Sosa was traded by Chicago during the off-season to the Baltimore Orioles of the American League. In his first season in Baltimore, Sosa suffered his worst campaign in nearly 15 years by smacking just 14 homers and spending the final month of the season on the disabled list. He might have several years left in the majors and has an outside chance of challenging Aaron's (or Bonds') all-time homer mark before his retirement. He is just about a sure bet for election to baseball's Hall of Fame but the steroid usage (of which Sosa has not been accused) by several contemporary players has called into question the offensive accomplishments many players achieved in the last 10 or so years.

122. Shawn Green

Born: November, 10, 1972, Des Plaines, Illinois *Bats*: Left *Throws*: Left *Height*: 6 feet, 4 inches *Weight*: 190 *Major league debut*: September 28, 1993 (Toronto at Milwaukee [AL]) *Last major league game*: (still active)

Major league Iron Man from: September 19, 2000, to September 26, 2001 *Consecutive games played*: 415 *Games as major league Iron Man*: 163 (consecutive games 253 through 415) *Teams played for during streak*: Toronto Blue Jays (AL) (1999) and Los Angeles Dodgers (NL) (2000–01) *Primary position played*: Outfield *Game missed before streak*: June 9, 1999 (Toronto [AL] at New York [NL]) *First game played of streak*: June 11, 1999 (Toronto [AL] at Philadelphia [NL]) *Last game played of streak*: September 25, 2001 (San Francisco at Los Angeles) *Game missed to end streak*: September 26, 2001 (San Francisco at Los Angeles)

Consecutive Game Streak's Statistical Totals

Year	G	AB	R	H	2B	3B	HR	RBI	BB	SO	AVG	SLG	SB
1999	101	406	91	123	27	0	27	75	44	78	.303	.569	10
2000	162	610	98	164	44	4	24	99	90	121	.269	.472	24
2001	152	580	113	173	27	3	48	119	71	100	.298	.603	19
Total	415	1596	302	460	98	7	99	293	205	299	.288	.544	53

One of the better all-around contemporary players with plenty of pop in his bat, Shawn Green was selected by the Toronto Blue Jays organization in the first round (and 16th overall) of the free agent draft in June 1991. When he was first drafted, the Blue Jays did not think they were getting a player with a lot of power, but Green can consistently hit 30 or more homers annually. Spending most of his first two years in pro ball in the minors, he made his major league debut in a Blue Jays uniform on September 28, 1993, against the Milwaukee Brewers. He played in only three games for Toronto that first year. He spent most of the next year with Syracuse (of the International League) before getting another call-up by the Blue Jays. He took in 14 contests but went 3 for 33 for a horrendous .091 batting average.

In 1995, Green made the Blue Jays' roster on a permanent basis and took over in right field. Over the next three seasons, his presence in the outfield ensured that the team had a consistent player as was evident by his batting average, which hovered around the .280 mark. Toronto was a little disappointed, though, in Green's run production because he drove in only 152 runs during these three years. Although his batting average dropped nearly 10 points in 1998, this season was his breakout year as he played in 158 games and clobbered 35 homers along with driving home 100 runners. His consecutive game streak started the next year on

June 11, 1999, when he returned to the lineup after missing nearly 10 games due to an injury. He did pinch-run in the previous game, but according to major league rule 10.24(C), pinch running appearances alone cannot start or extend a playing streak. He did not miss a game the rest of the year as he appeared in the final 101 games on the 1999 Blue Jays' schedule. He finished the season with 42 clouts, 123 RBI, and a .309 batting average. He led the American League with 45 doubles, 361 total bases, 87 extra-base hits and made an appearance in his first all-star game. He also had the second-highest total of runs scored (134) behind Cleveland's Roberto Alomar (138) and won a Gold Glove for his fielding excellence. This turned out to be his last year in Toronto because the Blue Jays traded Green to the Los Angeles Dodgers for Raul Mondesi in November 1999. The Dodgers inserted Green into their lineup as the club's new right fielder, replacing Mondesi. Green's first season in the National League was rocky as his hitting dropped 40 points. He also hit only 24 homers but did knock in 99 runs and topped all Dodgers with 44 doubles. Although he appeared in all 162 Dodgers' games in 2000, during the July 2 game at San Francisco, he did not get into the contest until the seventh inning. On September 19, 2000, with about 10 games left on the schedule, Green inherited the Iron Man title from the Cubs' Sammy Sosa. Green closed out the year with an active streak of 263 games played. Even though his home run and RBI stats were down a good amount from his 1999 totals, he helped lead the Dodgers to an 86–76 record and a second-place finish in the National League's Western Division. Early in the following year, his streak nearly ended in the Dodgers' loss to the Atlanta Braves on May 11, 2001. Green was used as a pinch hitter in the bottom of the ninth inning with two outs and he struck out to end the game. His Iron Man streak ended later in the year when after 415 contests he voluntarily sat out the Dodgers' home game on September 26, 2001, against the San Francisco Giants in observance of Yom Kippur (a Jewish holiday). Green is one of the few Jewish players in major league baseball. Although his streak had ended, Green still had quite the year by posting career highs in homers (49) and RBI (125) along with hitting for a .297 average. The Dodgers had another 86–76 won-loss record in 2001 and came in third, just six games behind the eventual World Series winner, the Arizona Diamondbacks.

In the next three seasons after his streak came to an end, Green had mixed reviews with the Dodgers. In 2002, he kept producing offensively by clouting 42 homers and driving in 114 runners. His 2003 and 2004 performances, however, did not go so well because his home run totals did not even reach the 30 homer level. After hitting over 35 or more clouts four out of five years from 1998 through 2002, he hit only 47 homers combined those two seasons. Because the Dodgers were concerned that Green's best playing days might be behind him, the club traded him to the Diamondbacks in early 2005. Although his 2005 run production totals suffered a slight dropoff from his previous year with the Dodgers, his batting and slugging averages improved nearly 20 points as he helped the Diamondbacks place second to the San Diego Padres in the final Western Division standings.

123. Luis Gonzalez

Born: September 3, 1967, Tampa, Florida *Bats*: Left *Throws*: Right *Height*: 6 feet, 2 inches *Weight*: 180 *Major league debut*: September 4, 1990 (Houston at Los Angeles [NL]) *Last major league game*: (still active)

Major league Iron Man from: September 26, 2001, to August 14, 2002 *Consecutive games played*: 446 *Games as major league Iron Man*: 130 (consecutive games 317 through 446) *Team played for during streak*: Arizona Diamondbacks (NL) *Primary position played*: Outfield *Game missed before streak*: September 30, 1999 (San Diego at Arizona) *First game played of streak*: October 1, 1999 (San Diego at Arizona) *Last game played of streak*: August 13, 2002 (Arizona at Cincinnati) *Game missed to end streak*: August 14, 2002 (Arizona at Cincinnati)

Consecutive Game Streak's Statistical Totals

Year	G	AB	R	H	2B	3B	HR	RBI	BB	SO	AVG	SLG	SB
1999	3	10	1	4	2	0	0	4	1	0	.400	.600	0
2000	162	618	106	192	47	2	31	114	78	85	.311	.544	2
2001	162	609	128	198	36	7	57	142	100	83	.325	.688	1
2002	119	426	76	125	18	3	24	87	77	57	.293	.519	7
Total	446	1663	311	519	103	12	112	347	256	225	.312	.590	10

Luis Gonzalez's baseball career has lasted 16 seasons and can be divided into two parts. During the first part of his big league career (from 1990 to 1998), he was the solid, above-average player who could be relied upon in the clutch. Since 1999 (his first year in an Arizona Diamondbacks uniform), he has performed at a level that makes him one of the top stars of the game. Selected by the Houston Astros organization in the 1988 amateur draft, he spent three seasons in the minors before getting his call-up to the majors in the last month of the 1990 season. On September 4, 1990, he made his major league debut by pinch-hitting for Astros pitcher Mark Portugal in the third inning of a 10–8 Houston victory against the Los Angeles Dodgers. Playing at either first or third base, he got into a dozen games and went 4 for 21 for a .190 average. Although these statistics were not very good, it did not matter much because Gonzalez made the club's starting lineup the following season.

In 1991, Gonzalez was inserted into the left field slot where he hit 13 homers and knocked in 69 runners his rookie year. Over the next several years, he maintained a consistent pattern of production by averaging around a dozen homers and 60 to 70 RBI. During the middle of his sixth season with Houston, he was traded to the Chicago Cubs on June 28, 1995. He spent the rest of that season and the following year playing in the outfield and dealing with the ivy-covered walls of Wrigley Field. After the 1996 season, he filed for free agency and wound up back in Houston by signing a one-year contract to rejoin the Astros. His second tour of duty in Houston lasted just one season because he filed for free agency again and this time left the National League and signed on to play for the American League's Detroit Tigers. While the Tigers finished as the cellar-dwellers of the American League's Central Division in 1998, Gonzalez started to hit for more power as he belted a career high (at that time) in homers with 23 blasts. After the season finished, Gonzalez found himself on the move again, only this time instead of leaving via the free agent route, he departed Motown via a trade to the second-year Arizona Diamondbacks. This situation had a big impact on his career as the Diamondbacks expected him to provide some leadership to their club along with Jay Bell and Randy Johnson. Gonzalez responded to the challenge by hitting a career-best .336 (finishing in second place behind Colorado's Larry Walker, who hit .379), knocking 26 pitches out of the park and driving in 111 runners. Additionally, he led the league with 206 hits and took part in his first all-star game. His consecutive-games streak started when he played the final three games on the 1999 schedule, beginning with the October 1 contest in Arizona against the San Diego Padres. Gonzalez's performance directly contributed to the vastly improved Diamondbacks as they went 100–62 (an improvement of 35 games in the win column from their inaugural season in 1998) and won the league's Western Division crown. In the best-of-five divisional series against the New York Mets, he hit .200 but Arizona lost the series in four games. In 2000, he played every one of the Diamondbacks' games in left field, hit for a solid .311 average, clubbed 31 homers and drove in a team-high 114 runners. Arizona regressed to third place as they finished a dozen games behind the San Francisco Giants. If there was ever a career year for a player, the 2001 season was it for Gonzalez. Again playing the full slate of scheduled games, the only game he was not found in left field was the May 27, 2001, contest. He pinch-hit for pitcher Brian Anderson in the top of the eighth of the Diamondbacks' 6–4 victory over the Padres to keep his streak alive. With about a week left in the season, Gonzalez became the Iron Man of the majors on September 26 when Shawn Green of the Dodgers voluntarily sat out a game in Los Angeles against the Giants because of a Jewish holiday. Gonzalez's 2001 season stats showed him hitting an amazing 57 homers (good for third place in the National League behind the Giants' Barry Bonds and the Cubs' Sammy Sosa) and driving home 142 runs. He also had other team highs in doubles (36) and batting average (.325). In addition, he finished in second place in times on base (312 — behind Bonds' 342) and total bases (419 — behind Sosa's 425). Gonzalez's spectacular year helped Arizona finish first in the league's Western Division as they plowed past the St. Louis Cardinals and Atlanta Braves to take on the New York Yankees in the World Series. The 2001 series was a classic and the championship came down to a seventh and winner-take-all contest in Arizona. In an extremely close game involving two of the game's better pitchers (Arizona's Curt Schilling and the Yanks' Roger Clemens), the Diamondbacks responded to the pressure and won the World Series, seizing victory in the final game 3–2 in the ninth inning on a bloop single by Gonzalez. For the series, he went 7 for 27 for a .259 average along with a homer and five RBI (which included the series-winning run). The following year (2002), his streak came close to ending in games on May 3 and 12, June 5, July 3 and August 10 when he was not in Arizona's starting lineup. Pinch-hitting appearances or defensive replacements late in each of these games kept the streak alive until he sat out the August 14, 2002, contest against the Cincinnati Reds because of a rib cage strain. This ended his playing streak at 446 straight games, the longest such streak since Cal Ripken ended his record run in September 1998. Although Gonzalez's production numbers were still impressive, all his figures were down considerably from his 2001 career year as he batted .288, knocked out 28 homers and drove home 103 runners. Since his most productive years as a player came during his playing streak, it looks like he actually thrived on playing every day without the occasional rest.

Since his streak has ended, he has continued to play in Arizona. The next two years were pretty consistent but his 2004 season was cut short when he went on the disabled list the first week of August 2004 to have Tommy John surgery for ligament damage in one of his arms. After his injury-shortened 2004 season, Gonzalez rebounded in 2005 by producing respectable numbers in his home run, RBI and batting average categories as he helped lead the Diamondbacks to a second-place finish in the National League's Western Division, just behind the San Diego Padres.

124. MIGUEL TEJADA

Born: May 25, 1976, Bani, Dominican Republic *Bats*: Right *Throws*: Right *Height*: 5 feet, 10 inches *Weight*: 170 *Major league debut*: August 27, 1997 (New York at Oakland [AL]) *Last major league game*: (still active)

Major league Iron Man from: August 14, 2002, to present *Consecutive games played*: 918 *Games as major league Iron Man*: 528 (consecutive games 391 through 918) *Teams played for during streak*: Oakland Athletics (AL) (2000–2003), Baltimore Orioles (AL) (2004–2005) *Primary position played*: Shortstop *Game missed before streak*: May 31, 2000 (Oakland at New York) *First game played of streak*: June

2, 2000 (San Francisco (NL) at Oakland) (AL) *Last game played of streak*: (streak is currently active)

Consecutive Game Streak's Statistical Totals

Year	G	AB	R	H	2B	3B	HR	RBI	BB	SO	AVG	SLG	SB
2000	108	403	69	117	25	0	23	80	49	68	.290	.524	2
2001	162	622	107	166	31	3	31	113	43	89	.267	.476	11
2002	162	662	108	204	30	0	34	131	38	84	.308	.508	7
2003	162	636	98	177	42	0	27	106	53	65	.278	.472	10
2004	162	653	107	203	40	2	34	150	48	73	.311	.534	4
2005	162	654	89	199	50	5	26	98	40	83	.304	.515	5
Total	918	3630	578	1066	218	10	175	678	271	462	.294	.504	39

Miguel Tejada is a shortstop in the tradition of the modern-day shortstops like Cal Ripken Jr. and Alex Rodriguez (good fielders who also can produce with the bat). Signed as a nondrafted free agent by the Oakland Athletics' organization in the summer of 1993, he spent most of his first four years of professional ball in Oakland's farm system until his call-up to the parent club in August 1997. He made his big league debut in Oakland against the New York Yankees on August 27, 1997. The Athletics used several players at shortstop that season because their regular shortstop the year before, Mike Bordick, had left to join the Baltimore Orioles. With his promotion to Oakland, Tejada took over the shortstop position on a permanent basis (even though he was a rookie and the youngest player in the American League that season). He played in 26 games and went 20 for 99 and finished with a rather unimpressive .202 batting average.

Tejada's first full year in the majors was delayed when he suffered a hand injury in preseason action that required him to go on the disabled list for the first two months of the 1998 season. After a 10-day rehabilitation assignment in the minors, he returned to Oakland and claimed his spot on the roster. He played in 105 contests and came in with a .233 batting average. During the 1999 season, Tejada started showing the signs of the durability and production that he has become noted for. He missed just three games in 1999, hit 21 homers, drove in 84 runners and hit a respectable .251 while contributing to Oakland's second-place finish in the league's Western Division behind the Texas Rangers. He also paced the league's shortstops in games played (159) and putouts (292). His consecutive-games-played streak commenced in Oakland against the National League's San Francisco Giants on June 2, 2000. The game he missed in New York against the

Miguel Tejada: As of August 2006, is baseball's current reigning Iron Man. At the end of the 2005 season, he had played in 918 straight contests. His streak is presently the seventh longest in big league history.

Yankees on May 31 was the only contest he sat out the entire season. Except for the first game of a double-header on July 17 where he pinch-hit and then went in as a defensive replacement, he started the rest of the 108 regular season games left on the 2000 schedule. His offensive numbers continued to improve as he hit .275, smacked 30 round-trippers and drove home 115 runs while helping Oakland win the junior circuit's Western Division title. Fieldingwise, he again led all the American League's shortstops in games played (160) and assists (501). In the first round of the playoffs, the Athletics met the defending world champion New York Yankees. The series went the full five games but the Athletics came out on the losing end. In his first experience in playoff competition, Tejada went 7 for 20 for a .350 average and led all division series players with five runs scored. Although his batting average dipped a little (.267) in 2001, he kept his power and clutch productive numbers consistent by clouting 31 home runs and driving in 113 runs. The closest he came to missing a game in 2001 were the June 23 and September 26 contests where he was inserted as a defensive replacement in the latter part of both games. For the third straight year, he led the league shortstops in games played (162). Oakland made the playoffs (via the wild card) and wound up having to face the mighty Yankees again. The Athletics were again eliminated from further competition by the Yankees in five games. Tejada had another good series, going 6 for 21 for a .286 average and tied with three other players for most doubles with three two-baggers. The 2002 season saw Tejada make his first all-star appearance for the American League squad. When the Diamondbacks' Luis Gonzalez sat out a game on August 14, 2002, Tejada assumed the role of major league Iron Man with a streak of 391 straight games played. His streak nearly ended on September 27, 2002, but he got into the game in the latter innings by pinch-hitting and then filling in at shortstop. With the closure of the 2002 season, his streak stood at 432 games. Pacing the Athletics in several offensive categories, he finished with 204 hits, 34 homers, 131 RBI, a .308 batting average and led Oakland to the American League's Western Division crown by four games over the Anaheim Angels. In the best-of-five divisional series against the Minnesota Twins, Oakland came out on the short end again and was eliminated. Tejada had a dreadful series as he went only 3 for 21 for a .143 average. While his performance figures dropped off considerably in 2003 (his batting average fell 30 points and RBI total was down by 25 runs) due primarily to his slow start at the beginning of the season, Tejada was kept in the lineup and extended his playing streak to 594 games. On June 17, he became the 34th major leaguer to cross the 500-consecutive-games-played barrier and the first to accomplish this since Toronto's Joe Carter did it on September 30, 1991. Tejada's leadership helped the Athletics win another divisional crown, but they were again eliminated from the playoffs by the Boston Red Sox in a five-game series. Tejada had another awful time with the bat as he went 2 for 23 for a .087 batting average.

Tejada left Oakland and signed a free agent contact with the Baltimore Orioles after the 2003 season. The Orioles again have another shortstop with a long-running consecutive-games streak. His streak came close to ending on two occasions in 2004. In spring training, he missed a few exhibition games because of a strained leg muscle. This same type of injury resulted in his leaving in the first inning of the May 11 game in Chicago against the White Sox, which Baltimore lost in a 15-0 blowout. Luckily, the injury did not require him to miss any further action. Tejada stretched his consecutive games streak to 756 games by the end of the 2004 season and 918 by the end of the 2005 season. At present, this streak (which is still active) qualifies as the seventh longest in major league history. He had another productive year with the bat for the Orioles, hitting over .300 again for the third time in four years plus leading the American League in two-base hits with 50 doubles. However, his RBI total plummeted to 98 RBI (a decrease of 52 RBI from his 2004 season totals).

Appendix A: Chronological Listing of Baseball Iron Men

Player's Name	Beginning/Ending Dates of Streak	Consecutive Games Played
Paul Hines	April 14, 1873, to September 12, 1876	226
Davy Force	July 21, 1873, to May 17, 1877	225
John Glenn	July 18, 1874, to August 25, 1877	209
John Peters	August 8, 1874, to August 31, 1878	274
Jim O'Rourke	August 4, 1875, to May 10, 1879	225
John Clapp	April 25, 1876, to June 24, 1879	212
Cal McVey	May 10, 1876, to September 30, 1879	262
Paul Hines	September 26, 1876, to June 28, 1880	242
John Morrill	April 30, 1877, to May 18, 1881	302
Jack Burdock	July 26, 1877, to June 4, 1881	276
Bill Phillips	July 23, 1879, to August 19, 1882	275
Jim O'Rourke	August 19, 1879, to July 2, 1883	319
Joe Hornung	September 1, 1879, to September 11, 1884	464
Bill Gleason*	May 2, 1882, to April 24, 1886	406
Jimmy Wolf*	May 5, 1882, to April 17, 1886	397
Steve Brady	May 1, 1883, to May 1, 1886	328
Charley Jones	August 21, 1883, to July 28, 1886	333
Curt Welch	May 1, 1884, to September 8, 1886 (2)	334
Jim O'Rourke	June 28, 1884, to September 16, 1886	288
Bill McClellan	July 30, 1884, to June 5, 1887	333
Henry Larkin	May 24, 1885, to August 13, 1887	318
George Pinkney	September 21, 1885, to April 30, 1890	577
Sid Farrar	June 23, 1887, to July 3, 1890	403
Dave Foutz	June 17, 1888, to June 3, 1891	398
Hub Collins	October 3, 1888, to July 20, 1891	351
Germany Smith	June 4, 1889, to July 4, 1892 (2)	433
Bid McPhee	June 2, 1890, to September 24, 1892	377

Appendix A

Tommy McCarthy	April 26, 1891, to September 13, 1893 (2)	392
Jake Beckley	April 16, 1892, to July 17, 1894	352
Hugh Duffy	October 11, 1892, (1) to August 8, 1894	225
Steve Brodie	April 27, 1893, to June 26, 1897	574
George Van Haltren	May 4, 1895, to July 16, 1897 (2)	324
Kid Gleason	June 28, 1895, to September 9, 1897 (2)	335
Gene DeMontreville	September 17, 1895, to August 4, 1898 (2)	365
Duff Cooley	July 8, 1896, to September 5, 1898 (1)	309
Hugh Duffy	May 6, 1897, to August 16, 1899 (2)	376
George Van Haltren	September 29, 1897, to May 7, 1901	462
Jimmy Slagle	May 8, 1899, to June 21, 1901	326
Jesse Burkett	June 18, 1899, to June 13, 1902	428
Jimmy Collins	April 19, 1900, to June 28, 1902	338
Jimmy Barrett	May 27, 1900, to August 25, 1902 (2)	352
Topsy Hartsel	September 21, 1900, to May 11, 1903	314
Freddy Parent	April 26, 1901, to September 25, 1903	413
Candy LaChance	June 24, 1901, to April 28, 1905	539
Buck Freeman	July 27, 1901, to June 5, 1905	536
Bill Bradley	August 1, 1903, to August 28, 1905	320
Lee Tannehill	May 12, 1904, to September 16, 1905	265
Freddy Parent	May 23, 1904, to September 4, 1906 (2)	408
Sherry Magee	July 22, 1904, to June 28, 1907	447
George Stone	August 14, 1905, to June 20, 1908	425
Jiggs Donahue	August 31, 1905, to June 23, 1908	413
Tom Jones	May 31, 1906, to May 19, 1909	451
Ed Konetchy	June 29, 1907, to July 27, 1909	327
John Hummel	August 28, 1907, to August 6, 1909	285
George McBride	April 14, 1908, to May 5, 1910	330
Eddie Grant	June 13, 1908, to June 28, 1910	324
Eddie Collins	October 7, 1908, (1) to October 4, 1910	308
Zack Wheat	September 11, 1909, (1) to August 15, 1911	287
George McBride	May 10, 1910, to April 20, 1912	295
Ed Konetchy	August 15, 1910, (1) to July 1, 1912	279
Clyde Milan	August 12, 1910, to October 3, 1913 (2)	511
Owen "Chief" Wilson	September 10, 1911, to October 3, 1914 (2)	484
Sam Crawford	April 10, 1913, to April 17, 1916	472
George Cutshaw†	June 13, 1914, to June 17, 1916	309
Ray Chapman†	June 15, 1914, to April 26, 1916	271
Del Pratt	September 4, 1914, to April 29, 1917	363
Eddie Collins	October 5, 1914, to May 2, 1918	478
Fred Luderus	June 2, 1916, to September 28, 1919 (2)	533
Everett Scott	June 20, 1916, to May 5, 1925	1.307
Joe Sewell	September 13, 1922, to April 30, 1930	1,103

Chronological Listing

Lou Gehrig	June 1, 1925, to April 30, 1939	2,130
Pete Fox	May 16, 1937, to May 6, 1939	306
Frankie Crosetti	July 9, 1937, to May 10, 1940	418
Stan Hack	April 22, 1938, to May 17, 1940	332
Frank McCormick	April 19, 1938, to May 24, 1942 (2)	652
Rudy York	April 16, 1940, to July 30, 1942 (2)	413
Danny Litwhiler	May 4, 1941, to June 2, 1943	325
Mickey Vernon§	September 16, 1941, to September 3, 1943	292
Billy Herman§	September 22, 1941, to October 3, 1943	313
Bill Nicholson	May 20, 1942, to July 9, 1944 (2)	348
Bobby Doerr	July 19, 1942, (1) to August 25, 1944 (1)	344
Stan Musial	September 4, 1942, to September 10, 1944 (2)	314
Phil Cavarretta	May 29, 1943, to September 14, 1944 (1)	259
Tommy Holmes	July 30, 1943, (1) to July 13, 1946 (2)	454
Eddie Lake	May 27, 1945, (1) to September 28, 1947	442
Mickey Vernon	April 28, 1946, to July 5, 1948 (2)	369
Frankie Gustine	September 11, 1946, (1) to July 19, 1948	260
Vern Stephens	June 17, 1947, to June 9, 1950	464
Gil Hodges	June 1, 1948, to July 17, 1950 (1)	352
Granny Hamner	September 14, 1948, to September 18, 1951	473
Eddie Yost	August 30, 1949, to May 11, 1955	829
Roy McMillan	September 16, 1951, (1) to August 7, 1955 (1)	584
Stan Musial	April 15, 1952, to August 22, 1957	895
Nellie Fox	August 7, 1955, to September 3, 1960	798
Ernie Banks	August 26, 1956, (2) to June 22, 1961	717
Vada Pinson	September 26, 1958, to May 30, 1962 (2)	508
Rocky Colavito	June 21, 1960, to May 21, 1963	458
Brooks Robinson	September 7, 1960, to September 2, 1963 (1)	483
Ron Santo	August 15, 1961, to April 17, 1964	371
Bill White	June 24, 1962, (2) to May 14, 1964	284
Ken Boyer	May 7, 1963, to April 21, 1965	306
Johnny Callison	June 9, 1963, (1) to June 9, 1965	323
Curt Flood	July 14, 1963, (1) to June 13, 1965 (2)	294
Leo Cardenas	August 4, 1963, (2) to September 1, 1965 (1)	344
Billy Williams	September 22, 1963, to September 2, 1970	1,117
Sandy Alomar	May 16, 1969, to May 20, 1973	648
Roy White	August 31, 1971, to May 21, 1974	388
Eddie Brinkman	September 26, 1971, to August 9, 1974	434
Mike Schmidt	September 1, 1973, to May 26, 1975	231
Dave Cash	September 18, 1973, to September 26, 1976 (1)	494
Pete Rose	September 28, 1973, to May 7, 1978 (1)	678
Steve Garvey	September 3, 1975, to July 29, 1983 (1)	1,207
Pete Rose	September 1, 1978, to August 23, 1983	745

Appendix A

Alfredo Griffin	September 7, 1981, to May 27, 1984 (1)	392
Dale Murphy	September 26, 1981, to July 8, 1986	740
Cal Ripken Jr.	May 30, 1982, to September 19, 1998	2,632
Albert Belle	September 19, 1996, to June 9, 1999	392
Vinny Castilla	June 26, 1997, to June 14, 1999	307
B. J. Surhoff**	March 31, 1998, to August 20, 2000	445
Johnny Damon**	March 31, 1998, to September 14, 1999 (1)	305
Sammy Sosa	July 9, 1998, to September 18, 2000	388
Shawn Green	June 11, 1999, to September 25, 2001	415
Luis Gonzalez	October 1, 1999, to August 13, 2002	446
Miguel Tejada	June 2, 2000, to present	918

Notes

* Wolf tied Gleason in number of consecutive games played on May 30, 1885. They stayed tied until June 6, 1885, when Gleason took the lead back and maintained it as Wolf missed a game on April 18, 1886.

† Chapman tied Cutshaw in number of consecutive games played on April 24, 1916. Chapman then took over the lead from Cutshaw in consecutive games played on April 25, 1916, and remained the major league baseball Iron Man for one more game on April 26, 1916. The next day, April 27, 1916, Chapman missed a game, ending his playing streak, and Cutshaw reclaimed the title.

§ When Litwhiler's streak ended on June 3, 1943, Vernon had a one-game lead on Herman in consecutive games played. On June 7, 1943, Herman tied Vernon. They stayed tied till June 9, 1943, when Vernon took the lead back. Vernon held the lead till Herman tied him again on June 24, 1943. The tie remained till June 30, 1943, when Herman took the lead for the first time. On July 7, 1943, Vernon tied Herman till July 15, 1943, when Vernon took the lead again. Vernon led till July 21, 1943, when Herman again tied him. This tie remained till July 22, 1943, when Vernon took the lead again and kept it till he missed a game on September 4, 1943, when Herman took the lead.

** When Castilla's streak ended on June 15, 1999, Surhoff had a two-game lead on Damon in consecutive games played. On July 3, 1999, Damon tied Surhoff in consecutive games played. They stayed tied till July 5, 1999, when Surhoff regained the lead in consecutive games played and continued to hold a slim lead until August 20, 1999, when Damon tied Surhoff again. On August 21, 1999, Surhoff took the lead again and kept it till August 30, 1999, when Damon again tied Surhoff. This tie remained through September 6, 1999, when Surhoff took the lead again and continued to hold a slim lead until Damon missed a game on September 14, 1999. At that time, Surhoff had no close competitor as the major league baseball Iron Man.

Appendix B: Season by Season Review of Baseball Iron Men

1876 — Paul Hines, Chicago White Stockings, NL (to September 13, 1876)
   Davy Force, Philadelphia Athletics, NL, and New York Mutuals, NL

1877 — Davy Force, St. Louis Brown Stockings, NL (to May 19, 1877)
   John Glenn, Chicago White Stockings, NL (to September 4, 1877)
   John Peters, Chicago White Stockings, NL

1878 — John Peters, Milwaukee Cream Citys, NL (to September 6, 1878)
   Jim O'Rourke, Boston Red Caps, NL

1879 — Jim O'Rourke, Providence Grays, NL (to May 13, 1879)
   John Clapp, Buffalo Bisons, NL (to June 25, 1879)
   Cal McVey, Cincinnati Reds, NL

1880 — Paul Hines, Providence Grays, NL (to June 29, 1880)
   John Morrill, Boston Red Caps, NL

1881 — John Morrill, Boston Red Caps, NL (to May 20, 1881)
   Jack Burdock, Boston Red Caps, NL (to June 7, 1881)
   Bill Phillips, Cleveland Blues, NL

1882 — Bill Phillips, Cleveland Blues, NL (to August 23, 1882)
   Jim O'Rourke, Buffalo Bisons, NL

1883 — Jim O'Rourke, Buffalo Bisons, NL (to July 3, 1883)
   Joe Hornung, Boston Beaneaters, NL

1884 — Joe Hornung, Boston Beaneaters, NL (to September 13, 1884)
   Bill Gleason, St. Louis Browns, AA

1885 — Bill Gleason, St. Louis Browns, AA (to May 30, 1885)
   Bill Gleason, St. Louis Browns, AA and Jimmy Wolf, Louisville Colonels, AA
     (to June 6, 1885)
   Bill Gleason, St. Louis Browns, AA

1886 — Bill Gleason, St. Louis Browns, AA (to April 25, 1886)
   Steve Brady, New York Metropolitans, AA (to May 3, 1886)
   Charley Jones, Cincinnati Reds, AA (to July 29, 1886)
   Curt Welch, St. Louis Browns, AA (to September 9, 1886)

APPENDIX B

        Jim O'Rourke, New York Gothams, NL (to September 17, 1886)
        Bill McClellan, Brooklyn Trolley Dodgers, AA

1887 — Bill McClellan, Brooklyn Trolley Dodgers, AA (to June 7, 1887)
        Henry Larkin, Philadelphia Athletics, AA (to August 15, 1887)
        George Pinkney, Brooklyn Trolley Dodgers, AA

1888 — George Pinkney, Brooklyn Bridegrooms, AA

1889 — George Pinkney, Brooklyn Bridegrooms, AA

1890 — George Pinkney, Brooklyn Bridegrooms, NL (to May 2, 1890)
        Sid Farrar, Philadelphia Quakers, PL (to July 4, 1890)
        Dave Foutz, Brooklyn Bridegrooms, NL

1891 — Dave Foutz, Brooklyn Bridegrooms, NL (to June 4, 1891)
        Hub Collins, Brooklyn Bridegrooms, NL (to July 21, 1891)
        Germany Smith, Cincinnati Reds, NL

1892 — Germany Smith, Cincinnati Reds, NL (to July 5, 1892)
        Bid McPhee, Cincinnati Reds, NL (to September 25, 1892)
        Tommy McCarthy, Boston Beaneaters, NL

1893 — Tommy McCarthy, Boston Beaneaters, NL (to September 14, 1893)
        Jake Beckley, Pittsburgh Pirates, NL

1894 — Jake Beckley, Pittsburgh Pirates, NL (to July 18, 1894)
        Hugh Duffy, Boston Beaneaters, NL (to August 9, 1894)
        Steve Brodie, Baltimore Orioles, NL

1895 — Steve Brodie, Baltimore Orioles, NL

1896 — Steve Brodie, Baltimore Orioles, NL

1897 — Steve Brodie, Pittsburgh Pirates, NL (to June 28, 1897)
        George Van Haltren, New York Giants, NL (to July 17, 1897)
        Kid Gleason, New York Giants, NL (to September 10, 1897)
        Gene DeMontreville, Washington Senators, NL

1898 — Gene DeMontreville, Baltimore Orioles, NL (to August 5, 1898)
        Duff Cooley, Philadelphia Phillies, NL (to September 5, 1898)
        Hugh Duffy, Boston Beaneaters, NL

1899 — Hugh Duffy, Boston Beaneaters, NL (to August 17, 1899)
        George Van Haltren, New York Giants, NL

1900 — George Van Haltren, New York Giants, NL

1901 — George Van Haltren, New York Giants, NL (to May 8, 1901)
        Jimmy Slagle, Philadelphia Phillies, NL (to June 22, 1901)
        Jesse Burkett, St. Louis Cardinals, NL

1902 — Jesse Burkett, St. Louis Browns, AL (to June 14, 1902)
        Jimmy Collins, Boston Americans, AL (to July 1, 1902)
        Jimmy Barrett, Detroit Tigers, AL (to August 26, 1902)
        Topsy Hartsel, Philadelphia Athletics, AL

1903 — Topsy Hartsel, Philadelphia Athletics, AL (to May 12, 1903)

Freddy Parent, Boston Americans, AL (to September 26, 1903)
Candy LaChance, Boston Americans, AL

1904 — Candy LaChance, Boston Americans, AL

1905 — Candy LaChance, Boston Americans, AL (to April 29, 1905)
Buck Freeman, Boston Americans, AL (to June 7, 1905)
Bill Bradley, Cleveland Naps, AL (to August 29, 1905)
Lee Tannehill, Chicago White Sox, AL (to September 17, 1905)
Freddy Parent, Boston Americans, AL

1906 — Freddy Parent, Boston Americans, AL (to September 5, 1906)
Sherry Magee, Philadelphia Phillies, NL

1907 — Sherry Magee, Philadelphia Phillies, NL (to July 1, 1907)
George Stone, St. Louis Browns, AL

1908 — George Stone, St. Louis Browns, AL (to June 21, 1908)
Jiggs Donahue, Chicago White Sox, AL (to June 24, 1908)
Tom Jones, St. Louis Browns, AL

1909 — Tom Jones, St. Louis Browns, AL (to May 20, 1909)
Ed Konetchy, St. Louis Cardinals, NL (to July 28, 1909)
John Hummel, Brooklyn Superbas, NL (to August 7, 1909)
George McBride, Washington Senators, AL

1910 — George McBride, Washington Senators, AL (to May 6, 1910)
Eddie Grant, Philadelphia Phillies, NL (to June 29, 1910)
Eddie Collins, Philadelphia Athletics, AL (to October 5, 1910)
Zack Wheat, Brooklyn Superbas, NL

1911 — Zack Wheat, Brooklyn Superbas, NL (to August 16, 1911)
George McBride, Washington Senators, AL

1912 — George McBride, Washington Senators, AL (to April 23, 1912)
Ed Konetchy, St. Louis Cardinals, NL (to July 4, 1912)
Clyde Milan, Washington Senators, AL

1913 — Clyde Milan, Washington Senators, AL (to October 4, 1913)
Owen Wilson, Pittsburgh Pirates, NL

1914 — Owen Wilson, St. Louis Cardinals, NL (to October 4, 1914)
Sam Crawford, Detroit Tigers, AL

1915 — Sam Crawford, Detroit Tigers, AL

1916 — Sam Crawford, Detroit Tigers, AL (to April 18, 1916)
George Cutshaw, Brooklyn Robins, NL (to April 24, 1916)
George Cutshaw, Brooklyn Robins, NL, and Ray Chapman, Cleveland Indians, AL
  (to April 25, 1916)
Ray Chapman, Cleveland Indians, AL (to April 27, 1916)
George Cutshaw, Brooklyn Robins, NL (to June 19, 1916)
Del Pratt, St. Louis Browns, AL

1917 — Del Pratt, St. Louis Browns, AL (to April 30, 1917)
Eddie Collins, Chicago White Sox, AL

Appendix B

1918 — Eddie Collins, Chicago White Sox, AL (to May 3, 1918)
  Fred Luderus, Philadelphia Phillies, NL

1919 — Fred Luderus, Philadelphia Phillies, NL

1920 — Everett Scott, Boston Red Sox, AL

1921 — Everett Scott, Boston Red Sox, AL

1922 — Everett Scott, New York Yankees, AL

1923 — Everett Scott, New York Yankees, AL

1924 — Everett Scott, New York Yankees, AL

1925 — Everett Scott, New York Yankees, AL (to May 6, 1925)
  Joe Sewell, Cleveland Indians, AL

1926 — Joe Sewell, Cleveland Indians, AL

1927 — Joe Sewell, Cleveland Indians, AL

1928 — Joe Sewell, Cleveland Indians, AL

1929 — Joe Sewell, Cleveland Indians, AL

1930 — Joe Sewell, Cleveland Indians, AL (to May 2, 1930)
  Lou Gehrig, New York Yankees, AL

1931 — Lou Gehrig, New York Yankees, AL

1932 — Lou Gehrig, New York Yankees, AL

1933 — Lou Gehrig, New York Yankees, AL

1934 — Lou Gehrig, New York Yankees, AL

1935 — Lou Gehrig, New York Yankees, AL

1936 — Lou Gehrig, New York Yankees, AL

1937 — Lou Gehrig, New York Yankees, AL

1938 — Lou Gehrig, New York Yankees, AL

1939 — Lou Gehrig, New York Yankees, AL (to May 2, 1939)
  Pete Fox, Detroit Tigers, AL (to May 7, 1939)
  Frankie Crosetti, New York Yankees, AL

1940 — Frankie Crosetti, New York Yankees, AL (to May 11, 1940)
  Stan Hack, Chicago Cubs, NL (to May 18, 1940)
  Frank McCormick, Cincinnati Reds, NL

1941 — Frank McCormick, Cincinnati Reds, NL

1942 — Frank McCormick, Cincinnati Reds, NL (to May 25, 1942)
  Rudy York, Detroit Tigers, AL (to July 31, 1942)
  Danny Litwhiler, Philadelphia Phillies, NL

1943 — Danny Litwhiler, Philadelphia Phillies, NL, and St. Louis Cardinals, NL
    (to June 3, 1943)
  Mickey Vernon, Washington Senators, AL (to June 7, 1943)

Mickey Vernon, Washington Senators, AL, and Billy Herman, Brooklyn Dodgers, NL, (to June 9, 1943)
Mickey Vernon, Washington Senators, AL (to June 24, 1943)
Mickey Vernon, Washington Senators, AL, and Billy Herman, Brooklyn Dodgers, NL (to June 30, 1943)
Billy Herman, Brooklyn Dodgers, NL (to July 7, 1943)
Mickey Vernon, Washington Senators, AL, and Billy Herman, Brooklyn Dodgers, NL (to July 15, 1943)
Mickey Vernon, Washington Senators, AL (to July 21, 1943)
Mickey Vernon, Washington Senators, AL, and Billy Herman, Brooklyn Dodgers, NL (to July 22, 1943)
Mickey Vernon, Washington Senators, AL (to September 4, 1943)
Billy Herman, Brooklyn Dodgers, NL

1944 — Bill Nicholson, Chicago Cubs, NL (to July 13, 1944)
Bobby Doerr, Boston Red Sox, AL (to August 25, 1944)
Stan Musial, St. Louis Cardinals, NL (to September 12, 1944)
Phil Cavarretta, Chicago Cubs, NL (to September 14, 1944)
Tommy Holmes, Boston Braves, NL

1945 — Tommy Holmes, Boston Braves, NL

1946 — Tommy Holmes, Boston Braves, NL (to July 14, 1946)
Eddie Lake, Detroit Tigers, AL

1947 — Eddie Lake, Detroit Tigers, AL

1948 — Mickey Vernon, Washington Senators, AL (to July 6, 1948)
Frankie Gustine, Pittsburgh Pirates, NL (to July 20, 1948)
Vern Stephens, Boston Red Sox, AL

1949 — Vern Stephens, Boston Red Sox, AL

1950 — Vern Stephens, Boston Red Sox, AL (to June 10, 1950)
Gil Hodges, Brooklyn Dodgers, NL (to July 17, 1950)
Granny Hamner, Philadelphia Phillies, NL

1951 — Granny Hamner, Philadelphia Phillies, NL (to September 19, 1951)
Eddie Yost, Washington Senators, AL

1952 — Eddie Yost, Washington Senators, AL

1953 — Eddie Yost, Washington Senators, AL

1954 — Eddie Yost, Washington Senators, AL

1955 — Eddie Yost, Washington Senators, AL (to May 12, 1955)
Roy McMillan, Cincinnati Reds, NL (to August 7, 1955)
Stan Musial, St. Louis Cardinals, NL

1956 — Stan Musial, St. Louis Cardinals, NL

1957 — Stan Musial, St. Louis Cardinals, NL (to August 23, 1957)
Nellie Fox, Chicago White Sox, AL

1958 — Nellie Fox, Chicago White Sox, AL

Appendix B

1959 — Nellie Fox, Chicago White Sox, AL

1960 — Nellie Fox, Chicago White Sox, AL (to September 4, 1960)
Ernie Banks, Chicago Cubs, NL

1961 — Ernie Banks, Chicago Cubs, NL (to June 23, 1961)
Vada Pinson, Cincinnati Reds, NL

1962 — Vada Pinson, Cincinnati Reds, NL (to May 31, 1962)
Rocky Colavito, Detroit Tigers, AL

1963 — Rocky Colavito, Detroit Tigers, AL (to May 22, 1963)
Brooks Robinson, Baltimore Orioles, AL (to September 2, 1963)
Ron Santo, Chicago Cubs, NL

1964 — Ron Santo, Chicago Cubs, NL (to April 18, 1964)
Bill White, St. Louis Cardinals, NL (to May 15, 1964)
Ken Boyer, St. Louis Cardinals, NL

1965 — Ken Boyer, St. Louis Cardinals, NL (to April 23, 1965)
Johnny Callison, Philadelphia Phillies, NL (to June 10, 1965)
Curt Flood, St. Louis Cardinals, NL (to June 14, 1965)
Leo Cardenas, Cincinnati Reds, NL (to September 1, 1965)
Billy Williams, Chicago Cubs, NL

1966 — Billy Williams, Chicago Cubs, NL

1967 — Billy Williams, Chicago Cubs, NL

1968 — Billy Williams, Chicago Cubs, NL

1969 — Billy Williams, Chicago Cubs, NL

1970 — Billy Williams, Chicago Cubs, NL (to September 3, 1970)
Sandy Alomar, California Angels, AL

1971 — Sandy Alomar, California Angels, AL

1972 — Sandy Alomar, California Angels, AL

1973 — Sandy Alomar, California Angels, AL (to May 22, 1973)
Roy White, New York Yankees, AL

1974 — Roy White, New York Yankees, AL (to May 22, 1974)
Eddie Brinkman, Detroit Tigers, AL (to August 10, 1974)
Mike Schmidt, Philadelphia Phillies, NL

1975 — Mike Schmidt, Philadelphia Phillies, NL (to May 27, 1975)
Dave Cash, Philadelphia Phillies, NL

1976 — Dave Cash, Philadelphia Phillies, NL (to September 26, 1976)
Pete Rose, Cincinnati Reds, NL

1977 — Pete Rose, Cincinnati Reds, NL

1978 — Pete Rose, Cincinnati Reds, NL (to May 7, 1978)
Steve Garvey, Los Angeles Dodgers, NL

1979 — Steve Garvey, Los Angeles Dodgers, NL

Season by Season Review

1980 — Steve Garvey, Los Angeles Dodgers, NL

1981 — Steve Garvey, Los Angeles Dodgers, NL

1982 — Steve Garvey, Los Angeles Dodgers, NL

1983 — Steve Garvey, San Diego Padres, NL (to July 29, 1983)
Pete Rose, Philadelphia Phillies, NL (to August 24, 1983)
Alfredo Griffin, Toronto Blue Jays, AL

1984 — Alfredo Griffin, Toronto Blue Jays, AL (to May 27, 1984)
Dale Murphy, Atlanta Braves, NL

1985 — Dale Murphy, Atlanta Braves, NL

1986 — Dale Murphy, Atlanta Braves, NL (to July 9, 1986)
Cal Ripken, Jr., Baltimore Orioles, AL

1987 — Cal Ripken, Jr., Baltimore Orioles, AL

1988 — Cal Ripken, Jr., Baltimore Orioles, AL

1989 — Cal Ripken, Jr., Baltimore Orioles, AL

1990 — Cal Ripken, Jr., Baltimore Orioles, AL

1991 — Cal Ripken, Jr., Baltimore Orioles, AL

1992 — Cal Ripken, Jr., Baltimore Orioles, AL

1993 — Cal Ripken, Jr., Baltimore Orioles, AL

1994 — Cal Ripken, Jr., Baltimore Orioles, AL

1995 — Cal Ripken, Jr., Baltimore Orioles, AL

1996 — Cal Ripken, Jr., Baltimore Orioles, AL

1997 — Cal Ripken, Jr., Baltimore Orioles, AL

1998 — Cal Ripken, Jr., Baltimore Orioles, AL (to September 20, 1998)
Albert Belle, Chicago White Sox, AL

1999 — Albert Belle, Baltimore Orioles, AL (to June 11, 1999)
Vinny Castilla, Colorado Rockies, NL (to June 15, 1999)
B.J. Surhoff, Baltimore Orioles, AL (to July 3, 1999)
B.J. Surhoff, Baltimore Orioles, AL, and Johnny Damon, Kansas City Royals, AL (to July 5, 1999)
B.J. Surhoff, Baltimore Orioles, AL (to August 20, 1999)
B.J. Surhoff, Baltimore Orioles, AL, and Johnny Damon, Kansas City Royals, AL (to August 21, 1999)
B.J. Surhoff, Baltimore Orioles, AL (to August 30, 1999)
B.J. Surhoff, Baltimore Orioles, AL, and Johnny Damon, Kansas City Royals, AL (to September 6, 1999)
B.J. Surhoff, Baltimore Orioles, AL

2000 — B.J. Surhoff, Baltimore Orioles, AL, and Atlanta Braves, NL (to August 21, 2000)
Sammy Sosa, Chicago Cubs, NL (to September 19, 2000)
Shawn Green, Los Angeles Dodgers, NL

Appendix B

2001 — Shawn Green, Los Angeles Dodgers, NL (to September 26, 2001)
Luis Gonzalez, Arizona Diamondbacks, NL

2002 — Luis Gonzalez, Arizona Diamondbacks, NL (to August 14, 2002)
Miguel Tejada, Oakland Athletics, AL

2003 — Miguel Tejada, Oakland Athletics, AL

2004 — Miguel Tejada, Baltimore Orioles, AL

2005 — Miguel Tejada, Baltimore Orioles, AL

Appendix C: Longest Playing Streaks (500 or More Games)

Games	Name	Dates of Streak
2,632	Cal Ripken, Jr.	May 30, 1982, to September 19, 1998
2,130	Lou Gehrig	June 1, 1925, to April 30, 1939
1,307	Everett Scott	June 20, 1916, to May 5, 1925
1,207	Steve Garvey	September 3, 1975, to July 29, 1983 (1)
1,117	Billy Williams	September 22, 1963, to September 2, 1970
1,103	Joe Sewell	September 13, 1922, to April 30, 1930
918	Miguel Tejada	June 2, 2000, to present (active streak)
895	Stan Musial	April 15, 1952, to August 22, 1957
829	Eddie Yost	August 30, 1949, to May 11, 1955
822	Gus Suhr*	September 11, 1931, to June 4, 1937
798	Nellie Fox	August 7, 1955, to September 3, 1960
745	Pete Rose	September 1, 1978, to August 23, 1983
740	Dale Murphy	September 26, 1981, to July 8, 1986
730	Richie Ashburn*	June 7, 1950, to September 26, 1954
717	Ernie Banks	August 26, 1956, (2) to June 22, 1961
678	Pete Rose	September 28, 1973, to May 7, 1978 (1)
673	Earl Averill*	April 14, 1931, to June 28, 1935
652	Frank McCormick	April 19, 1938, to May 24, 1942 (2)
648	Sandy Alomar	May 16, 1969, to May 20, 1973
618	Eddie Brown*	June 5, 1924, to June 7, 1928
584	Roy McMillan	September 16, 1951, (1) to August 7, 1955 (1)
577	George Pinkney	September 21, 1885, to April 30, 1890
574	Steve Brodie	April 27, 1893, to June 26, 1897
565	Aaron Ward*	July 11, 1920, to May 26, 1924
546	Alex Rodriguez*	July 25, 2000, to September 23, 2003
539	Candy LaChance	June 24, 1901, to April 28, 1905
536	Buck Freeman	July 27, 1901, to June 5, 1905
533	Fred Luderus	June 2, 1916, to September 28, 1919 (2)

Appendix C

511	Clyde Milan	August 12, 1910, to October 3, 1913 (2)
511	Charlie Gehringer*	September 3, 1927, to May 7, 1931
508	Vada Pinson	September 26, 1958, to May 30, 1962 (2)
507	Joe Carter*	September 13, 1988, to April 8, 1992
504	Tony Cuccinello*	July 9, 1930, to August 24, 1933 (2)
504	Charlie Gehringer*	June 25, 1932, to August 11, 1935
503	Omar Moreno*	June 19, 1979, to September 4, 1982

* Was not a major league baseball Iron Man because the streak was entirely overlapped by another player's consecutive-games-playing streak.

Appendix D: Start Dates for Streaks of 500 or More Consecutive Games Played

500 games (35 streaks)

George Pinkney	July 13, 1889
Steve Brodie	August 28, 1896
Candy LaChance	September 14, 1904 (first game)
Buck Freeman	April 14, 1905
Clyde Milan	September 19, 1913
Fred Luderus	August 23, 1919 (second game)
Everett Scott	August 28, 1919 (second game)
Aaron Ward	August 26, 1923
Joe Sewell	May 8, 1926
Eddie Brown	July 18, 1927
Lou Gehrig	July 8, 1928 (first game)
Charlie Gehringer (1)	April 25, 1931
Tony Cuccinello	August 19, 1933
Earl Averill	June 7, 1934
Gus Suhr	May 14, 1935
Charlie Gehringer (2)	August 4, 1935
Frank McCormick	May 28, 1941
Eddie Yost	April 19, 1953
Richie Ashburn	July 11, 1953
Roy McMillan	May 14, 1955
Stan Musial	May 27, 1955
Nellie Fox	September 13, 1958
Ernie Banks	April 13, 1960
Vada Pinson	May 22, 1962
Billy Williams	April 18, 1967
Sandy Alomar	June 2, 1972
Pete Rose (1)	April 17, 1977
Steve Garvey	September 19, 1978
Pete Rose (2)	May 23, 1982
Omar Moreno	August 31, 1982
Dale Murphy	April 14, 1985

Appendix D

Cal Ripken Jr. — June 15, 1985
Joe Carter — September 30, 1991
Miguel Tejada — June 17, 2003
Alex Rodriguez — August 5, 2003

600 games (20 streaks)

Everett Scott — July 14, 1920 (first game)
Joe Sewell — August 25, 1926
Eddie Brown — May 14, 1928
Lou Gehrig — May 15, 1929
Earl Averill — September 16, 1934
Gus Suhr — August 28, 1935 (first game)
Frank McCormick — September 13, 1941
Eddie Yost — August 2, 1953
Richie Ashburn — May 13, 1954
Stan Musial — September 5, 1955
Nellie Fox — July 17, 1959
Ernie Banks — August 6, 1960
Billy Williams — August 2, 1967 (second game)
Sandy Alomar — September 19, 1972
Pete Rose (1) — August 8, 1977
Steve Garvey — July 12, 1979
Pete Rose (2) — September 10, 1982
Dale Murphy — August 8, 1985
Cal Ripken Jr. — October 3, 1985 (second game)
Miguel Tejada — April 10, 2004

700 games (15 streaks)

Everett Scott — May 17, 1921
Joe Sewell — June 30, 1927
Lou Gehrig — August 29, 1929 (first game)
Gus Suhr — July 2, 1936
Eddie Yost — June 11, 1954
Richie Ashburn — August 27, 1954
Stan Musial — July 16, 1956
Nellie Fox — May 24, 1960
Ernie Banks — June 4, 1961 (second game)
Billy Williams — May 29, 1968 (first game)
Steve Garvey — May 11, 1980
Pete Rose (2) — July 10, 1983
Dale Murphy — May 26, 1986
Cal Ripken Jr. — July 26, 1986
Miguel Tejada — August 4, 2004

800 games (10 streaks)

Everett Scott — September 2, 1921
Joe Sewell — April 27, 1928
Lou Gehrig — June 30, 1930
Gus Suhr — May 11, 1937
Eddie Yost — September 22, 1954

Stan Musial	May 17, 1957
Billy Williams	September 4, 1968 (second game)
Steve Garvey	August 30, 1980
Cal Ripken, Jr.	May 15, 1987
Miguel Tejada	May 24, 2005

***900 games* (7 streaks)**

Everett Scott	June 24, 1922 (second game)
Joe Sewell	August 15, 1928
Lou Gehrig	April 28, 1931
Billy Williams	July 3, 1969
Steve Garvey	August 17, 1981
Cal Ripken, Jr.	September 5, 1987
Miguel Tejada	September 13, 2005

***1,000 games* (6 streaks)**

Everett Scott	May 2, 1923
Joe Sewell	June 26, 1929
Lou Gehrig	August 17, 1931
Billy Williams	April 30, 1970
Steve Garvey	June 7, 1982
Cal Ripken, Jr.	June 25, 1988

***1,100 games* (6 streaks)**

Everett Scott	August 23, 1923
Joe Sewell	April 27, 1930
Lou Gehrig	June 19, 1932
Billy Williams	August 14, 1970
Steve Garvey	September 26, 1982
Cal Ripken, Jr.	April 18, 1989

***1,200 games* (4 streaks)**

Everett Scott	June 28, 1924
Lou Gehrig	April 14, 1933
Steve Garvey	July 22, 1983
Cal Ripken, Jr.	August 9, 1989

***1,300 games* (3 streaks)**

Everett Scott	April 25, 1925
Lou Gehrig	August 7, 1933 (second game)
Cal Ripken, Jr.	June 3, 1990

***1,400 games* (2 streaks)**

Lou Gehrig	June 15, 1934
Cal Ripken, Jr.	September 22, 1990

***1,500 games* (2 streaks)**

Lou Gehrig	September 25, 1934
Cal Ripken, Jr.	July 19, 1991

***1,600 games* (2 streaks)**

Lou Gehrig	August 8, 1935
Cal Ripken, Jr.	May 6, 1992

1,700 games (2 streaks)

Lou GehrigJune 5, 1936
Cal Ripken Jr.August 26, 1992

1,800 games (2 streaks)

Lou GehrigSeptember 19, 1936
Cal Ripken Jr.June 16, 1993

1,900 games (2 streaks)

Lou GehrigAugust 3, 1937 (first game)
Cal Ripken Jr.April 8, 1994

2,000 games (2 streaks)

Lou GehrigMay 31, 1938
Cal Ripken Jr.August 1, 1994

2,100 games (2 streaks)

Lou GehrigSeptember 9, 1938
Cal Ripken Jr.August 5, 1995

2,200 games (1 streak)

Cal Ripken Jr.May 26, 1996

2,300 games (1 streak)

Cal Ripken Jr.September 12, 1996

2,400 games (1 streak)

Cal Ripken Jr.July 5, 1997

2,500 games (1 streak)

Cal Ripken Jr.April 25, 1998

2,600 games (1 streak)

Cal Ripken Jr.August 15, 1998

Appendix E: Miscellaneous Consecutive Games Played Records

1. Positional Records

National League

Catcher	217 games — Ray Mueller (Cincinnati), July 31, 1943, to October 1, 1944
First Base	652 games — Frank McCormick (Cincinnati), April 19, 1938, to May 24, 1942 (2)
Second Base	443 games — Dave Cash (Pittsburgh and Philadelphia), September 20, 1973, to August 5, 1976
Third Base	364 games — Ron Santo (Chicago), April 19, 1964, to May 31, 1966
Shortstop	584 games — Roy McMillan (Cincinnati), September 16, 1951, (1) to August 6, 1955
Outfield	897 games — Billy Williams (Chicago), September 22, 1963, to June 13, 1969

American League

Catcher	312 games — Frankie Hayes (St. Louis, Philadelphia and Cleveland), October 2, 1943, (2) to April 21, 1946
First Base	885 games — Lou Gehrig (New York), June 2, 1925, to September 27, 1930
Second Base	798 games — Nellie Fox (Chicago), August 7, 1955, to September 3, 1960
Third Base	576 games — Eddie Yost (Washington), July 3, 1951, to May 11, 1955
Shortstop	2,216 games — Cal Ripken Jr. (Baltimore), July 1, 1982, to July 14, 1996
Outfield	511 games — Clyde Milan (Washington), August 12, 1910, to October 3, 1913 (2)

2. Franchise Team Consecutive Games Played Records (Active Franchises)

National League

Arizona	446 games, Luis Gonzalez, October 1, 1999, to August 13, 2002
Atlanta	740 games, Dale Murphy, September 26, 1981, to July 8, 1986
Chicago	1,117 games, Billy Williams, September 22, 1963, to September 2, 1970
Cincinnati	678 games, Pete Rose, September 28, 1973, to May 7, 1978 (1)
Colorado	307 games, Vinny Castilla, June 26, 1997, to June 14, 1999
Florida	375 games, Juan Pierre, March 31, 2003, to June 2, 2005
Houston	494 games, Craig Biggio, August 1, 1995, to August 4, 1998
Los Angeles	1,107 games, Steve Garvey, September 3, 1975, to October 3, 1982

APPENDIX E

Milwaukee	276 games, Robin Yount, August 13, 1987, to June 14, 1989
New York	192 games, Felix Millan, October 2, 1974, to May 11, 1976
	192 games, Steve Henderson, July 5, 1977, to August 2, 1978
Philadelphia	731 games, Richie Ashburn, June 7, 1950, to September 26, 1954
Pittsburgh	822 games, Gus Suhr, September 11, 1931, to June 4, 1937
St. Louis	895 games, Stan Musial, April 15, 1952, to August 22, 1957
San Diego	305 games, Steve Garvey, September 23, 1984, to September 6, 1986
San Francisco	468 games, Bill Terry, April 15, 1930, to April 24, 1933*
Washington	276 games, Vladimir Guerrero, April 19, 1998, to August 30, 1999**

American League

Baltimore	2,632 games, Cal Ripken Jr., May 30, 1982, to September 19, 1998
Boston	832 games, Everett Scott, June 20, 1916, to October 2, 1921
Chicago	798 games, Nellie Fox, August 7, 1955, to September 3, 1960
Cleveland	1,103 games, Joe Sewell, September 13, 1922, to April 30, 1930
Detroit	511 games, Charlie Gehringer, September 3, 1927, to May 7, 1931
Kansas City	305 games, Johnny Damon, March 31, 1998, to September 14, 1999 (1)
Los Angeles	648 games, Sandy Alomar, May 16, 1969, to May 20, 1973†
Minnesota	829 games, Eddie Yost, August 30, 1949, to May 11, 1955§
New York	2,130 games, Lou Gehrig, June 1, 1925, to April 30, 1939
Oakland	594 games, Miguel Tejada, June 2, 2000, to September 28, 2003
Seattle	293 games, Edgar Martinez, June 12, 1994, to July 20, 1996
Tampa Bay	398 games, Aubrey Huff, May 28, 2002, to August 21, 2004
Texas	482 games, Alex Rodriguez, April 1, 2001, to September 23, 2003
Toronto	432 games, Carlos Delgado, April 3, 2000, to August 3, 2002

* Streak was compiled when San Francisco franchise was known as the New York Giants
† Streak was compiled when Los Angeles franchise was known as the California Angels
§ Streak was compiled when Minnesota franchise was known as the Washington Senators
** Streak was compiled when Washington franchise was known as the Montreal Expos.

3. Major Leaguers Who Played the Most Full Schedule Seasons (since 1876):

15	Cal Ripken, Jr. Baltimore, AL, 1983–1997
13	Lou Gehrig, New York, AL, 1926–1938
10	Pete Rose, Cincinnati and Philadelphia, NL, 1965; 1972; 1974–1977; 1979–1982
9	Stan Musial, St. Louis, NL, 1943; 1946; 1948–1949; 1952–1956
8	Jim O'Rourke, Buffalo, Boston and New York, NL, 1876–1878; 1880–1882; 1885; 1891
8	Everett Scott, Boston and New York, AL, 1917–1924
8	Joe Sewell, Cleveland, AL, 1921; 1923–1929
8	Steve Garvey, Los Angeles and San Diego, NL, 1976–1982; 1985
7	Cap Anson, Chicago, NL, 1876; 1880–1881; 1883–1884; 1890; 1892
7	Richie Ashburn, Philadelphia, NL, 1949; 1951–1954; 1956–1957
6	Roger Connor, Troy and New York, NL, 1880–1881; 1883–1884; 1889; 1892
6	George Van Haltren, Baltimore, AA and New York, NL, 1891; 1894; 1896; 1898–1900
6	Eddie Collins, Philadelphia and Chicago, AL, 1909; 1912; 1915–1917; 1919
6	Del Pratt, St. Louis, New York and Boston, AL, 1913; 1915–1916; 1918; 1920; 1922

6	Charlie Gehringer, Detroit, AL, 1928–1930; 1933–1934; 1936
6	Earl Averill, Cleveland, AL, 1929; 1931–1934; 1936
6	Ernie Banks, Chicago, NL, 1954–1955; 1957–1960
6	Billy Williams, Chicago, NL, 1964–1969
5	John Morrill, Boston, NL, 1877–1880, 1887
5	Paul Hines, Chicago and Boston, NL, 1877–1879; 1882; 1886
5	Jimmy Wolf, Louisville, AA, 1883–1885; 1887; 1890
5	Sam Crawford, Detroit, AL, 1903; 1905; 1913–1915
5	Rogers Hornsby, St. Louis, New York and Chicago, NL, 1919; 1921–1922; 1927; 1929
5	Gus Suhr, Pittsburgh, NL, 1932–1936
5	Billy Herman, Chicago and Brooklyn, NL, 1932; 1935; 1939; 1942–1943
5	Rudy York, Detroit, Boston and Chicago, AL, 1940–1941; 1943; 1945; 1947
5	Eddie Yost, Washington, AL, 1950–1954
5	Nellie Fox, Chicago, AL, 1954; 1956–1959
5	Eddie Murray, Baltimore, AL, and Los Angeles, NL, 1978–1979; 1984; 1988–1989
5	Miguel Tejada, Oakland and Baltimore, AL 2001–2005

4. All-Time Record Holders of Consecutive Games Played:

212 games, John Clapp, St. Louis, Indianapolis and Buffalo (NL),
   April 25, 1876, to June 24, 1879
(record holder to July 8, 1879)

262 games, Cal McVey, Chicago and Cincinnati (NL),
   May 10, 1876, to September 30, 1879
(record holder from July 8, 1879, to August 17, 1880)

302 games, John Morrill, Boston (NL), April 30, 1877, to May 18, 1881
(record holder from August 17, 1880, to June 8, 1883)

319 games, Jim O'Rourke, Providence, Boston and Buffalo (NL),
   August 19, 1879, to July 2, 1883
(record holder from June 8, 1883, to July 10, 1883)

464 games, Mike Hornung, Buffalo and Boston (NL),
   September 1, 1879, to September 11, 1884
(record holder from July 10, 1883, to May 27, 1889)

577 games, George Pinkney, Brooklyn (AA and NL),
   September 21, 1885, to April 30, 1890
(record holder from May 27, 1889, to June 21, 1920)

1,307 games, Everett Scott, Boston and New York (AL),
   June 20, 1916, to May 5, 1925
(record holder from June 21, 1920, to August 17, 1933)

2,130 games, Lou Gehrig, New York (AL), June 1, 1925, to April 30, 1939
(record holder from August 17, 1933, to September 6, 1995)

2,632 games, Cal Ripken Jr., Baltimore (AL), May 30, 1982, to September 19, 1998
(record holder from September 6, 1995, to present)

(Note: National Association games are not included.)

Appendix E

5. Most Consecutive Games Played at the Beginning of a Career

National League

424 games, Ernie Banks (Chicago Cubs), September 17, 1953, to August 10, 1956

American League

487 games, Hideki Matsui (New York Yankees), March 31, 2003 to present

6. Major League Baseball Iron Men Hall of Famers

Ernie Banks (1977 — BBWAA)
Jake Beckley (1971— Veterans Committee)
Jesse Burkett (1946 — Veterans Committee)
Eddie Collins (1939 — BBWAA)
Jimmy Collins (1945 — Veterans Committee)
Sam Crawford (1957 — Veterans Committee)
Bobby Doerr (1986 — Veterans Committee)
Hugh Duffy (1945 — Veterans Committee)
Nellie Fox (1997 — Veterans Committee)
Lou Gehrig (1939 — BBWAA)
Billy Herman (1975 — Veterans Committee)
Tommy McCarthy (1946 — Veterans Committee)
Bid McPhee (2000 — Veterans Committee)
Stan Musial (1969 — BBWAA)
Jim O'Rourke (1945 — Veterans Committee)
Brooks Robinson (1983 — BBWAA)
Mike Schmidt (1995 — BBWAA)
Joe Sewell (1977 — Veterans Committee)
Zack Wheat (1959 — Veterans Committee)
Billy Williams (1987 — BBWAA)

Appendix F: Season by Season Review of Major Leaguers Who Played All Their Team's Games

(Year, League, Name, Team, Number of Games Played)

1876 (22 players)

National League

Jack Manning, Boston, 70
Jim O'Rourke, Boston, 70
George Wright, Boston, 70
Harry Schafer, Boston, 70
Jack Burdock, Hartford, 69
Bob Ferguson, Hartford, 69
Jack Remsen, Hartford, 69
Deacon White, Chicago, 66
Ross Barnes, Chicago, 66
Cap Anson, Chicago, 66
John Peters, Chicago, 66
John Glenn, Chicago, 66
Al Spalding, Chicago, 66
John Clapp, St. Louis, 64
Herman Dehlman, St. Louis, 64
Joe Battin, St. Louis, 64
George Bradley, St. Louis, 64
Davy Force, Philadelphia-New York, 61
George Hall, Philadelphia, 60
Al Nichols, New York, 57
Fred Treacey, New York, 57
Eddie Booth, New York, 57

1877 (19 players)

National League

George Wright, Boston, 61
John Morrill, Boston, 61
Jim O'Rourke, Boston, 61
Tommy Bond, Boston, 61
Pop Snyder, Louisville, 61
George Hall, Louisville, 61
Orator Shafer, Louisville, 61
Bill Crowley, Louisville, 61
Jim Devlin, Louisville, 61
Joe Start, Hartford, 60
Tom Carey, Hartford, 60
John Cassidy, Hartford, 60
John Clapp, St. Louis, 60
Mike Dorgan, St. Louis, 60
Cal McVey, Chicago, 60
Al Spalding, Chicago, 60
John Peters, Chicago, 60
Paul Hines, Chicago, 60
Lip Pike, Cincinnati, 58

1878 (24 players)

National League

Silver Flint, Indianapolis, 63
Ned Williamson, Indianapolis, 63
Orator Shafer, Indianapolis, 63
Russ McKelvy, Indianapolis, 63
John Clapp, Indianapolis, 63
Bill Hague, Providence, 62
Dick Higham, Providence, 62
Paul Hines, Providence, 62
Tom York, Providence, 62
Deacon White, Cincinnati, 61
Chub Sullivan, Cincinnati, 61

APPENDIX F

Cal McVey, Cincinnati, 61
Billy Geer, Cincinnati, 61
Charley Jones, Cincinnati, 61
Joe Start, Chicago, 61
Bob Ferguson, Chicago, 61
Abner Dalrymple, Milwaukee, 61
Pop Snyder, Boston, 60
John Morrill, Boston, 60
Jack Burdock, Boston, 60
Ezra Sutton, Boston, 60
Andy Leonard, Boston, 60
Jack Manning, Boston, 60
Jim O'Rourke, Boston, 60

1879 (13 players)
National League

Mike McGeary, Providence, 85
George Wright, Providence, 85
Paul Hines, Providence, 85
Jack Burdock, Boston, 84
Ezra Sutton, Boston, 84
John Morrill, Boston, 84
Joe Quest, Chicago, 83
John Peters, Chicago, 83
Cal McVey, Cincinnati, 81
Pete Hotaling, Cincinnati, 81
Buttercup Dickerson, Cincinnati, 81
Davy Force, Buffalo, 79
Hardy Richardson, Buffalo, 79

1880 (15 players)
National League

Emil Gross, Providence, 87
Cap Anson, Chicago, 86
Abner Dalrymple, Chicago, 86
John Morrill, Boston, 86
Jack Burdock, Boston, 86
Jim O'Rourke, Boston, 86
Bill Phillips, Cleveland, 85
Fred Dunlap, Cleveland, 85
George Creamer, Worcester, 85
Art Irwin, Worcester, 85
Bill Crowley, Buffalo, 85
Joe Hornung, Buffalo, 85
Roger Connor, Troy, 83
John Cassidy, Troy, 83
Pop Smith, Cincinnati, 83

1881 (18 players)
National League

Jerry Denny, Providence, 85
Monte Ward, Providence, 85
Tom York, Providence, 85
Roger Connor, Troy, 85
Bob Ferguson, Troy, 85
Frank Hankinson, Troy, 85
John Cassidy, Troy, 85
Bill Phillips, Cleveland, 85
Jack Glasscock, Cleveland, 85
Orator Shafer, Cleveland, 85
Cap Anson, Chicago, 84
Tom Burns, Chicago, 84
Curry Foley, Buffalo, 83
Jim O'Rourke, Buffalo, 83
Hardy Richardson, Buffalo, 83
Ezra Sutton, Boston, 83
Joe Hornung, Boston, 83
Hick Carpenter, Worcester, 83

1882 (28 players)
National League

Lou Knight, Detroit, 86
Joe Hornung, Boston, 85
Fred Pfeffer, Troy, 85
Tom Burns, Chicago, 84
King Kelly, Chicago, 84
George Gore, Chicago, 84
Abner Dalrymple, Chicago, 84
Jack Farrell, Providence, 84
Jerry Denny, Providence, 84
Paul Hines, Providence, 84
Dan Brouthers, Buffalo, 84
Curry Foley, Buffalo, 84
Jim O'Rourke, Buffalo, 84
Blondie Purcell, Buffalo, 84
Fred Dunlap, Cleveland, 84
Jack Glasscock, Cleveland, 84
Mike Muldoon, Cleveland, 84
Orator Shafer, Cleveland, 84
Harry Stovey, Worcester, 84
Art Irwin, Worcester, 84

American Association

Hick Carpenter, Cincinnati, 80
Joe Sommer, Cincinnati, 80
George Strief, Pittsburgh, 79

Mike Mansell, Pittsburgh, 79
Bill Gleason, St. Louis, 79
Jud Birchall, Philadelphia, 75
Ed Whiting, Baltimore, 74
Charles Householder, Baltimore, 74

1883 (25 players)

National League

Martin Powell, Detroit, 101
Sadie Houck, Detroit, 101
Joe Farrell, Detroit, 101
Paul Hotaling, Cleveland, 100
Tom York, Cleveland, 100
Sid Farrar, Philadelphia, 99
Joe Hornung, Boston, 98
Cap Anson, Chicago, 98
Ned Williamson, Chicago, 98
King Kelly, Chicago, 98
Art Irwin, Providence, 98
Jerry Denny, Providence, 98
Dan Brouthers, Buffalo, 98
Roger Connor, New York, 98
Pete Gillespie, New York, 98

American Association

Bill Gleason, St. Louis, 98
Arlie Latham, St. Louis, 98
John Reilly, Cincinnati, 98
Jimmy Wolf, Louisville, 98
Joe Battin, Pittsburgh, 98
Steve Brady, New York, 97
Candy Nelson, New York, 97
Dude Esterbrook, New York, 97
Pop Smith, Columbus, 97
Tom Brown, Columbus, 97

1884 (22 players)

National League

Alex McKinnon, New York, 116
Roger Connor, New York, 116
Paul Hines, Providence, 114
Jim Lillie, Buffalo, 114
Ned Hanlon, Detroit, 114
George Wood, Detroit, 114
Cap Anson, Chicago, 112
Fred Pfeffer, Chicago, 112

American Association

Billy Geer, Philadelphia-Brooklyn, 116
Steve Brady, New York, 112
Dude Esterbrook, New York, 112
Bid McPhee, Cincinnati, 112
Charley Jones, Cincinnati, 112
Bill Kuehne, Columbus, 110
Jimmy Wolf, Louisville, 110
Bill Gleason, St. Louis, 110
Arlie Latham, St. Louis, 110
Hugh Nicol, St. Louis, 110
Curt Welch, Toledo, 109
Sadie Houck, Philadelphia, 108
Lou Knight, Philadelphia, 108

Union Association

Emmett Seery, Baltimore, 105

1885 (22 players)

National League

Ned Williamson, Chicago, 113
Abner Dalrymple, Chicago, 113
Joe Gerhardt, New York, 112
Jim O'Rourke, New York, 112
Jim Lillie, Buffalo, 112
Sid Farrar, Philadelphia, 111
Jim Fogarty, Philadelphia, 111
Jack Glasscock, St. Louis, 111

American Association

Bill Gleason, St. Louis, 112
Hugh Nicol, St. Louis, 112
Curt Welch, St. Louis, 112
Frank Fennelly, Cincinnati, 112
Hick Carpenter, Cincinnati, 112
Pop Corkhill, Cincinnati, 112
Charley Jones, Cincinnati, 112
Bill McClellan, Brooklyn, 112
Tom McLaughlin, Louisville, 112
John Kerins, Louisville, 112
Jimmy Wolf, Louisville, 112
Pete Browning, Louisville, 112
Joe Sommer, Baltimore, 110
Steve Brady, New York, 108

1886 (7 players)

National League

Ned Hanlon, Detroit, 126
Emmett Seery, St. Louis, 126

American Association

Bill Phillips, Brooklyn, 141
George Pinkney, Brooklyn, 141
Bill McClellan, Brooklyn, 141
Henry Larkin, Philadelphia, 139

Appendix F

Joe Sommer, Baltimore, 139

1887 (9 players)

National League

Monte Ward, New York, 129
Sam Thompson, Detroit, 127
Ned Williamson, Chicago, 127
Joe Morrill, Boston, 127
Dick Johnston, Boston, 127

American Association

George Pinkney, Brooklyn, 138
Jimmy Wolf, Louisville, 137
Chippy McGarr, Philadelphia, 137
Denny Lyons, Philadelphia, 137

1888 (8 players)

National League

Bill Kuehne, Pittsburgh, 138
Dummy Hoy, Washington, 136
Fred Pfeffer, Chicago, 135
Sid Farrar, Philadelphia, 131

American Association

George Pinkney, Brooklyn, 143
Charlie Comiskey, St. Louis, 137
Mike Griffin, Baltimore, 137
Curt Welch, Philadelphia, 136

1889 (19 players)

National League

Tom Burns, Chicago, 136
Hugh Duffy, Chicago, 136
Cub Stricker, Cleveland, 136
Paul Radford, Cleveland, 136
Patsy Tebeau, Cleveland, 136
Roger Connor, New York, 131
Sid Farrar, Philadelphia, 130
Dummy Hoy, Washington, 127

American Association

Ollie Beard, Cincinnati, 141
Shorty Fuller, St. Louis, 140
Tommy McCarthy, St. Louis, 140
Jim McTamany, Columbus, 139
Lefty Marr, Columbus, 139
Ecky Stearns, Kansas City, 139
Dave Foutz, Brooklyn, 138
Hub Colllins, Brooklyn, 138
George Pinkney, Brooklyn, 138
Pop Corkhill, Brooklyn, 138
Frank Fennelly, Philadelphia, 138

1890 (25 players)

National League

Tom Burns, Chicago, 139
Cap Anson, Chicago, 139
Walt Wilmot, Chicago, 139
Doggie Miller, Pittsburgh, 138
Will Smalley, Cleveland, 136
George Davis, Cleveland, 136
Ed McKean, Cleveland, 136
Pop Smith, Boston, 134
Bob Allen, Philadelphia, 133
Dave Foutz, Brooklyn, 129
Hub Collins, Brooklyn, 129
Germany Smith, Brooklyn, 129

American Association

Mike Lehane, Columbus, 140
Harry Taylor, Louisville, 134
Jimmy Wolf, Louisville, 134
Parson Nicholson, Toledo, 134
Frank Scheibeck, Toledo, 134
Harry Lyons, Rochester, 133

Players League

Hugh Duffy, Chicago, 138
Lou Bierbauer, Brooklyn, 133
Bill Joyce, Brooklyn, 133
Billy Shindle, Philadelphia, 132
George Wood, Philadelphia, 132
Joe Quinn, Boston, 130
Hardy Richardson, Boston, 130

1891 (15 players)

National League

Cupid Childs, Cleveland, 141
Ed McKean, Cleveland, 141
Tommy Tucker, Boston, 140
Billy Nash, Boston, 140
Bid McPhee, Cincinnati, 138
Germany Smith, Cincinnati, 138
Fred Pfeffer, Chicago, 137
Jim O'Rourke, New York, 136

American Association

Charlie Comiskey, St. Louis, 139
Dummy Hoy, St. Louis, 139

Perry Werden, Baltimore, 139
George Van Haltren, Baltimore, 139
Pete Gilbert, Baltimore, 139
Cub Stricker, Boston, 139
Jack Crooks, Columbus, 138

1892 (5 players)
National League

Roger Connor, Philadelphia, 155
Tommy McCarthy, Boston, 152
Lou Bierbauer, Pittsburgh, 152
Duke Farrell, Pittsburgh, 152
Cap Anson, Chicago, 146

1893 (8 players)
National League

Joe Quinn, St. Louis, 135
Steve Brodie, St. Louis-Baltimore, 132
Hugh Duffy, Boston, 131
Jake Beckley, Pittsburgh, 131
Denny Lyons, Pittsburgh, 131
Heinie Reitz, Baltimore, 130
Dave Foutz, Brooklyn, 130
Dummy Hoy, Washington, 130

1894 (11 players)
National League

George Van Haltren, New York, 139
Bobby Lowe, Boston, 133
Frank Shugart, St. Louis, 133
Patsy Donovan, Pittsburgh, 133
Ed Cartwright, Washington, 132
Billy Hamilton, Philadelphia, 132
Ed McKean, Cleveland, 130
Tom Brown, Louisville, 130
Joe Kelley, Baltimore, 129
Steve Brodie, Baltimore, 129
Willie Keeler, Baltimore, 129

1895 (14 players)
National League

Bill Everitt, Chicago, 133
Jack Boyle, Philadelphia, 133
Billy Nash, Boston, 133
Deacon McGuire, Washington, 133
Charlie Abbey, Washington, 133
Dusty Miller, Cincinnati, 132
Fred Clarke, Louisville, 132

Jesse Burkett, Cleveland, 132
Jimmy McAleer, Cleveland, 132
Ed McKean, Cleveland, 132
Steve Brodie, Baltimore, 131
Hugh Jennings, Baltimore, 131
Joe Kelley, Baltimore, 131
Willie Keeler, Baltimore, 131

1896 (8 players)
National League

Mike Tiernan, New York, 133
George Van Haltren, New York, 133
Kid Gleason, New York, 133
Gene DeMontreville, Washington, 133
Ed Cartwright, Washington, 133
Steve Brodie, Baltimore, 132
Bill Everitt, Chicago, 132
Patsy Donovan, Pittsburgh, 131

1897 (5 players)
National League

Charlie Irwin, Cincinnati, 134
Dick Padden, Pittsburgh, 134
Duff Cooley, Philadelphia, 133
Gene DeMontreville, Washington, 133
Bobby Wallace, Cleveland, 130

1898 (4 players)
National League

George Van Haltren, New York 156
Billy Clingman, Louisville, 154
Jimmy Collins, Boston, 152
Hugh Duffy, Boston, 152

1899 (3 players)
National League

Buck Freeman, Washington, 155
Monte Cross, Philadelphia, 154
George Van Haltren, New York, 152

1900 (5 players)
National League

Jimmy Collins, Boston, 142
George Van Haltren, New York, 141
Jimmy Slagle, Philadelphia, 141
Jesse Burkett, St. Louis, 141
Kip Selbach, New York, 141

Appendix F

1901 (17 players)
American League

Bill Hallman, Milwaukee, 139
Hobe Ferris, Boston, 138
Freddy Parent, Boston, 138
Jimmy Collins, Boston, 138
Tommy Dowd, Boston, 138
Sam Dungan, Washington, 138
Frank Isbell, Chicago, 137
Sam Mertes, Chicago, 137
Kid Gleason, Detroit, 135
Jimmy Barrett, Detroit, 135
Cy Seymour, Baltimore, 134

National League

Otto Krueger, St. Louis, 142
Jesse Burkett, St. Louis, 142
Claude Ritchey, Pittsburgh, 140
Honus Wagner, Pittsburgh, 140
Gene DeMontreville, Boston, 140
Topsy Hartsel, Chicago, 140

1902 (12 players)
American League

Barry McCormick, St. Louis, 139
Candy LaChance, Boston, 138
Freddy Parent, Boston, 138
Buck Freeman, Boston, 138
Monte Cross, Philadelphia, 137
Lave Cross, Philadelphia, 137
Socks Seybold, Philadelphia, 137
Topsy Hartsel, Philadelphia, 137
Bill Bradley, Cleveland, 137

National League

Cozy Dolan, Brooklyn, 141
Shad Barry, Philadelphia, 138
Roy Thomas, Philadelphia, 138

1903 (18 players)
American League

Candy LaChance, Boston, 141
Hobe Ferris, Boston, 141
Buck Freeman, Boston, 141
Elmer Flick, Cleveland, 140
Harry Bay, Cleveland, 140
Kip Selbach, Washington, 140
Frank Isbell, Chicago, 138
Lee Tannehill, Chicago, 138
Monte Cross, Philadelphia, 137
Lave Cross, Philadelphia, 137
Socks Seybold, Philadelphia, 137
Ollie Pickering, Philadelphia, 137
Sam Crawford, Detroit, 137

National League

Ginger Beaumont, Pittsburgh, 141
Ed Gremminger, Boston, 140
Jimmy Slagle, Chicago, 139
Jack Doyle, Brooklyn, 139
Jimmy Sheckard, Brooklyn, 139

1904 (8 players)
American League

Jimmy Barrett, Detroit, 162
Candy LaChance, Boston, 157
Buck Freeman, Boston, 157
Chick Stahl, Boston, 157
Tom Jones, St. Louis, 156
Lave Cross, Philadelphia, 155
Bill Bradley, Cleveland, 154

National League

Claude Ritchey, Pittsburgh, 156

1905 (8 players)
American League

Bobby Wallace, St. Louis, 156
Terry Turner, Cleveland, 155
Sam Crawford, Detroit, 154
Freddy Parent, Boston, 153

National League

Jimmy Slagle, Chicago, 155
Kid Gleason, Philadelphia, 155
Ernie Courtney, Philadelphia, 155
Sherry Magee, Philadelphia, 155

1906 (11 players)
American League

Elmer Flick, Cleveland, 157
Chick Stahl, Boston, 155
Jiggs Donahue, Chicago, 154
Charlie Hemphill, St. Louis, 154
George Stone, St. Louis, 154
John Anderson, Washington, 151

National League

Johnny Evers, Chicago, 154

Jim Nealon, Pittsburgh, 154
Mickey Doolan, Philadelphia, 154
Sherry Magee, Philadelphia, 154
Cozy Dolan, Boston, 152

1907 (7 players)
American League

Jiggs Donahue, Chicago, 157
Tom Jones, St. Louis, 155
George Stone, St. Louis, 155
Bob Ganley, Washington, 154
Claude Rossman, Detroit, 153

National League

Miller Huggins, Cincinnati, 156
Spike Shannon, New York, 155

1908 (9 players)
American League

Nap Lajoie, Cleveland, 157
Tom Jones, St. Louis, 155
George McBride, Washington, 155
Germany Schaefer, Detroit, 153

National League

Art Devlin, New York, 157
Hans Lobert, Cincinnati, 155
John Hummel, Brooklyn, 154
Ed Konetchy, St. Louis, 154
Red Murray, St. Louis, 154

1909 (4 players)
American League

George McBride, Washington, 156
Eddie Collins, Philadelphia, 153

National League

Owen Wilson, Pittsburgh, 154
Eddie Grant, Philadelphia, 154

1910 (2 players)
American League

None

National League

Mike Mitchell, Cincinnati, 156
Zack Wheat, Brooklyn, 156

1911 (4 players)
American League

George McBride, Washington, 154
Clyde Milan, Washington, 154

National League

Ed Konetchy, St. Louis, 158
Dode Paskert, Philadelphia, 153

1912 (6 players)
American League

Duffy Lewis, Boston, 154
Eddie Foster, Washington, 154
Clyde Milan, Washington, 154
Stuffy McInnis, Philadelphia, 153
Eddie Collins, Philadelphia, 153

National League

Owen Wilson, Pittsburgh, 152

1913 (3 players)
American League

Del Pratt, St. Louis, 155
Sam Crawford, Detroit, 153

National League

Owen Wilson, Pittsburgh, 155

1914 (7 players)
American League

Donie Bush, Detroit, 157
Sam Crawford, Detroit, 157
Roger Peckinpaugh, New York, 157
Eddie Foster, Washington, 157

National League

None

Federal League

Fred Beck, Chicago, 157
Al Wickland, Chicago, 157
Charlie Hanford, Buffalo, 155

1915 (18 players)
American League

Del Pratt, St. Louis, 159
Sam Crawford, Detroit, 156
Ty Cobb, Detroit, 156
Eddie Collins, Chicago, 155
Ray Chapman, Cleveland, 154

Appendix F

National League

Heinie Groh, Cincinnati, 160
Tommy Griffith, Cincinnati, 160
Red Smith, Boston, 157
Honus Wagner, Pittsburgh, 156
Bill Hinchman, Pittsburgh, 156
George Burns, New York 155
George Cutshaw, Brooklyn, 154
Dave Bancroft, Philadelphia, 153

Federal League

Babe Borton, St. Louis, 159
Jimmy Esmond, Newark, 155
Al Scheer, Newark, 155
George Perring, Kansas City, 153
Claude Cooper, Brooklyn, 153

1916 (6 players)

American League

Del Pratt, St. Louis, 158
Eddie Collins, Chicago, 155
Joe Jackson, Chicago, 155

National League

Ed Konetchy, Boston, 158
George Burns, New York, 155
Tommy Griffith, Cincinnati, 155

1917 (6 players)

American League

Everett Scott, Boston, 157
Eddie Collins, Chicago, 156
Ray Chapman, Cleveland, 156
Wally Pipp, New York, 155
Bobby Veach, Detroit, 154

National League

Fred Luderus, Philadelphia, 154

1918 (16 players)

American League

Joe Judge, Washington, 130
George Burns, Philadelphia, 130
Donie Bush, Detroit, 128
Everett Scott, Boston, 126
Harry Hooper, Boston, 126
Del Pratt, New York, 126
Frank Baker, New York, 126
Joe Gedeon, St. Louis, 123

National League

Charlie Hollocher, Chicago, 131
George Cutshaw, Pittsburgh, 126
Bill McKechnie, Pittsburgh, 126
Max Carey, Pittsburgh, 126
Ivy Olson, Brooklyn, 126
Fred Luderus, Philadelphia, 125
Dave Bancroft, Philadelphia, 125
Art Fletcher, New York, 124

1919 (13 players)

American League

Frank Baker, New York, 141
Duffy Lewis, New York, 141
Eddie Collins, Chicago, 140
Buck Weaver, Chicago, 140
Harry Heilmann, Detroit, 140
Wally Gerber, St. Louis, 140
Bill Wambsganss, Cleveland, 139
Larry Gardner, Cleveland, 139
Everett Scott, Boston, 138

National League

Jake Daubert, Cincinnati, 140
George Cutshaw, Pittsburgh, 139
Rogers Hornsby, St. Louis, 138
Fred Luderus, Philadelphia, 138

1920 (12 players)

American League

Larry Gardner, Cleveland, 154
Del Pratt, New York, 154
George Sisler, St. Louis, 154
Wally Gerber, St. Louis, 154
Baby Doll Jacobson, St. Louis, 154
Everett Scott, Boston, 154
Sam Rice, Washington, 153

National League

Jimmy Johnston, Brooklyn, 155
George Kelly, New York, 155
Milt Stock, St. Louis, 155
Pat Duncan, Cincinnati, 154
Tony Boeckel, Boston, 153

1921 (14 players)

American League

Jimmy Dykes, Philadelphia, 155
Joe Sewell, Cleveland, 154
Bucky Harris, Washington, 154

Howard Shanks, Washington, 154
Everett Scott, Boston, 154
Earl Sheely, Chicago, 154
Wally Pipp, New York, 153
Aaron Ward, New York, 153

National League

Rogers Hornsby, St. Louis, 154
Dave Bancroft, New York, 153
Frankie Frisch, New York, 153
Tony Boeckel, Boston, 153
Sam Bohne, Cincinnati, 153
Jimmy Johnston, Brooklyn, 152

1922 (16 players)

American League

Topper Rigney, Detroit, 155
Bobby Veach, Detroit, 155
Chick Galloway, Philadelphia, 155
Aaron Ward, New York, 154
Everett Scott, New York, 154
Marty McManus, St. Louis, 154
Bucky Harris, Washington, 154
Sam Rice, Washington, 154
Del Pratt, Boston, 154

National League

Dave Bancroft, New York, 156
Jake Daubert, Cincinnati, 156
Babe Pinelli, Cincinnati, 156
George Burns, Cincinnati, 156
Rabbit Maranville, Pittsburgh, 155
Max Carey, Pittsburgh, 155
Rogers Hornsby, St. Louis, 154

1923 (9 players)

American League

Earl Sheeley, Chicago, 156
Marty McManus, St. Louis, 154
Wally Gerber, St. Louis, 154
Joe Sewell, Cleveland, 153
Aaron Ward, New York, 152
Everett Scott, New York, 152
Babe Ruth, New York, 152

National League

George Burns, Cincinnati, 154
Jigger Statz, Chicago, 154

1924 (7 players)

American League

Wally Pipp, New York, 153
Everett Scott, New York, 153
Babe Ruth, New York, 153
Joe Sewell, Cleveland, 153
Al Simmons, Philadelphia, 152

National League

Jack Fournier, Brooklyn, 154
Glenn Wright, Pittsburgh, 153

1925 (12 players)

American League

Bob Meusel, New York, 156
Joe Sewell, Cleveland, 155
Bibb Falk, Chicago, 154
Marty McManus, St. Louis, 154
Gene Robertson, St. Louis, 154
Al Simmons, Philadelphia, 153
Sam Rice, Washington, 152

National League

Glenn Wright, Pittsburgh, 153
Kiki Cuyler, Pittsburgh, 153
Jim Bottomley, St. Louis, 153
Les Bell, St. Louis, 153
Eddie Brown, Brooklyn, 153

1926 (10 players)

American League

Lou Gehrig, New York, 155
Tony Lazzeri, New York, 155
Bibb Falk, Chicago, 155
Joe Sewell, Cleveland, 154
Homer Summa, Cleveland, 154
Phil Todt, Boston, 154
Sam Rice, Washington, 152

National League

Kiki Cuyler, Pittsburgh, 157
Tommy Thevenow, St. Louis, 156
Eddie Brown, Boston, 153

1927 (5 players)

American League

Lou Gehrig, New York, 155
Joe Sewell, Cleveland, 153

National League

Appendix F

Rogers Hornsby, New York, 155
Eddie Brown, Boston, 155
Frankie Frisch, St. Louis, 153

1928 (14 players)
American League

Willie Kamm, Chicago, 155
Joe Sewell, Cleveland, 155
Lou Gehrig, New York, 154
Babe Ruth, New York, 154
Lu Blue, St. Louis, 154
Heinie Manush, St. Louis, 154
Charlie Gehringer, Detroit, 154

National League

Del Bissonette, Brooklyn, 155
Taylor Douthit, St. Louis, 154
Hughie Critz, Cincinnati, 153
Les Bell, Boston, 153
Paul Waner, Pittsburgh, 152
Lloyd Waner, Pittsburgh, 152
Fresno Thompson, Philadelphia, 152

1929 (12 players)
American League

Dale Alexander, Detroit, 155
Charlie Gehringer, Detroit, 155
Lou Gehrig, New York, 154
Frank O'Rourke, St. Louis, 154
Joe Sewell, Cleveland, 152
Earl Averill, Cleveland, 152
Bill Cissell. Chicago, 152

National League

Rogers Hornsby, Chicago, 156
Don Hurst, Philadelphia, 154
Pinky Whitney, Philadelphia, 154
Lefty O'Doul, Philadelphia, 154
George Sisler, Boston, 154

1930 (14 players)
American League

Bing Miller, Philadelphia, 154
Joe Cronin, Washington, 154
Lou Gehrig, New York, 154
Johnny Hodapp, Cleveland, 154
Dale Alexander, Detroit, 154
Charlie Gehringer, Detroit, 154
Red Kress, St. Louis, 154

Tom Oliver, Boston, 154

National League

Woody English, Chicago, 156
Kiki Cuyler, Chicago, 156
Tommy Thevenow, Philadelphia, 156
Chuck Klein, Philadelphia, 156
Taylor Douthit, St. Louis, 154
Bill Terry, New York, 154

1931 (9 players)
American League

Joe Cronin, Washington, 156
Lou Gehrig, New York, 155
Lyn Lary, New York, 155
Earl Averill, Cleveland, 155

National League

Woody English, Chicago, 156
Wally Berger, Boston, 156
Pie Traynor, Pittsburgh, 155
Tony Cuccinello, Cincinnati, 154
Bill Terry, New York, 153

1932 (16 players)
American League

Lou Gehrig, New York, 156
Jimmie Foxx, Philadelphia, 154
Al Simmons, Philadelphia, 154
Oscar Melillo, St. Louis, 154
Earl Averill, Cleveland, 153
Joe Vosmik, Cleveland, 153

National League

Billy Herman, Chicago, 154
Gus Suhr, Pittsburgh, 154
Tony Piet, Pittsburgh, 154
Paul Waner, Pittsburgh, 154
Tony Cuccinello, Brooklyn, 154
Dick Bartell, Philadelphia, 154
Pinky Whitney, Philadelphia, 154
Chuck Klein, Philadelphia, 154
Bill Terry, New York, 154
Mel Ott, New York, 154

1933 (15 players)
American League

Charlie Gehringer, Detroit, 155
Billy Rogell, Detroit, 155

Played All Games

Joe Kuhel, Washington, 153
Heinie Manush, Washington, 153
Lou Gehrig, New York, 152
Pinky Higgins, Philadelphia, 152
Doc Cramer, Philadelphia, 152
Earl Averill, Cleveland, 151
Luke Appling, Chicago, 151
Jimmy Dykes, Chicago, 151

National League

Gus Suhr, Pittsburgh, 154
Pie Traynor, Pittsburgh, 154
Paul Waner, Pittsburgh, 154
Dick Bartell, Philadelphia, 152
Chuck Klein, Philadelphia, 152

1934 (13 players)

American League

Charlie Gehringer, Detroit, 154
Billy Rogell, Detroit, 154
Marv Owen, Detroit, 154
Lou Gehrig, New York, 154
Hal Trosky, Cleveland, 154
Earl Averill, Cleveland, 154
Jack Burns, St. Louis, 154
Doc Cramer, Philadelphia, 153

National League

Ripper Collins, St. Louis, 154
Jack Rothrock, St. Louis, 154
Bill Terry, New York, 153
Mel Ott, New York, 153
Gus Suhr, Pittsburgh, 151

1935 (11 players)

American League

Luke Appling, Chicago, 153
Hank Greenberg, Detroit, 152
Lou Gehrig, New York, 149
Red Rolfe, New York, 149
Doc Cramer, Philadelphia, 149

National League

Dolph Camilli, Philadelphia, 156
Ethan Allen, Philadelphia, 156
Billy Herman, Chicago, 154
Augie Galan, Chicago, 154
Joe Medwick, St. Louis, 154
Gus Suhr, Pittsburgh, 153

1936 (13 players)

American League

Lou Gehrig, New York, 155
Jimmie Foxx, Boston, 155
Lyn Lary, St. Louis, 155
Beau Bell, St. Louis, 155
Charlie Gehringer, Detroit, 154
Marv Owen, Detroit, 154

National League

Gus Suhr, Pittsburgh, 156
Arky Vaughan, Pittsburgh, 156
Buddy Hassett, Brooklyn, 156
Joe Medwick, St. Louis, 155
Burgess Whitehead, New York, 154
Frank Demaree, Chicago, 154
Leo Norris, Philadelphia, 154

1937 (13 players)

American League

Lou Gehrig, New York, 157
Lyn Lary, Cleveland, 156
Earl Averill, Cleveland, 156
Beau Bell, St. Louis, 156
Luke Appling, Chicago, 154
Dixie Walker, Chicago, 154
Wally Moses, Philadelphia, 154

National League

Joe Medwick, St. Louis, 156
Stan Hack, Chicago, 154
Frank Demaree, Chicago, 154
Paul Waner, Pittsburgh, 154
Burgess Whitehead, New York, 152
Tony Cuccinello, Boston, 152

1938 (6 players)

American League

Lou Gehrig, New York, 157
Frankie Crosetti, New York, 157
Hank Greenberg, Detroit, 155
Pete Fox, Detroit, 155

National League

Frank McCormick, Cincinnati, 151
Harry Craft, Cincinnati, 151

1939 (7 players)

American League

APPENDIX F

Ken Keltner, Cleveland, 154
Frankie Crosetti, New York, 152
Red Rolfe, New York, 152

National League

Dolph Camilli, Brooklyn, 157
Frank McCormick, Cincinnati, 156
Billy Herman, Chicago, 156
Stan Hack, Chicago, 156

1940 (9 players)

American League

Rudy York, Detroit, 155
Lou Boudreau, Cleveland, 155
Babe Dahlgren, New York, 155
Joe Gordon, New York, 155
Joe Kuhel, Chicago, 155
George Case, Washington, 154
Dick Siebert, Philadelphia, 154

National League

Arky Vaughan, Pittsburgh, 156
Frank McCormick, Cincinnati, 155

1941 (4 players)

American League

Joe Gordon, New York, 156
Rudy York, Detroit, 155

National League

Marty Marion, St. Louis, 155
Frank McCormick, Cincinnati, 154

1942 (6 players)

American League

Les Fleming, Cleveland, 156
Joe DiMaggio, New York, 154
Mickey Vernon, Washington, 151

National League

Billy Herman, Brooklyn, 155
Bert Haas, Cincinnati, 154
Danny Litwhiler, Philadelphia, 151

1943 (12 players)

American League

Billy Johnson, New York, 155
Luke Appling, Chicago, 155
Rudy York, Detroit, 155
Dick Wakefield, Detroit, 155

Bobby Doerr, Boston, 155
Ray Mack, Cleveland, 153

National League

Stan Musial, St. Louis, 157
Vince DiMaggio, Pittsburgh, 157
Bill Nicholson, Chicago, 154
Billy Herman, Brooklyn, 153
Whitey Wietelmann, Boston, 153
Chuck Workman, Boston, 153

1944 (9 players)

American League

Mickey Rocco, Cleveland, 155
Frankie Hayes, Philadelphia, 155
Nick Etten, New York, 154
Snuffy Stirnweiss, New York, 154

National League

Babe Dahlgren, Pittsburgh, 158
Woody Williams, Cincinnati, 155
Eddie Miller, Cincinnati, 155
Ray Mueller, Cincinnati, 155
Tommy Holmes, Boston, 155

1945 (8 players)

American League

Rudy York, Detroit, 155
Nick Etten, New York, 152
Snuffy Stirnweiss, New York, 152
Frankie Hayes, Philadelphia-Cleveland, 151
Mike Tresh, Chicago, 150

National League

Emil Verban, St. Louis, 155
George Hausmann, New York, 154
Tommy Holmes, Boston, 154

1946 (3 players)

American League

Eddie Lake, Detroit, 155

National League

Stan Musial, St. Louis, 156
Enos Slaughter, St. Louis, 156

1947 (6 players)

American League

Eddie Lake, Detroit, 158

Mickey Vernon, Washington, 154
Rudy York, Boston-Chicago, 150

National League

Frankie Gustine, Pittsburgh, 156
Emil Verban, Philadelphia, 155
Willard Marshall, New York, 155

1948 (6 players)

American League

Vern Stephens, Boston, 155
Dom DiMaggio, Boston, 155
Tony Lupien, Chicago, 154

National League

Ralph Kiner, Pittsburgh, 156
Stan Rojek, Pittsburgh, 156
Stan Musial, St. Louis, 155

1949 (12 players)

American League

Vic Wertz, Detroit, 155
Vern Stephens, Boston, 155
Ted Williams, Boston, 155
Cass Michaels, Chicago, 154
Sam Chapman, Philadelphia, 154

National League

Stan Musial, St. Louis, 157
Jackie Robinson, Brooklyn, 156
Gil Hodges, Brooklyn, 156
Bobby Thomson, New York, 156
Granny Hamner, Philadelphia, 154
Richie Ashburn, Philadelphia, 154
Del Ennis, Philadelphia, 154

1950 (15 players)

American League

Johnny Groth, Detroit, 157
George Kell, Detroit, 157
Jerry Priddy, Detroit, 157
Dave Philley, Chicago, 156
Al Rosen, Cleveland, 155
Phil Rizzuto, New York, 155
Eddie Yost, Washington, 155
Sam Dente, Washington, 155
Eddie Robinson, Washington-Chicago, 155

National League

Puddin Head Jones, Philadelphia, 157
Granny Hamner, Philadelphia, 157
Earl Torgeson, Boston, 156
Al Dark, New York, 154
Roy Smalley, Chicago, 154
Red Schoendienst, St. Louis, 153

1951 (6 players)

American League

Eddie Yost, Washington, 154
Jerry Priddy, Detroit, 154

National League

Carl Furillo, Brooklyn, 158
Gil Hodges, Brooklyn, 158
Earl Torgeson, Boston, 155
Richie Ashburn, Philadelphia, 154

1952 (7 players)

American League

Eddie Yost, Washington, 157

National League

Whitey Lockman, New York, 154
Stan Musial, St. Louis, 154
Connie Ryan, Philadelphia, 154
Richie Ashburn, Philadelphia, 154
Bobby Adams, Cincinnati, 154
Roy McMillan, Cincinnati, 154

1953 (13 players)

American League

Dave Philley, Philadelphia, 157
Jim Rivera, Chicago, 156
Al Rosen, Cleveland, 155
Billy Hunter, St. Louis, 154
Mickey Vernon, Washington, 152
Eddie Yost, Washington, 152

National League

Ray Jablonski, St. Louis, 157
Eddie Mathews, Milwaukee, 157
Joe Adcock, Milwaukee, 157
Stan Musial, St. Louis, 157
Richie Ashburn, Philadelphia, 156
Al Dark, New York, 155
Roy McMillan, Cincinnati, 155

1954 (12 players)

American League

Harvey Kuenn, Detroit, 155

Appendix F

Jim Busby, Washington, 155
Eddie Yost, Washington, 155
Chico Carrasquel, Chicago, 155
Nellie Fox, Chicago, 155

National League

Ernie Banks, Chicago, 154
Roy McMillan, Cincinnati, 154
Johnny Logan, Milwaukee, 154
Al Dark, New York, 154
Gil Hodges, Brooklyn, 154
Stan Musial, St. Louis, 153
Richie Ashburn, Philadelphia, 153

1955 (8 players)

American League

Al Smith, Cleveland, 154
Bill Tuttle, Detroit, 154

National League

Johnny Logan, Milwaukee, 154
Gus Bell, Cincinnati, 154
Wally Post, Cincinnati, 154
Gene Baker, Chicago, 154
Ernic Banks, Chicago, 154
Stan Musial, St. Louis, 154

1956 (5 players)

American League

Jimmy Piersall, Boston, 155
Nellie Fox, Chicago, 154

National League

Frank Thomas, Pittsburgh, 157
Stan Musial, St. Louis, 156
Richie Ashburn, Philadelphia, 154

1957 (5 players)

American League

Nellie Fox, Chicago, 155
Billy Gardner, Baltimore, 154

National League

Ernie Banks, Chicago, 156
Richie Ashburn, Philadelphia, 156
Don Blasingame, St. Louis, 154

1958 (4 players)

American League

Frank Malzone, Boston, 155
Nellie Fox, Chicago, 155
Frank Bolling, Detroit, 154

National League

Ernie Banks, Chicago, 154

1959 (6 players)

American League

Nellie Fox, Chicago, 156
Frank Malzone, Boston, 154
Rocky Colavito, Cleveland, 154

National League

Don Hoak, Pittsburgh, 155
Ernie Banks, Chicago, 155
Vada Pinson, Cincinnati, 154

1960 (4 players)

American League

Minnie Minoso, Chicago, 154

National League

Ernie Banks, Chicago, 156
Don Hoak, Pittsburgh, 155
Vada Pinson, Cincinnati, 154

1961 (4 players)

American League

Brooks Robinson, Baltimore, 163
Rocky Colavito, Detroit, 163

National League

Hank Aaron, Milwaukee, 155
Vada Pinson, Cincinnati, 154

1962 (8 players)

American League

Norm Siebern, Kansas City, 162
Brooks Robinson, Baltimore, 162
Rocky Colavito, Detroit, 161
Carl Yastrzemski, Boston, 160

National League

Maury Wills, Los Angeles, 165
Frank Robinson, Cincinnati, 162
Ron Santo, Chicago, 162
Dick Groat, Pittsburgh, 161

1963 (3 players)

American League

PLAYED ALL GAMES

None

National League

Ron Santo, Chicago, 162
Vada Pinson, Cincinnati, 162
Bill White, St. Louis, 162

1964 (9 players)

American League

Brooks Robinson, Baltimore, 163
Bobby Knoop, Los Angeles, 162

National League

Leo Cardenas, Cincinnati, 163
Ken Boyer, St. Louis, 162
Curt Flood, St. Louis, 162
Johnny Callison, Philadelphia, 162
Dick Allen, Philadelphia, 162
Bill Mazeroski, Pittsburgh, 162
Billy Williams, Chicago, 162

1965 (6 players)

American League

Don Wert, Detroit, 162
Ron Hansen, Chicago, 162
Rocky Colavito, Cleveland, 162

National League

Ron Santo, Chicago, 164
Billy Williams, Chicago, 164
Pete Rose, Cincinnati, 162

1966 (7 players)

American League

Don Buford, Chicago, 163
George Scott, Boston, 162
Jim Fregosi, California, 162
Harmon Killebrew, Minnesota, 162

National League

Billy Williams, Chicago, 162
Bill Mazeroski, Pittsburgh, 162
Leo Cardenas, Cincinnati, 160

1967 (3 players)

American League

Cesar Tovar, Minnesota, 164

National League

Bill Mazeroski, Pittsburgh, 163
Billy Williams, Chicago, 162

1968 (2 players)

American League

Brooks Robinson, Baltimore, 162

National League

Billy Williams, Chicago, 163

1969 (6 players)

American League

Sal Bando, Oakland, 162
Carl Yastrzemski, Boston, 162
Harmon Killebrew, Minnesota, 162

National League

Billy Williams, Chicago, 163
Felix Millan, Atlanta, 162
Matty Alou, Pittsburgh, 162

1970 (2 players)

American League

Sandy Alomar, California, 162

National League

Wes Parker, Los Angeles, 161

1971 (3 players)

American League

Sandy Alomar, California, 162
Paul Schaal, Kansas City, 161

National League

Rusty Staub, Montreal, 162

1972 (5 players)

American League

Eddie Brinkman, Detroit, 156
Roy White, New York, 155
Sandy Alomar, California, 155

National League

Pete Rose, Cincinnati, 154
Roger Metzger, Houston, 153

1973 (6 players)

American League

Sal Bando, Oakland, 162
Bobby Grich, Baltimore, 162

Appendix F

Roy White, New York, 162
Eddie Brinkman, Detroit, 162

National League

Ken Singleton, Montreal, 162
Bill Russell, Los Angeles, 162

1974 (5 players)

American League

Toby Harrah, Texas, 161

National League

Pete Rose, Cincinnati, 163
Larry Bowa, Philadelphia, 162
Dave Cash, Philadelphia, 162
Mike Schmidt, Philadelphia, 162

1975 (4 players)

American League

Willie Horton, Detroit, 159

National League

Dave Cash, Philadelphia, 162
Pete Rose, Cincinnati, 162
Felix Millan, New York, 162

1976 (5 players)

American League

Rusty Staub, Detroit, 161
Robin Yount, Milwaukee, 161
Buddy Bell, Cleveland, 159

National League

Steve Garvey, Los Angeles, 162
Pete Rose, Cincinnati, 162

1977 (4 players)

American League

Al Cowens, Kansas City, 162
Hal McRae, Kansas City, 162

National League

Steve Garvey, Los Angeles, 162
Pete Rose, Cincinnati, 162

1978 (5 players)

American League

Jim Rice, Boston, 163
Rusty Staub, Detroit, 162

Eddie Murray, Baltimore, 161

National League

Enos Cabell, Houston, 162
Steve Garvey, Los Angeles, 162

1979 (10 players)

American League

Rick Bosetti, Toronto, 162
Don Baylor, California, 162
Buddy Bell, Texas, 162
Roy Smalley, Minnesota, 162
Ruppert Jones, Seattle, 162
Willie Horton, Seattle, 162
Eddie Murray, Baltimore, 159
Ken Singleton, Baltimore, 159

National League

Pete Rose, Philadelphia, 163
Steve Garvey, Los Angeles, 162

1980 (9 players)

American League

Al Oliver, Texas, 163
Gorman Thomas, Milwaukee, 162
Jim Morrison, Chicago, 162
Mike Hargrove, Cleveland, 160
Toby Harrah, Cleveland, 160

National League

Steve Garvey, Los Angeles, 163
Pete Rose, Philadelphia, 162
Warren Cromartie, Montreal, 162
Omar Moreno, Pittsburgh, 162

1981 (18 players)

American League

Lou Whitaker, Detroit, 109
Tony Armas, Oakland, 109
Jim Rice, Boston, 108
Dwight Evans, Boston, 108
Tony Bernazard, Chicago, 106
Toby Harrah, Cleveland, 103
Rick Manning, Cleveland, 103

National League

Steve Garvey, Los Angeles, 110
Ozzie Smith, San Diego, 110
George Foster, Cincinnati, 108
Chris Chambliss, Atlanta, 107

Pete Rose, Philadelphia, 107
Bill Buckner, Chicago, 106
Ivan DeJesus, Chicago, 106
Doug Flynn, New York, 105
Keith Hernandez, St. Louis, 103
Tommy Herr, St. Louis, 103
Omar Moreno, Pittsburgh, 103

1982 (8 players)

American League

Alfredo Griffin, Toronto, 162
Dwight Evans, Boston, 162
Toby Harrah, Cleveland, 162

National League

Steve Garvey, Los Angeles, 162
Gary Matthews, Philadelphia, 162
Pete Rose, Philadelphia, 162
Dale Murphy, Atlanta, 162
Johnny Ray, Pittsburgh, 162

1983 (3 players)

American League

Cal Ripken, Jr., Baltimore, 162
Alfredo Griffin, Toronto, 162

National League

Dale Murphy, Atlanta, 162

1984 (5 players)

American League

Eddie Murray, Baltimore, 162
Cal Ripken, Jr., Baltimore, 162
Dwight Evans, Boston, 162
Gary Gaetti, Minnesota, 162

National League

Dale Murphy, Atlanta, 162

1985 (6 players)

American League

Greg Walker, Chicago, 163
Alfredo Griffin, Oakland, 162
Tony Fernandez, Toronto, 161
Cal Ripken, Jr., Baltimore, 161

National League

Steve Garvey, San Diego, 162
Dale Murphy, Atlanta, 162

1986 (5 players)

American League

Tony Fernandez, Toronto, 163
Alfredo Griffin, Oakland, 162
Cal Ripken, Jr., Baltimore, 162
Don Mattingly, New York, 162

National League

Dave Parker, Cincinnati, 162

1987 (2 players)

American League

Cal Ripken, Jr., Baltimore, 162

National League

Bill Doran, Houston, 162

1988 (4 players)

American League

Robin Yount, Milwaukee, 162
Eddie Murray, Baltimore, 161
Cal Ripken, Jr., Baltimore, 161

National League

Will Clark, San Francisco, 162

1989 (5 players)

American League

Cal Ripken, Jr., Baltimore, 162
Joe Carter, Cleveland, 162
Ruben Sierra, Texas, 162
Dave Gallagher, Chicago, 161

National League

Eddie Murray, Los Angeles, 160

1990 (3 players)

American League

Roberto Kelly, New York, 162
Cal Ripken, Jr., Baltimore, 161

National League

Joe Carter, San Diego, 162

1991 (4 players)

American League

Cal Ripken, Jr., Baltimore, 162
Joe Carter, Toronto, 162
Cecil Fielder, Detroit, 162

APPENDIX F

National League

Mark Grace, Chicago, 160

1992 (4 players)

American League

Cal Ripken, Jr., Baltimore, 162

National League

Jeff Bagwell, Houston, 162
Craig Biggio, Houston, 162
Steve Finley, Houston, 162

1993 (2 players)

American League

Cal Ripken, Jr., Baltimore, 162

National League

Jeff Conine, Florida, 162

1994 (5 players)

American League

Paul Molitor, Toronto, 115
Mike Bordick, Oakland, 114
Frank Thomas, Chicago, 113
Cal Ripken, Jr., Baltimore, 112

National League

Jeff Conine, Florida, 115

1995 (9 players)

American League

Edgar Martinez, Seattle, 145
Frank Thomas, Chicago, 145
Cal Ripken, Jr., Baltimore, 144
Travis Fryman, Detroit, 144
Chad Curtis, Detroit, 144
Ed Sprague, Toronto, 144

National League

Fred McGriff, Atlanta, 144
Barry Bonds, San Francisco, 144
Sammy Sosa, Chicago, 144

1996 (3 players)

American League

Cal Ripken, Jr., Baltimore, 163

National League

Jeff Bagwell, Houston, 162
Craig Biggio, Houston, 162

1997 (7 players)

American League

Cal Ripken, Jr., Baltimore, 162
Brian Hunter, Detroit, 162
Albert Belle, Chicago, 161

National League

Jeff Bagwell, Houston, 162
Craig Biggio, Houston, 162
Sammy Sosa, Chicago, 162
Eric Karros, Los Angeles, 162

1998 (8 players)

American League

Albert Belle, Chicago, 163
Rafael Palmeiro, Baltimore, 162
B.J. Surhoff, Baltimore, 162
Ken Griffey Jr., Seattle, 161
Alex Rodriguez, Seattle, 161
Johnny Damon, Kansas City, 161

National League

Vinny Castilla, Colorado, 162
Neifi Perez, Colorado, 162

1999 (4 players)

American League

B. J. Surhoff, Baltimore, 162

National League

Sammy Sosa, Chicago, 162
Jeff Bagwell, Houston, 162
Andruw Jones, Atlanta, 162

2000 (6 players)

American League

Carlos Delgado, Toronto, 162
Jose Cruz Jr., Toronto, 162

National League

Neifi Perez, Colorado, 162
Luis Gonzalez, Arizona, 162
Shawn Green, Los Angeles, 162
Preston Wilson, Florida, 161

2001 (7 players)

American League

Carlos Delgado, Toronto, 162
Terrence Long, Oakland, 162
Miguel Tejada, Oakland, 162
Alex Rodriguez, Texas, 162

National League

Luis Gonzalez, Arizona, 162
Orlando Cabrera, Montreal, 162
Bobby Abreu, Philadelphia, 162

2002 (6 players)

American League

Miguel Tejada, Oakland, 162
Terrence Long, Oakland, 162
Carlos Beltran, Kansas City, 162
Alex Rodriguez, Texas, 162

National League

Derrek Lee, Florida, 162
Aaron Boone, Cincinnati, 162

2003 (6 players)

American League

Hideki Matsui, New York, 163
Miguel Tejada, Oakland, 162
Aubrey Huff, Tampa Bay, 162

National League

Orlando Cabrera, Montreal, 162
Richie Sexson, Milwaukee, 162
Juan Pierre, Florida, 162

2004 (4 players)

American League

Miguel Tejada, Baltimore, 162
Hideki Matsui, New York, 162

National League

Juan Pierre, Florida, 162
Carlos Beltran, Kansas City-Houston, 159

2005 (10 players)

American League

Miguel Tejada, Baltimore, 162
Hideki Matsui, New York, 162
Alex Rodriguez, New York, 162
Ichiro Suzuki, Seattle, 162
Raul Ibanez, Seattle, 162
Mark Teixeira, Texas, 162

National League

Juan Pierre, Florida, 162
Carlos Lee, Milwaukee, 162
Bobby Abreu, Philadelphia, 162
Jason Bay, Pittsburgh, 162

Bibliography

Books

Neft, David S., Richard M. Cohen, and Michael L. Neft. *The Sports Encyclopedia: Baseball.* 22nd ed. New York: St. Martin's, 2002.

Nemec, David. *The Great Encyclopedia of 19th Century Major League Baseball.* New York: Penguin, 1997.

Palmer, Pete, and Gary Gillette, eds. *The Baseball Encyclopedia.* New York: Barnes and Noble, 2004.

Thorn, John, and Pete Palmer, eds. *Total Baseball.* 2nd ed. New York: Time Warner, 1991.

Wright, Marshall D. *Nineteenth Century Baseball.* Jefferson, NC: McFarland, 1996.

Newspapers and Periodicals

New York Clipper, 1876–1884
New York Times, 1900–1962
The Sporting Life, 1883–1917
The Sporting News, 1886–1986
USA Today Baseball Weekly, 1998–2005

Other Sources

ICI sheets, National League, 1891–1902
ICI sheets, American League, 1901–1904
ICI sheets, American Association, 1882–1891
ICI sheets, Players League, 1890
Official National League batting log sheets, 1903–1986
Official American League batting log sheets, 1905–1986
Society for American Baseball Research Publications
Baseball's First Stars, 1996
Deadball Stars of the National League, 2004
Nineteenth Century Stars, 1989
Tattersall Collection of newspaper National League box scores from 1876 to 1890
Tattersall-McConnell Home Run Log

Web Sites

www.Baseballreference.com
www.Retrosheet.org (the information used from this website was obtained free of charge and is copyrighted by Retrosheet. Interested parties may contact Retrosheet at 20 Sunset Road, Newark, DE 19711)

Index

Aaron, Hank 175, 225, 266
Abbey, Charles 257
Abreu, Bobby 271
Adams, Ace 147
Adams, Bobby 265
Adcock, Joe 159, 265
Addy, Bob 14, 20
Alexander, Dale 262
Alexander, Manny 214, 215
Allen, Bob 51, 76, 256
Allen, Dick 267
Allen, Ethan 263
Alomar, Roberto 193, 226
Alomar, Sandy 192–195, 233, 240, 243, 245, 246, 250, 267
Alomar, Sandy, Jr. 193
Alou, Matty 267
Alperman, Whitey 98
Alston, Walt 203
Altizer, Dave 99
Anderson, Brady 218
Anderson, Goat 110
Anderson, John 69, 95, 258
Angelos, Peter 215
Anson, Cap 7, 9, 16, 33, 35, 55, 250, 253–257
Aparicio, Luis 177
Appling, Luke 141, 263, 264
Armas, Tony 268
Ashburn, Richie 243, 245, 246, 250, 265, 266
Averill, Earl 243, 245, 246, 251, 262, 263

Bagwell, Jeff 270
Baker, Del 140, 141
Baker, Frank 102, 103, 260
Baker, Gene 266
Bancroft, Dave 260, 261
Bando, Sal 267, 268
Banks, Ernie 97, 136, 174–176, 233, 240, 243, 245, 246, 251, 252, 266
Barnes, Ross 4, 5, 7, 9, 11, 16, 253

Barnie, Billy 46
Barrett, Jimmy 75, 76, 78, 232, 236, 258
Barrow, Ed 123
Barry, Jack 102
Barry, Shad 70, 258
Bartell, Dick 262, 263
Bassett, Charley 42
Battin, Joe 253, 255
Bay, Harry 258
Bay, Jason 271
Baylor, Don 224, 268
Beard, Ollie 49, 256
Beaumont, Ginger 112, 258
Beck, Fred 259
Beckley, Jake 53–56, 96, 232, 236, 252, 257
Bell, Beau 263
Bell, Buddy 268
Bell, Gus 266
Bell, Jay 227
Bell, Les 261, 262
Belle, Albert 216–219, 234, 241, 270
Beltran, Carlos 222, 271
Berardino, John 161
Berger, Wally 262
Bernazard, Tony 268
Berra, Yogi 134, 169
Berry, Jack 125
Berry, Neil 157
Bichette, Dante 219
Bierbauer, Lou 256, 257
Biggio, Craig 249, 270
Birchall, Jud 255
Birmingham, Joe 117
Bissonette, Del 262
Blackburne, Lena 120
Blasingame, Don 201, 266
Blomberg, Ron 186, 195
Blue, Lu 262
Bluege, Ossie 144, 158
Boeckel, Tony 260, 261
Bohne, Sam 261

Bolling, Frank 266
Bond, Tommy 253
Bonds, Barry 225, 228, 270
Bonds, Bobby 167
Bonilla, Bobby 221
Boone, Aaron 271
Booth, Eddie 253
Bordick, Mike 216, 221, 229, 270
Borton, Babe 260
Bosetti, Rick 268
Bottomley, Jim 261
Boudreau, Lou 264
Bowa, Larry 200, 268
Boyer, Clete 184
Boyer, Cloyd 184
Boyer, Ken 184–186, 233, 240, 267
Boyle, Jack 33, 257
Bradley, Bill 84, 85, 87, 232, 237, 258
Bradley, George 253
Brady, Steve 29, 30, 32, 231, 235, 255
Bransfield, Kitty 122
Brinkman, Eddie 195–198, 233, 240, 267, 268
Brodie, Steve 56–59, 61, 81, 123, 125, 232, 236, 243, 245, 257
Brouthers, Dan 19, 20, 45, 56, 254, 255
Brown, Eddie 59, 243, 245, 246, 261, 262
Brown, Tom 255, 257
Browning, Pete 28, 32, 39, 53, 255
Buckenberger, Al 54
Buckner, Bill 203, 269
Buford, Don 267
Burdock, Jack 19–21, 37, 38, 47, 231, 235, 253, 254
Burkett, Jesse 70–72, 75, 91, 232, 236, 252, 257, 258
Burns, George (New York and Cincinnati) 260, 261

INDEX

Burns, George (Philadelphia) 260
Burns, Jack 263
Burns, Tom 254, 256
Burns, Tommy "Oyster" 42, 47
Burroughs, Jeff 210
Busby, Jim 266
Bush, Donie 109, 113, 259, 260
Bushong, Doc 38
Butler, Brett 210
Byrne, Charlie 37

Cabell, Enos 268
Cabrera, Orlando 271
Callahan, Nixey 86
Callison, Johnny 185–187, 233, 240, 267
Cameron, Mike 178
Camilli, Dolph 263, 264
Camp, Llewellyn 42
Campanella, Roy 163
Cantillon, Joe 99, 109
Cardenas, Leo 188, 189, 191, 233, 240, 267
Carey, Max 111, 115, 260, 261
Carey, Tom 14, 253
Carlton, Steve 207
Carpenter, Hick 254, 255
Carrasquel, Chico 172, 266
Carrigan, Bill 125
Carter, Joe 230, 244, 246, 269, 270
Cartwright, Ed 257
Caruthers, Bob 38, 44, 45, 52, 75
Case, George 264
Cash, Dave 199–202, 233, 240, 249, 268
Cassidy, John 253, 254
Castilla, Vinny 218–220, 234, 241, 249, 270
Castino, John 208
Cater, Danny 181
Cates, Eli 95
Cavarretta, Phil 86, 87, 137, 152–155, 233, 239
Cepeda, Orlando 183
Cey, Ron 203
Chambliss, Chris 269
Chance, Frank 122
Chandler, Spud 141
Chapman, Ben 128
Chapman, Ray 114–118, 126, 232, 234, 237, 259, 260
Chapman, Sam 265
Childs, Cupid 256
Cissell, Bill 262
Clapp, John 11–13, 15, 231, 235, 251, 253
Clark, Bob 38
Clark, Will 269
Clarke, Fred 110, 111, 257

Clarke, Horace 193, 194
Clemens, Roger 224, 228
Clement, Wally 104
Clemente, Roberto 177
Clingman, Billy 257
Cobb, Ty 71, 92, 102, 109, 112, 113, 120, 170, 259
Cochrane, Mickey 133
Cogswell, Ed 18
Colavito, Rocky 177–180, 233, 240, 266, 267
Coleman, Jack 43
Collins, Eddie 102–104, 113, 118–121, 123, 172, 232, 237, 238, 250, 252, 259, 260
Collins, Hub 45–47, 49, 231, 236, 256
Collins, Jimmy 70, 72–76, 78, 79, 81–83, 88, 232, 236, 257, 258
Collins, Ripper 153, 263
Comiskey, Charlie 33, 41, 51, 52, 55, 86, 256
Conine, Jeff 270
Connor, Roger 47, 250, 254–257
Cooley, Duff 64–67, 232, 236, 257
Cooper, Claude 260
Corbett, Joe 71
Corkhill, Pop 255, 256
Coscarart, Pete 146
Courtney, Ernie 100, 101, 258
Cowens, Al 268
Cox, Bobby 208–210, 221
Craft, Harry 263
Cramer, Doc 137, 263
Crane, Sam 23
Cravath, Gavvy 122, 123
Crawford, Sam 76, 79, 92, 111–115, 117, 232, 237, 251, 252, 258, 259
Creamer, George 254
Criger, Lou 84
Critz, Hughie 262
Cromartie, Warren 268
Cronin, Joe 149, 156, 161, 262
Crooks, Jack 257
Crosetti, Frankie 133–135, 137, 233, 238, 263, 264
Cross, Lave 85, 258
Cross, Monte 257, 258
Crowley, Bill 253, 254
Cruz, Jose, Jr. 270
Cuccinello, Tony 244, 245, 262, 263
Cullen, Tim 192, 196
Curtis, Chad 270
Cutshaw, George 114–117, 119, 232, 234, 237, 260
Cuyler, Kiki 261, 262

Dahlen, Bill 98, 115
Dahlgren, Babe 264
Dalrymple, Abner 16, 24, 254, 255
Damon, Johnny 220–223, 234, 241, 250, 270
Dark, Alvin 265, 266
Daubert, Jake 260, 261
Davis, George 66, 73, 86, 88, 93, 256
Davis, Harry 92, 103
Davis, Willie 186
Dean, Dizzy 133
DeCinces, Doug 212
Dehlman, Herman 253
DeJesus, Ivan 269
Delahanty, Ed 64, 69, 71, 72, 82
Delgado, Carlos 178, 250, 270, 271
Demaree, Frank 263
DeMontreville, Gene 63–65, 232, 236, 257, 258
Denny, Jerry 254, 255
Dente, Sam 166, 265
Devlin, Art 259
Devlin, Jim 253
Dexter, Charlie 77
Dickerson, Buttercup 254
DiMaggio, Dom 134, 149, 265
DiMaggio, Joe 134, 264
DiMaggio, Vince 264
Doerr, Bobby 134, 148–150, 152, 233, 239, 252, 264
Dolan, Cozy 258, 259
Donahue, Jiggs 92–95, 232, 237, 258, 259
Donovan, Patsy 42, 97, 98, 257
Dooin, Red 122
Doolan, Mickey 101, 259
Doran, Bill 269
Dorgan, Mike 253
Dougherty, Patsy 79
Douglas, Klondike 66
Douthit, Taylor 262
Dowd, Tommy 258
Doyle, Denny 200
Doyle, Jack 258
Doyle, Larry 101, 123
Dressen, Charlie 167
Driessen, Dan 202
Dropo, Walt 162
Duffy, Hugh 52, 55, 56, 58, 66–68, 74, 90, 232, 236, 252, 256, 257
Duncan, Pat 260
Dungan, Sam 258
Dunlap, Fred 254
Durocher, Leo 163, 176, 191
Dykes, Jimmy 260. 263

Edwards, Bruce 163

Index

Eggler, Dave 1
English, Woody 136, 262
Ennis, Del 265
Erstad, Darin 223
Esmond, Jimmy 260
Esterbrook, Dude 28, 255
Etten, Nick 264
Evans, Dwight 268, 269
Evans, Steve 107
Everitt, Bill 257
Evers, Johnny 258
Ewing, Buck 35

Fain, Ferris 144
Falk, Bibb 261
Farrar, Geraldine 43
Farrar, Sid 42, 43, 45, 231, 236, 255, 256
Farrell, Duke 56, 257
Farrell, Jack 254
Farrell, Joe 255
Feller, Bob 149
Fennelly, Frank 255, 256
Ferguson, Bob 36, 253, 254
Fernandez, Tony 209, 269
Ferris, Hobe 258
Fielder, Cecil 270
Finley, Steve 270
Finneran, Bill 90
Fisher, Ray 90
Fleming, Les 264
Fletcher, Art 131, 260
Flick, Elmer 258
Flint, Silver 253
Flood, Curt 184, 187–189, 233, 240, 267
Flynn, Doug 269
Fogarty, Jim 255
Foley, Curry 254
Force, Davy 5, 6, 8, 231, 235, 253, 254
Fosse, Ray 201
Foster, Eddie 259
Foster, George 269
Fournier, Jack 261
Foutz, Dave 38, 44–47, 49, 52, 56, 80, 231, 236, 256, 257
Fox, Nellie 171–173, 175, 233, 239, 240, 243, 245, 246, 249–252, 266
Fox, Pete 132, 133, 135, 233, 238, 263
Foxx, Jimmie 262, 263
Frank, Charlie 65
Freeman, Buck 74, 78, 79, 81–85, 123, 232, 237, 243, 245, 257, 258
Freese, Gene 186
Fregosi, Jim 267
Frisch, Frankie 153, 159, 160, 261, 262

Fryman, Travis 270
Fuller, Shorty 256
Fultz, Dave 78
Furillo, Carl 265

Gaetti, Gary 269
Galan, Augie 263
Galehouse, Denny 142
Gallagher, Dave 269
Galloway, Chick 261
Ganley, Bob 259
Ganzel, John 95
Garber, Gene 210
Gardner, Billy 266
Gardner, Larry 260
Garms, Debs 152
Garvey, Steve 2, 192, 203–205, 207, 214, 233, 240, 241, 243, 245–247, 249, 250, 268, 269
Gedeon, Joe 260
Geer, Billy 48, 254, 255
Gehrig, Lou 1, 124, 126, 129–135, 162, 166, 167, 178, 191, 213–216, 233, 238, 243, 245–252, 261–263
Gehringer, Charlie 133, 244, 245, 250, 251, 262, 263
Gerber, Wally 260, 261
Gerhardt, Joe 255
Giamatti, Bart 183, 207
Gifford, Jim 30
Gilbert, Pete 257
Gillespie, Pete 255
Glasscock, Jack 254, 255
Gleason, Bill 26–28, 30, 231, 234, 235, 255
Gleason, Jack 26
Gleason, Kid 61–64, 121, 232, 236, 257, 258
Glenn, John 6–9, 231, 235, 253
Gomez, Luis 208
Gonzalez, Juan 218
Gonzalez, Luis 226–228, 230, 234, 242, 249, 270, 271
Gordon, Joe 135, 264
Gore, George 254
Grabarkewitz, Billy 193
Grace, Mark 270
Grant, Eddie 98, 100, 101, 103, 232, 237, 259
Green, Danny 86
Green, Shawn 225, 226, 228, 234, 241, 242, 270
Greenberg, Hank 140, 263
Greenwood, Bill 40
Gremminger, Ed 258
Grich, Bobby 268
Griffey, Ken, Jr. 270
Griffin, Alfredo 208–211, 234, 241, 269
Griffin, Mike 256

Griffith, Clark 106, 109
Griffith, Tommy 260
Grimm, Charlie 136, 137, 152
Groat, Dick 266
Groh, Heinie 260
Gross, Emil 254
Groth, Johnny 265
Guerrero, Vladimir 250
Gustine, Frankie 159–161, 233, 239, 265
Gutierrez, Cesar 197

Haas, Bert 264
Haas, Eddie 211
Hack, Stan 136, 137, 139, 142, 154, 233, 238, 263, 264
Hague, Bill 253
Hall, George 253
Hallman, Bill 258
Hamilton, Billy 64, 66, 257
Hamner, Granny 164–166, 233, 239, 265
Handley, Lee 160
Hanford, Charlie 259
Hankinson, Frank 254
Hanlon, Ned 62, 97, 255
Hansen, Ron 196, 267
Hardy, Dr. Steve 161
Hargrove, Mike 217, 268
Harrah, Toby 268, 269
Harris, Bucky 144, 166, 167, 260, 261
Hart, Jim 46
Hartnett, Gabby 153
Hartsel, Topsy 77–79, 92, 232, 236, 258
Hartsfield, Roy 208
Hassett, Buddy 263
Hatfield, John 20
Hausmann, George 264
Hayes, Charlie 219
Hayes, Frankie 249, 264
Hebner, Richie 200, 206
Heidrick, Snags 95
Heilmann, Harry 260
Helton, Todd 224
Hemphill, Charlie 258
Hemus, Solly 184
Henderson, Dave 250
Hendrix, Claude 110
Herman, Billy 143–147, 233, 234, 239, 251, 252, 262–264
Hernandez, Keith 269
Hernandez, Roberto 215
Herr, Tom 269
Herzog, Whitey 185
Higgins, Pinky 141, 263
Higham, Dick 11, 253
Hinchman, Bill 260
Hines, Paul 2–4, 6, 15–18, 23, 57, 231, 235, 251, 253–255

Index

Hitchcock, Bill 180
Hoak, Don 266
Hodapp, Johnny 262
Hodges, Gil 2, 159, 162–165, 167, 196, 233, 239, 265, 266
Hoffer, Bill 71
Hollocher, Charlie 260
Holmes, Tommy 154, 155, 157, 172, 233, 239, 264
Hooper, Harry 260
Hopp, Johnny 151
Horner, Bob 210
Hornsby, Rogers 71, 105, 251, 260–262
Hornung, Joe 10, 23–26, 41, 231, 235, 251, 254, 255
Horton, Willie 268
Hotaling, Pete 254, 255
Houck, Sadie 255
Hough, Charlie 205
Houk, Ralph 195
Householder, Charlie 255
Hoy, Dummy 256, 257
Huff, Aubrey 250, 271
Huggins, Miller 111, 126, 129, 131, 259
Hughes, Mickey 38
Hummel, John 97, 98, 100, 104, 115, 232, 237, 259
Hunter, Billy 265
Hunter, Brian 270
Hunter, Catfish 192
Hurst, Don 262
Hutchinson, Fred 170, 189

Ibanez, Raul 271
Irwin, Art 254, 255
Irwin, Charlie 257
Isbell, Frank 86, 93, 258

Jablonski, Ray 184, 265
Jackson, Joe 260
Jackson, Reggie 204
Jacobson, Baby Doll 260
Jamieson, Charlie 105
Jennings, Hughie 113, 257
John, Tommy 228
Johnson, Ban 75, 80, 106
Johnson, Billy 264
Johnson, Bob 144
Johnson, Randy 227
Johnson, Walter 87
Johnston, Dick 256
Johnston, Jimmy 260, 261
Jones, Andruw 270
Jones, Charley 30–33, 231, 235, 254, 255
Jones, Fielder 93
Jones, Nippy 170
Jones, Puddin Head 265
Jones, Ruppert 268

Jones, Tom 94–97, 232, 237, 258, 259
Joost, Eddie 157
Joyce, Bill 256
Judge, Joe 260
Jurges, Billy 136, 141

Kaat, Jim 200
Kamm, Willie 262
Karros, Eric 270
Kasko, Eddie 184, 189
Keane, Johnny 185
Keeler, Willie 58, 202, 257
Kell, George 180, 265
Kelley, Joe 58, 257
Kelly, George 260
Kelly, King 22, 34, 57, 254, 255
Kelly, Roberto 269
Keltner, Ken 264
Kemmerer, Russ 167
Kennedy, Doc 21
Kennedy, John F. 179
Kerins, John 255
Killebrew, Harmon 178, 267
Kiner, Ralph 265
Kinugasa, Sachio 215
Klein, Chuck 262, 263
Kluszewski, Ted 163
Knickerbocker, Bill 135
Knight, Lou 254, 255
Knoop, Bobby 193, 267
Konetchy, Ed 96–98, 107–109, 232, 237, 259, 260
Kress, Red 262
Krueger, Otto 258
Kuehne, Bill 255, 256
Kuenn, Harvey 178, 266
Kuhel, Joe 158, 263, 264

LaChance, Candy 74, 79–81, 83, 85, 123, 232, 237, 243, 245, 258
LaGuardia, Fiorello 131
Lajoie, Nap 75, 83, 85, 113, 259
Lake, Eddie 156–158, 233, 239, 264
Lane, Frank 178
LaPorte, Frank 118
Larkin, Henry 37–41, 231, 236, 255
Lary, Lyn 134, 262, 263
Latham, Arlie 50, 255
Lavan, Doc 117
Lazzeri, Tony 135, 261
Lee, Carlos 271
Lee, Derrek 271
Lehane, Mike 256
Leiber, Hank 137
Leonard, Andy 31, 254
Lewis, Duffy 259, 260
Lewis, Fred 33

Leyland, Jim 219
Lillie, Jim 255
Litwhiler, Danny 141, 142, 144, 233, 234, 238, 264
Lobert, Hans 101, 142, 259
Lockman, Whitey 265
Logan, Johnny 266
Lolich, Mickey 188
Lombardi, Ernie 154
Lonberg, Jim 200
Long, Terrence 271
Lopes, Davy 203
Lopez, Al 172
Louden, Baldy 113
Lowe, Bobby 178, 257
Luderus, Fred 121–123, 125, 232, 238, 243, 245, 260
Lumley, Harry 98
Lupien, Tony 265
Luque, Dolf 90
Luzinski, Greg 206
Lynch, Thomas 101
Lyons, Denny 52, 256, 257
Lyons, Harry 60, 256

Mack, Connie 63, 78, 102, 103, 120, 121
Mack, Denny 4, 6
Mack, Ray 264
Maddox, Garry 206
Magee, Sherry 89–92, 116, 232, 237, 258, 259
Mahler, Bruce 211
Malay, Charlie 97
Malone, Fergy 12
Malzone, Frank 266
Manning, Jack 37, 253, 254
Manning, Rick 268
Mansell, Mike 255
Mantle, Mickey 178
Manush, Heinie 262, 263
Maranville, Rabbit 261
Marion, Marty 148, 172, 264
Maris, Roger 178, 219, 224
Marquard, Rube 102
Marr, Lefty 256
Marshall, Willard 265
Martin, Billy 197
Martinez, Edgar 217, 250
Mathews, Eddie 175, 265
Matsui, Hideki 252, 271
Matthews, Gary 269
Mattick, Bobby 208
Mattingly, Don 269
Mauch, Gene 186
Mays, Carl 116, 117, 126
Mays, Willie 174
Mazeroski, Bill 199, 267
McAleer, Jimmy 71, 91, 93, 95, 257
McAuliffe, Dick 197

INDEX

McBride, Bake 206
McBride, George 98–101, 105–107, 232, 237, 259
McCallister, Jack 128
McCarthy, Jack 77
McCarthy, Joe 130, 131, 135, 161
McCarthy, Tommy 51–54, 56, 232, 236, 252, 256, 257
McClellan, Bill 20, 36–39, 41, 231, 236, 255
McCloskey, John 73
McCormick, Barry 258
McCormick, Frank 137–139, 141, 233, 238, 243, 245, 246, 249, 263, 264
McCreery, Tom 61
McGann, Dan 80
McGarr, Chippy 256
McGeary, Mike 12, 254
McGraw, John 72, 81
McGriff, Fred 270
McGuire, Deacon 257
McGunnigle, Bill 37, 41, 47, 49
McGwire, Mark 219, 224
McInnis, Stuffy 103, 259
McIntyre, Matty 78
McKean, Ed 256, 257
McKechnie, Bill 260
McKelvy, Russ 253
McKinnon, Alex 255
McLain, Denny 188
McLaughlin, Tom 255
McLean, Larry 101
McManus, Marty 261
McMillan, Roy 167–170, 189, 233, 239, 243, 245, 249, 265, 266
McNair, Eric 149
McPhee, Bid 49–52, 60, 69, 231, 236, 252, 255, 256
McRae, Hal 268
McTamany, Jim 256
McVey, Cal 4, 7, 9, 11–16, 18, 31, 231, 235, 251, 253, 254
Medwick, Joe 139, 263
Melillo, Oscar 149, 262
Mertes, Sam 258
Metzger, Roger 267
Meusel, Bob 261
Meyer, Billy 160
Meyerle, Levi 5, 14
Michaels, Cass 172, 265
Milan, Clyde 108, 109, 111, 232, 237, 244, 245, 249, 259
Millan, Felix 250, 267, 268
Miller, Bing 262
Miller, Doggie 256
Miller, Dusty 257
Miller, Eddie 164, 264
Miller, Ray 216, 218, 221
Miller, Stu 180

Minoso, Minnie 172, 266
Mitchell, Mike 259
Mize, Johnny 139, 147, 156
Molitor, Paul 270
Mondesi, Raul 226
Money, Don 198
Montanez, Willie 210
Moran, Pat 122
Morgan, Joe 202
Moreno, Omar 244, 245, 268, 269
Morrill, John 17–20, 23, 231, 235, 251, 253, 254, 256
Morris, Ed 44
Morrison, Jim 268
Moses, Wally 263
Mueller, Ray 249, 264
Muldoon, Mike 254
Murphy, Dale 2, 209–211, 213, 234, 241, 243, 245, 246, 249, 269
Murphy, Danny 103
Murray, Billy 100, 101
Murray, Eddie 251, 268, 269
Murray, Red 259
Muser, Tony 222
Musial, Stan 147, 148, 150–153, 163, 169–172, 174, 175, 183, 184, 190, 191, 201, 206, 233, 239, 243, 245–247, 250, 252, 264–266
Mutrie, Jim 30, 35

Nash, Billy 35, 73, 256, 257
Nealon, Jim 259
Nelson, Candy 255
Newhouser, Hal 150
Newsome, Skeeter 156
Nichols, Al 253
Nicholson, Bill 146, 147, 150, 233, 239, 264
Nicholson, Parson 256
Nicol, Hugh 255
Norris, Leo 263
Northrup, Jim 188

Oates, Johnny 214
O'Brien, Darby 38
O'Brien, Tom 66
O'Doul, Lefty 262
Oliver, Al 268
Oliver, Tom 262
Olson, Ivy 115, 116, 260
O'Neill, Paul 217
O'Neill, Steve 105, 141
O'Neill, Tip 33
O'Rourke, Frank 262
O'Rourke, Jim 9–13, 18, 22, 23, 25, 34–37, 231, 235, 236, 250–256
O'Rourke, John 23, 30, 31

Orr, Dave 38, 45
Ott, Mel 262
Owen, Marv 263
Owens, Paul 207
Ozark, Danny 198, 200, 206

Padden, Dick 257
Palmeiro, Rafael 270
Parent, Freddy 74, 78, 79, 81, 87, 88, 90, 232, 237, 258
Parker, Dave 269
Parker, Wes 267
Paskert, Dode 101, 259
Patterson, Ham 95
Pearce, Dickey 1, 4, 19
Peckinpaugh, Roger 116, 125, 128, 259
Peoples, Jimmy 38
Perez, Neifi 270
Perez, Pascual 205
Perrine, Fred 99
Perring, George 85, 260
Pesky, Johnny 149, 150
Peters, John 8, 9, 11, 37, 231, 235, 253, 254
Pettit, Bob 55
Pfeffer, Fred 254–256
Philley, Dave 265
Phillips, Bill 21–23, 231, 235, 254, 255
Phillips, Tony 209
Pickering, Ollie 258
Pierre, Juan 249, 271
Piersall, Jim 266
Piet, Tony 262
Pike, Lip 12, 253
Pinelli, Babe 261
Piniella, Lou 195
Pinkney, George 25, 37, 38, 40–43, 45, 49, 58, 59, 81, 123, 125, 231, 236, 243, 245, 251, 255, 256
Pinson, Vada 176–178, 233, 240, 244, 245, 266, 267
Pipp, Wally 129, 260, 261
Pitler, Jake 116
Portugal, Mark 227
Post, Wally 266
Powell, Boog 180
Powell, Martin 255
Power, Vic 159
Pratt, Del 113, 118, 119, 232, 237, 250, 259–261
Priddy, Jerry 265
Purcell, Blondie 254

Quest, Joe 36, 254
Quinn, Joe 256, 257

Radcliff, Rip 141
Radford, Paul 38, 256

INDEX

Rapp, Vern 185, 207
Raschi, Vic 163
Ray, Johnny 269
Reilly, "Long" John 50, 255
Reiser, Pete 142
Reitz, Heinie 62, 64, 257
Remsen, Jack 253
Rice, Harry 130
Rice, Jim 268
Rice, Sam 260, 261
Richardson, Hardy 254, 256
Rigney, Topper 261
Ripken, Cal, Jr. 1, 2, 131, 180, 211–216, 218, 221, 224, 228, 229, 234, 241, 243, 246–251, 269, 270
Ripken, Cal, Sr. 213
Ritchey, Claude 258
Rivera, Jim 265
Rizzo, Johnny 142
Rizzuto, Phil 135, 183, 265
Robertson, Gene 261
Robinson, Bill 194
Robinson, Brooks 179–181, 212, 233, 240, 252, 266, 267
Robinson, Eddie 265
Robinson, Frank 177, 213, 214, 266
Robinson, Jackie 265
Robinson, Wilbert 60, 105, 115
Rocco, Mickey 264
Rodriguez, Alex 229, 243, 246, 250, 270, 271
Rogell, Billy 262, 263
Rohe, George 93
Rojek, Stan 265
Rolfe, Red 130, 263, 264
Rose, Pete 2, 154, 155, 196, 201, 202, 204, 206–208, 233, 240, 241, 243, 245, 246, 249, 250, 267–269
Roseman, Chief 30
Rosen, Al 265
Rossman, Claude 95, 259
Rothrock, Jack 263
Rowe, Jack 21
Rowland, Pants 63, 121
Russell, Bill 203, 268
Ruth, Babe 91, 114, 125, 129, 131, 134, 178, 261, 262
Ryan, Connie 265

Saltzgaver, Jack 130
Sanders, Ray 169
Santo, Ron 181–183, 191, 233, 240, 249, 266, 267
Sawyer, Eddie 164
Schaal, Paul 267
Schaefer, Germany 259
Schafer, Harry 1, 253
Scheer, Al 260

Scheffing, Bob 179
Scheibeck, Frank 64, 256
Schilling, Curt 228
Schmidt, Mike 178, 197–200, 206, 210, 233, 240, 252, 268
Schoendienst, Red 160, 185, 188, 265
Schroeder, Bill 221
Schulte, Wildfire 110, 122
Scott, Everett 40, 58, 116, 123–130, 133, 191, 214, 232, 238, 243, 245–247, 250, 251, 260, 261
Scott, George 267
Seery, Emmett 255
Selbach, Kip 257, 258
Selee, Frank 56, 57
Sewell, Joe 118, 126–130, 133, 172, 191, 232, 238, 243, 245–247, 250, 252, 260–262
Sewell, Luke 161
Sexson, Richie 271
Seybold, Socks 258
Seymour, Cy 258
Shafer, Orator 253, 254
Shanks, Howie 106, 261
Shannon, Dan 29
Shannon, Spike 259
Shawkey, Bob 131
Shay, Danny 99
Sheckard, Jimmy 258
Sheely, Earl 261
Shettsline, Bill 65, 69
Shindle, Billy 60, 256
Shugart, Frank 257
Siebern, Norm 266
Siebert, Dick 264
Sierra, Ruben 269
Simmons, Al 261, 262
Singleton, Ken 212, 268
Sisler, George 260, 262
Sisti, Sibby 159
Slagle, Jimmy 69, 70, 72, 76, 232, 236, 257, 258
Slaughter, Enos 150, 170, 264
Smalley, Roy, Jr. 174, 265
Smalley, Roy, III 268
Smalley, Will 256
Smith, Al 173, 266
Smith, Dave 2
Smith, Germany 38, 45, 47–50, 231, 236, 256
Smith, Ozzie 48, 268
Smith, Pop 254–256
Smith, Red 260
Snyder, Pop 253, 254
Sommer, Joe 254–256
Sosa, Sammy 219, 223–226, 228, 234, 241, 270
Southworth, Billy 155
Spalding, Al 1, 4, 7, 11, 14, 15, 253

Speaker, Tris 118, 127, 128, 207
Sprague, Ed 270
Stafford, General 60
Stahl, Chick 75, 82, 88, 258
Stallcup, Virgil 168
Stanky, Eddie 170
Start, Joe 253, 254
Statz, Jigger 261
Staub, Rusty 267, 268
Stearns, Ecky 256
Stengel, Casey 115
Stennett, Rennie 200
Stenzel, Jake 58
Stephens, Vern 160, 161, 163, 233, 239, 265
Stirnweiss, Snuffy 264
Stock, Milt 260
Stone, George 91, 92, 94, 95, 232, 237, 258, 259
Stovey, Harry 23, 31, 32, 35, 39, 45, 52, 54, 254
Stricker, Cub 256, 257
Strief, George 254
Suhr, Gus 171, 243, 245, 246, 250, 251, 262, 263
Sullivan, Billy 88
Sullivan, Chub 253
Sullivan, Marty 59
Summa, Homer 261
Surhoff, B.J. 218, 220–222, 224, 234, 241, 270
Surhoff, Rich 220
Sutton, Ezra 34, 254
Suzuki, Ichiro 271
Swartwood, Ed 41

Tannehill, Jesse 86
Tannehill, Lee 85–88, 232, 237, 258
Tanner, Chuck 211
Taylor, Harry 256
Taylor, Tony 197
Tebbetts, Birdie 168
Tebeau, Patsy 40, 256
Teixeira, Mark 271
Tejada, Miguel 2, 209, 228–230, 234, 242, 243, 246, 247, 250, 251, 271
Terry, Adonis 38
Terry, Bill 250, 262, 263
Terwilliger, Wayne 167
Thevenow, Tommy 261, 262
Thomas, Frank (Chicago) 270
Thomas, Frank (Pittsburgh) 266
Thomas, Gorman 268
Thomas, Roy 70, 76, 258
Thompson, Fresco 262
Thompson, Hank 168
Thompson, Sam 27, 256
Thomson, Bobby 265
Tiernan, Mike 257

INDEX

Tipton, Joe 172
Titus, John 90
Todt, Phil 261
Torgeson, Earl 139, 265
Torre, Joe 211
Tovar, Cesar 193, 267
Traynor, Pie 73, 159, 262, 263
Treacey, Fred 253
Tresh, Mike 264
Trosky, Hal 263
Tucker, Tommy 256
Turner, Terry 258
Tuttle, Bill 266

Van Haltren, George 59–62, 67, 68, 70, 74, 76, 232, 236, 250, 257
Vaughan, Arky 263, 264
Vaughn, Farmer 54
Vaughn, Hippo 115
Veach, Bobby 260, 261
Verban, Emil 264, 265
Vernon, Mickey 143–146, 157–160, 163, 164, 167, 233, 234, 238, 239, 264, 265
Veryzer, Tom 197
Virdon, Bill 186, 195, 200
Vosmik, Joe 262

Wagner, Heinie 88, 124
Wagner, Honus 90, 112, 258, 260
Wakefield, Dick 264
Walker, Dixie 263
Walker, Greg 269
Walker, Harry 170
Walker, Larry 227
Walker, Tilly 118

Wallace, Bobby 82, 257, 258
Waltz, John 60
Wambsganss, Bill 127, 260
Waner, Lloyd 262
Waner, Paul 262, 263
Wanninger, Peewee 129
Ward, Aaron 243, 245, 261
Ward, Monte 45, 49, 254, 256
Warner, Fred 37
Weaver, Buck 260
Weaver, Earl 212, 213
Webb, Skeeter 156
Welch, Curt 32–35, 39, 231, 235, 255, 256
Werden, Perry 257
Wert, Don 267
Wertz, Vic 157, 265
West, Sammy 143
Westervelt, Fred 106
Wheat, Zack 104–106, 115, 232, 237, 252, 259
Whitaker, Lou 268
White, Bill 182–184, 233, 240, 267
White, Deacon 4, 7, 9, 11, 12, 14–16, 253
White, Roy 194, 195, 233, 240, 267, 268
Whitehead, Burgess 263
Whiting, Ed 255
Whitney, Pinky 262
Wickland, Al 259
Wietelmann, Whitey 264
Williams, Billy 151, 182, 189–193, 205, 233, 240, 243, 245–247, 249, 251, 252, 267
Williams, Jimmy 82, 95

Williams, Ted 134, 148–150, 157, 161, 162, 173, 196, 197, 265
Williams, Woody 264
Williamson, Ned 253, 255, 256
Wills, Maury 186, 266
Wilmot, Walt 256
Wilson, Jimmie 137, 153
Wilson, Owen 110, 111, 113, 115, 232, 237, 259
Wilson, Preston 270
Wine, Bobby 211
Winkles, Billy 193
Wolf, Jimmy 27–30, 52, 231, 234, 251, 255, 256
Wolverton, Harry 84
Wood, George 255, 256
Woodling, Gene 165
Workman, Chuck 264
Wright, George 20, 253, 254
Wright, Glenn 261
Wright, Harry 11, 14, 17, 19, 23, 43, 62
Wynn, Early 172

Yastrzemski, Carl 266, 267
York, Rudy 139–142, 156, 233, 238, 251, 264, 265
York, Tom 20, 253–255
Yost, Eddie 165–168, 233, 239, 243, 245, 246, 249–251, 265, 266
Young, Nick 4
Youngblood, Joel 207
Yount, Robin 250, 268, 269

Zimmer, Chief 67
Zimmerman, Heinie 111, 115

www.ingramcontent.com/pod-product-compliance
Lightning Source LLC
Chambersburg PA
CBHW081544300426
44116CB00015B/2743